Language
Network

Grammar • Writing • Communication

McDougal Littell
A HOUGHTON MIFFLIN COMPANY

Language
Network

- **Grammar, Usage, and Mechanics**
- **Essential Writing Skills**
- **Writing Workshops**
- **Communicating in the Information Age**

McDougal Littell
A HOUGHTON MIFFLIN COMPANY

2004 Impression.

Acknowledgments begin on page 682.

ISBN-13: 978-0-395-96737-9   ISBN-10: 0-395-96737-6

16 17 18 19 – DCI – 09 08 07 06

Teacher Panels

The teacher panels helped guide the conceptual development of *Language Network*. They participated actively in shaping and reviewing prototype materials for the pupil edition, determining ancillary and technology components, and guiding the development of the scope and sequence for the program.

Gloria Anderson, Campbell Junior High School, Houston, Tex.
Luke Atwood, Park Junior High School, LaGrange, Ill.
Donna Blackall, Thomas Middle School, Arlington Heights, Ill.
Karen Bostwick, McLean Middle School, Fort Worth, Tex.
Rebecca Hadavi, Parkland Middle School, El Paso, Tex.
Sandi Heffelfinger, Parkland Junior High School, McHenry, Ill.
Diane Hinojosa, Alamo Middle School, Pharr, Tex.
Patricia Jackson, Pearce Middle School, Austin, Tex.
Sue Kazlusky, Lundahl Middle School, Crystal Lake, Ill.
Tom Kiefer, Cary Junior High School, Cary, Ill.
Keith Lustig, Hill Middle School, Naperville, Ill.
Joanna Martin, Haines Middle School, St. Charles, Ill.
Sandy Mattox, Coppell Middle School, Lewisville, Tex.
Susan Mortensen, Deer Path Junior High School, Lake Forest, Ill.
Adrienne Myers, Foster Middle School, Longview, Tex.
Kathy Powers, Welch Middle School, Houston, Tex.
Patricia Smith, Tefft Middle School, Streamwood, Ill.
Frank Westerman, Jackson Middle School, San Antonio, Tex.
Bessie Wilson, Greiner Middle School, Dallas, Tex.
Kimberly Zeman, Hauser Junior High School, Riverside, Ill.

Content Specialists

Dr. Mary Newton Bruder, former Professor of Linguistics at University of Pittsburgh (creator of the Grammar Hotline Web site), Pittsburgh, Penn.
Rebekah Caplan, High School and Middle Grades English/Language Arts Specialist for the New Standards Project, National Center on Education and the Economy, Washington, D.C.
Dr. Sharon Sicinski Skeans, Assistant Professor, University of Houston–Clear Lake, Houston, Tex.
Richard Vinson, Retired Teacher, Provine High School, Jackson, Miss.

Technology Consultants

Dr. David Considine, Media Studies Coordinator, Appalachian State University, Boone, NC (author of *Visual Messages: Integrating Imagery into Instruction*)

Heidi Whitus, Teacher, Communication Arts High School, San Antonio, Tex.

Anne Clark, Riverside-Brookfield High School, Riverside, Ill.

Pat Jurgens, Riverside-Brookfield High School, Riverside, Ill.

Ralph Amelio, Former teacher, Willowbrook High School, Villa Park, Ill.

Cindy Lucia, Horace Greeley High School, New York, N.Y.

Aaron Barnhart, Television writer for the *Kansas City Star* and columnist for *Electronic Media,* Kansas City, Mo.

ESL Consultants

Dr. Andrea B. Bermúdez, Professor of Studies in Language and Culture; Director, Research Center for Language and Culture; Chair, Foundations and Professional Studies, University of Houston-Clear Lake, Clear Lake, Tex.

Inara Bundza, ESL Director, Kelvyn Park High School, Chicago, Ill.

Danette Erickson Meyer, Consultant, Illinois Resource Center, Des Plaines, Ill.

John Hilliard, Consultant, Illinois Resource Center, Des Plaines, Ill.

John Kibler, Consultant, Illinois Resource Center, Des Plaines, Ill.

Barbara Kuhns, Camino Real Middle School, Las Cruces, N.M.

Teacher Reviewers

Gloria Anderson, Campbell Junior High School, Houston, TX

Patricia Jackson, Pearce Middle School, Austin, TX

Sandy Mattox, Coppell Middle School, Lewisville, TX

Adrienne Myers, Foster Middle School, Longview, TX

Frank Westerman, Jackson Middle School, San Antonio, TX

Bessie Wilson, Greiner Middle School, Dallas, TX

Student Reviewers

Saba Abraham, Chelsea High School

Julie Allred, Southwest High School

Nabiha Azam, East Kentwood High School

Dana Baccino, Downington High School

Christianne Balsamo, Nottingham High School

Luke Bohline, Lakeville High School

Nathan Buechel, Providence Senior High School

Melissa Cummings, Highline High School

Megan Dawson, Southview Senior High School

Michelle DeBruce, Jurupa High School

Brian Deeds, Arvada West High School

Ranika Fizer, Jones High School

Ashleigh Goldberg, Parkdale High School

Jacqueline Grullon, Christopher Columbus High School

Dimmy Herard, Hialeah High School

Sean Horan, Round Rock High School

Bob Howard, Jr., Robert E. Lee High School

Rebecca Iden, Willowbrook High School
Agha's Igbinovia, Florin High School
Megan Jones, Dobson High School
Ed Kampelman, Parkway West High School
David Knapp, Delmar High School
Eva Lima, Westmoor High School
Ashley Miers, Ouachita High School
Raul Morffi, Shawnee Mission West High School
Sakenia Mosley, Sandalwood High School
Sergio Perez, Sunset High School
Jackie Peters, Westerville South High School
Kevin Robischaud, Waltham High School
Orlando Sanchez, West Mesa High School
Selene Sanchez, San Diego High School
Sharon Schaefer, East Aurora High School
Mica Semrick, Hoover High School
Julio Sequeira, Belmont High School
Camille Singleton, Cerritos High School
Solomon Stevenson, Ozen High School
Tim Villegas, Dos Pueblos High School
Shane Wagner, Waukesha West High School
Swenikqua Walker, San Bernardino High School
Douglas Weakly, Ray High School
Lauren Zoric, Norwin High School

Student Writers

Elizabeth Albertson, Chute Middle School
Britney Chilcote, Fort Morgan Middle School
Joe Clark, Springfield Junior High
Kate Frasca, John Jay Middle School
Rachel Smith, King Philip Middle School
Andy Sturgeon, Thomas Middle School
Aaron Vinson, Northbrook Junior High
Dan Walsh, Hauser Junior High
Caroline Watkins, Lake Forest Country Day School

Contents Overview

Grammar, Usage, and Mechanics

Essential Writing Skills

Grammar, Usage, and Mechanics

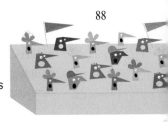

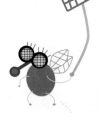

8 Sentence Structure

July 30   2:30 P.M.
Congress Center
Seat 1379
The Opening Ceremonies

11 Punctuation 248

Quick-Fix Editing Machine

Essential Writing Skills

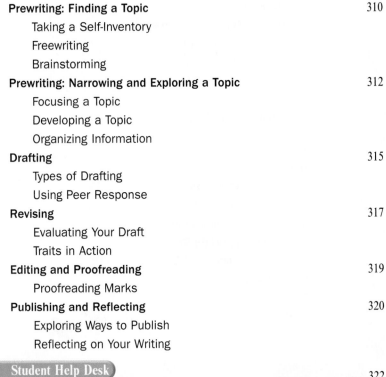
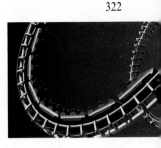

14 Building Paragraphs

Writing Workshops

Communicating in the Information Age

Special Features

Grammar Across the Curriculum

Grammar in Literature

Power Words: Vocabulary for Precise Writing

Quick-Fix Editing Machine

Student Resources

Grammar, Usage, and Mechanics

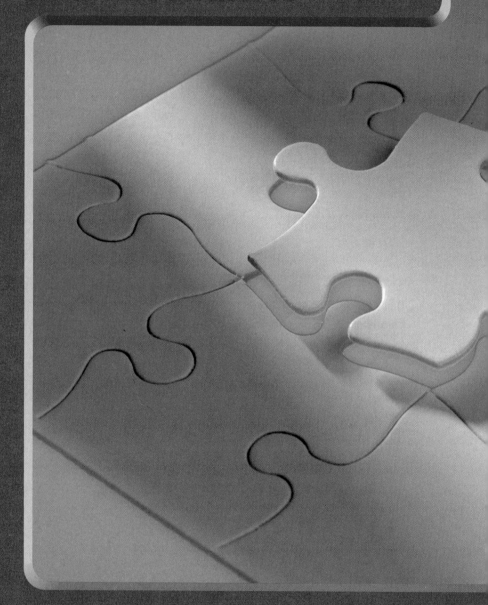

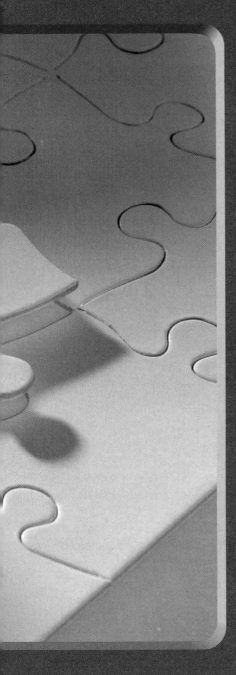

Putting the Pieces Together

When the pieces of a puzzle come together correctly, they form a clear picture. When words come together correctly, they form a clear message. By following the rules of grammar, you can be sure you've put it all together the right way.

The Sentence and Its Parts

Theme: There's No Place Like Home

If You Build It . . .

A pile of bricks is not a home. To be a home, the bricks must be assembled and combined with doors and windows to make a building that will house a family.

In the same way, the pair of words *"Home is"* is not a sentence. To be a sentence, the words must be combined with other words to make a complete thought.

Write Away: Home Is . . . ?

Where do you feel most at home? Why? Write a paragraph answering these questions and place it in your 📁 **Working Portfolio.**

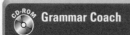

Grammar Coach

4

Choose the letter that correctly identifies each underlined item.

> What is a home? That depends on the home. Skyscrapers, space
> (1)   (2)
> stations, burrows, and nests are all homes to living things. People
> and animals build homes from many different materials. However,
>   (3)   (4)
> for human beings a home is more than a building. For some people
>   (5)
> home may be the place where they were born. For others home is
>   (6)
> the place where they feel most comfortable. We use the word in
>   (7)   (8)
> many ways. Expressions like *home team, home plate, home page.*
>   (9)
> You will learn a lot about people by discussing their idea of home.
>   (10)

1. A. declarative sentence
   B. interrogative sentence
   C. exclamatory sentence
   D. imperative sentence

2. A. compound subject
   B. main verb
   C. helping verb
   D. indirect object

3. A. compound subject
   B. main verb
   C. helping verb
   D. object

4. A. simple subject
   B. direct object
   C. compound verb
   D. compound subject

5. A. simple subject
   B. simple predicate
   C. compound verb
   D. compound subject

6. A. indirect object
   B. subject
   C. direct object
   D. verb phrase

7. A. compound subject
   B. compound verb
   C. predicate noun
   D. verb phrase

8. A. subject
   B. predicate
   C. direct object
   D. indirect object

9. A. run-on sentence
   B. interrogative sentence
   C. sentence fragment
   D. exclamatory sentence

10. A. main verb
    B. helping verb
    C. complement
    D. subject

Complete Subjects and Predicates

LESSON 1

❶ Here's the Idea

In order to share ideas and information successfully, you need to use complete sentences.

▶ **A sentence is a group of words that expresses a complete thought.**

Here is a group of words.

These words are good building blocks, but to get a message across, they need a structure. Here is a sentence built from the words. Notice that the sentence communicates a complete idea.

| Architects | can | surprise | us |

▶ **Every complete sentence has two basic parts: a subject and a predicate.**

1. The **complete subject** includes all the words that tell whom or what the sentence is about.

COMPLETE SUBJECT

| Some architects | bring nature indoors. |

2. The **complete predicate** includes the verb and all the words that complete the verb's meaning.

COMPLETE PREDICATE

| Some architects | bring nature indoors. |

Here's How Finding Complete Subjects and Predicates

Some architects bring nature indoors.

1. **To find the complete subject, ask who or what does something (or is something).**
   Who brings nature indoors? **Some architects**

2. **To find the complete predicate, ask what the subject does (or is).**
   What do some architects do? bring nature indoors

❷ Why It Matters in Writing

Jotting down ideas is a good way to prepare to write. For example, you might write down *Frank Lloyd Wright, didn't copy,* and *unique buildings* as you take notes or brainstorm. To share these ideas with others, though, you need both subjects and predicates. Notice what the writer has added in the paragraph below.

PROFESSIONAL MODEL

Frank Lloyd Wright was different from other architects. **This dreamer from the prairie states** didn't copy other people's designs. **He** created his own unique buildings instead.

—M. Carton

SENTENCE PARTS

❸ Practice and Apply

CONCEPT CHECK: Complete Subjects and Predicates

In separate columns on a sheet of paper, write the complete subjects and complete predicates of these sentences.

Amazing Designs
1. Frank Lloyd Wright designed an unusual home in the Pennsylvania woods.
2. The owners called the house Fallingwater.
3. Sections of the house jut over a waterfall.
4. Its stone walls blend in with the natural surroundings.
5. More than 130,000 people visit the site each year.
6. Tourists can see a very different house near Spring Green, Wisconsin.
7. The architect Alex Jordan built House on the Rock on a column of sandstone.
8. Its many rooms contain unique furnishings.
9. An automated band plays music all day for the tourists.
10. This odd house attracts half a million visitors a year.

Fallingwater

➡ **For a SELF-CHECK and more practice, see the EXERCISE BANK, p. 584.**

Simple Subjects

❶ Here's the Idea

You have learned that one basic part of a sentence is the complete subject. Now you will learn about the key part of the complete subject.

▶ **The simple subject is the main word or words in the complete subject.** Descriptive words are not part of the simple subject.

COMPLETE SUBJECT

An expectant seal builds a shelter in a snowdrift.
    ↑ SIMPLE SUBJECT

The cozy shelter hides her newborn pup.
    ↑ SIMPLE SUBJECT

When a proper name is used as a subject, all parts of the name make up the simple subject.

Robert Peary explored the North Pole.
SIMPLE SUBJECT

❷ Why It Matters in Writing

The simple subject tells the reader whom or what the sentence is about. Be sure to choose as accurate a word as possible for this key part.

STUDENT MODEL

Polar bears' ˄ *noses* stand out against the white snow. When

bears lie in wait for a seal, their white ~~fur~~ *paws* serve$ as a mask.

Then their ~~enemy~~ *prey* cannot see them.

CHAPTER 1

A. CONCEPT CHECK: Simple Subjects

Write the simple subject of each sentence. Remember, descriptive words are not part of the simple subject.

Example: The river beavers built a new lodge.
Simple subject: beavers

Winter Lodges
1. Many animals need shelter from cold and predators.
2. Lodges on islands often give beavers the best protection.
3. These homes are built up from the bottom of the pond.
4. Strong saplings are anchored into the mud.
5. The sturdy rodents then pile debris into a mound.
6. Branches buried in the mud are food for the winter.
7. The whole family lives together in the snug burrow.
8. Their warm bodies keep the temperature comfortable.
9. Predators can claw at the frozen lodge.
10. The crafty beavers stay safe and warm inside.

➡ **For a SELF-CHECK and more practice, see the EXERCISE BANK, p. 584.**

B. WRITING: Synthesizing Information in Science

A classmate did research on how long young animals stay with their parents. Write one sentence about each animal described below. Underline the simple subject.

Example: An arctic seal <u>pup</u> spends two weeks in a shelter with its mother.

Leaving Home		
Animal	**Name of Young**	**Length of Time Spent with Parents**
Arctic seal	pup	2 weeks in shelter with mother
Penguin	chick	23 days with parents
Kangaroo	joey	7 to10 months in mother's pouch
Beaver	kitten	more than a year with parents
Human	child	usually 18 years at home

SENTENCE PARTS

Simple Predicates, or Verbs

LESSON 3

❶ Here's the Idea

You have learned about the simple subject of a sentence. You also need to know about the simple predicate.

▶ **The simple predicate, or verb, is the main word or words in the complete predicate.**

COMPLETE PREDICATE

Prairie pioneers **lived in sod houses.**

SIMPLE PREDICATE

Few trees grow **in the prairie grasslands.**

SIMPLE PREDICATE

▶ **A verb is a word used to express an action, a condition, or a state of being.** A **linking verb** tells what the subject *is.* An **action verb** tells what the subject *does,* even when the action cannot be seen.

Pioneers made **sod bricks.** (action you can see)

They wanted **a sturdy home.** (action you cannot see)

Sod houses stayed **cool in hot weather.** (linking)

❷ Why It Matters in Writing

You can make your writing more interesting by substituting strong verbs for weaker ones. Strong verbs can add important information about the subject.

STUDENT MODEL

A prairie fire ~~burned~~ *destroyed* almost everything in its path. The fire ~~was~~ *grew* enormous. It ~~went~~ *stretched* from one end of the horizon to the other.

CHAPTER 1

❸ Practice and Apply

A. CONCEPT CHECK: Simple Predicates, or Verbs

Write the simple predicate, or verb, in each sentence.

On the Lone Prairie

1. My great-grandparents lived in a sod house, or "soddy," on the Kansas prairie.
2. They traveled west from their home in Tennessee.
3. The men used nearly an acre of sod for the house.
4. The home had only two windows and one door.
5. My family built their soddy in the side of a hill.
6. Sometimes the cows ate the grass on the roof.
7. Once, a cow fell through the roof into the house!
8. Heavy rains at times soaked through the sod.
9. The dirt floor turned into a giant mud puddle.
10. Still, sod houses protected my family from harsh winters.

➜ **For a SELF-CHECK and more practice, see the EXERCISE BANK, p. 585.**

B. WRITING: Preparing a Science Report

A science student drew this diagram and took notes about the soil in her neighborhood. Use a different verb with each note to create three sentences that describe the soil.

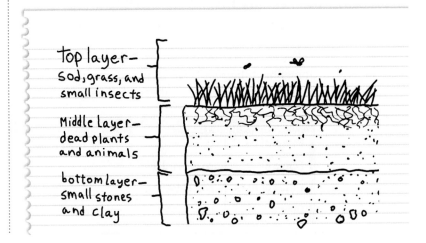

top layer—
sod, grass, and
small insects

Middle Layer—
dead plants
and animals

bottom layer—
small stones
and clay

SENTENCE PARTS

Verb Phrases

❶ Here's the Idea

The simple predicate, or verb, may consist of two or more words. These words are called a verb phrase.

▶ **A verb phrase is made up of a main verb and one or more helping verbs.**

VERB PHRASE

A "smart house" may cook your food for you.

HELPING VERB ⬈ ⬉ MAIN VERB

Main Verbs and Helping Verbs

A **main verb** can stand by itself as the simple predicate of a sentence.

Computer networks run smart houses. (action)

MAIN VERB

The network is the brain of the house. (linking)

MAIN VERB

One or more **helping verbs** help main verbs express action or show time.

VERB PHRASE

Computer networks will run smart houses.

HELPING VERB ⬈ ⬉ MAIN VERB

The network has been turning the lights on and off.

It will have been programmed for all seasons.

Sometimes the main verb changes form when used with a helping verb. For more on these changes, see pages 108–110.

Common Helping Verbs	
Forms of *be*	is, am, are, was, were, be, been
Forms of *do*	do, does, did
Forms of *have*	has, have, had
Others	may, might, can, should, could, would, shall, will

❷ Why It Matters in Writing

Writers often use verb phrases to help show time. Notice how the verb phrases in the paragraph below show past, present, and future time.

Long before scientists or architects had considered the possibility, the author Ray Bradbury wrote about a smart house. In a 1950 story, he described a kind of super-automated house that technologists now are hoping they will make a reality.

PAST

PRESENT

FUTURE

—J. Timothy Bagwell

SENTENCE PARTS

❸ Practice and Apply

CONCEPT CHECK: Verb Phrases

Write the verb phrase in each sentence below. Be sure to include all the helping verbs.

Smart Houses
1. The first "smart house" was developed in the early 1980s.
2. Its appliances could communicate with each other.
3. Suppose you were running the vacuum cleaner.
4. The noise might keep you from hearing the phone.
5. In that situation the house would stop the vacuum cleaner automatically.
6. Those with disabilities may benefit the most from a smart house.
7. The house will perform some of the tasks beyond their capability.
8. For example, meals could be brought to a person's bed.
9. The food will have been prepared by a smart kitchen.
10. Surely you can imagine other uses for a smart house.

➡ For a SELF-CHECK and more practice, see the EXERCISE BANK, p. 585.

Compound Sentence Parts

❶ Here's the Idea

Sentences can have **compound subjects** and **compound verbs**.

▶ **A compound subject is made up of two or more subjects that share the same verb.** The subjects are joined by a conjunction, or connecting word, such as *and, or,* or *but.*

COMPOUND SUBJECT

Salyut 1 **and** *Skylab* were **the first space stations.**
SUBJECT   SUBJECT

American astronauts or Russian cosmonauts lived **aboard the stations.**

▶ **A compound verb is made up of two or more verbs that have the same subject.** The verbs are joined by a conjunction such as *and, or,* or *but.*

COMPOUND VERB

The *Skylab* **crew** worked **and** slept **in close quarters.**
VERB   VERB

They worked **hard but** slept **little.**

❷ Why It Matters in Writing

You can use compound subjects and verbs to combine sentences and avoid repetition in your writing.

STUDENT MODEL

Weightlessness is fun. ~~Weightlessness can have serious~~ ^but is dangerous^
~~side effects.~~ In zero gravity, your muscles ^and bones^ do less work. ~~Your bones do less work, too.~~ Without exercise, they lose strength quickly.

CHAPTER 1

❸ Practice and Apply

A. CONCEPT CHECK: Compound Sentence Parts

Write the compound subject or the compound verb in each sentence.

Home Away from Home
1. Space stations and orbiting platforms are our first step away from Earth.
2. In the future, we may design and build outer-space cities.
3. Several nations or international groups could pool their resources.
4. They could create and manage a colony on the moon.
5. Minerals and other raw materials would be shipped to colonies in space.
6. We already design and plan model cities.
7. In one design, two huge cylinders and their solar panels form the main body of the space city.
8. The cylinders rotate and create an artificial gravity.
9. Special greenhouses shelter and sustain the city's food.
10. These cities or other space colonies could bring us closer to the stars!

➜ For a SELF-CHECK and more practice, see the EXERCISE BANK, p. 586.

B. REVISING: Using Compound Subjects and Verbs

Combine each pair of sentences, following the instructions in parentheses.

1. A group of nations is building an international space station. They are supplying it too. (Use a compound verb.)
2. Astronauts will be carried up on the space shuttle. Their supplies also will be carried on the shuttle. (Use a compound subject.)
3. Scientists will grow plants in zero gravity. They will study plants in zero gravity as well. (Use a compound verb.)

Skylab

SENTENCE PARTS

Kinds of Sentences

❶ Here's the Idea

▶ **A sentence can be used to make a statement, to ask a question, to make a request or give a command, or to show strong feelings.**

Four Kinds of Sentences

	What It Does	Examples
Declarative .	Makes a statement; always ends with a period.	I see something weird in that tree. It looks like a gray basketball.
Interrogative ?	Asks a question; always ends with a question mark.	What do you think it is? Is it a hornet's nest?
Imperative . or !	Tells or asks someone to do something; usually ends with a period but may end with an exclamation point.	Please don't get too close to it. Be careful!
Exclamatory !	Shows strong feeling; always ends with an exclamation point.	I see hornets flying out! I'm getting out of here!

CHAPTER 1

❷ Why It Matters in Writing

You can use different kinds of sentences to imitate the way people really talk. Notice how three kinds of sentences are used in this conversation between Ebenezer Scrooge and his nephew, Fred.

LITERARY MODEL

   Scrooge .... Come, come, what is it you want? Don't waste all day, Nephew.
   Fred. I only want to wish you a Merry Christmas, Uncle. Don't be cross.

INTERROGATIVE
IMPERATIVE
DECLARATIVE

—Charles Dickens, *A Christmas Carol*, dramatized by Frederick Gaines

❸ Practice and Apply

A. CONCEPT CHECK: Kinds of Sentences

Identify each of the following sentences as declarative (D), interrogative (INT), exclamatory (E), or imperative (IMP).

Dangerous Nests

1. Did you know that some wasps build round, gray nests that can be as big as beach balls?
2. The nests are made from cellulose and are very strong.
3. Stay away from wasps.
4. Their sting is very painful!
5. Yellow jackets are really yellow and black.
6. Do they eat many insect pests?
7. They live in colonies and build papery nests in spaces underground or in walls and attics.
8. Did you know that their nests may have from 300 to more than 100,000 cells?
9. Yellow jackets are dangerous only if you get too close to their nest.
10. Don't ever try to move a nest yourself.

➡ **For a SELF-CHECK and more practice, see the EXERCISE BANK, p. 586.**

B. WRITING: Creating Dialogue

Read the following *Fox Trot* comic strip. Notice the kinds of sentences used in the first two frames. Then, on a sheet of paper, write dialogue for the last two frames. Use complete sentences and as many sentence types as you can.

Fox Trot by Bill Amend

SENTENCE PARTS

Subjects in Unusual Order

① Here's the Idea

In most declarative sentences, subjects come before verbs. In some kinds of sentences, however, subjects can come between verb parts, follow verbs, or not appear at all.

Questions

▶ **In a question, the subject usually comes after the verb or between parts of the verb phrase.**

Is she ready?

┌──── VERB PHRASE ────┐
Does the weather look good for the game?
    ↑ SUBJECT

To find the subject, turn the question into a statement. Then ask who or what is or does something.

Are you staying home?

You are staying home. (Who is staying? *you*)

Commands

▶ **The subject of a command, or imperative sentence, is usually *you.*** Often, *you* doesn't appear in the sentence because it is implied.

(You) Meet us at the concession stand.
   ↑ IMPLIED SUBJECT

(You) Bring money for snacks!

Inverted Sentences

In an inverted sentence, the subject comes after the verb. Writers use inverted sentences to emphasize particular words or ideas.

Inverted Subject and Verb	
Normal	The first **batter** *walked* up to the plate.
Inverted	Up to the plate *walked* the first **batter**.
Normal	The **fans** *cheered* loud and long.
Inverted	Loud and long *cheered* the **fans**.

Sentences Beginning with *Here* or *There*

▶ **In some sentences beginning with *here* or *there*, subjects follow verbs. To find the subject in such a sentence, look for the verb and ask the question *who* or *what*.** Find the subject by looking at the words that follow the verb.

WHO COMES?

Here comes **your all-state championship team.**
VERB   SUBJECT

WHO GOES?

There goes **our best rebounder.**
VERB   SUBJECT

❷ Why It Matters in Writing

You can add variety and interest to your sentences by changing the order of subjects and verbs. Notice how the inverted sentences in the revision below create a more suspenseful tone.

STUDENT MODEL

DRAFT

    It was the bottom of the ninth inning, the score was tied, and two men were on base. Then the Yankees' best hitter stepped up to the plate. A deafening roar rolled from the upper decks.

REVISION

    It was the bottom of the ninth inning, the score was tied, and two men were on base. **Then up to the plate stepped the Yankees' best hitter. From the upper decks rolled a deafening roar.**

❸ Practice and Apply

A. CONCEPT CHECK: Subjects in Unusual Order

In separate columns on a sheet of paper, write the subjects and the verbs (or verb phrases) in these sentences.

Home Field Advantage

1. There are some benefits to games at the home stadium.
2. In the bleachers sit all your fans.
3. There are fewer hostile fans from the other team.
4. Is travel time shorter to and from the game?
5. On the field can be seen special landscaping.
6. Will the umpires give the home team a break?
7. Does the team usually play better on its own field?
8. Look at the team's record for the season.
9. There are more wins at home.
10. Plan more home games for next year.

➜ For a SELF-CHECK and more practice, see the EXERCISE BANK, p. 586.

B. REVISING: Adding Variety

Rewrite the following sentences according to the instructions given in parentheses.

1. You watched the Women's World Cup soccer games. (Change the sentence to a question.)
2. Women's soccer is becoming more popular for two reasons. (Begin the sentence with *There are*.)
3. Women with different backgrounds come from all over the United States. (Invert subject and verb, and begin with *From all over the United States*.)
4. Their schools have strong soccer programs for all grades. (Change the sentence to a question.)
5. The undefeated U.S. team ran onto the field. (Invert subject and verb, and begin with *Onto the field*.)

In your ⬦ **Working Portfolio,** find the paragraph that you wrote for the **Write Away** on page 4. Add variety to the sentences by changing the position of the subjects in some of them.

Complements: Subject Complements

❶ Here's the Idea

A complement is a word or a group of words that completes the meaning of a verb. Two kinds of complements are **subject complements** and **objects of verbs.**

▶ **A subject complement is a word or group of words that follows a linking verb and renames or describes the subject.** A linking verb links the subject with a noun or an adjective that tells more about it.

LINKING VERB ↘
Butterflies are fragile.
SUBJECT ↗   ↖ COMPLEMENT

Common Linking Verbs	
Forms of *be*	am, is, are, was, were, be, been
Other linking verbs	appear, become, feel, look, sound, seem, taste

Predicate Nouns and Predicate Adjectives

Both nouns and adjectives can serve as subject complements.

▶ **A predicate noun follows a linking verb and defines or renames the subject.**

DEFINES
Monarch butterflies are insects.
    SUBJECT ↗   ↖ PREDICATE NOUN

RENAMES
Cocoons become butterfly nurseries.

▶ **A predicate adjective follows a linking verb and describes a quality of the subject.**

DESCRIBES
Monarchs look beautiful.
SUBJECT ↗   ↖ PREDICATE ADJECTIVE

❷ Why It Matters in Writing

Subject complements can provide important information and vivid details about your subjects.

> **PROFESSIONAL MODEL**
>
> Arctic terns **are** marathoners of the bird world.   **PREDICATE NOUN**
> They **appear** too small and insignificant to be   **PREDICATE ADJECTIVES**
> great athletes, but every year they fly from the
> Arctic to the Antarctic and back again.
>
> —S. Baugh

❸ Practice and Apply

A. CONCEPT CHECK: Subject Complements

Write the underlined word in each sentence, and identify it as a predicate noun (PN) or a predicate adjective (PA).

Migration Matters
1. Migration routes are <u>highways</u> in the sky for birds.
2. The migration of songbirds is <u>difficult</u> to track.
3. The birds are too <u>little</u> to carry radio transmitters.
4. Identification bands can be <u>useful</u> in tracking migration.
5. The bands often become <u>loose</u>, however.
6. Fortunately, the isotope deuterium has been <u>helpful</u>.
7. Deuterium is a <u>form</u> of hydrogen found in rainwater.
8. Deuterium becomes <u>part</u> of plants, insects, and birds.
9. Deuterium levels become <u>higher</u> as you go farther south.
10. Now scientists feel <u>hopeful</u> about tracking migrations.

➔ For a SELF-CHECK and more practice, see the EXERCISE BANK, p. 587.

B. REVISING: Adding Subject Complements

Choose the word *time, residents,* or *remarkable* to fill in each missing subject complement below.

> Monarch butterflies are **(1)** (predicate adjective). In the summer, the adults in the northern United States lay their eggs. Then, it is **(2)** (predicate noun) for them to die. By late summer, the great-grandchildren of the original butterflies migrate. They become **(3)** (predicate noun) of Mexico.

Complements: Objects of Verbs

❶ Here's the Idea

In addition to subject complements, there are objects of verbs. Action verbs often need complements called direct objects and indirect objects to complete their meaning.

Direct Objects

▶ **A direct object is a word or group of words that names the receiver of the action of an action verb.** A direct object answers the question *what* or *whom*.

BORROW WHAT?

Movie producers often borrow real homes.
DIRECT OBJECT

The right house can charm viewers. (can charm whom? *viewers*)

Indirect Objects

▶ **An indirect object is a word or group of words that tells to whom or what (or for whom or what) an action is performed.** An indirect object usually comes between a verb and a direct object.

TO WHOM?

We lent the producer our house.
INDIRECT OBJECT   DIRECT OBJECT

She offered us free movie passes.

Verbs that are often followed by indirect objects include *bring, give, hand, lend, make, offer, send, show, teach, tell, write,* and *ask*.

Here's How Finding Direct and Indirect Objects

The producer paid us rent money.

1. Find the action verb in the sentence. *paid*
2. To find the direct object, ask, Paid what? *money*
3. To find the indirect object, ask, Paid to or for whom? *us*

---

❷ Why It Matters in Writing

By using both direct and indirect objects, a writer can describe complicated events clearly and simply.

> **LITERARY MODEL**
>
> She **heated** some lima **beans** and **ham** she had in the icebox, **made** the **cocoa,** and **set** the **table.** The woman **did** not **ask** the **boy** **anything** about where he lived, or his folks, or anything else that **would embarrass** **him.**
>
> —Langston Hughes, "Thank You, M'am"

DIRECT OBJECTS

INDIRECT OBJECT

❸ Practice and Apply

CONCEPT CHECK: Objects of Verbs

Write the objects in these sentences, identifying each as a direct object (DO) or an indirect object (IO).

One Person's Dream House

1. Bill Gates owns a very technologically advanced house.
2. The house gives its inhabitants a high level of comfort and convenience.
3. Each visitor to the house carries an electronic identifier.
4. The device gives the house information.
5. The house can then grant the visitor's wishes.
6. Such a house can teach researchers many things about homes for people with disabilities.
7. For example, the house can bring you music in every room.
8. A similar house could provide aids for the visually challenged.
9. Voice instructions could give a visually challenged person information about running appliances.
10. Gates's house also has a 32-screen video wall.

➜ For a SELF-CHECK and more practice, see the EXERCISE BANK, p. 587.

Fragments and Run-Ons

❶ Here's the Idea

Sentence fragments and run-on sentences are writing errors that can make your writing difficult to understand.

Sentence Fragments

▶ **A sentence fragment is a part of a sentence that is written as if it were a complete sentence.** A sentence fragment is missing a subject, a predicate, or both.

FRAGMENTS

The Rungus people in Malaysia. (missing a predicate)

Build traditional homes called longhouses. (missing a subject)

On top of stilts away from floodwaters. (missing both)

To make a complete sentence, add a subject, a predicate, or both.

REVISION

The Rungus people live in Malaysia.

They build traditional homes called longhouses.

These homes often are constructed on top of stilts, away from floodwaters.

Run-On Sentences

▶ **A run-on sentence is two or more sentences written as though they were a single sentence.**

RUN–ON

The longhouse roof is made **of palm leaves, the walls** are made **of tree bark.**

REVISION

The longhouse roof is made **of palm leaves . The walls** are made **of tree bark.**

REVISION

The longhouse roof is made **of palm leaves , and the walls** are made **of tree bark.**

When combining two sentences with a conjunction, use a comma before the conjunction.

❷ Why It Matters in Writing

Fragments and run-on sentences can make your writing confusing and difficult to read. If you fix these problems, your writing will read more clearly.

STUDENT MODEL

DRAFT

Each Rungus family has its own apartment the family shares a common living area with other families. Many may live in a longhouse. Twenty to 40 families. In each apartment, a raised sleeping and dining area.

REVISION

Each Rungus family has its own apartment, **but** the family shares a common living area with other families. Twenty to 40 families **may live in a longhouse.** In each apartment **there is** a raised sleeping and dining area.

❸ Practice and Apply

A. CONCEPT CHECK: Sentence Fragments and Run-Ons

Identify each of the following sentences as a fragment (F), a run-on (RO), or a complete sentence (CS).

Mayan Homes
1. The Maya live in Mexico.
2. Their traditional homes.
3. Have been much the same for centuries.
4. Some were made of stucco or stone.
5. Today Mayan houses have electricity and telephones other things haven't changed.
6. Modern building materials.
7. The Maya now use such materials as cinder blocks and cement for walls.
8. They build roofs from corrugated metal they also use tarpaper.
9. The tombstones in some Mayan cemeteries.
10. Are shaped like little houses.

➜ For a SELF-CHECK and more practice, see the EXERCISE BANK, p. 588.

B. REVISING: Clearing Up Confusion

You are out hiking on a beautiful sunny day when suddenly a thunderstorm rolls in. You pull out a friend's notes on building a temporary shelter. Yikes! The notes are hard to understand. Revise them so that the next person to use them won't be frustrated by fragments and run-ons.

BUILDING A TEMPORARY SHELTER
    First, you need to find a small tree. Away from open areas. Won't be hit by lightning. Second, drive a three-foot stick into the ground nearby take out your rain poncho. Tie a string between the tree and the stick. Drape over the string. Sit underneath the poncho "tent" lie down if you hear thunder.

Grammar in Literature

Varying Your Sentences

Writers use sentences of different types to keep their writing interesting and to call attention to certain ideas. In the following passage, notice how Anna Quindlen varies her sentences effectively to describe and give readers a feel for her subject.

from

Homeless

by Anna Quindlen

Her name was Ann, and we met in the Port Authority Bus terminal several Januarys ago. I was doing a story on homeless people. She said I was wasting my time talking to her; she was just passing through, although she'd been passing through for more than two weeks. To prove to me that this was true, she rummaged through a tote bag... and brought out her photographs.

They were not pictures of family, or friends.... They were pictures of a house. The house was yellow. I looked on the back for a date or name, but neither was there. There was no need for discussion. I knew what she was trying to tell me, for it was something I had often felt. She was not adrift, alone, anonymous, although her bags and her raincoat with the grime shadowing its creases had made me believe she was. She had a house, or at least once upon a time had had one. Inside were curtains, a couch, a stove, potholders. You are where you live. She was somebody.

SHORT DECLARATIVE SENTENCES
help proclaim these simple statements of fact.

INVERTED SENTENCE
draws the reader into the house.

SHORT SENTENCES
neatly summarize the writer's feelings about Ann.

Practice and Apply

A. Using Sentence Variety

Follow the directions below to revise this passage by varying sentences.

(1) The temperature of 17 degrees below zero was dangerous. (2) People could die from exposure in only a few hours. (3) Volunteers tried to get homeless people into the city shelters. (4) The police tried to get them to go, too. (5) Homeless people could warm up. (6) They could eat hot meals, also. (7) A stubborn homeless man was on one street. (8) He refused to move, and at first no one knew why. (9) His wife was afraid to go to the shelter he wouldn't leave her, home was where she was, he said. (10) Volunteers finally got them into a warm shelter.

1. Revise sentences 1 and 2 to express a complete thought.
2. Revise sentences 3 and 4 by using a compound subject.
3. Use a compound predicate to combine sentences 5 and 6.
4. Revise sentence 7 by reversing the subject and the verb and beginning with *On one street*.
5. Revise run-on sentence 9 by creating three shorter sentences.

B. WRITING: Description

Use the ideas from this chapter or your own ideas to write a paragraph describing your ideal room or home. Save your paragraph in your 🗀 **Working Portfolio.**

A. Subjects, Predicates, and Compound Sentence Parts Read the passage, then write the answers to the questions below it.

(1) The skies over many big cities echo with the cries of peregrine falcons. **(2)** These birds are raptors, or birds of prey. **(3)** Falcons and hawks were once nearly extinct in the eastern United States. **(4)** However, a restoration program has increased their numbers. **(5)** Falcons like the high ledges of skyscrapers and tall bridges. **(6)** There are perfect nesting sites in these places. **(7)** The birds' favorite foods are pigeons and starlings. **(8)** What happens when a soaring falcon spots its prey? **(9)** Down drops the hunter at nearly 200 miles an hour! **(10)** Falcons can live and hunt with ease in major cities.

1. What is the simple subject of sentence 1?
2. What kind of sentence is sentence 2?
3. What is the compound part in sentence 3?
4. What is the simple predicate of sentence 4?
5. What is the complete predicate of sentence 5?
6. What is the simple subject of sentence 6?
7. What is the complete subject of sentence 7?
8. What kind of sentence is sentence 8?
9. What is the simple subject of sentence 9?
10. What is the compound part in sentence 10?

B. Complements Identify each underlined word as a predicate noun (PN), a predicate adjective (PA), an indirect object (IO), or a direct object (DO).

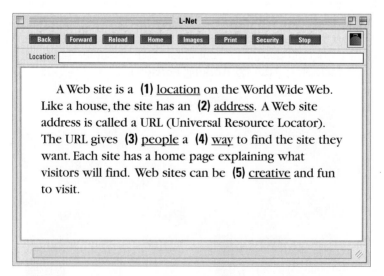

A Web site is a **(1)** <u>location</u> on the World Wide Web. Like a house, the site has an **(2)** <u>address</u>. A Web site address is called a URL (Universal Resource Locator). The URL gives **(3)** <u>people</u> a **(4)** <u>way</u> to find the site they want. Each site has a home page explaining what visitors will find. Web sites can be **(5)** <u>creative</u> and fun to visit.

Choose the letter of the term that correctly identifies each underlined part of this passage.

Elevators made skyscrapers and high-rises possible. Why? There
(1)
is a simple reason. Few people would want to walk up 30 or 40
(2)
flights to their office or home each day. Elevators offer other
(3)
benefits too. Their automated cars are actually safer than stairs.
(4)   (5)
Every three days, elevators collect and transport the equivalent of
(6)
the world's population. The fastest elevator ever built is in

Yokohama, Japan. It carries people up 68 floors in 40 seconds. Don't
(7)
think this invention is always a convenience, though. Elevators can
(8)
also cause passengers real trouble. A man in England was trapped
(9)   (10)
in an elevator for 62 hours! He was finally rescued.

1. A. declarative sentence
   B. interrogative sentence
   C. exclamatory sentence
   D. imperative sentence

2. A. main verb
   B. helping verb
   C. complete predicate
   D. verb phrase

3. A. imperative sentence
   B. interrogative sentence
   C. exclamatory sentence
   D. declarative sentence

4. A. subject
   B. predicate
   C. complement
   D. indirect object

5. A. compound subject
   B. predicate noun
   C. simple subject
   D. predicate adjective

6. A. simple subject
   B. complement
   C. compound verb
   D. compound subject

7. A. simple subject
   B. verb phrase
   C. direct object
   D. indirect object

8. A. declarative sentence
   B. interrogative sentence
   C. exclamatory sentence
   D. imperative sentence

9. A. simple predicate
   B. direct object
   C. predicate noun
   D. indirect object

10. A. declarative sentence
    B. interrogative sentence
    C. exclamatory sentence
    D. imperative sentence

SENTENCE PARTS

Student Help Desk

The Sentence at a Glance

A sentence has two basic parts, a complete subject and a complete predicate.

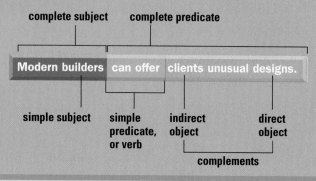

complete subject   complete predicate

Modern builders | **can offer** | **clients unusual designs.**

simple subject   simple predicate, or verb   indirect object   direct object

complements

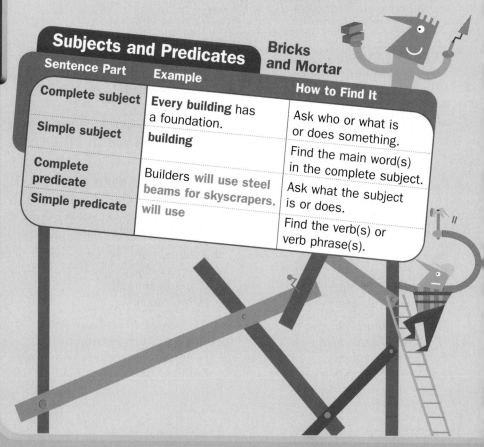

Subjects and Predicates — Bricks and Mortar

Sentence Part	Example	How to Find It
Complete subject	Every building has a foundation.	Ask who or what is or does something.
Simple subject	building	Find the main word(s) in the complete subject.
Complete predicate	Builders will use steel beams for skyscrapers.	Ask what the subject is or does.
Simple predicate	will use	Find the verb(s) or verb phrase(s).

Complements Finishing the Job

	Type of Complement	Example	What It Does
Linking verbs	Predicate noun	This building is my **home.**	Renames or defines the subject
	Predicate adjective	It is **gorgeous.**	Describes the subject
Action verbs	Direct object	We painted the **house.**	Completes the action of the verb
	Indirect object	A neighbor gave **us** some blue shutters.	Tells to whom/what or for whom/what the action is done

Kinds of Sentences Adding Interest

Declarative sentence	Someone is coming.
Interrogative sentence	Are you the repairman**?**
Imperative sentence	**(You)** Fix our furnace.
Exclamatory sentence	We are freezing**!**

The Bottom Line

Checklist for Editing Sentences

Have I . . .

____ made sure that each sentence has a subject and a predicate?

____ corrected any fragments or run-on sentences?

____ combined sentences with similar ideas by using compound subjects or verbs?

____ used different kinds of sentences and different orders of sentence parts for variety?

____ used complements to make the meanings of sentences clear?

Nouns

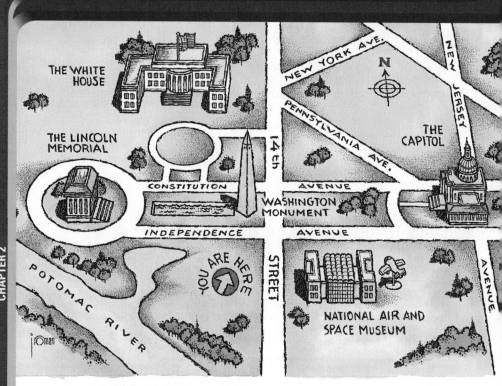

Topic: U.S. Landmarks and Attractions

You Are Here

If you were visiting Washington, D.C., a map like the one above could help you get to all the important sites. Using the map, explain how you would get from the White House to the National Air and Space Museum. What roads would you use? Which landmarks would you pass?

The labels for the roads and landmarks are nouns—important words that allow us to name persons, places, things, and ideas. Without nouns we'd all have trouble finding our way around.

Write Away: Roll Out the Plans

Write about a landmark you would design. What would it look like? Whom or what might it honor? Save your work in your
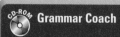 **Working Portfolio.**

Grammar Coach

For each underlined item, choose the letter of the term that correctly identifies it.

Each year, millions of <u>people</u> visit the remarkable <u>National Air</u>
$\quad\quad\quad\quad\quad\quad\quad$(1)
<u>and Space Museum</u> in Washington, D.C. Opened in 1976, this
$\quad\quad$(2)
museum is part of the Smithsonian Institution. It features more

than 20 <u>galleries</u>, a <u>theater</u>, and a planetarium. Among its displays
$\quad\quad\quad\quad$(3)$\quad\quad\quad$(4)
of early aircraft are the Wright <u>brothers'</u> original 1903 <u>airplane</u>,
$\quad\quad\quad\quad\quad\quad\quad\quad\quad\quad$(5)$\quad\quad\quad\quad\quad\quad$(6)
Flyer, and <u>Charles Lindbergh's</u> *Spirit of St. Louis.* Other exhibits
$\quad\quad\quad\quad\quad$(7)
include <u>spacecraft</u> from various missions, including *Columbia,* the
$\quad\quad\quad$(8)
command module of the *Apollo 11* spacecraft that carried

astronauts <u>Neil Armstrong</u>, Buzz Aldrin, and Michael Collins to
$\quad\quad\quad\quad\quad$(9)
the moon and back. Those who want to learn more about the

<u>courage</u> of pilots and the history of flying should really stop in.
$\quad$(10)

---

1. A. proper noun
   B. plural noun
   C. possessive noun
   D. compound noun

2. A. noun as subject
   B. noun as direct object
   C. noun as indirect object
   D. noun as predicate noun

3. A. collective noun
   B. plural noun
   C. possessive noun
   D. compound noun

4. A. common noun
   B. abstract noun
   C. proper noun
   D. compound noun

5. A. singular possessive noun
   B. plural possessive noun
   C. compound noun
   D. abstract noun

6. A. singular possessive noun
   B. plural possessive noun
   C. singular compound noun
   D. plural compound noun

7. A. singular common noun
   B. plural proper noun
   C. singular possessive noun
   D. plural possessive noun

8. A. proper noun
   B. abstract noun
   C. possessive noun
   D. compound noun

9. A. common noun
   B. abstract noun
   C. proper noun
   D. possessive noun

10. A. concrete noun
    B. abstract noun
    C. possessive noun
    D. compound noun

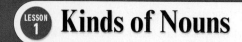

LESSON 1 — Kinds of Nouns

① Here's the Idea

▶ **A noun is a word that names a person, place, thing, or idea.**

PLACES
park
Sierra Nevada

THINGS
sequoia
backpack

IDEAS
curiosity
surprise

PERSONS
guide
Terry

Common and Proper Nouns

A **common noun** is a general name for a person, place, thing, or idea. Common nouns are usually not capitalized. A **proper noun** is the name of a particular person, place, thing, or idea. Proper nouns are always capitalized.

Common	leader	forest	mountain
Proper	Sequoya	Giant Forest	Mount Whitney

Concrete and Abstract Nouns

A **concrete noun** names a thing that can be seen, heard, smelled, touched, or tasted. Examples include *rainbow, thunder, sapling, feather,* and *blueberry.*

On the path we spotted a large, slithery snake.

CHAPTER 2

An **abstract noun** names an idea, feeling, quality, or characteristic. Examples include *happiness, beauty, freedom, humor,* and *greed.*

We felt tremendous relief after the snake passed us.

Every noun is either common or proper and either concrete or abstract. For example, *desert* is common and concrete; *Mohave Desert* is proper and concrete. *Nature* is common and abstract.

Collective Nouns

A **collective noun** is a word that names a group of people or things. Examples include *class, crowd, family, staff, trio,* and *team.*

Our family gathered around the campfire for breakfast.

Some collective nouns name specific groups of animals. Examples include *school, herd, pack,* and *colony.*

At night, a pack of wolves howled at the moon.

NOUNS

❷ Why It Matters in Writing

Although common nouns can be very specific, the proper nouns in the passage below leave no doubt about exactly what trail or tree the writer means.

> **PROFESSIONAL MODEL**
>
> I began my park explorations on the **Congress Trail**—just up the road from my cabin in **Giant Forest**—for nowhere can you get a quicker grasp of the life cycle of the big trees. I set out early, when the air was bracing and few people stirred. For companions I had fussy Steller's jays and a trio of mule deer. The two-mile paved walkway starts right at the base of the **Sherman Tree.**
>
> —Paul Martin, "California's Wilderness Sisters"

❸ Practice and Apply

A. CONCEPT CHECK: Kinds of Nouns

Write the nouns in these sentences, identifying each as common or proper. Then identify the two collective nouns.

California's Living Monuments
1. Among the largest living things on our planet are sequoias.
2. They are named for Sequoya, a Cherokee scholar and leader.
3. The most impressive example is the General Sherman Tree.
4. It bears the name of a Northern commander of the Civil War.
5. This sequoia weighs 12 million pounds and soars 275 feet, a symbol of strength and endurance.
6. The size of its trunk, as wide as a highway with three lanes, comes as a great surprise to many people.
7. A team of researchers estimated its age as between 2,200 and 2,500 years.
8. In past centuries sequoias grew across the Northern Hemisphere.
9. Now they are found chiefly in national reserves in California.
10. The beauty of these trees amazes crowds every day.

Find two abstract nouns in the sentences above.

➡ For a SELF-CHECK and more practice, see the EXERCISE BANK, p. 588.

B. WRITING: Collective Nouns

Flock is a collective noun referring to a group of birds. Of all the collective nouns, those referring to groups of animals may be the most unusual. Write a funny piece of dialogue about or between two members of an animal group. Be sure to use the right collective noun.

Farcus

by David Waisglass
Gordon Coulthart

© 1993 Farcus Cartoons   WAISGLASS/COULTHART

"Some of the guys in the flock think you're showing off."

Singular and Plural Nouns

(LESSON 2)

❶ Here's the Idea

▶ **A singular noun names one person, place, thing, or idea. A plural noun names more than one person, place, thing, or idea.**

> **One tourist noticed a statue.** (singular nouns)
>
> **Many tourists looked at statues.** (plural nouns)

One of the hardest things about plural nouns is spelling them correctly. Use these rules in the Quick-Fix Spelling Machine.

QUICK–FIX SPELLING MACHINE: PLURALS OF NOUNS

	SINGULAR	RULE	PLURAL
❶	statue dream	Add -s to most nouns.	statues dreams
❷	wish sandwich	Add -es to a noun that ends in s, sh, ch, x, or z.	wishes sandwiches
❸	photo	Add -s to most nouns that end in o.	photos
	hero	Add -es to a few nouns that end in o.	heroes
❹	city	For most nouns ending in y, change the y to an i and add -es.	cities
	valley	When a vowel comes before the y, just add -s.	valleys
❺	wolf life	For most nouns ending in f or fe, change the f to v and add -es or -s.	wolves lives
	chief	Just add -s to a few nouns that end in f or fe.	chiefs
❻	deer buffalo	For some nouns, keep the same spelling.	deer buffalo

NOUNS

> **The plurals of some nouns are formed in irregular ways.**

Singular	man	child	foot	mouse
Plural	men	children	feet	mice

❷ Why It Matters in Writing

Imagine writing without plural nouns! Writers use so many plurals that learning the spelling rules is important.

> **LITERARY MODEL**
>
> **Passengers** all about us were crowding against the rail. Jabbered conversation, sharp **cries, laughs** and **cheers**—a steadily rising din filled the air. **Mothers** and **fathers** lifted up **babies** so that they too could see, off to the left, the Statue of Liberty.
>
> —Russell Freedman, *Immigrant Kids*

❸ Practice and Apply

A. CONCEPT CHECK: Singular and Plural Nouns

Write the plural forms of the nouns in parentheses.

A Makeover for Lady Liberty

1. When the Statue of Liberty was almost a century old, (engineer) began to worry about her.
2. The copper (covering) had worn down, and (piece) of the torch were falling.
3. Photos showed that the head was 24 (inch) out of line.
4. This caused one of the (ray) in the crown to rub against the copper cover of the right arm.
5. Money for repairs came from (corporation), (individual), and (schoolchild).
6. A major job was repairing the arm and the torch, which had endured many (stress) over the (year).
7. Thin (leaf) of gold were applied to the torch's "flame" so that it would reflect the sun.

8. In addition to the anniversary celebration in New York, many (community) around the country held their own (celebration).
9. On July 3, 1986, (speech), (concert), and (party) were held.
10. Lady Liberty began her second century on July 4, 1986, with many (festivity) and fireworks (display).

→ For a SELF-CHECK and more practice, see the EXERCISE BANK, p. 589.

B. PROOFREADING: Spelling Plural Nouns

Ten plural nouns in the following passage are misspelled. Find them and write the correct spellings.

Show Me Your Golden Gate

San Francisco is one of California's largest citys. It has bunchs of attractions, including cable cars, ferrys, and wharfes. Its most popular sight, however, is the Golden Gate Bridge. Completed in 1937, the bridge connects San Francisco to northern communitys. Its main span stretches more than 4,200 feet across the Golden Gate waterway. The bridge has withstood bad weather, strong winds, and earthquakies. Its steel structure remains solid, protected by coates of orange rustproof paint. The lifes of residents and touristes alike seem affected by the bridge's beauty. Few can resist snapping photoes of it.

C. WRITING: Interpreting Data

Using the table below, write a few sentences comparing two famous suspension bridges—New York City's Brooklyn Bridge and San Francisco's Golden Gate Bridge. Use a variety of plural nouns in your sentences.

Comparing Two Bridges	Brooklyn Bridge	Golden Gate Bridge
Length of main span	1,595 feet	4,200 feet
Years to complete	14	4
Total cost	$15,000,000	$35,500,000
Construction deaths	21	0

Possessive Nouns

❶ Here's the Idea

▶ **The possessive form of a noun shows ownership or relationship.**

I held Corey's camera as she tied her shoe.
          OWNERSHIP

Rick's parents met us at the train station.
          RELATIONSHIP

You may use possessive nouns in place of longer phrases.

                              George Washington Carver's home.
We visited ~~the home of George Washington Carver.~~

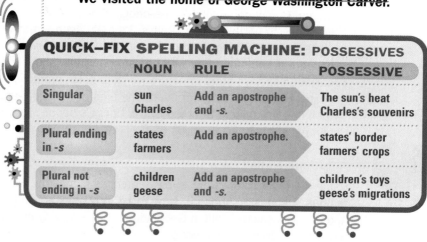

QUICK–FIX SPELLING MACHINE: POSSESSIVES

	NOUN	RULE	POSSESSIVE
Singular	sun Charles	Add an apostrophe and -s.	The sun's heat Charles's souvenirs
Plural ending in -s	states farmers	Add an apostrophe.	states' border farmers' crops
Plural not ending in -s	children geese	Add an apostrophe and -s.	children's toys geese's migrations

❷ Why It Matters in Writing

Possessive nouns can help writers show even the most unusual relationships, as in the model below.

PROFESSIONAL MODEL

In Ashburn, Georgia, stands an unusual monument. Here you will find the **world's** largest sculpture of a peanut, the local **growers'** pride. The **peanut's** length is an amazing ten feet, seven feet greater than that of its rival, **Oklahoma's** "big peanut."

❸ Practice and Apply

A. CONCEPT CHECK: Possessive Nouns

Write the possessive form of each noun in parentheses. Then label each possessive form as singular or plural.

George Washington Carver Slept Here

1. In (Missouri) southwestern corner stands a modest frame home.
2. The (farmhouse) appearance is like that of many others.
3. Visitors may not recognize one of our (country) monuments.
4. Yet, within its walls lived one of (history) finest agricultural scientists, George Washington Carver.
5. As a young boy he survived most (children) worst nightmare, the loss of both parents.
6. (Neighbors) actions helped him to overcome his greatest difficulties.
7. At the monument, children can walk through the (area) many woods and fields.
8. Here (Carver) own interest in plants and agriculture began.
9. In time his work benefited many (farmers) lives.
10. The (home) simplicity reminds visitors of this great (person) humble background.

➡ **For a SELF-CHECK and more practice, see the EXERCISE BANK, p. 589.**

B. REVISING: Using Possessive Nouns

Use possessive nouns to make these phrases short enough to fit on signposts.

Example: The Mammoth Caves of Kentucky
Answer: Kentucky's Mammoth Caves

1. the Space Needle in Seattle
2. Preservation Hall in New Orleans
3. the beaches of California
4. the Hermitage of Andrew Jackson
5. the Gateway Arch in St. Louis

A. Kinds of Nouns Write the 12 nouns that appear in the message on the postcard below. Identify each as common or proper. Then identify two collective nouns.

MESSAGE

Dear Esperanza,

My family and I are here in Grand Canyon National Park. In an hour, we'll be riding a team of mules down into the actual canyon. I can't wait to see Phantom Ranch! I wonder if it will be scary. Ha! The whole experience has been like a dream.

See you later,

Taneah

P.S. Tell the class I say "Hi."

ADDRESS

Esperanza Diaz

154 Elm Street

Encinitas, California

91303

B. Plural and Possessive Nouns Choose the correct word in parentheses, and identify it as plural or possessive.

1. An incomplete sculpture of Chief Crazy Horse stands in the (Black Hills, Black Hill's) several (miles, mile's) from Mount Rushmore.
2. The (Lakotas, Lakota's) chose to celebrate the great (warriors, warrior's) spirit with this sculpture.
3. Work began over 50 years ago, and many (hands, hand's) continue to help in the process.
4. In 1998 the (statues, statue's) massive face was unveiled.
5. The (monuments, monument's) final form will show the (chiefs, chief's) entire figure seated on a horse.

In your 📁 **Working Portfolio,** return to the writing you did for the **Write Away** on page 34. Revise it to make the nouns more specific.

Compound Nouns

LESSON 4

❶ Here's the Idea

▶ **A compound noun is made of two or more words used together as a single noun.** The parts of a compound noun may be written as

- a single word: **toothbrush, watermelon**
- two or more separate words: **sleeping bag, dining room**
- a hyphenated word: **runner-up, great-aunt**

Plural Compound Nouns

QUICK–FIX SPELLING MACHINE: COMPOUND NOUNS			
	SINGULAR	**RULE**	**PLURAL**
One word	rooftop	Add *-s* to most words.	rooftops
	paintbrush	Add *-es* to a word that ends in *s, sh, ch, x,* or *z*.	paintbrushes
Two or more words or hyphenated words	compact disc lily of the valley sixteen-year-old sister-in-law	Make the main noun plural. The main noun is the noun that is modified.	compact discs lilies of the valley sixteen-year-olds sisters-in-law

❷ Why It Matters in Writing

Compound nouns are very descriptive—they actually describe themselves. They also help writers paint clear pictures.

PROFESSIONAL MODEL

Dreamland Amusement Park is closed for the winter. . . . Taffy stands are shuttered, no teenagers screaming on the roller coaster, . . . and at the merry-go-round, the exquisite carousel which has been right here since 1915, the horses are frozen in their classical posture, waiting for another spring.

—Charles Kuralt, *On the Road with Charles Kuralt*

A. CONCEPT CHECK: Compound Nouns

Write each compound noun in the sentences below, indicating whether it is singular or plural.

Not Corny to Farmers

1. The plains produce foodstuffs such as corn, wheat, and rye.
2. The cornstalks stand tall in South Dakota, a state that loves corn.
3. The Corn Palace is a famous building in Mitchell, a prairie town that welcomes cornhuskers.
4. Today it is called the agricultural show place of the world.
5. Each spring, the outside of the concrete building is covered with wall designs made of sweet corn, grains, and grasses.
6. Corn is so popular in Mitchell that the local radio station uses the call letters KORN.
7. Sportswriters cover the local high school's teams, which are named the Kernels.
8. Corn Palace Week celebrates harvest home, the end of the harvest, with themes such as "South Dakota birds."
9. The state produces other products: livestock are fattened in feedlots in eastern South Dakota.
10. Even though meatpacking is a major industry in Sioux Falls, corncribs throughout the state remind visitors that corn is king.

➡ **For a SELF-CHECK and more practice, see the EXERCISE BANK, p. 590.**

B. REVISING: Adding Compound Nouns

Read the following description. Then choose five compound nouns from the list to replace the words in parentheses.

During our summer vacation, my family usually visits the annual state fair. **(1)** Mom, Dad, and Cindy like to start off by riding the **(singular compound)**. **(2)** Cindy also enjoys petting animals, especially furry ones—sheep, rabbits, and **(plural compound)**. **(3)** My brother Tom and I, however, like to tear up the **(singular compound)** on our **(plural compound)**. **(4)** By evening, we all look forward to the rodeo and loud, sparkling **(plural compound)**.

skateboard
billy goats
thunderstorm
Ferris wheel
dirt bikes
fireworks
barnyard
rattlesnakes
racetrack

Nouns and Their Jobs

❶ Here's the Idea

Because they name many things, nouns have different jobs in sentences.

Nouns as Subjects

A **subject** tells whom or what a sentence is about. Nouns are often subjects, as this description shows.

> **PROFESSIONAL MODEL**
>
> **Independence Hall** in Philadelphia is one of the nation's most popular landmarks. Here, the **Declaration of Independence** was approved by the 13 colonies on July 4, 1776.

Nouns as Complements

A **complement** is a word that completes the meaning of a verb. Three kinds of complements are predicate nouns, direct objects, and indirect objects.

Nouns as Complements		
Predicate noun	Renames, identifies, or defines the subject after a linking verb.	Benjamin Franklin was a **Founding Father** of our country.
Direct object	Names the receiver of the action after an action verb.	Thomas Jefferson wrote the **Declaration of Independence.**
Indirect object	Tells to whom or what or for whom or what an action is done.	Mom gave my **brother** a miniature replica of the Liberty Bell.

Nouns as Objects of Prepositions

An **object of a preposition** is the noun or pronoun that follows a preposition.

Paul Revere left on his ride.

PREPOSITION ⬆   ⬆ OBJECT OF PREPOSITION

You'll learn more about prepositions on pp. 152–157.

NOUNS

❷ Why It Matters in Writing

Specific complements can help you create a
sharp picture. Notice how the complements in
this description add specific details.

PROFESSIONAL MODEL

In the nation's capital, the Washington
Monument seems a giant arrow, piercing the
highest skies. This tremendous column climbs
555 feet into the air. The monument's sparkling
beauty still astounds children and adults more
than a century after its completion.

> PREDICATE
> NOUN

> DIRECT
> OBJECTS

❸ Practice and Apply

A. CONCEPT CHECK: Nouns and Their Jobs

Identify each underlined noun as a subject, a complement, or
an object of a preposition.

Maya Lin and the Vietnam Veterans Memorial
1. The Vietnam War brought our country much sorrow.
2. More than 58,000 Americans died or remained missing
   in action.
3. Veterans of the war wished to honor those who died.
4. A committee set up a contest to choose someone to
   design a memorial.
5. Maya Lin, a young architect, visited Washington, D.C., to
   view the memorial site.
6. The landscape gave Lin an idea.
7. The architect designed a memorial of two marble walls.
8. She created a meeting place between earth and sky.
9. The names of dead and missing Americans appear on
   the walls.
10. Visits to the memorial have been healing experiences for
    millions of Americans.

➜ **For a SELF-CHECK and more practice, see the EXERCISE BANK, p. 591.**

Label each complement as a predicate noun, a direct object,
or an indirect object.

B. REVISING: Identifying Complements

Identify each underlined complement as a predicate noun, a direct object, or an indirect object.

The Cradle of Liberty

1. Boston, Massachusetts, is the <u>city</u> where American independence began.
2. Today, the Freedom Trail gives <u>tourists</u> a <u>walk</u> through history.
3. At Faneuil Hall colonists regularly protested the British <u>king</u> and his <u>taxation</u>.
4. In 1773, at Griffin's Wharf, patriots boarded three <u>ships</u>.
5. The patriots were active <u>participants</u> in the destruction of British property—tea.

C. WRITING: Using Nouns in Directions

A Tour of the White House

Imagine that you have been asked to prepare directions for tour guides at the White House. The tour begins in the Rose Garden and continues clockwise through the first floor. Using the floor plan shown below, write simple directions for the guides. Include nouns used as subjects, complements, and objects of prepositions. Then identify and label each.

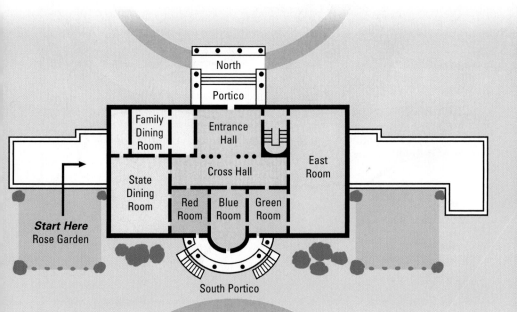

Grammar in Social Studies

Using Nouns Effectively

In social studies classes you learn about important people, places, and things,—and you use nouns to name them. Creating a map is a good way to show information rather than talking about it. Mapmaking allows you to present clearly where important places are and where important events took place. Notice how common and proper nouns are used on this map of the famous Route 66.

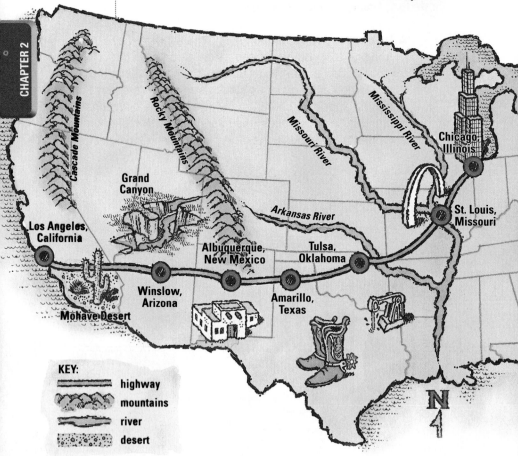

KEY:

≈≈≈≈≈ highway

🗻🗻🗻 mountains

≈≈≈ river

⋯⋯⋯ desert

Practice and Apply

A. REVISING: Using Proper Nouns

The message below is hard to understand because the writer uses many common nouns rather than specific proper ones. On a separate sheet of paper, write proper nouns to replace the underlined common nouns. Use the map to find the proper nouns.

Dear Anya,
   Driving on <u>this road</u> is so cool. We started out at <u>a lake</u> and ended up at <u>the ocean</u>. We went through eight states and crossed <u>two of the country's major rivers</u>. <u>One city on a river</u> had a huge arch sticking up into the sky. Near the end of the trip, we passed by <u>one desert</u> and finally jumped into the surf at our final destination.
   I wish you could have come with us.
   See you soon,
         Winona

Anya Taylor
501 S. Francisco Ave.
Chicago, IL 60601

B. WRITING: Make a map of your own.

Draw a map of your neighborhood, a nearby park, zoo, or any other area. Include the following landmarks:

- natural features such as rivers, lakes, and mountains
- streets
- buildings
- other interesting attractions

Be sure to label each landmark with an appropriate proper noun. Use different colors or symbols for features like streets, rivers, and bike paths. Use common nouns to create a key that explains the symbols.

A colorful strip along Route 66.

A. Plurals, Possessives, and Compounds Read the following sign advertising a roadside attraction, and correct ten errors in spelling. Then identify each corrected noun as plural, possessive, or compound. For some of the nouns, you will use more than one label.

Freds' Famous Fantastic Museum!

★ *Come see our attractions:*

Queen Victoria's neck lace

Antique watchs and grandfatherclocks

★ A base ball autographed by Babe Ruth

Settlers' original diarys

An entire school house from 1900

Elvis' white scarfs

★ The Beatles's bus from their first U.S. tour

B. Nouns and Their Jobs In the following sentences, nouns are used in various ways. Identify each underlined noun as a subject, a predicate noun, a direct object, an indirect object, or an object of a preposition.

1. A favorite site of many tourists is the <u>Everglades.</u>
2. The <u>Everglades</u> are wetlands in southern Florida.
3. The naturalist Marjory Stoneman Douglas saved the <u>Everglades</u> from <u>destruction</u> several decades ago.
4. Still, the <u>Everglades</u> continued to be drained, and much of the habitat of <u>alligators</u> and wading birds disappeared.
5. Now a congressional agreement gives the <u>Everglades</u> millions of dollars for preservation.
6. Every tourist should honor <u>John Muir</u> for his life and work.
7. <u>Muir</u> was a lifelong tourist himself.
8. His parents brought <u>Muir</u> and his sisters from Scotland to Wisconsin as children.
9. <u>Muir</u> later traveled the country and was responsible for saving Yosemite as a national park.
10. The conservationist who founded the Sierra Club was <u>John Muir.</u>

Mastery Test: What Did You Learn?

For each underlined item, choose the letter of the term that correctly identifies it.

> In the East and the <u>Midwest</u>, travelers can visit many <u>sites</u>
> (1)   (2)
> associated with the Underground Railroad. This "railroad" consisted
> of people and places that helped Southern slaves escaping to the
> North and to Canada. Both blacks and whites were "<u>conductors</u>"
> (3)
> and guided the <u>runaways</u>. Some conductors were slaves who had
> (4)
> already escaped and then traveled back south to lead others to
> safety. Over 2,000 slaves passed through <u>Levi Coffin's</u> home in
> (5)
> Newport, Indiana. A <u>light</u> in the <u>window</u> of John Rankin's home in
> (6)   (7)
> Ohio showed slaves that no slave catchers were nearby. Today the
> homes of <u>Levi Coffin</u>, John Rankin, and others are open so that the
> (8)
> <u>public</u> can learn about the "railroad" of <u>courage</u>.
> (9)   (10)

1. A. singular common noun
   B. plural common noun
   C. singular proper noun
   D. plural proper noun

2. A. noun as subject
   B. noun as predicate noun
   C. noun as direct object
   D. nouns as indirect object

3. A. noun as subject
   B. noun as predicate noun
   C. noun as direct object
   D. noun as indirect object

4. A. singular possessive noun
   B. plural possessive noun
   C. singular compound noun
   D. plural compound noun

5. A. singular collective noun
   B. plural collective noun
   C. singular possessive noun
   D. plural possessive noun

6. A. noun as subject
   B. noun as predicate noun
   C. noun as direct object
   D. noun as indirect object

7. A. concrete noun
   B. abstract noun
   C. possessive noun
   D. compound noun

8. A. noun as direct object
   B. noun as subject
   C. noun as predicate noun
   D. noun as object of a preposition

9. A. compound noun
   B. collective noun
   C. proper noun
   D. possessive noun

10. A. compound noun
    B. concrete noun
    C. abstract noun
    D. possessive noun

Student Help Desk

Nouns at a Glance

A noun names a person, place, thing, or idea. There are several ways to classify nouns.

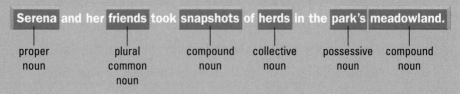

Serena and her friends took snapshots of herds in the park's meadowland.

| proper noun | plural common noun | compound noun | collective noun | possessive noun | compound noun |

QUICK–FIX SPELLING MACHINE: PLURALS OF NOUNS

	SINGULAR	RULE	PLURAL
1	tent	Add -s to most nouns.	tents
2	fox	Add -es to nouns that end in s, sh, ch, x, or z.	foxes
3	photo	Add -s to most nouns that end in o.	photos
	tomato	Add -es to a few nouns that end in o.	tomatoes
4	butterfly	For most nouns ending in y, change the y to i and add -es.	butterflies
	alley	When a vowel comes before the y, just add -s.	alleys
5	leaf	For most nouns ending in f or fe, change the f to v and add -es.	leaves
6	campfire	Add -s to most compound nouns.	campfires
7	pup tent	For a hyphenated compound or one written as separate words, make the main noun plural.	pup tents

Classifying Nouns Sorting Your Stuff

Possessives of Nouns

Relationship	Ownership
Douglas's sister	Natalie's marshmallow

Collective Nouns

Collective Noun	Group of Animals
colony	colony of ants, badgers, or frogs
flock	flock of birds or sheep
school	school of fish
herd	herd of cattle, deer, or elephants

More Noun Types

Concrete	Abstract
tent	nature
lake	beauty

Nouns and Their Jobs What's Happening at Camp?

Use of Noun	Example
Subject	**Mosquitoes** swarmed around Meg's head.
Predicate noun	The bullfrogs were our **entertainers** for the night.
Direct object	Tim tipped his **canoe** over in the icy river.
Indirect object	Kyra just handed **Jordan** a moldy plum.
Object of a preposition	We're hiking to **Old Faithful** this afternoon.

The Bottom Line

Checklist for Nouns

Have I . . .

____ chosen precise nouns?

____ spelled plural nouns correctly?

____ spelled possessive nouns correctly?

____ used possessive nouns to shorten my sentences?

____ spelled compound nouns correctly?

Pronouns

There it goes!
I can see it.
Quick, bring your
light over here!

What *is* that?
Maybe we
should get help.

Theme: It's a Mystery
Who Did What?

Imagine this conversation without the words *it, I, your, what, that,* and *we.* These words, called **pronouns,** can streamline your writing by taking the place of nouns or other pronouns. Be careful though. If you don't use pronouns correctly, you may create a mystery for your readers.

Write Away: Real-Life Mysteries
You don't need to be a detective to solve mysteries. In a sense, you solve a mystery whenever you find the answer to a math problem or succeed in locating your new homeroom. Write a paragraph describing a mystery you've solved. Place the paragraph in your 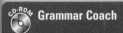 **Working Portfolio.**

CD-ROM **Grammar Coach**

Choose the letter that correctly identifies each underlined word.

> Ball lightning is one of nature's most baffling mysteries. Small glowing spheres appear during violent thunderstorms. No one knows what causes <u>them</u>. <u>Their</u> behavior is truly weird. One
> (1)   (2)
> eyewitness said <u>he</u> saw a blue sphere go right through <u>his</u>
> (3)   (4)
> windowpane, burning a neat hole in the glass. If <u>you</u> are in an
> (5)
> airplane during a thunderstorm, you <u>yourself</u> might see ball
> (6)
> lightning rolling down the aisle! <u>This</u> has actually happened on
> (7)
> some flights. In one city, a multicolored sphere entered a factory, traveled along the metal girders, hit a window, and disappeared. The workers must have argued among <u>themselves</u> about whether
> (8)
> to tell <u>anyone</u>. <u>Who</u> would believe such a strange story?
> (9)   (10)

1. A. subject pronoun
   B. object pronoun
   C. possessive pronoun
   D. demonstrative pronoun

2. A. indefinite pronoun
   B. subject pronoun
   C. demonstrative pronoun
   D. possessive pronoun

3. A. first-person pronoun
   B. second-person pronoun
   C. third-person pronoun
   D. plural pronoun

4. A. plural possessive pronoun
   B. singular possessive pronoun
   C. plural object pronoun
   D. singular object pronoun

5. A. personal pronoun
   B. interrogative pronoun
   C. reflexive pronoun
   D. demonstrative pronoun

6. A. indefinite pronoun
   B. reflexive pronoun
   C. intensive pronoun
   D. interrogative pronoun

7. A. demonstrative pronoun
   B. intensive pronoun
   C. complement pronoun
   D. interrogative pronoun

8. A. personal pronoun
   B. indefinite pronoun
   C. reflexive pronoun
   D. possessive pronoun

9. A. demonstrative pronoun
   B. indefinite pronoun
   C. reflexive pronoun
   D. interrogative pronoun

10. A. demonstrative pronoun
    B. interrogative pronoun
    C. indefinite pronoun
    D. reflexive pronoun

at Is a Pronoun?

❶ Here's the Idea

▶ **A pronoun is a word that is used in place of a noun or another pronoun.** A pronoun can refer to a person, place, thing, or idea. The word that a pronoun refers to is called its **antecedent.**

REFERS TO

Ramon visited Death Valley, and he was impressed.

REFERS TO

Death Valley is mysterious. It is silent.

Personal Pronouns

▶ **Pronouns such as *we, I, he, them*, and *it* are called personal pronouns.** Personal pronouns have a variety of forms to indicate different **persons, numbers,** and **cases.**

Person and Number There are first-person, second-person, and third-person personal pronouns, each having both singular and plural forms.

Singular	Plural
I went out.	**We** left early.
You left too.	**You** are leaving.
He came by bus.	**They** came by car.

Case Each personal pronoun has three cases: subject, object, and possessive. Which form to use depends on the pronoun's function in a sentence.

Subject: **He read about Death Valley.**

Object: **Julie asked him about the rocks.**

Possessive: **Ramon brought his book.**

The chart on the next page shows all the forms of the personal pronouns.

Personal Pronouns			
	Subject	**Object**	**Possessive**
Singular			
First person	I	me	my, mine
Second person	you	you	your, yours
Third person	he, she, it	him, her, it	his, her, hers, its
Plural			
First person	we	us	our, ours
Second person	you	you	your, yours
Third person	they	them	their, theirs

❷ Why It Matters in Writing

Pronouns help you talk about people concisely when you're telling a story. Notice how pronouns are used in this passage.

> **LITERARY MODEL**
>
> I knew I had to be honest with Grandpa; it was my only chance. He saw my shadow and looked up.
>   He waited for me to speak. I cleared my throat nervously. . . .
>
> —Marta Salinas, "The Scholarship Jacket"

❸ Practice and Apply

A. CONCEPT CHECK: What Is a Pronoun?

Write the personal pronouns in these sentences.

Mystery in Death Valley
1. Death Valley is famous for its strange moving boulders.
2. They are found in a dry lake bed called Racetrack Playa.
3. The rocks slide on their own, leaving long tracks behind them.
4. Can you think of an explanation for this curious event?
5. Investigators offer two major theories for us to consider.

6. One geologist thinks that when floodwater freezes, an ice sheet can form under a rock and help it slide.
7. Other scientists disagree with his theory.
8. They believe that the wind alone can move the rocks.
9. Some scientists have hedged their bets, telling us that both theories could be true.
10. We still don't know for sure how the rocks move.

Name the antecedents of the personal pronouns in sentences 1, 3, 6, 7, and 8.

→ For a SELF-CHECK and more practice, see the EXERCISE BANK, p. 591.

B. REVISING: Substituting Pronouns for Nouns

Rewrite this draft of a social studies report by changing each underlined noun to a pronoun.

STUDENT MODEL

Death Valley is a land of extremes. <u>Death Valley</u> contains the lowest point in the United States. Temperatures reflect the harsh, arid landscape. <u>Temperatures</u> range from 125°F in summer to near freezing in winter.

The valley was named in 1849 by pioneers after <u>the pioneers'</u> long, hard journey. In 1868 a California state geologist mentioned the valley in <u>the geologist's</u> published paper. The valley interested other geologists when <u>the geologists</u> heard about the valuable minerals discovered there.

C. WRITING: Dialogue

Use the information in exercise A to write a short dialogue between two people who are visiting Racetrack Playa. Use personal pronouns to make the dialogue sound natural.

Example:

SPEAKER 1. Did **you** see that boulder move?

SPEAKER 2. No, **I** didn't. Maybe **it** just wobbled a little.

SPEAKER 1. Don't tell **me** that. **You** can see the track!

Death Valley

LESSON 2 Subject Pronouns

❶ Here's the Idea

▶ A subject pronoun is used as a subject in a sentence or as a predicate pronoun after a linking verb.

Subject Pronouns	
Singular	**Plural**
I	we
you	you
he, she, it	they

Pronouns as Subjects

Use a subject pronoun when the pronoun is a subject or part of a compound subject.

The Hope diamond has a fascinating history.

It has been bad luck for many owners.
(*It*, referring to *The Hope diamond,* is the subject of the sentence.)

You and he think the diamond is cursed.

Predicate Pronouns

A predicate pronoun follows a linking verb and identifies the verb's subject. Use the subject case for predicate pronouns.

The owner was he.
    ↑ SUBJECT   ↑ PREDICATE PRONOUN

The buyers are you and she.

The royal jewelers are they.

Remember, the most common linking verbs are forms of the verb *be*, including *is, am, are, was, were, been, has been, have been, can be, will be, could be,* and *should be.*

PRONOUNS

❷ Why It Matters in Writing

A subject pronoun may not sound right to you. But as the writer of the passage below discovered, you can't always rely on sound to choose the correct case.

> The huge French Blue diamond, later recut into the Hope diamond, was certainly bad luck for Marie Antoinette. The rulers of France in the years before the French Revolution were ~~her~~ she and Louis XVI. Marie Antoinette and ~~him~~ he were executed during the revolution.

❸ Practice and Apply

CONCEPT CHECK: Subject Pronouns

Write the correct pronoun form to complete each sentence.

Investigating the Hope Diamond Legend

1. The diamond detectives were Carla and (I, me).
2. According to legend the huge blue diamond has had many owners, and (they, them) all came to a bad end.
3. Jean Baptiste Tavernier brought the original blue diamond from India; the first owner to die was (him, he).
4. (He, him) is said to have been killed in India by wild dogs.
5. Marie Antoinette and Louis XVI inherited the diamond; (we, us) know that the next victims were (them, they).
6. Carla and (me, I) learned that a Dutch diamond cutter may have recut the stone to disguise it.
7. His son and (he, him) died tragically soon afterward.
8. In the 1830s Henry Hope bought the recut gem; the person for whom the diamond was named was (he, him).
9. (We, Us) discovered that the Hope diamond is now in the Smithsonian Institution in Washington, D.C.
10. "Hope diamond experts" are (us, we)!

➜ **For a SELF-CHECK and more practice, see the EXERCISE BANK, p. 592.**

Object Pronouns

LESSON 3

❶ Here's the Idea

▶ **An object pronoun is used as a direct object, an indirect object, or an object of a preposition.**

Object Pronouns	
Singular	**Plural**
me	us
you	you
him, her, it	them

Direct Object The pronoun receives the action of a verb and answers the question *whom or what.*

The mysterious death of King Tut fascinates me.
FASCINATES
DIRECT OBJECT

Did someone murder him? (murder whom? *him*)

Indirect Object The pronoun tells to whom or what or for whom or what an action is performed.

TO
Chu lent me a video on the topic.
INDIRECT OBJECT   DIRECT OBJECT

I told her the whole story.

Object of a Preposition The pronoun follows a preposition (such as *to, from, for, against, by,* or *about*).

Will you save the video for them?
PREPOSITION
I can tell the story to you and him.

Always use object pronouns after the preposition *between.*

This secret is between you and me. (not *between you and I*)

❷ Why It Matters in Writing

In conversation, people sometimes misuse subject and object pronouns ("Him and me went to the store"). When you write for school, however, you should always use the correct forms.

> The Egyptologist Bob Brier studied King Tut's mummy.
> Evidence uncovered by ~~he~~ *him* suggests that Tut was killed by a blow to the head. Others say he was poisoned. Brier and ~~them~~ *they* agree, however, that the king was murdered.

❸ Practice and Apply

MIXED REVIEW: Subject and Object Pronouns

Choose the correct pronoun in these sentences, and identify them as subject or object pronouns.

Who Killed King Tut?

1. King Tutankhamen was only about nine years old when the priests crowned (he, him) as the new pharaoh.
2. (He, Him) and his wife were not in power long before the young pharaoh died.
3. (I, Me) saw a video showing x-ray pictures of Tut's skull.
4. (They, Them) revealed that someone had struck Tut on the back of the head.
5. It occurred to (I, me) that only someone the king knew could get so close to (he, him).
6. There are several possible suspects, but two of (them, they) had the best opportunity—the queen and the royal minister, Ay.
7. (She, Her) and Ay married when Ay became pharaoh.
8. A ring discovered in 1931, however, shows that Ay married another queen after (she, her).
9. Just between you and (me, I), I believe that Ay is the most likely killer.
10. All the suspects may be long dead, but the evidence has outlived (they, them).

➡ **For a SELF-CHECK and more practice, see the EXERCISE BANK, p. 592.**

Possessive Pronouns

① Here's the Idea

▶ **A possessive pronoun is a personal pronoun used to show ownership or relationship.**

Possessive Pronouns	
Singular	**Plural**
my, mine	our, ours
your, yours	your, yours
her, hers, his, its	their, theirs

The possessive pronouns *my, your, her, his, its, our,* and *their* come before nouns.

OWNERSHIP

The Chinese museum kept its amazing secret for years.

OWNERSHIP

No one saw the mummies in their colorful clothes.

RELATIONSHIP

Then Professor Mair and his tour group arrived.

The possessive pronouns *mine, yours, hers, his, ours* and *theirs* can stand alone in a sentence.

The secret was theirs. Now the secret is ours.

Is that book yours? No, mine has a blue cover.

His looks torn. Is hers in better shape?

Possessive Pronouns and Contractions

Some possessive pronouns sound like contractions (*its/it's, your/you're, their/they're*). Because these pairs sound alike, writers often confuse possessive pronouns with contractions.

Remember, a possessive pronoun *never* has an apostrophe. A contraction, however, *always* has an apostrophe. The apostrophe shows where a letter or letters have been left out after combining two words.

QUICK–FIX SPELLING MACHINE

Possessive pronouns		Contractions	
its	Its clothes look great.	it's	It's well preserved.
your	Your pictures are great.	you're	You're talented!
their	Their colors are vivid.	they're	They're beautiful.

❷ Why It Matters in Writing

Proofread your work carefully to be sure you haven't confused possessive pronouns with contractions. The spell-checker on a computer will not catch these mistakes.

> **STUDENT MODEL**
>
> The desert, with ~~it's~~ *its* dry air, salt, and sand, is the best preserver of ancient textiles. Once these materials are uncovered, however, ~~their~~ *they're* easily damaged. Even the moisture from ~~you're~~ *your* hands and breath can harm the fibers. For this reason, archaeologists always wear masks when they work with ancient cloth.

Experts use tools in *their* work.

❸ Practice and Apply

A. CONCEPT CHECK: Possessive Pronouns

Choose the pronoun or contraction to complete each sentence.

> **The Amazing Mummies of Ürümqi**
> **1.** Imagine (your, you're) visiting a museum in Ürümqi, in the desert of northwest China.
> **2.** In one room, you find remarkable mummies in (their, they're) cases.
> **3.** The leggings, shirts, and cloaks on the mummies look as colorful as (your, you're) clothes today.
> **4.** This experience really happened to Professor Mair and his tour group on (their, they're) trip to China in 1987.
> **5.** The mummies are about 3,000 years old, and (they're, their) European, not Chinese!
> **6.** (It's, Its) a mystery why these Europeans went all the way to China.
> **7.** Mair's astonishing report made (its, it's) way around the world.
> **8.** Some 3,000 years ago, a group of European Celts may have started trading with (their, they're) Chinese neighbors.
> **9.** When one of the Celts was buried, the dry, salty desert preserved the body and (it's, its) clothing perfectly.
> **10.** You can satisfy (your, you're) curiosity about these mummies of Ürürmqi by reading articles about them.

➡ For a SELF-CHECK and more practice, see the EXERCISE BANK, p. 593.

B. PROOFREADING: Using Possessive Pronouns

Correct the errors in the use of pronouns and contractions in the paragraph below. If a sentence contains no error, write *Correct*.

(1) Its common for archaeologists to name the mummies they find. (2) Sometimes they're named for the way they look, other times for a person or place. (3) Your probably not aware that three mummies in the Smithsonian Institution are named Indiana Jones, Ancient Annie, and Minister Cox. (4) You can guess how the first two got they're names, but how did Minister Cox get him? (5) The mummy was named after a former diplomat, Mr. Cox, who donated the mummy to the museum for it's Egyptian collection.

Reflexive and Intensive Pronouns

1 Here's the Idea

A pronoun that ends in *self* or *selves* is either a reflexive or an intensive pronoun.

Reflexive and Intensive Pronouns		
myself	yourself	herself, himself, itself
ourselves	yourselves	themselves

Reflexive Pronouns

▶ **A reflexive pronoun refers to the subject and directs the action of the verb back to the subject.** Reflexive pronouns are necessary to the meaning of a sentence.

 REFLECTS

Houdini **called himself a master escape artist.**

REFLECTS

Lynne **dedicated herself to learning Houdini's secrets.**

Notice that if you drop a reflexive pronoun, a sentence no longer makes sense ("Lynne dedicated to learning Houdini's secrets").

Intensive Pronouns

▶ **An intensive pronoun emphasizes a noun or another pronoun in the same sentence.** Intensive pronouns are not necessary to the meaning of a sentence.

You yourselves **have seen magic shows on TV.**

I myself **like to perform magic tricks.**

Notice that when you drop an intensive pronoun, a sentence still makes sense ("I like to perform magic tricks").

Hisself and *theirselves* may look like real words, but they are not. Use *himself* and *themselves* instead.

68 Grammar, Usage, and Mechanics

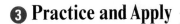

❷ Why It Matters in Writing

You can use reflexive pronouns to describe a person's actions more clearly.

> **PROFESSIONAL MODEL**
>
> In the Water Torture Cell, Houdini doubled **himself** up and picked the lock that held his feet. Then, still holding his breath, he stood and unlocked the top of the tank. He hauled **himself** out.
>
> —L. S. Baugh

❸ Practice and Apply

CONCEPT CHECK: Reflexive and Intensive Pronouns

Write the reflexive or intensive pronoun in each sentence. Then label it *reflexive* or *intensive*.

Houdini's Great Escapes

1. During the 1920s, Harry Houdini labeled himself "the most daring escape artist in the world."
2. His name itself makes people think of magic.
3. In one famous trick, Houdini freed himself from a tank that was filled to the top with water and securely locked.
4. He also called himself "the handcuff king" and said no handcuffs in the world could hold him.
5. The police officers themselves were amazed at Houdini.
6. Some people convinced themselves that Houdini really had mysterious powers.
7. The magician himself said that wasn't true.
8. He said people could develop these skills themselves.
9. Still, we probably couldn't become Houdinis even if we taught ourselves his secrets.
10. Even today's professional magicians themselves don't try Houdini's dangerous escapes.

➡ For a SELF-CHECK and more practice, see the EXERCISE BANK, p. 593.

LESSON 6 Interrogatives and Demonstratives

❶ Here's the Idea

Interrogative Pronouns

▶ **An interrogative pronoun is used to introduce a question.**

Who made up this riddle?

Which riddle are you talking about?

Using Interrogative Pronouns	
Interrogative Pronoun	**Use**
who, whom	refers to people
what	refers to things
which	refers to people or things
whose	indicates ownership or relationship

Using *Who* and *Whom*

▶ ***Who* is always used as a subject or a predicate pronoun.**

Subject: **Who knows the answer to the riddle?**

Predicate pronoun: **Your favorite comedian is who?**

▶ ***Whom* is always used as an object.**

Direct object: **Whom did you tell?**

Indirect object: **You gave whom the answer?**

Object of preposition: **To whom did you give my name?**

Don't confuse *whose* with *who's*. *Whose* is a pronoun. ("Whose book did you borrow?") *Who's* is a contraction that means *who is* or *who has*. ("Who's missing a book"? "Who's returned my book?")

CHAPTER 3

Demonstrative Pronouns

▶ **A demonstrative pronoun points out a person, place, thing, or idea.**

The demonstrative pronouns—*this, that, these,* and *those*—are used alone in a sentence, as shown below.

Singular

This is the game
that we created.

That is the spinner.

Plural

These are the rules.

Those are the
playing pieces.

Never use *here* or *there* with a demonstrative pronoun. The pronoun already tells which one or ones. *This* and *these* point out people or things that are near, or *here. That* and *those* point out people or things that are far away, or *there.*

This ~~here~~ is my playing piece.

That ~~there~~ is your playing piece.

❷ Why It Matters in Writing

Demonstrative pronouns call readers' attention to the people or things being discussed. In the riddles below, the demonstrative pronouns serve as the subjects of the riddles.

> **STUDENT MODEL**
>
> **This** has 18 legs and
> catches flies.
>
> Answer: baseball team
>
> **These** may fall far, but they
> never break.
>
> Answer: leaves
>
> Although **this** is small, it
> fills the house.
>
> Answer: a lamp's light
>
> **These** are bought by the
> yard and worn by the foot.
>
> Answer: floor carpets

❸ Practice and Apply

A. CONCEPT CHECK: Interrogatives and Demonstratives

Write the correct word to complete each sentence.

Inventors' Guide to Creating Board Games

1. To create a great board game, you need to answer some basic questions. First, (what, who) is the goal of the game?
2. If several people make up rules, (who's, whose) will you follow?
3. (Who, What) will you use to represent each player?
4. (Who, Whom) will go first?
5. You have to think up penalties. (That, Those) are important to any game.
6. Also, to (who, whom) will you give extra points or turns?
7. You need to create some kind of trap along the way. (These, This) makes the game more challenging.
8. Be careful (which, what) people you tell about the game before you finish it.
9. (Who, Whom) knows—someone might try to copy it.
10. Once you finish the game, (who, whom) will you invite to play it?

➔ **For a SELF-CHECK and more practice, see the EXERCISE BANK, p. 594.**

B. WRITING: What's Missing?

Geometry is important to quilters. Notice the many geometric pieces in the quilt. Can you find the sections that are missing from this quilt? Write a sentence about each missing section, describing its shape and telling how many sides it has. Then write another sentence to compare the missing sections to each other. Use four demonstrative pronouns in your sentences. Underline the demonstrative pronouns.

Pronoun Agreement

① Here's the Idea

▶ **The antecedent is the noun or pronoun that a pronoun replaces or refers to.** The antecedent and the pronoun can be in the same sentence or in difference sentences.

REFERS TO

Louis writes his own detective stories.
⬆ ANTECEDENT   ⬆ PRONOUN

REPLACES

Agatha Christie writes mysteries. Her stories are famous.

Pronouns must agree with their antecedents in number, person, and gender.

Agreement in Number

▶ **Use a singular pronoun to refer to a singular antecedent.**

REFERS TO

One story has its setting in Egypt.

▶ **Use a plural pronoun to refer to a plural antecedent.**

REFERS TO

The characters have their motives for murder.

Agreement in Person

▶ **The pronoun must agree in person with the antecedent.**

3RD PERSON

Louis likes his mysteries to have surprise endings.

2ND PERSON

You want a story to grab your attention.

Avoid switching from one person to another in the same sentence or paragraph.

INCORRECT:

> Readers **know you shouldn't read the ending first.**
> (*Readers* is third person; *you* is second person.)

CORRECT:

> Readers **know they shouldn't read the ending first.**
> (*Readers* and *they* are both third person.)

Agreement in Gender

▶ **The gender of a pronoun must be the same as the gender of its antecedent.**

Personal pronouns have three gender forms: masculine (*he, his, him*), feminine (*she, her, hers*), and neuter (*it, its*).

> **Agatha Christie sets many of her stories in England.**

> **The hero has to use all his wits to solve the crime.**

Don't use only masculine or only feminine pronouns when you mean to refer to both genders.

DRAFT:

Each **character** has **his** alibi ready.
(character could be masculine or feminine.)

There are two ways to make this sentence gender free.

1. Use the phrase *his or her*.
Each character has his or her alibi ready.

2. Rewrite the sentence, using a plural antecedent and a plural pronoun. Be careful! Other words may also need to be changed.
The characters have their alibis ready.

❷ Why It Matters in Writing

In your writing, you will sometimes refer to several people or groups of people. Correct pronoun-antecedent agreement will help your readers keep track of who is who in your writing.

STUDENT MODEL

> **Mystery lovers** should read novels by Agatha Christie. ~~You~~ *They*
>
> will never guess who is the real **killer** in any of these stories.
>
> *He or she*
> ~~They~~ usually turn~s~ out to be a surprise.

❸ Practice and Apply

CONCEPT CHECK: Pronoun Agreement

Write the pronouns and their antecedents in these sentences.

Agatha Christie: Amateur Archaeologist

1. Agatha Christie loved real-life mysteries of the past. She helped to investigate them in the Middle East.
2. Max Mallowan was an English archaeologist. He was married to Christie for 45 years.
3. The couple went on many archaeological trips and found them exciting and a real source of inspiration.
4. Christie and Mallowan made important discoveries about Assyria. It was a wealthy country in the ancient world.
5. Pottery pieces revealed their secrets about the powerful Assyrian civilization.
6. Although Christie helped Mallowan at the site, she also kept writing mysteries.
7. A mystery writer may use exotic places as background for his or her stories.
8. Christie started *Murder in Mesopotamia* in the desert, but she finished it in England.
9. The story takes place at an archaeological dig. One of its main characters is Dr. Leidner.
10. When Mrs. Leidner is murdered, the detective Hercule Poirot must catch her killer.

Write the number and gender of each personal pronoun.

➡ **For a SELF-CHECK and more practice, see the EXERCISE BANK, p. 594.**

LESSON 8 Indefinite-Pronoun Agreement

❶ Here's the Idea

▶ **An indefinite pronoun does not refer to a specific person, place, thing, or idea.**

Indefinite pronouns often do not have antecedents.

> **Something unusual is going on in Loch Ness.**

> **Has anyone photographed the Loch Ness monster?**

▶ **Some indefinite pronouns are always singular, some are always plural, and some can be either singular or plural.**

Indefinite Pronouns

Singular		Plural	Singular or Plural
another	neither	both	all
anybody	nobody	few	any
anyone	no one	many	most
anything	nothing	several	none
each	one		some
either	somebody		
everybody	someone		
everyone	something		
everything			

Any pronoun containing *one*, *thing*, or *body* is singular.

Singular Indefinite Pronouns

▶ **Use a singular personal pronoun to refer to a singular indefinite pronoun.**

REFERS TO

> **Everyone took his or her camera to the lake.**

(*Everyone* could be masculine or feminine.)

REFERS TO

> **One dropped his camera in the water by mistake.**

Plural Indefinite Pronouns

▶ **Use a plural personal pronoun to refer to a plural indefinite pronoun.**

REFERS TO

Several reported their sightings of the monster.

REFERS TO

Many could not believe their own eyes!

Singular or Plural Indefinite Pronouns

▶ **Some indefinite pronouns can be singular or plural.** The phrase that follows the indefinite pronoun will often tell you whether the pronoun is singular or plural.

Most of the monster story has its origin in fantasy.
↟SINGULAR INDEFINITE PRONOUN   ↟SINGULAR PERSONAL PRONOUN

Most of the monster stories have their origins in fantasy.
↟ PLURAL INDEFINITE PRONOUN   ↟PLURAL PERSONAL PRONOUN

❷ Why It Matters in Writing

Keep your facts and ideas clear. Make sure that all pronouns agree in number with their indefinite antecedents.

STUDENT MODEL

Not everyone has made up ~~their minds~~ *his or her mind*

about the existence of the Loch Ness

monster. A few have ~~his or her~~ *their* own ~~theory~~ *theories*.

> Use singular pronoun to agree with *everyone*

> Use plural pronoun to agree with *few*

PRONOUNS

❸ Practice and Apply

A. CONCEPT CHECK: Indefinite-Pronoun Agreement

Choose the pronoun that agrees with the indefinite pronoun antecedent.

The Quest for "Nessie"

1. All of the tourists want (his or her, their) own monster stories to tell.
2. None of the tourists have (his or her, their) questions answered.
3. Tourists wonder what the Loch Ness creature is. One said that in (their, her) opinion, it was an ancient reptile.
4. Several claim to have photos of (his or her, their) sightings.
5. Many display (his or her, their) very blurry photographs.
6. No one has proved that (their, his or her) pictures are genuine.
7. Everyone around Loch Ness has a nickname for the monster; (he or she, they) calls it "Nessie."
8. Scientists are curious about the mystery, and several have done (his or her, their) own underwater investigations.
9. Each has presented (his or her, their) theory about Nessie.
10. Most of the evidence has (their, its) problems, however.

➜ **For a SELF-CHECK and more practice, see the EXERCISE BANK, p. 595.**

B. PROOFREADING: Agreement Errors

Rewrite the paragraph, correcting errors in pronoun-antecedent agreement.

Famous Photo a Fake!

No one could believe their eyes when this famous photo was published. Most of the people had his or her opinions about the picture. Finally, the photographer, R. Kenneth Wilson, admitted it was a fake! Many were crushed that his or her favorite photo of Nessie was not real.

🗐 Return to your **Write Away** and correct any errors in pronoun-antecedent agreement.

Pronoun Problems

❶ Here's the Idea

We and *Us* with Nouns

The pronoun *we* or *us* is sometimes followed by a noun that identifies the pronoun (*we* students, *us* students).

▶ **Use *we* when the pronoun is a subject or a predicate pronoun. Use *us* when the pronoun is an object.**

We owners don't always understand our pets.
　　↖ SUBJECT

Dogs and cats often surprise us owners.
　　　　　　　　　↖ OBJECT OF VERB

> **Here's How** Choosing *We* or *Us*
>
> **Dogs think of (us, we) humans as their leaders.**
> **1.** Drop the identifying noun from the sentence.
> ---
> **Dogs think of (us, we) as their leaders.**
> **2.** Decide whether the sentence calls for a subject pronoun or an object pronoun. This sentence calls for the pronoun that is the object of the preposition *of*.
> **Dogs think of us as their leaders.**
> ---
> **3.** Use the correct pronoun with the noun.
> **Dogs think of us humans as their leaders.**

Unclear Reference

▶ **Be sure that each personal pronoun refers clearly to only one person, place, or thing.** If there is any chance your reader will be confused about whom or what you are talking about, use a noun instead of a pronoun.

Confusing: Tony and Fred want to become veterinarians. He now works at an animal shelter. (Who works? Tony or Fred?)

Clear: Tony and Fred want to become veterinarians. Fred now works at an animal shelter.

❷ Why It Matters in Writing

When you write a paper for school, or when you want to persuade someone in authority, your use of correct pronouns will help the reader take your ideas more seriously.

STUDENT MODEL

Dear Mayor Trimble:

~~Us~~ *We* students have some ideas about a

special dog park for the city. Sarah Fein

and Tanya Roberts have written a report

on our ideas. ~~She~~ *Tanya* will send it to you soon.

> Use *we*—*students* is a subject.

> *She* could refer either to Sarah or to Tanya. Name the person to avoid confusion.

❸ Practice and Apply

A. CONCEPT CHECK: Pronoun Problems

Choose the correct word in parentheses.

Mysterious Cat Behavior

1. Cats baffle (us, we) owners by the things they do.
2. They often rub themselves against (we, us) humans.
3. My two cats, Pickles and Bert, do this. Surprisingly, (he, Bert) does this even with strangers.
4. However, (he, Pickles) hides when guests arrive.
5. This rubbing is simple. (We, Us) humans are being marked by the cat as part of its territory.

➡ **For a SELF-CHECK and more practice, see the EXERCISE BANK, p. 596.**

B. REVISING: Correcting Pronoun Errors

Correct the pronoun errors in the following paragraph.

A Cat's Point of View

Us cats have rights, too. A new puppy or pet bird in the house can upset us. It has very poor manners and will eat our food in one gulp. It will sit singing in its cage and drive us crazy. It will chase us through the house for fun. Owners need to consider the needs of we cats.

CHAPTER 3

More Pronoun Problems

LESSON 10

❶ Here's the Idea

Pronouns in Compounds

Pronouns sometimes cause difficulty when they are parts of compound subjects and compound objects.

▶ **Use the subject pronouns *I*, *she*, *he*, *we*, and *they* in a compound subject or with a predicate noun or pronoun.**

Kathy and he decided to research a mystery.

The research team was Jim and I.

▶ **Use the object pronouns *me*, *her*, *him*, *us*, and *them* in a compound object.**

Samantha asked Jim and me about the Bermuda Triangle.

Kathy loaned our report to Mac and her.

To choose the correct case of a pronoun in a compound part, read the sentence with only the pronoun in the compound part. Mentally screen out the noun. Then choose the correct case.

Intervening Phrases

Sometimes words and phrases come between a subject and a pronoun that refers to it. Don't be confused by those words in between. Mentally cross out the phrase to figure out agreement.

REFERS TO

Jim, ~~like the others,~~ brought his map. (*His* agrees with *Jim*, not with *others*.)

REFERS TO

Five planes ~~from a Navy airfield~~ lost their way in the Bermuda Triangle. (*Their* agrees with *planes*, not with *airfield*.)

PRONOUNS

❷ Why It Matters in Writing

Some writers think that *between you and I* sounds more formal than *between you and me* and therefore is correct. Don't make that mistake in your writing—*between you and me* is correct.

STUDENT MODEL

To begin our project, my partner and ~~me~~ *I* did some

research. However, between you and ~~I~~ *me*, I found many more

sources than she did.

❸ Practice and Apply

A. CONCEPT CHECK: More Pronoun Problems

Choose the correct word to complete each sentence.

The Bermuda Triangle: Mystery or Misinformation?

1. Terry, Kathy, Jim and (I, me) led a discussion about the Bermuda Triangle.
2. One student asked Jim and (I, me) where the Bermuda Triangle is.
3. Terry and (I, me) pointed out Bermuda, Puerto Rico, and the southeast coast of Florida.
4. The triangle, having three geographic boundaries, is named for (its, their) shape.
5. Another student asked Kathy and (we, us) about the strange disappearances that give the Bermuda Triangle its spooky reputation.
6. Jim and (I, me) explained that some ships and planes have mysteriously vanished in that area.
7. Angela, like several other classmates, had (her, their) doubts about the Bermuda Triangle stories.
8. Jim and (I, me) explained that many investigators agree with Angela.
9. Experts on the Bermuda Triangle said that in (its, their) opinion, many reports had been greatly exaggerated.
10. Between you and (I, me), I'm not sure how seriously to take this legend either.

➡️ For a SELF-CHECK and more practice, see the EXERCISE BANK, p. 596.

B. PROOFREADING: Correct Use of Pronouns

Rewrite the passage below, correcting the pronoun errors.

Flight 19: The Mystery Is Solved!

Claire and me read about the mysterious disappearance of Flight 19 in the Bermuda Triangle. Us students discovered that Flight 19 consisted of five Avenger bombers led by Lt. Charles Taylor. Hours after they're take-off from Fort Lauderdale, Florida, they vanished in the Atlantic Ocean.

Whom is responsible for the bizarre disappearance of Flight 19? Interestingly, some think that UFOs may have been responsible. Which actually happened is less dramatic.

Lt. Taylor thought he was flying southwest when he really was flying east. Taylor, unlike two other crew members, did not recognize their mistake. It's clear Taylor led the team farther out into the Atlantic. His men and he finally crashed in the ocean.

The facts about Flight 19 taught Claire and I not to believe in the myth of the Bermuda Triangle.

C. WRITING: Interpreting a Map

This map illustrates what may have happened to Flight 19. Working with a partner, use the map and the information in exercise B to write a paragraph, explaining in your own words what probably happened to Flight 19.

Underline the pronouns you use. Proofread your work to be sure you have used the pronouns correctly.

Flight 19's Path

★ Starting point ✗ Probable crash site

Example: The planes of Flight 19 left *their* base at the Naval Air Station in Fort Lauderdale, Florida.

·········· Taylor's planned flight path, heading southwest

·········· Taylor's actual flight path

Using Pronouns in Dialogue

Look at the following sentences. Then, compare them with the dialogue in the following passage. How do pronouns change the effect of the words?

"The guard told Jimmy to go out in the morning, brace up, and make a man of himself. The guard told Jimmy he wasn't a bad fellow at heart."

from:

A Retrieved Reformation

by O. Henry

"Now, Valentine," said the warden, "**you**'ll go out in the morning. Brace up and make a man of **yourself**. **You**'re not a bad fellow at heart. Stop cracking safes, and live straight.

"**Me**?" said Jimmy, in surprise. "Why, **I** never cracked a safe in **my** life."

"Oh, no," laughed the warden. "Of course not, Let's see now. How was it **you** happened to get sent up on that Springfield job? Was it because you wouldn't prove an alibi for fear of compromising **somebody** in extremely high-toned society? Or was it simply a case of a mean old jury that had it in for **you**? It's always one or the other with **you** innocent victims."

"**Me**?" said Jimmy, still blankly virtuous. "Why, warden, **I** never was in Springfield in **my** life."

Portrait of Prince Eristoff (1925) Tamara de Lempicka. Private collection, New York. Copyright © 1996 Artists Rights Society (ARS), New York/SPADEM, Paris.

Practice and Apply

The following passage from "A Retrieved Reformation" does not include dialogue. Read the passage and follow the steps to create a dialogue for a skit about the passage.

> The Elmore Bank had just put in a new safe and vault. Mr. Adams was very proud of it, and insisted on an inspection by everyone. The vault was a small one, but it had a new patented door. It fastened with three solid steel bolts thrown simultaneously with a single handle, and had a time lock.... The two children, May and Agatha, were delighted by the shining metal and funny clock and knobs....
>
> Suddenly there was a scream or two from the women, and a commotion. Unperceived by the elders, May, the nine-year-old girl, in a spirit of play, had shut Agatha in the vault. She had then shot the bolts and turned the knob of the combination as she had seen Mr. Adams do.
>
> The old banker sprang to the handle and tugged at it for a moment. "The door can't be opened," he groaned. "The clock hasn't been wound nor the combination set."

Writing About Literature

1. Identify the characters who will speak in your skit. You should include Mr. Adams, Agatha, and May. You might choose to add other visitors to the bank.
2. Write one or two lines of dialogue for each character you choose. Try reading your dialogue aloud to see if it sounds like a real conversation. Check to see if using pronouns instead of nouns will make your dialogue more natural.

Save your dialogue in your ▱ **Working Portfolio.**

A. Pronouns Read this passage from "Waiting" by Budge Wilson. Then identify each underlined word as a subject pronoun, object pronoun, possessive pronoun, or contraction.

When the spring came, a gang of **(1)** <u>us</u> would always start going out to The Grove on weekends to start practicing for **(2)** <u>our</u> summer play. Year after year **(3)** <u>we</u> did this, and it had nothing to do with those school plays in which I made such a hit. **(4)** <u>We'd</u> all talk about what stories we liked, and then we'd pick one of **(5)** <u>them</u> and make a play out of **(6)** <u>it</u>. I would usually select the play because I was always the one who directed **(7)** <u>it</u>, so it was only fair that I'd get to do the choosing. If there was a king or a queen, I'd usually be the queen. If **(8)** <u>you're</u> the director, you can't be something like a page or a minor fairy, because then you don't seem important enough to be giving out instructions and bossing people around, and the kids maybe won't pay attention to all the orders. Besides, as **(9)** <u>my</u> mother pointed out, **(10)** <u>I</u> was smart and I could learn my lines fast....

—Budge Wilson, "Waiting"

B. Pronoun Use This passage about theater superstitions contains ten errors in pronoun usage. Rewrite the paragraph, correcting the errors.

When an actor goes on stage, their fellow actors don't say "Good luck." They say "Break a leg." Whom would wish someone a broken leg? What does this expression mean? To find out, my friend Kevin and me interviewed Ms. Kay Gilbert, an expert on theater traditions.

She told him and I, "Us theater people are more superstitious than people in most other fields. I think it's because plays are so unpredictable. If their a hit, everything is fine. If not, your out of work.

"We try to give ourself any advantage we can. All of the actors tell his or her fellow actors something insulting in order to confuse the forces of bad luck. Acting, like other jobs, has their own traditions to uphold."

So the next time you go on stage, don't worry if someone tells you to "break a leg"!

Choose the correct replacement for each underlined word, or indicate that the word is correct as is.

Think of all the information that you have collected and saved over time. <u>Who</u> was the first president of the United States? Name
(1)
a favorite CD and picture <u>their</u> cover. Recall for a moment what
(2)
<u>you're</u> elementary school looked like. You might say that <u>we</u>
(3) (4)
humans are a little bit like computers; everyone stores countless memories in <u>their</u> brain. If you wonder exactly how we store these
(5)
memories in <u>my</u> brains, you are not alone. <u>These</u> is a question that
(6) (7)
scientists have asked <u>theirselves</u> for years. Will <u>themselves</u> find
(8) (9)
the explanation in the brain's physical structure, its complex chemistry, or both? <u>It's</u> one more mystery that modern science has
(10)
yet to solve.

PRONOUNS

1. A. Whom
   B. Whose
   C. Which
   D. Correct as is

2. A. his
   B. her
   C. its
   D. Correct as is

3. A. you
   B. your
   C. your are
   D. Correct as is

4. A. us
   B. they
   C. them
   D. Correct as is

5. A. his or her
   B. his
   C. her
   D. Correct as is

6. A. our
   B. their
   C. your
   D. Correct as is

7. A. What
   B. This
   C. Them
   D. Correct as is

8. A. theirs
   B. yourselves
   C. themselves
   D. Correct as is

9. A. them
   B. they
   C. he
   D. Correct as is

10. A. It
    B. Its
    C. Itself
    D. Correct as is

Student Help Desk

Pronouns at a Glance

Subject Case

I	it
you	we
he	you
she	they

Use this case when
- the pronoun is a **subject**
- the pronoun is a **predicate pronoun**

Object Case

me	it
you	us
him	you
her	them

Use this case when
- the pronoun is a **direct object**
- the pronoun is an **indirect object**
- the pronoun is the **object of a preposition**

Possessive Case

my/mine	its
your/yours	our/ours
his	your/yours
her/hers	their/theirs

Use this case for
- pronouns that show **ownership or relationship**

Types of Pronouns

Who Did It?

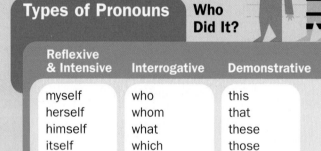

Reflexive & Intensive	Interrogative	Demonstrative	Indefinite
myself	who	this	someone
herself	whom	that	anyone
himself	what	these	each
itself	which	those	several
yourself	whose		many
themselves			all
ourselves			most
yourselves			none

For a full list of indefinite pronouns, see page 76.

Pronoun-Antecedent Agreement

A pronoun should agree with its antecedent in number, person, and gender.

A singular antecedent takes a singular pronoun.

Jewell is always writing **her** mystery stories. **(singular)**

A plural antecedent takes a plural pronoun.

The **plots** have **their** twists and turns. **(plural)**

Make sure you use the correct gender.

Each has **his or her** special skill.

They have **their** special skills.

Pronoun Problems   Solving the Case

We: Subject/predicate pronoun **Us:** Object	**We** students saw Nessie. No one believed **us** students.
Who: Subject/predicate pronoun **Whom:** Object	**Who** wants our story? To **whom** shall we write?

The Bottom Line

Checklist for Pronouns

Have I . . .

____ used the subject case for pronouns that are subjects and predicate pronouns?

____ used the object case for pronouns that are objects?

____ used the possessive case to show ownership or relationship?

____ made sure that pronouns agree with their antecedents in number, person, and gender?

____ used *who* and *whom* correctly?

Verbs

Theme: Lights, Camera, Action

A Giant Ape Did What?

Think about going with friends to see a really great movie. Talking about the movie afterward is almost as much fun as seeing it for the first time. You'll have to use plenty of verbs to recreate what you saw. In fact, whenever you speak or write, you use verbs to let people know exactly what is happening and how things look, feel, smell, sound, and taste.

Write Away: Tell Me a Movie
Write a paragraph describing an action scene from your favorite movie or one describing the scene from *King Kong* shown above. Put the paragraph in your ▭ **Working Portfolio.**

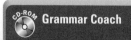

CD-ROM **Grammar Coach**

Choose the best way to rewrite each underlined word or group of words.

Spending on entertainment <u>will increase</u> sharply over the last
(1)
several decades. In 1997 the average American household <u>spends</u>
(2)
almost as much on entertainment as it did on health care. Families

now <u>choose</u> from a wide selection of entertainment options. These
(3)
<u>included</u> books, TV, movies, games, CDs, and theme parks, to name
(4)
a few. Think about how prices <u>have rised</u> over the years. In 1939 a
(5)
movie ticket to *Gone With The Wind* <u>costed</u> 75 cents. When a major
(6)
theme park first opened in 1955, visitors <u>paid</u> only $1 to enter
(7)
the park. Although people <u>earned</u> more money today, many
(8)
<u>are spending</u> more of that money on entertainment. Can you
(9)
predict how much prices <u>raise</u> in the future?
(10)

1. A. increases
   B. has increased
   C. does increase
   D. Correct as is

2. A. spending
   B. spent
   C. will spend
   D. Correct as is

3. A. chose
   B. have choosen
   C. chosed
   D. Correct as is

4. A. will include
   B. include
   C. had included
   D. Correct as is

5. A. have rose
   B. raised
   C. have risen
   D. Correct as is

6. A. cost
   B. has cost
   C. will cost
   D. Correct as is

7. A. pay
   B. payed
   C. are paying
   D. Correct as is

8. A. will earn
   B. earn
   C. have earned
   D. Correct as is

9. A. spent
   B. have spent
   C. spended
   D. Correct as is

10. A. will rise
    B. will raise
    C. rise
    D. Correct as is

What Is a Verb?

❶ Here's the Idea

▶ **A verb is a word used to express an action, a condition, or a state of being.** The two main types of verbs are **action verbs** and **linking verbs.** Both kinds can be accompanied by helping verbs.

Action Verbs

An **action verb** tells what its subject does. The action it expresses can be either **physical** or **mental.**

King Kong stomps through the streets of New York. (physical action)

He climbs the Empire State Building. (physical action)

Everyone fears Kong. (mental action)

Kong loves a woman. (mental action)

Linking Verbs

A **linking verb** links its subject to a word in the predicate. The most common linking verbs are forms of the verb *be.*

Linking Verbs	
Forms of *be*	is, am, are, was, were, been, being
Verbs that express condition	appear, become, feel, grow, look, remain, seem, smell, sound, taste

LINKS

King Kong is a huge gorilla.
↑ LINKING VERB

He seems angry.

Some verbs can serve as either action or linking verbs.

LINKS

Kong looks at Ann Darrow. She looks frightened.
ACTION VERB   LINKING VERB

LINKS

He feels sad. She feels his hot breath.
LINKING VERB   ACTION VERB

Helping Verbs and Verb Phrases

Helping verbs help main verbs express precise shades of meaning. The combination of one or more helping verbs with a main verb is called a **verb phrase**.

VERB PHRASE

We have watched the movie *King Kong* four times.
HELPING   MAIN

I can rent it any time.

Some verbs can serve both as main verbs and as helping verbs. For example, *has* stands alone in the first sentence below but is a helping verb in the second sentence.

King Kong has no chance of survival.
MAIN VERB

He has angered too many people.
HELPING VERB

Common Helping Verbs	
Forms of *be*	be, am, is, are, was, were, been, being
Forms of *do*	do, does, did
Forms of *have*	have, has, had
Others	could, should, would, may, might, must, can, shall, will

Kong has terrorized New Yorkers.

VERBS

❷ Why It Matters in Writing

Strong verbs can make your writing powerful. Try to use verbs that are as specific as possible. Notice the difference that a change to a more precise verb makes in the sentence below.

grabbed
The movie ~~had~~ my attention.

❸ Practice and Apply

A. CONCEPT CHECK: What Is a Verb?

Write the verb or verb phrase in each of the following sentences.

The King of the Monster Movies
1. *King Kong* may be the most famous monster movie ever.
2. At the start of the film, a producer is planning a movie.
3. He and a film crew sail to Skull Island.
4. There they find a giant ape, Kong.
5. Kong falls in love with Ann, the movie's star.
6. The producer takes Kong to New York in chains.
7. Kong escapes from his chains.
8. He climbs to the top of the Empire State Building.
9. There, he must struggle against fighter planes.
10. Kong's enemies win in the end.

Identify as action or linking each of the verbs you wrote.

➡ **For a SELF-CHECK and more practice, see the EXERCISE BANK, p. 597.**

B. WRITING: Using Specific Verbs

Special Effects
Write a more specific verb to replace each underlined verb in the paragraph below.

Willis O'Brien <u>did</u> the special effects for the *King Kong* movie of 1933. O'Brien <u>made</u> miniature models, including an 18-inch-tall Kong. To make Kong's muscles, he carefully <u>put</u> latex strips under the model's skin. Then he added air bladders in its chest. Now the model <u>was</u> real. O'Brien <u>took</u> many long hours at his task.

Action Verbs and Objects

LESSON 2

❶ Here's the Idea

Action verbs are often accompanied by words that complete their meaning. These complements are **direct objects** and **indirect objects.**

Direct Objects

▶ **A direct object is a noun or pronoun that names the receiver of an action.** The direct object answers the question *what* or *whom.*

BEGINS WHAT?

The scriptwriter begins the process.
 ACTION VERB   DIRECT OBJECT

The scriptwriter develops a story idea.

Indirect Objects

▶ **An indirect object tells *to what* or *whom* or *for what* or *whom* an action is done.** Verbs that often take indirect objects include *bring, give, hand, lend, make, send, show, teach, tell,* and *write.*

The scriptwriter sends a script. (sends to whom?)

TO WHOM?

The scriptwriter sends the director a script.
 INDIRECT   DIRECT
 OBJECT   OBJECT

The director gives the scriptwriter some advice.

If the preposition *to* or *for* appears in a sentence, the word that follows it is *not* an indirect object. It is the object of the preposition.

Tell the movie ending to us.
                      OBJECT OF PREPOSITION

Tell us the movie ending.
 INDIRECT OBJECT

Transitive and Intransitive Verbs

An action verb that has a direct object is called a **transitive verb.** A verb that does not have a direct object is called an **intransitive verb.**

Scriptwriters set the pace of their movies.
TRANSITIVE VERB ⬈   ⬉ DIRECT OBJECT

The action moves quickly or slowly.
              ⬉ INTRANSITIVE VERB (NO OBJECT)

Sometimes an intransitive verb is followed by a word that looks like a direct object but is really an adverb. An adverb tells where, when, how, or to what extent; a direct object answers the question whom or what.

CHOOSE WHAT?
Directors choose camera angles.
TRANSITIVE VERB ⬈   ⬉ DIRECT OBJECT

CHOOSE HOW?
The good ones choose wisely.
INTRANSITIVE VERB ⬈   ⬉ ADVERB

❷ Why It Matters in Writing

The correct use of direct objects can help you give clear directions or specific advice. Notice how in the model below, Bradbury uses direct objects to show what he wants you to read and see.

> **LITERARY MODEL**
>
> Read all the great **books.** Read all the great **poetry.** See all the great **films.** Fill your **life** with metaphors.
>
>   —Ray Bradbury, "An Interview with Ray Bradbury"

❸ Practice and Apply

A. CONCEPT CHECK: Action Verbs and Objects

Write the 15 complements in these sentences, identifying each as a direct object or an indirect object.

A Crew of Dozens
1. A movie crew includes many people.
2. The director usually tells crew members their assignments.
3. The director of photography gives the director the film footage.
4. The sound crew includes a boom operator.
5. The director tells the composer the mood of the movie.
6. Members of the art department have an important function.
7. They show the director of photography the special effects.
8. The crew also includes wardrobe assistants.
9. Makeup artists give the actors the right look.
10. A movie set provides many creative jobs.

➜ **For a SELF-CHECK and more practice, see the EXERCISE BANK, p. 597.**

B. REVISING: Adding Direct Objects

Read the movie proposal below. From the list at the top, select a direct object to fill in each blank.

world, powers, legs, evil, weights

Proposal for New Film

The movie begins as a sequel to *The Little Mermaid*. Ariel has changed, however. No longer a fragile little mermaid, she has two strong __1__. She lifts __2__ as a hobby. Now she has amazing __3__. She can switch back and forth from a mermaid to a human. She travels the __4__. She fights __5__ everywhere.

Linking Verbs and Predicate Words

❶ Here's the Idea

The word that a linking verb connects its subject to is called a **subject complement.** The subject complement identifies or describes the subject. Some common linking verbs are *is, feel, seem,* and *look.*

IDENTIFIES

A movie is a complicated project.
SUBJECT   VERB   SUBJECT COMPLEMENT

DESCRIBES

A movie must seem real.
SUBJECT   VERB   SUBJECT COMPLEMENT

Predicate Nouns and Predicate Adjectives

A subject complement can be a **predicate noun** or a **predicate adjective.**

▶ **A predicate noun is a noun that follows a linking verb and identifies, renames, or defines the subject.**

IDENTIFIES

***Star Wars* is a science fiction film.**
SUBJECT   VERB   PREDICATE NOUN

I am a science fiction fan.

▶ **A predicate adjective is an adjective that follows a linking verb and modifies the subject.**

MODIFIES

Science fiction films are popular.
SUBJECT   VERB   PREDICATE ADJECTIVE

They look so futuristic.

❷ Why It Matters in Writing

Predicate adjectives let you describe subjects with just a word or two. They can help you create vivid descriptions. Notice how predicate adjectives are used in the model below to contrast the characters and briefly convey the situation.

Look at the characters in *Star Wars.* Princess Leia is **brave.** Luke Skywalker is **tough.** And Han Solo is basically **honest.** Throughout the movie their situation seems **hopeless.** But their cause is **just.** In the end, they triumph.

> Predicate adjectives describe the subjects.

VERBS

❸ Practice and Apply

CONCEPT CHECK: Linking Verbs and Predicate Words

Identify each linking verb, predicate noun, and predicate adjective in the sentences below.

Creature Features
1. Not all creatures in science fiction movies are scary.
2. Some seem downright friendly.
3. For example, *E.T. the Extra-Terrestrial* was a hit.
4. The movie's alien creature appeared lovable.
5. E.T. seemed afraid of the children at first.
6. In *Close Encounters of the Third Kind* the aliens were a mystery for most of the movie.
7. In the end the inhabitants of the giant UFO were friendly to humans.
8. In *The Empire Strikes Back* one alien was very wise.
9. Yoda was a 900-year-old Jedi sage.
10. With Yoda's help Luke Skywalker became a Jedi too.

➡ **For a SELF-CHECK and more practice, see the EXERCISE BANK, p. 598.**

Principal Parts of Verbs

❶ Here's the Idea

▸ **Every verb has four basic forms, called its principal parts: the present, the present participle, the past, and the past participle.** These principal parts are used to make all of the forms and tenses of the verb. Here are some examples.

> **Stunt people take risks on screen.**
> PRESENT

> **Stunt people are doing dangerous things all the time.**
> PRESENT PARTICIPLE

> **Polly Berson performed stunts for 27 years.**
> PAST

> **Most stunt people have trained for many years.**
> PAST PARTICIPLE

The Four Principal Parts of a Verb			
Present	**Present Participle**	**Past**	**Past Participle**
jump	(is) jump**ing**	jump**ed**	(has) jump**ed**
crash	(is) crash**ing**	crash**ed**	(has) crash**ed**

Notice that helping verbs are used with the present participle and the past participles.

Regular Verbs

There are two kinds of verbs: regular and irregular.

▸ **A regular verb is a verb whose past and past participle are formed by adding -ed or -d to the present.** The present participle is formed by adding -ing to the present.

Present	**Present Participle**	**Past**	**Past Participle**
look	(is) look + **-ing**	look + **-ed**	(has) look + **-ed**

You will learn about irregular verbs in the next lesson.

❷ Why It Matters in Writing

The principal parts of verbs let you express changes in time in your writing. In the model below, notice how the writer uses the past and the present to show a shift in time.

PROFESSIONAL MODEL

An accident paralyzed stuntwoman Heidi von Beltz during a car stunt for the movie *The Cannonball Run*. Still, she exercises daily with a special trainer.

—S. Atlas

PAST

PRESENT

VERBS

❸ Practice and Apply

CONCEPT CHECK: Principal Parts of Verbs

Identify each underlined principal part as the present, the present participle, the past, or the past participle.

Stunt Stand-ins

Stunt people **(1)** <u>perform</u> the dangerous scenes in movies and TV shows. Many are athletes who have **(2)** <u>decided</u> to pursue careers in show business. When the hero of a movie is **(3)** <u>leaping</u> from a galloping horse or the villain is **(4)** <u>jumping</u> out of a burning helicopter, the person you see is probably a stunt person. Most stunts **(5)** <u>belong</u> to five categories: falls, fights, fires, car stunts, and horse stunts. A safety crew **(6)** <u>stays</u> on hand in case of problems. Some stunt people have fatally **(7)** <u>injured</u> themselves. For example, Vic Rivers once **(8)** <u>jumped</u> a truck into a lake and **(9)** <u>drowned</u>. Despite the dangers, most stunters **(10)** <u>love</u> their exciting jobs.

➜ For a SELF-CHECK and more practice, see the EXERCISE BANK, p. 598.

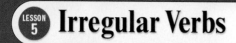

Irregular Verbs

LESSON 5

❶ Here's the Idea

▶ **Irregular verbs are verbs whose past and past participle forms are not made by adding -ed or -d to the present.**
The following chart shows you how to form the past and past-participle forms of many irregular verbs.

Common Irregular Verbs			
	Present	**Past**	**Past Participle**
Group 1 The forms of the present, the past, and the past participle are all the same.	burst cost cut hit hurt let put set shut	burst cost cut hit hurt let put set shut	(has) burst (has) cost (has) cut (has) hit (has) hurt (has) let (has) put (has) set (has) shut
Group 2 The forms of the past and the past participle are the same.	bring build buy catch feel have keep lay leave lose make pay say sell shine sit sleep teach think win wind	brought built bought caught felt had kept laid left lost made paid said sold shone sat slept taught thought won wound	(has) brought (has) built (has) bought (has) caught (has) felt (has) had (has) kept (has) laid (has) left (has) lost (has) made (has) paid (has) said (has) sold (has) shone (has) sat (has) slept (has) taught (has) thought (has) won (has) wound

CHAPTER 4

Common Irregular Verbs *(continued)*

	Present	Past	Past Participle
Group 3 The past participle is formed by adding -*n* or -*en* to the past.	bite break choose freeze lie speak steal tear wear	bit broke chose froze lay spoke stole tore wore	(has) **bitten** (has) broken (has) chosen (has) frozen (has) lain (has) spoken (has) stolen (has) torn (has) worn
Group 4 The past participle is formed from the present, usually by adding -*n* or -*en*.	blow do draw drive eat fall give go grow know rise run see take throw write	blew did drew drove ate fell gave went grew knew rose ran saw took threw wrote	(has) **blown** (has) done (has) drawn (has) driven (has) eaten (has) fallen (has) given (has) gone (has) grown (has) known (has) risen (has) run (has) seen (has) taken (has) thrown (has) written
Group 5 A vowel in the verb changes from *i* in the present to *a* in the past and to *u* in the past participle.	begin drink ring shrink sing sink spring swim	began drank rang shrank sang sank sprang swam	(has) **begun** (has) drunk (has) rung (has) shrunk (has) sung (has) sunk (has) sprung (has) swum

The Irregular Verb *Be*

	Present	Past	Past Participle
The past and past participle do not follow any pattern.	am, are, is	was, were	(has) **been**

❷ Why It Matters in Writing

To be a skilled writer, you need to use irregular verb forms correctly. They can be tricky, though. The best way to avoid mistakes is to memorize the principal parts of the most common irregular verbs.

STUDENT MODEL

Special effects ~~maked~~ *made* a skyscraper fall in an instant. Then a gigantic tornado ~~blowed~~ *blew* away the rubble.

❸ Practice and Apply

CONCEPT CHECK: Irregular Verbs

In the sentences below, choose the correct forms of the verbs in parentheses.

Movie Magic

1. Movies can convince us that we have (saw, seen) real events on screen.
2. Special effects have (let, letted) filmmakers fool us.
3. They have (bringed, brought) to the screen cloud cities, giant apes, and telephones with teeth.
4. Even in the early days of movies, directors (made, maked) impossible scenes look real.
5. A famous story shows that the Lumière brothers (knowed, knew) how to create a special effect in 1896.
6. A pile of rubble quickly (built, builded) itself into a wall.
7. The brothers had filmed as workers (teared, tore) down a wall.
8. Then they (runned, ran) the film backward.
9. Often filmmakers have (shrank, shrunk) huge monsters to miniature size for filming.
10. In the 1990s filmmakers (beginned, began) using computer-generated effects.

➜ For a SELF-CHECK and more practice, see the EXERCISE BANK, p. 599.

Simple Tenses

❶ Here's the Idea

> **A tense is a verb form that shows the time of an action or condition.** Verbs have three **simple tenses:** the present, the past, and the future.

Understanding Simple Tenses

Simple Tenses

The water **rushes** swiftly by the raft.	The **present tense** shows that an action or condition occurs now.
The raft **passed** the point of no return earlier.	The **past tense** shows that an action or condition was completed in the past.
Soon someone **will fall** into the water.	The **future tense** shows that an action or condition will occur in the future.

A **progressive** form of a tense expresses an action or condition in progress. The progressive forms of the three simple tenses are used to show that actions or conditions are, were, or will be in progress.

Progressive Forms

People on shore **are calling** for help.	Present Progressive
They **were fishing** before.	Past Progressive
They **will be watching** for the rescue boat.	Future Progressive

Forming Simple Tenses

The present tense of a verb is the present principal part. The past tense is the past principal part. To form the future tense, add *will* to the present principal part.

Forming Simple Tenses

	Singular	Plural
Present (present principal part)	I direct you direct he, she, it directs	we direct you direct they direct
Past (past principal part)	I directed you directed he, she, it directed	we directed you directed they directed
Future (*will* + present principal part)	I will direct you will direct he, she, it will direct	we will direct you will direct they will direct

To make the progressive form of one of these tenses, add the present, past, or future form of *be* to the present participle.

Present progressive: **I am directing.**

Past progressive: **I was directing.**

Future progressive: **I will be directing.**

❷ Why It Matters in Writing

Changing tenses allows you to be clear about the order in which things happen. Notice how the writer uses the past, the present, and the future tense in the sentence below.

PROFESSIONAL MODEL

Until recently, people considered digital films   **PAST**
inferior. Now better cameras produce good, clear   **PRESENT**
images. Soon many filmmakers will produce their   **FUTURE**
movies digitally.

—Eliza Blackburn

❸ Practice and Apply

A. CONCEPT CHECK: Simple Tenses

Identify each underlined verb as present, past, future, present progressive, past progressive, or future progressive.

The Digital Revolution Arrives

1. Digital videodiscs (DVDs) <u>will be</u> standard someday.

2. These shiny platters <u>will transform</u> movie distribution.

3. A digital videodisc <u>holds</u> up to 25 times as much information as a CD.

4. It <u>provides</u> high-quality video images, interactive multimedia features, and surround sound.

5. The movie *Ghostbusters* <u>came</u> out in 1984.

6. It <u>did</u> well at the box office.

7. Now it <u>is</u> available in DVD format.

8. Besides the movie, the DVD <u>contains</u> commentary by the director, production notes, and a photo gallery.

9. It also <u>includes</u> a complete script and ten scenes that were cut from the movie.

10. In the next few years, companies <u>will be releasing</u> nearly 100,000 movies on DVD.

➡ For a SELF-CHECK and more practice, see the EXERCISE BANK, p. 599.

🗂 **Working Portfolio:** Find the paragraph you wrote for the **Write Away** on page 90 or a sample of your most recent work. Identify any errors in the use of simple tenses and correct them.

B. REVISING: Correcting Simple Tenses

Rewrite the following paragraph, correcting the tenses of the underlined verbs.

The Cost of DVD

Today, movie distributors **(1)** <u>will spend</u> hundreds of millions of dollars on copies of films for theaters. In the next few years, most of them **(2)** <u>began</u> sending the movies digitally by satellite. When they do so, sending a movie out **(3)** <u>costs</u> them only about $150,000. Stefan Avalos and Lance Weiler **(4)** <u>release</u> an all-digital movie by satellite in 1999. They **(5)** <u>will shoot</u> the all-digital movie on borrowed digital cameras.

VERBS

Perfect Tenses

❶ Here's the Idea

Understanding Perfect Tenses

The **present perfect tense** places an action or condition in a stretch of time leading up to the present.

The scientist has created a monster.

The scientist created the monster at some unspecified time before the present.

The **past perfect tense** places a past action or condition before another past action or condition.

When the scientist had tinkered with him, the monster awakened.

The tinkering occurred before the awakening.

The **future perfect tense** places a future action or condition before another future action or condition.

The monster will have escaped before the scientist notices.

The escaping will occur before the scientist's noticing.

The monster has walked here.

The monster will have walked here.

Forming Perfect Tenses

To form the present perfect, past perfect, or future perfect
tense of a verb, add the present, past, or future form of *have*
to the past participle.

Forming Perfect Tenses		
	Singular	**Plural**
Present perfect (*has* or *have* + past participle)	I have screamed you have screamed he, she, it has screamed	we have screamed you have screamed they have screamed
Past perfect (*had* + past participle)	I had screamed you had screamed he, she, i t had screamed	we had screamed you had screamed they had screamed
Future perfect (*will* + *have* + past participle)	I will have screamed you will have screamed he, she, it will have screamed	we will have screamed you will have screamed they will have screamed

In perfect forms of verbs, the tense of the helping verb *have*
shows the verb's tense.

❷ Why It Matters in Writing

By using perfect tenses, you can help your readers understand
when events occur in relation to other events. Notice the
effective use of the past perfect and present perfect tenses in
the model.

PROFESSIONAL MODEL

Within a year the brute **had returned**
in *Godzilla's Counterattack* and over the
years he **has battled** The Thing.

—Jeremy Pascall, *The King Kong Story*

This action occurred
before other events
in the past.

This action occurred
sometime between
the previous action
and the present.

VERBS

❸ Practice and Apply

A. CONCEPT CHECK: Perfect Tenses

Identify the verb in each sentence, and indicate whether its tense is present perfect, past perfect, or future perfect.

Horrors!
1. For years we had looked for a funny werewolf movie.
2. Now we have found *An American Werewolf in London.*
3. By tomorrow morning we will have watched it four times.
4. *Young Frankenstein* has amused us too.
5. Many serious Frankenstein movies had appeared before that comedy.
6. Filmmakers had created the first such horror films not long after the invention of movies.
7. Even before the 1931 *Frankenstein* there had been a silent version of the Frankenstein story.
8. All Frankenstein movies have drawn on Mary Shelley's 1818 novel.
9. Filmmakers have produced at least eight versions of *Dr. Jekyll and Mr. Hyde.*
10. What new versions of horror classics will have come out by next year?

➡ **For a SELF-CHECK and more practice, see the EXERCISE BANK, p. 600.**

B. WRITING: Using Perfect Tenses

The scene described below could happen in a horror movie. Rewrite each underlined verb in the tense named in parentheses.

Horror Scene: Take One

Three girls <u>cut</u> (present perfect) through a cemetery. They <u>thought</u> (past perfect) it would be a good shortcut, but they <u>were</u> (present perfect) sorry ever since. Suddenly they see a strange light that <u>appeared</u> (present perfect) ahead of them. By the time they round the next tombstone, they <u>discovered</u> (future perfect) the light's source—a mummy!

Using Verb Tenses

❶ Here's the Idea

A good writer uses different verb tenses to indicate that events occur at different times. If you do not need to indicate a change of time, do not switch from one tense to another.

Writing About the Present

You can write about the present using the present tense, the present perfect tense, and the present progressive form.

Motion pictures work because of our vision.

The brain sees a series of still pictures as moving.

> The **present tense** places the actions in the present.

Filmmakers have created fantastic special effects.

They have brought dinosaurs and alien beings to life.

> The **present perfect tense** places the actions in the period of time leading up to the present.

Directors are learning the use of computer effects.

They are becoming extremely skilled artists.

> The **present progressive forms** show the actions are in progress now.

Many futuristic movies are becoming classics.

VERBS

Writing About the Past

▶ **The past tense conveys actions and conditions that came to an end in the past.** When you write about the past, you can use past verb forms to indicate the order in which events occurred. Using these forms correctly will make it easier for readers to follow the events.

Thomas Edison's company launched the motion-picture industry.

His employee William Dickson devised a way of moving film through a camera.

The **past tense** shows action that began and was completed in the past.

Other inventors had put sound with pictures before Edison did.

After the Lumière brothers had developed a projector, Edison began projecting his films.

The **past perfect tense** places the actions before other past actions.

Filmmakers were inventing new technologies for years before they began using computers.

They were trying to make unreal events look real.

The **past progressive forms** show that the actions in the past were in progress.

More than 30 years ago, filmmakers were creating realistic space scenes.

Writing About the Future

▶ **The future tenses convey actions and conditions that are yet to come.** By using the different future verb forms, you can show how future events are related in time.

Maybe everyone will make movies someday.

The line between home movies and professional ones will blur.

> The **future tense** shows that the actions have not yet occurred.

Before they can read, children already will have learned to use a camera.

Studio films will be less important because the Internet will have increased people's access to one another's films.

> The **future perfect tense** places the actions before other future actions.

People will be making movies ever more cheaply.

Everyone will be watching everyone else's movies.

> The **future progressive forms** show that the actions in the future will be continuing.

VERBS

❷ Why It Matters in Writing

When you use the right tenses, you help your readers keep sequences of events straight.

1850
No movies existed.

1900
Few people owned cameras and projectors.

Today
Big studios make movies for profit.

2050
Anyone will be able to make movies.

❸ Practice and Apply

A. CONCEPT CHECK: Using Verb Tenses

In each sentence, choose the correct verb form in parentheses.

Hollywood Goes High-Tech

1. In the 1930s, makers of monster movies (were using, will be using) laughably bad special effects.
2. They (lacked, have lacked) the technology to create realistic monsters.
3. Recently filmmakers (have improved, improved) special-effects technology considerably.
4. As early as the 1980s, filmmakers (will be using, were using) computer-generated, or CG, graphics.
5. They (added, will have added) effects on a background.
6. Now they (are refining, were refining) CG technology further.
7. They (will build, are building) characters on a computer.
8. They already (create, will create) everything from aliens to giant gorillas.
9. Soon they (had shown, will show) realistic animated human figures.
10. Yet the story (will remain, remained) the most important element.

Name the tense or form of each verb you chose in the sentences above.

➡ **For a SELF-CHECK and more practice, see the EXERCISE BANK, p. 600.**

B. EDITING: Arranging Verb Tenses

Pretend you are a film director. List the numbers of the following directions in a logical order, so that the tenses of the verbs make sense. (Hint: Read all the sentences before you begin.)

1. Now that you know what the scene is about, we will begin.
2. This scene starts just after an alien has made video contact with the reporter Colleen McKay.
3. Colleen is surprised because she expected the alien to look like a bug.
4. First, Colleen sees the alien, who looks like a cat.
5. The alien will tell Colleen his name, Rxxd.

Troublesome Verb Pairs

LESSON 9

① Here's the Idea

Some pairs of verbs seem similar but are actually different words with different meanings. Troublesome verb pairs include *lie* and *lay*, *sit* and *set*, *rise* and *raise*, and *may* and *can*.

Lie and *Lay*

Lie means "to rest in a flat position." It does not take an object. *Lay* means "to put or place." It does take an object.

The tigers lie at the trainer's feet.

The trainer lays the tiger treats on a tray.

Lie and *Lay*		
Present	**Past**	**Past Participle**
lie Fido **lies** down.	lay Fido **lay** down.	lain Fido has **lain** down.
lay Fido **lays** the toy down.	laid Fido **laid** the toy down.	laid Fido has **laid** the toy down.

Lie and lay are confusing because the present principal part of *lay* is spelled the same as the past principal part of *lie*.

Sit and *Set*

Sit means "to be seated." It does not take an object.

Set means "to put or place." It does take an object.

My cat, Luna, sits on the couch.

I set the flea powder down somewhere.

Sit and *Set*		
Present	**Past**	**Past Participle**
sit We **sit** on the floor.	sat We **sat** on the floor.	sat I had **sat** for hours.
set Tiff **sets** down the bug.	set Tiff **set** down the bug.	set Tiff had **set** down the bug.

Rise and *Raise*

Rise means "to move upward" or "to get out of bed." It does not take an object. *Raise* means "to lift" or "to care for or bring up." It does take an object.

The sun rises every morning.

King Kong raises a car easily.

Rise and **Raise**		
Present	**Past**	**Past Participle**
rise The water **rises**.	rose The water **rose**.	risen The water had **risen** earlier.
raise Kong **raises** the car.	raised Kong **raised** the car.	raised Kong had **raised** the car earlier.

May and *Can*

May means "to be allowed to" or "to be likely to." *Can* means "to be able to." *Might* and *could* serve as the past tense forms of *may* and *can*.

May I pet your dog?

Can he do any tricks?

Can and *may* do not have past participles. They are usually used as helping verbs.

❷ Practice and Apply

Choose the correct word in parentheses in each of the following sentences.

The Gentle Jungle

1. With love, patience, understanding, and respect, you (can, may) teach an animal almost anything.
2. The animal trainer Ralph Helfer teaches his animals what they (can, may) do with a system called affection training.
3. To show affection, Helfer (lies, lays) down with a lion.
4. Helfer (lies, lays) his hands on his animals carefully.
5. When Helfer's daughter Tana was little, she often (sat, set) on the trunk of Margie the elephant.
6. Margie the elephant (rose, raised) her trunk.
7. Tana would (rise, raise) in the air.
8. Then Margie would (sit, set) the child on her back.
9. Helfer (rose, raised) the orangutan who costarred with Clint Eastwood in two movies.
10. He even taught a sick chimp to (lie, lay) down and give itself a shot.

➡ For a SELF-CHECK and more practice, see the EXERCISE BANK, p. 601.

B. PROOFREADING: What Do They Mean?

List the five verbs that are used incorrectly in the following paragraph. Then change them to the correct verb forms.

Elvis and the Chimp

May you believe this story about Elvis Presley? Elvis used to set on Helfer's floor and play with baby tigers. One day when Elvis arrived, a chimp named Coffee jumped off the roof and knocked him down. Elvis laid on the ground while Coffee jumped up and down on him. After Helfer helped rise Elvis to his feet, Coffee apologized by brushing the dust off the singer. Coffee learned that he should not sit his feet on Elvis Presley!

Grammar in Fine Arts

Using Verbs in Drama

When you present a dramatic scene, you perform actions. When you write a dramatic scene, you use verbs to indicate those actions. Stage directions are very important because they tell the actors exactly what to do. The verbs in stage directions must clearly describe the desired movements. Notice the verbs in these scenes from *A Christmas Carol.*

CHAPTER 4

(*The spirit motions for Scrooge to turn. Scrooge trembles and shakes his head.*)

(*Dancers whirl around the stage. Fezziwhig's wife applauds.*)

Practice and Apply

A. WRITING: Describing a Scene

Use your own ideas and the actions shown on page 118 to write a one-minute scene. Include interesting, scary, or funny actions in your scene. Write clear stage directions for your actors. You may use some of the sentences beside the characters to get started.

B. Creating a Blocking Diagram

A director's plans for how actors should move on stage are called blocking. When you are working on a dramatic performance, you may need to write plans for blocking the action. The picture shows a blocking diagram for another scene in the play.

Make your own diagram showing the blocking for your scene. In your diagram, include each of the actors who will be on stage. Indicate who should move. Use arrows to indicate directions. Add verbs on labels that give additional information about how actors should move.

VERBS

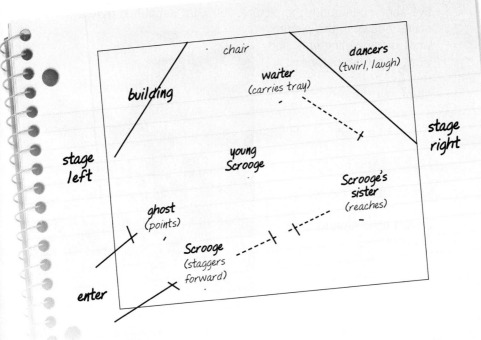

A. Revising Incorrect Verbs Find and correct the incorrect verb in each of the following sentences. Watch out for irregular verbs, troublesome verbs, and incorrect verb tenses.

Preserving Our Past in Movies

1. Today, some movie fans currently have worried about the rate at which movie prints are deteriorating.
2. They rose the alarm when they found that many early movies have disappeared forever.
3. Already, time will be destroying nine-tenths of all the movies from the 1920s.
4. The world has lost half of all the movies that were maked before 1950.
5. Thousands of movies are being losed in studios' vaults right now.
6. The biggest problem had been the decay of the film that moviemakers use.
7. Most directors in the future filmed digitally, without celluloid.
8. Yet electronic ways of recording movies were becoming out of date very fast.
9. Because equipment has changed, most TV stations today were unable to broadcast from the movie tape of 20 years ago.
10. Film restorers work hard now so that people have enjoyed today's movies in the future.

B. Using Tenses Using the ideas in the phrases listed below, write five sentences about the picture. Tell what happened before the scene shown in the picture, what is happening in it, and what might happen next.

steps out the window

reaches for the clock hands

fixes the clock

jumps onto the ledge

climbs up a rope to the flagpole

CHAPTER 4

Choose the best way to rewrite each underlined word or group of words.

Money <u>has been</u> an issue in movies since the beginning. In fact,
(1)

before movies became popular, Thomas Edison <u>vows</u> never to invent
(2)

anything he couldn't sell. He <u>seen</u> the movie camera as a product
(3)

that would make money. As technology improved, some costs

decreased. Other costs <u>rised</u>. For example, in 1959 it <u>costed</u> about
(4)   (5)

$70,000 to film a minute of the epic movie *Ben-Hur.* In 1998 the

filming of *Titanic* cost $1 million per minute. However, soon the cost

of special effects <u>will come</u> down as computer-generated graphics
(6)

are used more widely. In the next 25 years the cost of effects

<u>had dropped</u> by half. Today, all the studios together <u>spent</u> $400
(7)   (8)

million each year on prints of their movies. Soon filmmakers <u>sent</u>
(9)

their movies worldwide by satellite, and the cost <u>sinks</u>.
(10)

---

1. A. had been
   B. will be
   C. was
   D. Correct as is

2. A. will vow
   B. has vowed
   C. had vowed
   D. Correct as is

3. A. saw
   B. has seen
   C. had saw
   D. Correct as is

4. A. rise
   B. rose
   C. raised
   D. Correct as is

5. A. cost
   B. will cost
   C. is costing
   D. Correct as is

6. A. came
   B. are coming
   C. have come
   D. Correct as is

7. A. drop
   B. have dropped
   C. will drop
   D. Correct as is

8. A. spend
   B. spended
   C. will spend
   D. Correct as is

9. A. send
   B. have sent
   C. will send
   D. Correct as is

10. A. sank
    B. have sunk
    C. will sink
    D. Correct as is

VERBS

Student Help Desk

Verbs at a Glance

A verb expresses action, condition, or state of being.

People **eat** popcorn at the movies.
  ACTION VERB

Popcorn **is** a noisy treat.
  LINKING VERB

They **have eaten** too much popcorn.
  HELPING ⬈   ⬉ MAIN
   VERB   VERB

Principal Parts of Regular Verbs

Present	Present Participle	Past	Past Participle
present	present + *-ing*	present + *-ed* or *-d*	present + *-ed* or *-d*
act	(is) acting	acted	(has) acted
bellow	(is) bellowing	bellowed	(has) bellowed
cry	(is) crying	cried	(has) cried
drag	(is) dragging	dragged	(has) dragged
emote	(is) emoting	emoted	(has) emoted
film	(is) filming	filmed	(has) filmed
gesture	(is) gesturing	gestured	(has) gestured
help	(is) helping	helped	(has) helped
imitate	(is) imitating	imitated	(has) imitated
join	(is) joining	joined	(has) joined

Keeping Tenses Straight

....*It's about Time!*....

Tense	What It Conveys	Example
Present	Action or condition occurring in the present	I **watch** movies.
Past	Action or condition occurring in the past	I **watched** a movie.
Future	Action or condition occurring in the future	I **will watch** a movie.
Present perfect	Action or condition occurring in the period leading up to the present	I **have watched** movies.
Past perfect	Past action or condition preceding another past action or condition	I **had watched** the movie before I went to bed.
Future perfect	Future action or condition preceding another future action or condition	I **will have watched** five movies by next Tuesday.

The Bottom Line

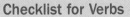

Checklist for Verbs

Have I . . .

____ used action verbs to express actions?

____ used linking verbs with predicate nouns and predicate adjectives?

____ used direct objects and indirect objects to answer the questions *whom, what,* and *to whom* or *to what?*

____ used the correct principal parts of irregular verbs?

____ used tenses correctly to express the times of actions and conditions?

____ used *sit* and *set, lie* and *lay, rise* and *raise,* and *may* and *can* correctly?

Adjectives and Adverbs

Theme: Accidents and Inventions

Back to the Drawing Board

How did inventors bring us from a primitive glider that barely carried one person to the incredibly sophisticated Boeing 777 that easily carries 300 passengers? It took a long time—and many modifications, or changes. Otto Lilienthal, who invented the first piloted glider (on the left above) in 1891, died after crashing one of his gliders. But other eager inventors continued to fine-tune their vehicles until they created the huge, fast, sleek jets of today.

Writers, like inventors, are fine-tuners. They use adjectives and adverbs to modify, or make more specific, their words. What words would you use to describe the three aircraft above?

Write Away: Moving into the Future
Imagine a transportation invention of the future. Freewrite a paragraph that describes what it does and how it looks. Save the paragraph in your 📁 **Working Portfolio.**

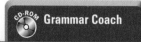

CD-ROM **Grammar Coach**

For each underlined item, choose the letter of the term that correctly identifies it.

In the late 1700s two <u>French</u> brothers, Jacques and Joseph

(1)
Montgolfier, began experiments that led to the invention of the

<u>modern</u> hot-air balloon. <u>The</u> brothers started <u>really</u> simply, using

(2)   (3)   (4)
small paper bags and wood fires. In <u>these</u> tests the Montgolfiers

(5)
saw that a bag would rise when <u>completely</u> filled with hot air. The

(6)
brothers conducted a <u>more important</u> experiment when they filled

(7)
a large cloth balloon with hot air and launched it. The flight was

<u>successful</u>! Today's balloonists <u>couldn't hardly fly</u> without the

(8)   (9)
methods perfected by the Montgolfiers. Today, by using modern

technologies, modern balloonists fly even <u>farther</u> than the

(10)
Montgolfiers flew.

ADJ. & ADV.

1. A. adverb
   B. comparative adjective
   C. proper adjective
   D. predicate adjective

2. A. adjective
   B. comparative adjective
   C. proper adjective
   D. predicate adjective

3. A. proper adjective
   B. definite article
   C. predicate adjective
   D. indefinite article

4. A. adverb describing *simply*
   B. adverb describing *started*
   C. adverb describing *brothers*
   D. adverb describing *bags*

5. A. pronoun used as adjective
   B. noun used as adjective
   C. pronoun used as adverb
   D. noun used as adverb

6. A. adverb telling how
   B. adverb telling when
   C. adverb telling where
   D. adverb telling to what extent

7. A. comparative adjective
   B. superlative adjective
   C. comparative adverb
   D. superlative adverb

8. A. adverb
   B. comparative adjective
   C. proper adjective
   D. predicate adjective

9. A. adjective
   B. double negative
   C. statement
   D. question

10. A. comparative adverb
    B. superlative adverb
    C. comparative adjective
    D. superlative adjective

What Is an Adjective?

LESSON 1

❶ Here's the Idea

▶ **An adjective is a word that modifies, or describes, a noun or a pronoun.**

MODIFIES

The noisy crowd cheered for Daria.
ADJECTIVE ⬆   ⬆ NOUN

Adjectives help you see, feel, taste, hear, and smell all the things you read about. Notice how adjectives make the second sentence in the following pair more descriptive.

She sped along the track on her bicycle.

She sped along the narrow track on her sleek bicycle.

Adjectives answer the questions *what kind, which one, how many,* and *how much.*

Adjectives			
What kind?	**fast** riders	**crowded** stadium	**steamy** afternoon
Which one or ones?	**first** lap	**inner** lanes	**final** race
How many or how much?	**five** teams	**many** fans	**more** applause

What kind?
green bicycle
sturdy frame

Which one or ones?
second tire
any seat

How many?
21 speeds
several reflectors

CHAPTER 5

Articles

The most commonly used adjectives are the **articles** *a, an,* and *the. A* and *an* are forms of the **indefinite article.** The indefinite article is used before a noun that names a nonspecific person, place, thing, or idea.

A sudden turn can cause an accident.
   ⬆ INDEFINITE ARTICLE   ⬆ INDEFINITE ARTICLE

Use *a* before a word beginning with a consonant sound ("a ball"); use *an* before a word beginning with a vowel sound ("an egg").

   The is the **definite article.** It points to a particular person, place, thing, or idea.

The competition continued through the afternoon.
   ⬆ DEFINITE ARTICLE   ⬆ DEFINITE ARTICLE

Forming Adjectives

Many adjectives are formed from common nouns.

Nouns and Adjectives	
Noun	**Adjective**
storm	stormy
child	childish
music	musical
beauty	beautiful

A **proper adjective** is formed from a proper noun. Proper adjectives are always capitalized.

Proper Nouns and Proper Adjectives	
Proper Noun	**Proper Adjective**
Shakespeare	Shakespearean
Asia	Asian
Spain	Spanish
Islam	Islamic

ADJ. & ADV.

❷ Why It Matters in Writing

Adjectives can provide important details. Imagine this description without adjectives.

> **PROFESSIONAL MODEL**
>
> The **first** bicycle was made of wood. This model was **hard** on shoes. Riders moved the bike in an **awkward** way. They pushed their feet backward against the ground. Later, a **Scottish** blacksmith made a **better** model, one with **two** pedals. This **new** bicycle was **easier** to ride and **easier** on shoes.
>
> —L.C. Chaveriat

❸ Practice and Apply

CONCEPT CHECK: What Is an Adjective?

Write each adjective in these sentences, along with the noun or pronoun it modifies. Do not include articles.

Cold Ears, Warm Invention

1. Some successful inventors are mature scientists.
2. Chester Greenwood, however, was a creative teenager when he made the first pair of earmuffs.
3. Chester's cold, red ears bothered him during the harsh Northeastern winters.
4. He didn't like itchy woolen mufflers.
5. One day, Chester had a brilliant idea.
6. He took a piece of flexible wire.
7. His grandmother sewed soft fur to the wire.
8. Chester then put on the strange contraption.
9. Earmuffs made Chester a rich man.
10. Chester received an American patent for the earmuffs at the age of 18.

➡ **For a SELF-CHECK and more practice, see the EXERCISE BANK, p. 602.**

Identify the proper adjectives in the sentences above. For each, write the proper noun from which it is formed.

Predicate Adjectives

LESSON 2

❶ Here's the Idea

▶ **A predicate adjective is an adjective that follows a linking verb and describes the verb's subject.** The linking verb connects the predicate adjective with the subject.

DESCRIBES

The airplanes were strange.
SUBJECT   LINKING VERB

DESCRIBE

They were large, heavy, and often dangerous.

Predicate adjectives can follow linking verbs other than forms of *be.* Forms of *taste, smell, feel, look, become,* and *seem* are often used as linking verbs.

DESCRIBES

Sam felt anxious about the airplane flight.
LINKING VERB   PREDICATE ADJECTIVE

DESCRIBES

The airplane's compartments felt warm.

For more about linking verbs, see page 98.

❷ Why It Matters in Writing

Predicate adjectives help you paint pictures with words. Notice how the adjectives in this passage help you visualize the wings.

LITERARY MODEL

> The wings themselves were **finer** than the finest rice paper, and yet they were **strong**. . . .
>   Right then I spread my wings and saw the glory of them! They had been **gold** at first, but now I saw how they shone iridescently—like the rainbow colors you see on a soap bubble. . . .
>
>   —Laurence Yep, *Dragonwings*

ADJ. & ADV.

❸ Practice and Apply

A. CONCEPT CHECK: Predicate Adjectives

Write each predicate adjective in these sentences, along with the noun or pronoun it modifies. There may be more than one predicate adjective in a sentence.

Clear and Safe

1. Because of a trolley rider's fear, windshield wipers are common today.
2. To Mary Anderson electric trolleys seemed dangerous.
3. The drivers were alert.
4. The windshields, however, looked blurry and cloudy.
5. The windshields became clean when drivers rubbed them with damp tobacco and onions.
6. Anderson was creative, so she invented a windshield wiper.
7. Her first wiper was clumsy.
8. It was manual, and the driver had to crank a handle.
9. Today's wipers are automatic.
10. Because of Mary Anderson's invention, transportation became safer than it had been.

→ **For a SELF-CHECK and more practice, see the EXERCISE BANK, p. 602.**

Write the linking verb in each sentence above.

B. WRITING: Creating Riddles

Choose three of the common inventions in the list below. For each, write a riddle containing one or more predicate adjectives. Then exchange riddles with a partner. Solve your partner's riddles, and underline the predicate adjectives in them.

Example: What is <u>shiny</u> and <u>twisted</u> and keeps papers together? (a paper clip)

television set	toaster
portable radio	doorbell
pencil	bubble gum
computer	cereal
in-line skates	wristwatch

Other Words Used as Adjectives

LESSON 3

❶ Here's the Idea

In addition to their usual uses, many nouns and pronouns can be used as adjectives. They can modify nouns to make their meanings more specific.

Pronouns as Adjectives

Demonstrative Pronouns *This, that, these,* and *those* are demonstrative pronouns that can be used as adjectives.

MODIFIES
This phone has a dial.

MODIFIES
That phone has a keypad.

This phone has a cord.

That phone has a battery.

Possessive Pronouns *My, our, your, her, his, its,* and *their* are possessive pronouns that are used as adjectives.

MODIFIES   MODIFIES
Your phone is lighter. My phone has better reception.

Indefinite Pronouns Indefinite pronouns such as *all, each, both, few, most,* and *some* can be used as adjectives.

MODIFIES
Originally, few people believed in the idea of the telephone.

MODIFIES
Today, most households have at least two phones.

ADJ. & ADV.

Nouns as Adjectives

Like pronouns, nouns can be used as adjectives. In the expression "computer keyboard," for example, the word *computer* (normally a noun) is used to modify *keyboard*. Notice the following examples of nouns used as adjectives.

MODIFIES

Renata's family just opened up an Internet account.

MODIFIES

This account should help her complete school projects.

➋ Why It Matters in Writing

You can't gesture in writing the way you can in a face-to-face conversation. But you can use demonstrative pronouns as adjectives to "point to" people, and possessive pronouns in order to make relationships clear.

LITERARY MODEL

Transistors, chips, integrated circuits, Teflon, new medicines, new ways of treating diseases, new ways of performing operations, . . . are linked to the space effort. Most of these developments have been so incorporated into our day-to-day life that they are taken for granted, their origin not considered.

DEMONSTRATIVE PRONOUN

POSSESSIVE PRONOUNS

—Louis L'Amour, "The Eternal Frontier"

➌ Practice and Apply

A. CONCEPT CHECK: Other Words Used as Adjectives

Write each noun or pronoun that is used as an adjective in these sentences.

Inventions from Nature
1. Most inventions are made by human beings.
2. But beavers may have inspired those huge dams that we build across rivers.

3. Our inventions often imitate the contrivances of nature.
4. To escape their enemies, insects mimic flowers and tree limbs.
5. A human army uses camouflage to hide its tanks.
6. Birds adjust their wings to the airflow as they fly.
7. Most airplanes have adjustable wing surfaces, too.
8. Bats use sound waves to locate their prey.
9. With sonar, we use sound waves to map the ocean floor.
10. I'm watching my cat for new ideas!

➜ For a SELF-CHECK and more practice, see the EXERCISE BANK, p. 603.

B. REVISING: Adding Pronouns Used as Adjectives

Write a demonstrative, possessive, or indefinite pronoun that can be used as an adjective to fill in each blank in this paragraph.

Young Inventors

    Some late-night talk shows feature child inventors. __1__ children use __2__ imaginations to solve everyday problems. Many of __3__ inventions have to do with pets. For example, one girl who didn't like putting __4__ hand on cat food invented a device that feeds __5__ cat automatically. Another invented a doggie entertainment center for times when a dog's owners are away from __6__ home. A boy created a device for petting __7__ dog. __8__ children have used ordinary household items to create __9__ unusual inventions. For __10__ clever ideas, they have sometimes won prizes.

C. WRITING: Using Nouns as Adjectives

Many nouns used as adjectives name the materials used to make something. Write a different noun used as an adjective for each of the following phrases.

Example   stone   wall
                brick   wall

glass door   gravel road

paper bag   plastic tube

marble statue   leather jacket

What Is an Adverb?

❶ Here's the Idea

▶ An adverb is a word that modifies a verb, an adjective, or another adverb.

MODIFIES

Historians **strongly believe** that the Chinese invented rockets. ⬆ADVERB ⬆VERB

MODIFIES

Ancient Chinese warriors fired **very powerful** rockets. ADVERB⬆ ⬆ADJECTIVE

MODIFIES

Today, rockets **almost always** power missiles and spacecraft. ⬆ADVERB ⬆ADVERB

Adverbs answer the questions *how, when, where,* and *to what extent*.

Adverbs	
How?	patiently, loudly, carefully
When?	sometimes, daily, always
Where?	inside, there, everywhere
To what extent?	extremely, nearly, almost

The position of adverbs can vary. An adverb that modifies an adjective or another adverb is generally placed just before the word it modifies. An adverb that modifies a verb can be placed after the verb, before the verb, or at the beginning of the sentence.

The rocket ascended suddenly. (after verb)

The rocket suddenly ascended. (before verb)

Suddenly, the rocket ascended. (at beginning of sentence)

Intensifiers are adverbs that modify adjectives or other adverbs. They are usually placed directly before the words they modify. Intensifiers usually answer the question *to what extent.*

We covered our ears very quickly at the shuttle launch.

MODIFIES

Intensifiers				
almost	extremely	quite	so	usually
especially	nearly	really	too	very

Forming Adverbs

Many adverbs are formed by adding the suffix -*ly* to adjectives. Sometimes a base word's spelling changes when -*ly* is added.

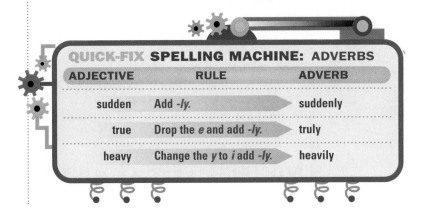

QUICK-FIX SPELLING MACHINE: ADVERBS

ADJECTIVE	RULE	ADVERB
sudden	Add -*ly*.	suddenly
true	Drop the *e* and add -*ly*.	truly
heavy	Change the *y* to *i* add -*ly*.	heavily

ADJ. & ADV.

❷ Why It Matters in Writing

You will find adverbs helpful when you're writing about historical events. The adverbs in this model help tell readers when and how blue jeans were invented.

PROFESSIONAL MODEL

During the California gold rush, a tailor named Levi Strauss saw miners daily. Their pants were often extremely worn. Strauss worked very carefully to fashion stiff canvas into overalls. These tough pants ultimately became today's blue jeans.

TELLS WHEN

TELLS TO WHAT EXTENT

TELLS HOW

❸ Practice and Apply

→ For a SELF-CHECK and more practice, see the EXERCISE BANK, p. 603.

A. CONCEPT CHECK: What Is an Adverb?

Write each adverb and the word it modifies. Identify the modified word as a verb, an adjective, or an adverb. There may be more than one adverb in a sentence.

Like the Birds
1. People were flying gliders experimentally in the early 1900s.
2. No one had yet flown a powered aircraft successfully.
3. In Dayton, Ohio, Orville and Wilbur Wright expertly repaired bicycles.
4. They were quite popular members of the community.
5. They bicycled enthusiastically and also studied gliders there.
6. The brothers worked fanatically to invent a powered aircraft.
7. Their first plane, which was quite crude, was made from wood, wire, and cotton sheets.
8. They very carefully added two propellers and hitched them together with bicycle chains.
9. In 1903 the Wright brothers flew and landed their *Flyer* quite successfully.
10. Each brother flew the plane twice.

B. WRITING: Adding Adverbs

Read the paragraph below. Choose five adverbs from the following list to replace the words in parentheses.

thoughtfully	cruelly	there	almost	soon
energetically	tiredly	very	daily	

Shopping-Cart Convenience
(1) Sylvan Goldman lived in Oklahoma City and owned a grocery store (answers *where*). **(2)** He watched shoppers (answers *how*) carry items from aisle to aisle. **(3)** To help his customers, Goldman (answers *how*) set out wheeled carts for them to use. **(4)** He (answers *to what extent*) sadly noted that no one wanted the carts. Goldman outsmarted them, however. He hired phony shoppers to push around the carts. **(5)** The real shoppers (answers *when*) began to use the carts throughout the store.

Making Comparisons

❶ Here's the Idea

Adjectives and adverbs can be used to compare people or things. Special forms of these words are used to make comparisons.

▶ **Use the comparative form of an adjective or adverb when you compare a person or thing with one other person or thing.**

The *Titanic* was larger than the *Olympic*.

It traveled faster than the other ship.

▶ **Use the superlative form of an adjective or adverb when you compare someone or something with more than one other thing.**

In fact, the *Titanic* was the largest ship of all.

Of the fleet's ships, the *Titanic* raced the fastest.

Regular Forms of Comparison

For most one-syllable modifiers, add -*er* to form the comparative and -*est* to form the superlative.

One-Syllable Modifiers	Base Form	Comparative	Superlative
Adjectives	tall shiny	taller shinier	tallest shiniest
Adverbs	close soon	closer sooner	closest soonest

You can also add -*er* and -*est* to some two-syllable adjectives. With others, and with two-syllable adverbs, use the words *more* and *most*.

Two-Syllable Modifiers	Base Form	Comparative	Superlative
Adjectives	easy cheerful	easier more cheerful	easiest most cheerful
Adverbs	brightly swiftly	more brightly more swiftly	most brightly most swiftly

ADJ. & ADV.

With adjectives and adverbs having three or more syllables, use *more* and *most*.

Modifiers with More Than Two Syllables			
	Base Form	**Comparative**	**Superlative**
Adjectives	powerful energetic	**more** powerful **more** energetic	**most** powerful **most** energetic
Adverbs	peacefully comfortably	**more** peacefully **more** comfortably	**most** peacefully **most** comfortably

Use only one sign of comparison at a time. Don't use *more* and *-er* together or *most* and *-est* together.

INCORRECT: **The *Titanic* was the most greatest ship.**

CORRECT: **The Titanic was the greatest ship.**

Irregular Forms of Comparison

The comparatives and superlatives of some adjectives and adverbs are formed in irregular ways.

Irregular Modifiers			
	Base Form	**Comparative**	**Superlative**
Adjectives	good bad	better worse	best worst
Adverbs	well much little	better more less	best most least

❷ Why It Matters in Writing

Use comparative and superlative forms of modifiers when you need to compare or contrast things in history or science class.

STUDENT MODEL

Although the *Californian* was the ship **nearest** the *Titanic,* it was the *Carpathia* that rescued the survivors. Those in the lifeboats were **most likely** to survive.

❸ Practice and Apply

ADJ. & ADV.

A. CONCEPT CHECK: Making Comparisons

Choose the correct comparative or superlative form to complete each sentence.

Stronger Than Steel

1. Stephanie Kwolek invented one of the (more original, most original) materials ever developed.
2. She believed that creativity was (more important, most important) for an inventor than technical knowledge.
3. Kwolek planned to study medicine, but she found chemistry (more interesting, most interesting).
4. She was intrigued by all the (most new, newest) chemical processes.
5. She studied the (best, most best) ways of making artificial materials.
6. When Kwolek was working with chemicals, petroleum was the (more, most) common source of plastic.
7. Kwolek invented a chemical fiber called Kevlar, which is five times (more strong, stronger) than steel.
8. Kevlar was one of the (more, most) influential inventions of the 20th century.
9. Kevlar vests are (most, more) famous as police vests.
10. Kwolek's work inventing Kevlar and other materials made her one of the (better-known, best-known) chemists in the United States.

➡ For a **SELF-CHECK** and more practice, see the **EXERCISE BANK, p. 604.**

B. WRITING: Creating Comparisons

Examine the three photographs of different kinds of boats. Write five sentences comparing them in terms of appearance, speed, power, or capacity. Use comparative and superlative forms in your writing.

Adjective or Adverb?

LESSON 6

CHAPTER 5

❶ Here's the Idea

Some pairs of adjectives and adverbs are often a source of confusion and mistakes in speaking and writing.

Good and *Well*

Good is always an adjective; it modifies a noun or pronoun. *Well* is usually an adverb, modifying a verb, an adverb, or an adjective. *Well* is an adjective when it refers to health.

MODIFIES

The ice-cream sundae was a good invention.
ADJECTIVE   NOUN

MODIFIES   MODIFIES

Ice cream sold well.   **He doesn't feel well.**
VERB   ADVERB   PRONOUN   ADJECTIVE

Real and *Really*

Real is always an adjective; it modifies a noun or pronoun. *Really* is always an adverb; it modifies a verb, an adverb, or an adjective.

MODIFIES

Medical inventions can make a real difference.
ADJECTIVE   NOUN

MODIFIES

A few inventions have really changed how we live.
ADVERB   VERB

Bad and *Badly*

Bad is always an adjective; it modifies a noun or pronoun. *Badly* is always an adverb; it modifies a verb, an adverb, or an adjective.

MODIFIES

A bad illness can require medicine.
ADJECTIVE   NOUN

MODIFIES

I did badly on the last science quiz.
VERB   ADVERB

❷ Why It Matters in Writing

Watch out for these tricky pairs of adjectives and adverbs. Mistakes are so common that you need to double-check your work every time you use a form of good, real, or bad.

> I want to enter this year's science fair because I think my experiment on lasers will be ~~real~~ *really* interesting. I'm planning on talking about the different uses of lasers in grocery stores, hospitals, and banks. All of the lasers seem to work ~~good~~ *well*.
>
> Sincerely,
>
> Jamie D.

ADJ. & ADV.

❸ Practice and Apply

CONCEPT CHECK: Adjective or Adverb?

For each sentence, choose the correct modifier from those given in parentheses. Identify each word you choose as an adjective or an adverb.

Medicine's History—Good or Bad?

1. Today we take (real, really) good medical care for granted, but history is full of examples of ineffective medicine.
2. Many early treatments were (badly, bad).
3. Unsuccessful treatments were (bad, badly) for both patients and doctors.
4. But if they got well, patients thought their doctors were (good, well).
5. The ancient Greek physician Hippocrates helped rid medicine of magic, superstition, and other (real, really) bad elements.

➜ **For a SELF-CHECK and more practice, see the EXERCISE BANK, p. 604.**

Avoiding Double Negatives

 LESSON 7

❶ Here's the Idea

A **negative word** is a word that implies that something does not exist or happen. Some common negative words are listed below.

Common Negative Words				
barely	hardly	never	none	nothing
can't	hasn't	no	no one	nowhere
don't	neither	nobody	not	scarcely

If two negative words are used where only one is needed, the result is a **double negative.** Avoid double negatives in your speaking and writing.

Nonstandard

    I can't hardly believe someone created pajamas for dogs.

Standard

    I can hardly believe someone created pajamas for dogs.

    I can't believe someone created pajamas for dogs.

❷ Why It Matters in Writing

Don't let double negatives creep into your writing when you're trying to make an important point. Double negatives are almost always nonstandard.

> **STUDENT MODEL**
>
> During World War II, pilots flew planes higher than ever before. They didn't have ~~no~~ *enough* air to breathe at very high altitudes. Alice Chatham, a sculptor, designed a mask to supply pilots with oxygen so that they wouldn't ~~never~~ *ever* black out from lack of oxygen.

❸ Practice and Apply

A. CONCEPT CHECK: Avoiding Double Negatives

Write the word in parentheses that correctly completes each sentence.

> **Sticky Stuff**
> **1.** You (can, can't) scarcely imagine a time before sticky notes, can you?
> **2.** You (can't, can) barely put a note in a book without them.
> **3.** Sticky notes (aren't, are) nothing like other bookmarks.
> **4.** They (were, weren't) scarcely Art Fry's first invention.
> **5.** In the 1970s Fry (hadn't, had) nothing but pieces of paper for bookmarks.
> **6.** These scraps of paper (could, couldn't) hardly stay in a book.
> **7.** Fry wanted something that (wouldn't, would) never fall out but wouldn't harm the page.
> **8.** His colleague discovered a glue that (did, didn't) not stick as tightly as other glues.
> **9.** Nobody had (never, ever) made a sticky bookmark that you could pull off a page.
> **10.** Now there (aren't, are) hardly any homes or offices without sticky notes.

➜ **For a SELF-CHECK and more practice, see the EXERCISE BANK, p. 605.**

B. PROOFREADING: Eliminating Double Negatives

Find and correct the double negatives in the paragraph below.

> **Cat Feeding for Fun**
>   Suzanna Goodin never wanted to feed her cats. Was she a cat hater? No, she loved her cats. She just didn't want nothing to do with feeding them. One day Suzanna's teacher told the class to think of problems they hadn't never been able to solve. Then they should invent solutions. Suzanna invented a cat-feeding spoon that didn't leave nothing to clean up. The spoon was made from dough baked in the oven.

Grammar in Literature

Inventing with Adjectives and Adverbs

One of the gifts an inventor needs is the ability to notice details. Writers use the same gift when they create literature. In your own writing, you can use adjectives and adverbs to help communicate details and convey the tone of your passage.

In the following excerpt, Gish Jen uses adjectives and adverbs to describe an umbrella. Her use of details lets readers sense the speaker's feelings of wonder.

The White Umbrella

by Gish Jen

I stared at the umbrella. I wanted to open it, twirl it around by its slender silver handle....

ADJECTIVE

I could not believe that I was actually holding the umbrella, opening it. It sprang up by itself as if it were alive, as if that were what it wanted to do—as if it belonged in my hands, above my head. I stared at the network of silver spokes, and then spun the umbrella around and around and around. It was so clean and white that it seemed to glow, to illuminate everything around it. "It's beautiful," I said.

ADVERB

Practice and Apply

A. DRAFTING: Write a Description

As the speaker and her sister wait for a ride, it begins to rain. Follow the directions to invent two descriptions about rain.

1. First describe two characters waiting for a ride in the rain. Use modifiers that help you create a joyful mood. Think of good descriptive words of your own, or try some of these:

soothing	gently
cool	quietly
clean	briefly
clear	softly
warm	

2. Now use different modifiers to create a depressing mood. Try some of these modifiers:

cold	prickly
soggy	sharply
clammy	steadily
heavy	

ADJ. & ADV.

B. WRITING: Create a Scene

Put ideas from your two descriptions together to create a scene in which two people are together in the rain and waiting for a ride. One of the people is enjoying the rain. The other is miserable. Save your descriptions in your 🗂 **Working Portfolio.**

Mixed Review

A. Using Modifiers Read this passage and answer the questions below it.

(1) Ruth Wakefield, owner of the Toll House Inn, <u>frequently</u> baked a kind of cookie that had melted chocolate in <u>its</u> batter. (2) One day she didn't have <u>enough</u> time to melt the chocolate. (3) So she cut the large slab of chocolate into <u>smaller</u> bits and added them to the batter. (4) She thought they would melt in the oven just as if she had melted the chocolate <u>first</u>. (5) But the <u>chocolate</u> bits didn't melt. (6) They poked up <u>here</u> and <u>there</u> in the cookies' surface. (7) Presto! Wakefield had invented <u>chocolate chip</u> cookies, an invention for which we are all <u>hungrily</u> <u>grateful</u>.

1. In sentence 1, is *frequently* an adjective or an adverb?
2. In sentence 1, what kind of word is *its*? How is it used?
3. In sentence 2, which word does *enough* modify?
4. In sentence 3, what form of adjective is *smaller*?
5. In sentence 4, is *first* an adjective or an adverb? How do you know?
6. In sentence 5, how is *chocolate* used?
7. In sentence 6, what kind of words are *here* and *there,* and what question do they answer?
8. In sentence 7, how is *chocolate chip* used?
9. In sentence 7, which word does *hungrily* modify? What part of speech is *hungrily?*
10. In sentence 7, is *grateful* an adjective or adverb? Which word does it modify?

B. Choosing the Right Modifier Choose the correct words from those given in parentheses.

1. George Crum, a chef, made a (real, really) good discovery in 1853.
2. One guest complained (loud, loudly) that his French fries were too (large, larger).
3. Crum sliced some (thinner, more thin) ones, but the guest (wouldn't say nothing, wouldn't say anything) good about the potatoes.
4. Finally Crum (angerly, angrily) sliced some potatoes (real, really) thin and fried them.
5. The guest loved the dish so (good, well) that potato chips became a specialty of the restaurant.

For each underlined item, choose the letter of the term that correctly identifies it.

We don't never run out of discoveries about space. Space is really
(1)   (2)
infinite. Recently in the *New York Times Magazine,* James Gleick
(3)
stated: "It wasn't until the year 4.5 billion or so . . . that an earthly

life form managed to hurl some stuff into orbit . . . high enough to
(4)
look down and see our tiny globe for what it is. Counted another way,
(5)
it was Oct. 4, 1957 [when Russian scientists launched the artificial
(6)
satellite *Sputnik.*] . . . Plenty of scientists and rocket buffs were

listening down below and hatching grander plans. Already, Arthur C.
(7)   (8)
Clarke, the science-fiction writer, had performed one of the

millennium's most astounding feats of invention. In 1945, he . . .
(9)
published a complete plan for using satellites to relay radio "signals."
(10)

1. A. adjective
   B. double negative
   C. statement
   D. question

2. A. adverb
   B. adjective
   C. demonstrative pronoun
   D. predicate adjective

3. A. adverb
   B. predicate adjective
   C. proper adjective
   D. demonstrative pronoun

4. A. pronoun used as adjective
   B. noun used as adjective
   C. pronoun used as adverb
   D. noun used as adverb

5. A. adverb telling when
   B. adverb telling how
   C. adverb telling how much
   D. adverb telling where

6. A. possessive pronoun
   B. adverb
   C. predicate adjective
   D. proper adjective

7. A. comparative adverb
   B. superlative adverb
   C. comparative adjective
   D. superlative adjective

8. A. adverb describing *Clarke*
   B. adverb describing *had performed*
   C. adjective describing *writer*
   D. adjective describing *Clarke*

9. A. comparative adverb
   B. superlative adverb
   C. comparative adjective
   D. superlative adjective

10. A. pronoun used as adjective
    B. noun used as adjective
    C. pronoun used as adverb
    D. noun used as adverb

ADJ. & ADV.

Student Help Desk

Adjectives and Adverbs at a Glance

Adjectives modify nouns and pronouns.

The nifty invention was helpful. It was silver.

Adverbs modify verbs, adjectives, and other adverbs.

The unusually quiet hole puncher worked very efficiently.

Modifier Problems   Fix-It Mechanics

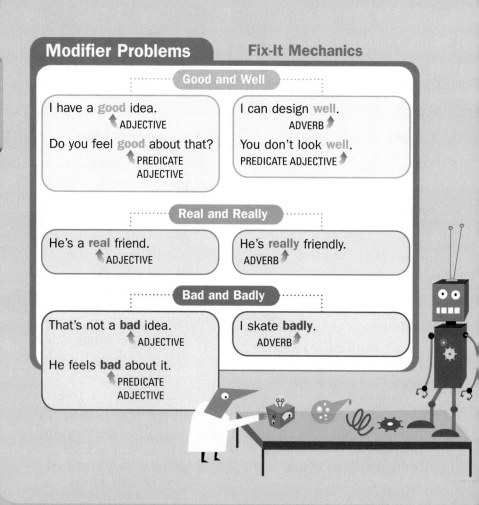

Good and Well

I have a good idea.
↑ ADJECTIVE

Do you feel good about that?
↑ PREDICATE
ADJECTIVE

I can design well.
ADVERB ↑

You don't look well.
PREDICATE ADJECTIVE ↗

Real and Really

He's a real friend.
↑ ADJECTIVE

He's really friendly.
ADVERB ↗

Bad and Badly

That's not a bad idea.
↑ ADJECTIVE

He feels bad about it.
↑ PREDICATE
ADJECTIVE

I skate badly.
ADVERB ↗

Modifiers in Comparisons

Size Adjustments

	Comparative	Superlative
far	farther	farthest
shiny	shinier	shiniest
useful	more useful	most useful
intelligent	more intelligent	most intelligent
happily	more happily	most happily
good	better	best
bad	worse	worst

Avoiding Double Forms

Double Trouble

Double Negative	Fix
we can't never	we can never we can't
we don't hardly	we hardly we don't

Double Comparison	Fix
more better	better
most luckiest	luckiest

The Bottom Line

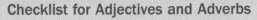

Checklist for Adjectives and Adverbs

Have I remembered to . . .

____ use adjectives to fine-tune my nouns?

____ capitalize proper adjectives?

____ use adverbs to fine-tune descriptions of actions?

____ use correct forms of adverbs and adjectives in comparisons?

____ avoid double negatives?

Prepositions, Conjunctions, Interjections

Yikes!

Theme: Bugs!
Little Things Mean a Lot

What would you say if you came face to face with this bug? You might express yourself with a small but powerful interjection like the one in the balloon above. Like bugs, interjections, conjunctions, and prepositions are often small but powerful. They not only express emotion but also connect other words and show relationships between words.

Write Away: What Bugs You?
Recall a time when you were up close and personal with a bug. Was the bug disgusting? fascinating? weird? beautiful, perhaps? Write a short paragraph about your bug. Save the paragraph in your 📁 **Working Portfolio.**

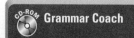
Grammar Coach

Choose the letter of the term that correctly identifies each underlined item.

Bugs! Ugh! Do you shriek in horror when you see bugs? Many
     (1)   (2)
people are terrified of bugs. Their alien shapes inspire fear, and
              (3)   (4)
the way they swarm around their target often causes panic. Bugs
                   (5)
include both 700,000 known species of insects and more than
      (6)   (6)
30,000 known species of spiders. Ecologists are glad that bugs live

among us. Their contributions to the environment are important.
(7)   (8)
For example, bees pollinate flowers. Bugs may seem strange, but
                                            (9)
life as we know it would be impossible without them.
                                   (10)

1. A. preposition
   B. interjection
   C. conjunction
   D. adverb

2. A. preposition
   B. object of a preposition
   C. prepositional phrase
   D. interjection

3. A. preposition
   B. object of a preposition
   C. conjunction
   D. interjection

4. A. coordinating conjunction
   B. correlative conjunction
   C. adjective phrase
   D. preposition

5. A. conjunction
   B. interjection
   C. adjective phrase
   D. adverb phrase

6. A. preposition
   B. object of a preposition
   C. coordinating conjunction
   D. correlative conjunction

7. A. preposition
   B. interjection
   C. coordinating conjunction
   D. prepositional phrase

8. A. conjunction
   B. interjection
   C. adjective phrase
   D. adverb phrase

9. A. coordinating conjunction
   B. correlative conjunction
   C. preposition
   D. interjection

10. A. interjection
    B. preposition
    C. object of a preposition
    D. adjective

PREP. & CONJ.

What Is a Preposition?

LESSON 1

❶ Here's the Idea

▶ **A preposition is a word that shows a relationship between a noun or pronoun and some other word in the sentence.** A preposition is always followed by an object, either a noun or a pronoun.

The article about insects is interesting.
　　　　　　↑ PREPOSITION

Here, the preposition *about* shows the relationship between the words *article* and *insects.* In the sentences below, notice how each preposition expresses a different relationship between the worm and the apple.

The worm is on the apple.

The worm is beside the apple.

The worm is under the apple.

The worm is in the apple.

Common Prepositions				
about	at	despite	like	to
above	before	down	near	toward
across	behind	during	of	under
after	below	except	off	until
against	beneath	for	on	up
along	beside	from	out	with
among	between	in	over	within
around	beyond	inside	past	without
as	by	into	since through	

This jewelry is inspired by a beetle.

Prepositional Phrases

▶ **A prepositional phrase consists of a preposition, its object, and any modifiers of the object.** The object of the preposition is the noun or pronoun following the preposition.

PREPOSITIONAL PHRASE

Some peoples have depicted insects in art.

PREPOSITION ▲   ▲ OBJECT

Beetle images decorate the jewelry of many cultures.

PREPOSITION ▲ ▲ MODIFIER ▲ OBJECT

Some believed that dreams come from a butterfly.

Use *between* when the object of the preposition refers to two people or things. Use *among* when speaking of three or more.

Ants share food *between* two nestmates.

Ants share food *among* all the colony members.

Preposition or Adverb?

Sometimes the same word can be used as a preposition or as an adverb. If the word has no object, then it is an adverb.

PREPOSITIONAL PHRASE

The ant scurried out the door.

PREPOSITION ▲   ▲ OBJECT

The ant scurried out.

▲ ADVERB

For more on adverbs, see pp. 134–136.

PREPOSITIONS

➋ Why It Matters in Writing

Use prepositional phrases in descriptive writing to add detailed information to sentences. For example, a prepositional phrase can tell an exact location. The prepositional phrases in this model tell where the ant found the grain and where she put it.

LITERARY MODEL

... she had taken it from the fields and stowed it away in a hole in the bank, under a hawthorn bush.

PREPOSITIONAL PHRASES

—Aesop, "Ant and Grasshopper,"
retold by James Reeves

➌ Practice and Apply

CONCEPT CHECK: What Is a Preposition?

Write the preposition in each sentence, along with its object.

Smoky the Beetle
1. Some jewel beetles are attracted to forest fires.
2. They can sense a forest fire from 30 miles.
3. Often they fly straight into the flames.
4. Sometimes they swarm around firefighters!
5. With their own infrared detectors, they sense heat.
6. Some scientists now believe that the beetles smell fire through their antennae.
7. Information from the beetles may improve the accuracy of fire alarms.
8. Currently, many fire alarms detect carbon dioxide levels in the air.
9. But the alarms can be fooled by car fumes.
10. Scientists are testing a more accurate alarm that is outfitted with actual insect antennae.

➜ For a SELF-CHECK and more practice, see the EXERCISE BANK, p. 606.

Using Prepositional Phrases

LESSON 2

❶ Here's the Idea

A prepositional phrase is always related to another word in a sentence. It modifies the word in the same way an adjective or adverb would.

Adjective Phrases

▶ **An adjective prepositional phrase modifies a noun or a pronoun.** Like an adjective, a prepositional phrase can tell which one, how many, or what kind.

WHAT KIND?

This spider is a type **of jumping spider.**
　　　　　　　NOUN　　　　　ADJECTIVE PHRASE

WHICH ONE?

The tiny bug **on the windowsill** is also a jumping spider.

Adverb Phrases

▶ **An adverb prepositional phrase modifies a verb, an adjective, or an adverb.** Like an adverb, a prepositional phrase can tell where, when, how, why, or to what extent.

WHERE?

Jumping spiders live **in many places.**
　　　　　　　VERB　　　ADVERB PHRASE

WHY?

These spiders are famous **for their eight eyes.**
　　　　　ADJECTIVE

HOW?

They jump far **for their size.**
　　　ADVERB

Several prepositional phrases can work together. Each phrase after the first often modifies the object of the phrase before it.

A spider sat **on the tip** **of a twig** **in a tree.**

PREPOSITIONS

Placement of Prepositional Phrases

When you write, try to place each prepositional phrase as close as possible to the word it modifies. Otherwise, you may confuse—or unintentionally amuse—your readers.

Unclear

With eight hairy legs, the bird chased the spider.

(This must be the world's weirdest bird!)

Clear

The bird chased the spider with eight hairy legs.

(Now the reader can tell who has the hairy legs!)

❷ Why It Matters in Writing

When you write about science, use prepositional phrases to answer such questions as *where, how, which one,* and *what kind.* Notice how much information the prepositional phrases supply in the caption of the photograph below.

From one berry and *to another* tell where.

A jumping spider, photographed while jumping from one berry to another.

❸ Practice and Apply

A. CONCEPT CHECK: Using Prepositional Phrases

Write the prepositional phrase in each sentence, along with the word it modifies. Then indicate whether the phrase is an adjective phrase or an adverb phrase. Warning: One sentence contains two prepositional phrases.

Eight-Legged Heroes
1. Nearly 36,000 known kinds of spiders inhabit the earth.
2. Very few spiders are dangerous to people.
3. Spiders eat millions of disease-bearing mosquitoes.
4. They also control huge populations of garden pests.
5. The spider, with its many useful qualities, is often helpful.
6. Spiders live in many habitats.
7. Some spiders survive in cold climates.
8. Spiders with brilliant colors are beautiful.
9. Dewdrops on spider webs sparkle in the morning light.
10. The dewdrops usually evaporate by afternoon.

➡ For a SELF-CHECK and more practice, see the EXERCISE BANK, p. 606.

B. WRITING: Using Prepositional Phrases in Science

Suppose that on a field trip you discovered an interesting spider and took this photograph of it. Write a very detailed description of the spider and of the place where you found it. Use adverb phrases to answer questions like *how, when,* and *where.*

LESSON 3 Conjunctions

1 Here's the Idea

▶ **A conjunction is a word used to join words or groups of words.** Different kinds of conjunctions are used in different ways.

Coordinating Conjunctions

▶ **A coordinating conjunction connects words used in the same way.** The words joined by a conjunction can be subjects, objects, predicates, or any other kind of sentence parts.

┌─── SUBJECTS ───┐
Insects and crustaceans have eyes with many lenses.
▲ COORDINATING CONJUNCTION

┌─── OBJECTS ───┐
Light enters the front or the side of their eyes.
▲ COORDINATING CONJUNCTION

Common Coordinating Conjunctions						
and	but	or	nor	yet	so	for

Use *and* to connect similar ideas. Use *but* to contrast ideas.

Each lens can receive light and form a separate image.
(*And* connects two things each lens can do.)

Insects' eyes are smaller than ours, but their vision is more complex.
(*But* contrasts vision in insects and people.)

A greenbottle fly is small, but its eyes contain many lenses.

Correlative Conjunctions

▶ **Correlative conjunctions are pairs of words that connect words used in the same way.** Like coordinating conjunctions, correlative conjunctions can join subjects, objects, predicates, and other sentence parts.

SUBJECTS
Both flies and mosquitoes have compound eyes.
CORRELATIVE
CONJUNCTION

PREDICATE ADJECTIVES
Their eye lenses are not only long but also cylindrical.
CORRELATIVE
CONJUNCTION

Common Correlative Conjunctions		
both . . . and	either . . . or	not only . . . but also
neither . . . nor	whether . . . or	

CONJUNCTIONS

❷ Why It Matters in Writing

A writer's use of the right conjunction helps readers know which words or ideas are joined together and how they relate to each other. Notice how conjunctions in the model connect similar ideas.

PROFESSIONAL MODEL

Insects **and** spiders have many different kinds of eyes. Some spiders have eight eyes, **so** they can see in several directions at once. Some insects have two compound eyes **and** three simple eyes called ocelli.

—S. Lieb

And connects two subjects in the sentence.

So connects two complete ideas.

And connects the two objects of *have*.

❸ Practice and Apply

A. CONCEPT CHECK: Conjunctions

Write the conjunction in each sentence, along with the words or groups of words that it joins.

Seeing with Electrons
1. To magnify things, optical microscopes make use of lenses and light waves.
2. Light waves show the details of ordinary objects, but the waves are too long to reveal the smallest structures.
3. Electron microscopes open new worlds, for they show smaller details.
4. They use magnetic "lenses" and electron beams instead of light waves.
5. The beams of electrons have only 1/8,000 the wavelength of visible light, so they can show much more detail.
6. Electron microscopes can be scanning or transmission microscopes.
7. Scanning microscopes and transmission microscopes are much more powerful than optical microscopes.
8. Scanning microscopes not only magnify but also produce a TV picture.
9. They can magnify an object over 100,000 times, but transmission microscopes can magnify up to 1 million times.
10. Bugs can keep no secrets from either scanning or transmission microscopes!

➜ For a SELF-CHECK and more practice, see the EXERCISE BANK, p. 606.

B. REVISING: Changing Conjunctions

The right conjunctions help you say what you mean. Rewrite the conjunctions so that the meaning is clear.

Catch Me If You Can
Flies always see the swatter <u>but</u> flit away from it. Are flies smart <u>and</u> alert? Which characteristic do they have? They are probably alert <u>but</u> sharp-eyed. Their eyes have many parts, <u>or</u> they can see motion even at the edges of their vision. You can hide the swatter, <u>and</u> the fly might still see it.

LESSON 4   Interjections

❶ Here's the Idea

▶ **An interjection is a word or phrase used to express emotion.**

Hey, look at that bug.

It's a cockroach! Yuck!

❷ Why It Matters in Writing

The Far Side   by Gary Larson

Larson S-31 © 1983 FarWorks Inc. All Rights Reserved.

"Spiders, scorpions, and insecticides, oh my! . . . Spiders, scorpions, and insecticides, oh my! . . ."

Writers often use interjections to express strong emotions, such as concern, terror, anger, and disgust.

Oh my is an interjection.

❸ Practice and Apply

In the cartoon above, the interjection *oh my* shows fear, since spiders, scorpions, and insecticides are all dangerous to insects. Try writing your own caption for the cartoon, using at least one interjection. Add your caption to your 📁 **Working Portfolio.**

Grammar in Science

➊ Using Prepositions to Write about Science

When you write your observations and conclusions in a lab report, the proper use of prepositions can make a difference. Prepositions are especially important if you are describing the physical features of animals or their behavior. In the notebook below, a student has used arrows on her drawing to show the location of certain features. For her field notes, she has used prepositional phrases to express the information shown in her drawing.

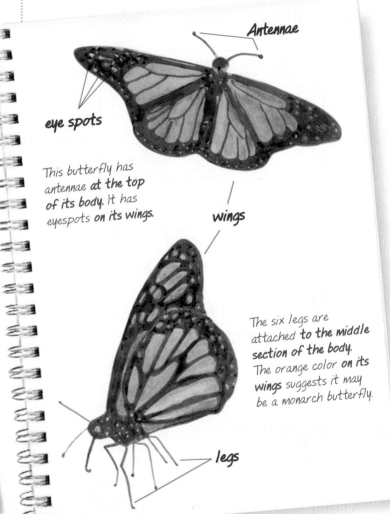

Antennae

eye spots

This butterfly has antennae **at the top of its body**. It has eyespots **on its wings**.

wings

The six legs are attached **to the middle section of the body**. The orange color **on its wings** suggests it may be a monarch butterfly.

legs

CHAPTER 6

❷ Practice and Apply

USING PREPOSITIONS

For a project on insect metamorphosis, your class has observed videos of caterpillars developing into butterflies and moths. You have taken notes on your observations. Write a summary of your observations using your notes as a guide. Use prepositional phrases to explain details about the caterpillar's behavior, the cocoon or pupa stage, and the butterfly or moth. Useful prepositions might include the words *around, inside, before, after, from.* Underline the prepositional phrases in your summary. Save your work in your 🗂 **Working Portfolio.**

- caterpillar stuck to the leaf
- film formed around caterpillar

- insect begins breaking from pupa or cocoon

- insect out of pupa or cocoon
- pumps fluids through its wings

PREP. & CONJ.

163

Mixed Review

A. Prepositions, Conjunctions, Interjections Choose the correct word in parentheses to complete each sentence. Then identify the word as a preposition, a conjunction, or an interjection.

1. New Orleans has many wooden buildings built (on, out) swampland.
2. (For, Off) termites these buildings are like a buffet.
3. The Algiers Public Library (near, up) New Orleans had 79 antitermite treatments.
4. Yet experts examined the ground afterward and found 70 million Formosan termites (beneath, above) the library.
5. (Ugh!, To!) It was the largest known termite colony on earth.
6. Each of the termites was small, (or, yet) together they were like a 500-pound animal eating the building 24 hours a day.
7. A typical Formosan colony is made up of 5 million termites (and, but) eats 1,000 pounds of wood a year.
8. The termites probably traveled (to, until) the United States in wooden crates after World War II.
9. People thought they were relatively harmless, (not, but) by 1965 they had infested a Houston warehouse.
10. (Except, Both) Galveston, Texas, (for, and) Charleston, South Carolina, are also victims of Formosan termites.

B. Prepositional Phrases Write the prepositional phrases in the paragraph below. Identify each as an adjective or an adverb phrase.

(1) Butterflies are the darlings of the insect world. (2) Like bugs in elaborate costumes, they grace our gardens. (3) Yet butterflies work hard despite their delicate appearance. (4) Some migrate for 2,000 miles. (5) They can soar 7,000 feet above the earth. (6) There are more than 20,000 species of butterflies. (7) But environmental changes in the modern world have reduced their numbers. (8) Industrial and residential development destroys the food and shelter needed by butterflies. (9) Pesticides are deadly to them. (10) However, "habitat gardening" helps provide butterflies with shelter and food plants.

Choose the letter of the term that correctly identifies each underlined item.

Jumping spiders are the cats <u>of the spider world</u>. Their quick gait

(1)

<u>and</u> short, sudden jumps help them catch their prey. When they get

(2)

close <u>to</u> an insect, they pounce. A jumping spider can leap 40 times

(3)

its body length. In human terms, it is like a person 6 feet tall who

can jump 240 feet. <u>Wow!</u> The spider is also famous <u>for its excellent</u>

(4)   (5)

<u>vision</u>. <u>With</u> four <u>of</u> its eight eyes very large, it has the best vision of

     (6)   (7)

any <u>spider</u> its size. Jumping spiders do not build webs. They spin a

(8)

dragline attached to a wall <u>or</u> a tree. Jumping spiders live in almost

(9)

every environment—you can find them <u>both</u> on your own windowsill

(10)

<u>and</u> 22,000 feet up the slopes of Mount Everest.

(10)

1. A. adjective phrase
   B. adverb phrase
   C. coordinating conjunction
   D. correlative conjunction

2. A. preposition
   B. object of a preposition
   C. coordinating conjunction
   D. correlative conjunction

3. A. interjection
   B. preposition
   C. correlative conjunction
   D. object of a preposition

4. A. object of a preposition
   B. coordinating conjunction
   C. correlative conjunction
   D. interjection

5. A. conjunction
   B. interjection
   C. adverb phrase
   D. adjective phrase

6. A. preposition
   B. conjunction
   C. adverb
   D. interjection

7. A. object of a preposition
   B. preposition
   C. correlative conjunction
   D. coordinating conjunction

8. A. interjection
   B. conjunction
   C. prepositional phrase
   D. object of a preposition

9. A. preposition
   B. adverb
   C. conjunction
   D. interjection

10. A. coordinating conjunction
    B. correlative conjunction
    C. preposition
    D. object of a preposition

Student Help Desk

Prepositions, Conjunctions, Interjections at a Glance

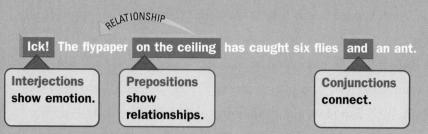

Ick! The flypaper on the ceiling has caught six flies and an ant.

RELATIONSHIP

Interjections show emotion.

Prepositions show relationships.

Conjunctions connect.

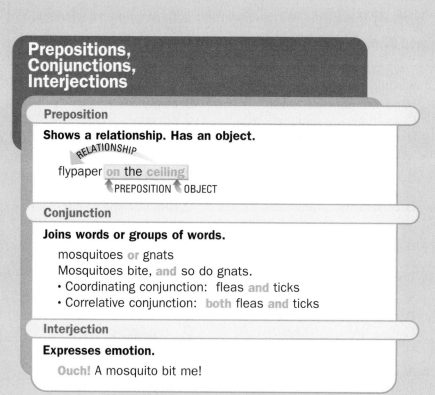

Prepositions, Conjunctions, Interjections

Preposition

Shows a relationship. Has an object.

RELATIONSHIP

flypaper on the ceiling

PREPOSITION · OBJECT

Conjunction

Joins words or groups of words.

mosquitoes or gnats
Mosquitoes bite, and so do gnats.
- Coordinating conjunction: fleas and ticks
- Correlative conjunction: both fleas and ticks

Interjection

Expresses emotion.

Ouch! A mosquito bit me!

CHAPTER 6

Prepositional Phrases

What Do They Do?

Adjective Phrase

Modifies a noun or a pronoun

Tells which one	That little spider on the wall
Tells what kind	is a type of jumping spider.

Adverb Phrase

Modifies a verb, an adjective, or an adverb

Tells when	During our recent picnic,
Tells where	ants came from everywhere
Tells why	for the free food
Tells how	in a big rush.

Interjections!

Splat! Just a Few Ideas . . .

To express concern	oh-oh, oh no, oops
To express disgust	yuck, ick, gross
To express joy	awesome, hooray, yea
To express surprise	wow, what, whoops
To draw attention to	hey, yo, look, wait

The Bottom Line

Checklist for Prepositions, Conjunctions, Interjections

Have I . . .

____ used prepositions to show relationships between things?

____ placed prepositional phrases close to the words they modify?

____ used coordinating conjunctions to connect words and groups of words?

____ used correlative conjunctions correctly?

____ used interjections to express strong emotion?

Verbals and Verbal Phrases

Fallen Boy Saved by Gorilla!

CHICAGO–
The spectators at the Brookfield Zoo

Theme: Animals to the Rescue

A Surprising Event!

Look at the photograph and newspaper headline above. We can see that the boy is in the gorilla's living area, but how did he get there? How do you know? *Fallen* clearly conveys that he accidentally tumbled in. Although we often use *fallen* as part of a verb, it works here as an adjective, describing the boy. Verb forms that serve as other parts of speech are called verbals. Using them can add excitement and grace to your writing.

Write Away: Caring and Helping

Think about a time when you received help or comfort from an animal. The animal may have been real, a toy, or a character in a book. Write a paragraph that describes the event. Save the paragraph in your 🗂 **Working Portfolio.**

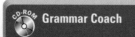

Grammar Coach

Choose the letter of the answer that correctly identifies each underlined item.

Brookfield Zoo visitor Eric Allison noticed a small boy climbing
$\qquad$ (1)
the fence at the Tropic World exhibit. Eric watched the boy trying

to lift himself toward the top. He wondered with growing anxiety, is
(2) (3)

he going to go higher? The boy, losing his balance, suddenly
(4) (5)

tumbled into the gorilla enclosure. A terrified crowd watched a
(6)

gorilla named Binti approach him. Eric's father, Bob Allison,

started to photograph the event. Watching in horror was all anyone
(7) (8)

could do. Would Binti hurt the boy? Carrying her own baby, Binti
(9)

came near the boy. Her gentle handling of the boy made newspaper
(10)

headlines.

---

1. A. gerund phrase
   B. participial phrase
   C. infinitive phrase
   D. helping verb

2. A. gerund
   B. gerund phrase
   C. infinitive
   D. infinitive phrase

3. A. gerund
   B. present participle
   C. past participle
   D. infinitive

4. A. gerund
   B. gerund phrase
   C. infinitive
   D. infinitive phrase

5. A. gerund
   B. gerund phrase
   C. participle
   D. participial phrase

6. A. gerund
   B. gerund phrase
   C. participle
   D. verb

7. A. gerund
   B. participle
   C. infinitive
   D. helping verb

8. A. infinitive phrase as subject
   B. gerund phrase as subject
   C. participial phrase as adjective
   D. gerund phrase as object of preposition

9. A. gerund
   B. gerund phrase
   C. participial phrase
   D. infinitive phrase

10. A. gerund phrase as subject
    B. gerund phrase as object
    C. participial phrase
    D. infinitive phrase

Gerunds

❶ Here's the Idea

A **verbal** is a word that is formed from a verb and that acts as a noun, an adjective, or an adverb. There are three kinds of verbals: gerunds, participles, and infinitives.

▶ **A gerund is a verbal that ends in *ing* and acts as a noun.** A **gerund phrase** consists of the gerund with its modifiers and complements. Like nouns, gerunds and gerund phrases may be subjects, predicate nouns, direct objects, indirect objects, or objects of prepositions.

GERUND PHRASE

The loud barking of the dogs woke up our neighbors.
GERUND

Using Gerunds	
Subject	**Herding** is something that border collies do well.
Predicate noun	It is their **running** that directs other animals.
Direct object	These dogs like **working**.
Indirect object	They give **herding** their full attention.
Object of a preposition	They are expert at **controlling** sheep and cows.

❷ Why It Matters in Writing

Gerunds are good words for describing activities because they imply action. Notice how the writer of the sentence below used gerunds and gerund phrases to discuss the many activities of beavers.

> **PROFESSIONAL MODEL**
>
> **Felling** timber and ornamental or orchard trees, **damming** ditches and culverts, **digging** and **tunneling**, and **eating** food crops make the beaver an unpopular neighbor.
>
> —Peg Boulay, "Beaver!"

❸ Practice and Apply

A. CONCEPT CHECK: Gerunds

Write the gerunds in these sentences.

The Horse Therapist

1. Horseback riding has many benefits for people with disabilities.
2. People with physical or emotional problems can enjoy moving around.
3. One horse, named Silver, was especially good at walking slowly and carefully.
4. Waiting took patience, but Silver let the teachers lift a woman named Maria onto his back.
5. When Maria started riding, she had never walked in her life.
6. Her activity had been limited to rolling in her wheelchair.
7. From Silver, she learned balancing.
8. After building her strength, she could even walk (with a little help).
9. Silver contributed to Maria's healing.
10. As a result of training with Silver, Maria now lives independently.

CHALLENGE Write the entire gerund phrase in each of the sentences above.

➡ For a SELF-CHECK and more practice, see the EXERCISE BANK, p. 607.

B. WRITING: Understanding Gerunds

Write about your typical day. Make a list, using gerunds to describe your activities at 9:00 A.M., 12:00 noon, 5:00 P.M., and 8:00 P.M.

9:00 A.M. Waking up

12:00 noon Still waking up

5:00 P.M. Falling asleep

8:00 P.M. Staying awake

LESSON 2 Participles

❶ Here's the Idea

▶ **A participle is a verb form that acts as an adjective.**
A **participial phrase** consists of a participle along with its modifiers and complements. Like other adjectives, participles and participial phrases can modify nouns and pronouns.

MODIFIES   MODIFIES

A tired hiker woke a sleeping bear.
   PARTICIPLE   PARTICIPLE

Present and Past Participles

A **present participle** always ends in *ing*.

MODIFIES

Growling, the bear rose from his slumber.

The **past participle** of a regular verb ends in *ed*. Past participles of irregular verbs, such as *freeze,* are formed in a variety of ways.

MODIFIES

The terrified traveler wanted to run.

MODIFIES

Frozen by fear, he was grateful that the bear only licked him.

A word that ends in *ing* may be a gerund, a participle, or part of a verb phrase. Here's how you can tell the difference.

Words That End in *ing*		
	Example	**Clue**
Gerund	We were annoyed by the moth's **fluttering**.	Could be replaced by a noun
Participle	The moth's **fluttering** wings were white.	Could be replaced by an adjective
Present Participle of Verb	The moth was **fluttering** in the breeze.	Always preceded by a helping verb.

Need help in forming past participles of irregular verbs? See page 102–104.

❷ Why It Matters in Writing

If your descriptive writing seems dull, use participles to liven up your sentences. Notice how strongly the participles in the following sentence convey sounds and actions.

> **LITERARY MODEL**
>
> There was a **snarling** growl that seemed to come from the bowels of the earth, **followed** by the sound of **ripping** cloth, screams, and then the **fading** slap of footsteps **running** away.
>
> —Gary Paulsen, "Dirk the Protector"

❸ Practice and Apply

VERBALS

MIXED REVIEW: Gerund or Participle?

Write the verbals in these sentences. Identify each verbal as a gerund or participle.

Animal Actors
1. Many TV commercials feature acting animals.
2. There are bell-ringing turkeys and typing chickens.
3. Training any type of animal requires patience.
4. Have you seen the dog-food commercial that shows a dog chasing a chuck wagon?
5. The trainer aroused yearning in the dog by hiding a squeaky toy in a closet.
6. Then the excited dog was let loose.
7. The dog reacted by racing around the corner, dashing across the kitchen, and skidding to a stop.
8. Staring at the door, the dog waited for the trainer to open it.
9. In the finished commercial, the chuck wagon disappears right through the cabinet door.
10. Working comes naturally to most animal actors.

For each participle, write the noun it modifies.

➡ **For a SELF-CHECK and more practice, see the EXERCISE BANK, p. 607.**

Infinitives

LESSON 3

❶ Here's the Idea

▶ **An infinitive is a verb form that usually begins with the word *to* and that acts as a noun, an adjective, or an adverb.** An **infinitive phrase** consists of an infinitive along with its modifiers and complements.

INFINITIVE
Sam has always wanted to work on his own farm.

Using Infinitives	
Noun	**To run** his farm takes Sam's full energy. (Subject)
	His challenge is **to handle** large animals. (Predicate noun)
	Often, bulls begin **to charge** for no reason. (Direct object)
Adjective	They can be creatures **to fear.**
Adverb	However, the bulls calm down **to receive** food.

HOT TIP

How can you tell the difference between an infinitive and a prepositional phrase that begins with *to*? If a verb follows *to*, the words are an infinitive. If a noun or pronoun follows *to*, the words are a prepositional phrase.

INFINITIVE
Sam's dog runs to distract the bulls.
↳ VERB

PREPOSITIONAL PHRASE
The dog runs to the pen.
↳ NOUN

❷ Why It Matters in Writing

Infinitives are often used to talk about goals, dreams, and wishes.

Sam hopes to buy more land and to increase his herd.

❸ Practice and Apply

A. CONCEPT CHECK: Infinitives

Write the infinitives in the following sentences. For sentences without an infinitive, write *none*.

The Cat's Meow

1. Ringo the cat liked to nap indoors every morning.
2. To play outside was for afternoons.
3. Yet one morning he was determined to get out.
4. His owners, Carol and Ray, were too sick to let him out.
5. Carol finally managed to open the door.
6. Meowing, the cat went to the gas meter and began to dig.
7. Carol thought he was trying to tell her about a gas leak.
8. She called the gas company, but the technician didn't find anything—until he checked the hole Ringo had been digging.
9. "Your house is about to blow up!" the technician shouted.
10. Ringo's instinct to warn his owners had saved their lives.

For each infinitive, indicate whether it serves as a noun, an adjective, or an adverb.

➜ For a SELF-CHECK and more practice, see the EXERCISE BANK, p. 608.

B. REVISING: Using Infinitives

Revise this paragraph by substituting infinitives for the underlined words.

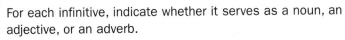

(1) Having a dog or a gerbil was out of the question for Duane Wright. He had trouble breathing whenever he came in contact with animal fur. So he found Goliath, a female iguana. (2) She seemed happy while keeping Duane company. One night, Duane had stopped breathing. (3) With her sharp claws Goliath started scratching hard with the hope of waking Duane. (4) She also began whipping his face with her scaly tail. Eventually, Duane began to breathe again. (5) Who would believe that an iguana would come around rescuing a man?

VERBALS

CHAPTER 7

❶ Here's the Idea

▶ **A verbal phrase includes a verbal and any modifiers or complements it may have.** As you have seen in the preceding lessons, there are three types of verbal phrases: gerund phrases, participial phrases, and infinitive phrases.

A **gerund phrase** consists of a gerund plus its modifiers and complements. Like a gerund itself, the entire phrase is used as a noun.

GERUND PHRASE (subject)

Sunning himself is Silas the snake's favorite activity.

GERUND PHRASE (object of a preposition)

He likes it so much he forgets about eating his dinner.

A **participial phrase** consists of a participle plus its modifiers and complements. The entire phrase modifies a noun or pronoun.

PARTICIPIAL PHRASE

Finishing his run, the horse walked for a few minutes.

His trainer, stunned by his speed, checked her stopwatch.

An **infinitive phrase** consists of an infinitive plus its modifiers and complements. The entire phrase functions as a noun, an adjective, or an adverb.

INFINITIVE PHRASE (subject)

To run free in peace and solitude was Luna's greatest goal.

INFINITIVE PHRASE (adjective)

She took every chance to escape from the house.

❷ Why It Matters in Writing

You can use verbals and verbal phrases to make your descriptions flow. Notice how the revised description at the top of the next page flows better and conveys greater excitement than the draft.

DRAFT

Noble Cause galloped down 46th Street. He was racing after the criminal, hoping to catch him. The police horse panted and snorted. Finally, he stopped the villain in his tracks.

REVISION

Galloping down 46th Street, Noble Cause raced to catch the criminal. Finally, the police horse, **panting and snorting,** stopped the villain in his tracks.

❸ Practice and Apply

A. CONCEPT CHECK: Verbal Phrases

Write the verbal phrase in each sentence, and identify it as a gerund phrase, a participial phrase, or an infinitive phrase.

Priscilla the Piglet

1. Strolling around the neighborhood pleased Priscilla, a three-month-old piglet.
2. Her owner, Victoria Herberta, would walk the slightly spoiled piglet on a purple leash.
3. Victoria taught Priscilla to swim with the family dogs.
4. One day a friend, Carol, took Priscilla to the lake to swim with her son Anthony.
5. Carol told Anthony to stay in the shallow water.
6. He decided to follow Carol and the pig into the deep water.
7. Unfortunately, Anthony felt himself sinking fast.
8. Rescuing Anthony was now necessary.
9. Grabbing Priscilla's leash, the boy held on tightly.
10. The 45-pound piglet began pulling the 90-pound boy back to shore.

→ For a SELF-CHECK and more practice, see the EXERCISE BANK, p. 608.

B. REVISING: Understanding Verbal Phrases

Return to the paragraph your wrote for the **Write Away** on page 168. Add three verbal phrases to make your writing more interesting and fluent.

VERBALS

Grammar in Literature

Using Verbals to Write About Action

Because verbals are formed from verbs, writers often find them especially helpful in writing about action. Notice the way Kipling's use of gerunds, infinitives, and participles adds life to this description. As we enter the story, a tailor bird named Darzee has just warned Rikki-Tikki-Tavi, the story's mongoose hero, that the cobra Nagaina is about to pounce.

Rikki-tikki-tavi
by Rudyard Kipling

Rikki-Tikki knew better than to waste time in staring. He jumped up in the air as high as he could go, and just under him whizzed by the head of Nagaina, Nag's wicked wife. She had crept up behind him as he was talking, to make an end of him; and he heard her savage hiss as the stroke missed. He came down almost across her back, and if he had been an old mongoose, he would have known that then was the time to break her back with one bite; but he was afraid of the terrible lashing return stroke of the cobra. He bit, indeed, but did not bite long enough; and he jumped clear of the whisking tail, leaving Nagaina torn and angry.

"Wicked, wicked Darzee!" said Nag, lashing up as high as he could reach toward the nest in the thorn bush; but Darzee had built it out of reach of snakes, and it only swayed to and fro.

> **GERUND** names an activity. What gerund names the activity Rikki-Tikki actually does?

> **INFINITIVE PHRASES** explain Rikki's and Nagaina's behaviors.

> **PARTICIPLES** describe the rapid movements of the animals as they fight.

CHAPTER 7

178 Grammar, Usage, and Mechanics

Practice and Apply

Using Verbals in Writing

Follow the directions to write your own action story about animals. You can write about the animals in Rikki Tikki Tavi, or you can write about more familiar animals, like cats, dogs, or birds.

1. List four gerunds naming the activities that the animals might do.
2. List four participles you might use as adjectives to describe each of the animals.
3. Briefly explain what would happen. Use at least one infinitive phrase as you describe the action.
4. Evaluate your work. How would your writing be different if you hadn't used participles? Put your writing and your evaluation in your ⬛ **Working Portfolio.**

VERBALS

1. Gerunds	2. Participles
1. hissing	1. fallen ____
2.	2. defeated ____
3.	3.
4.	4.

3. The hissing of the cat startled the fallen bird.

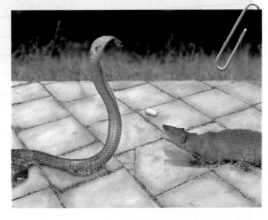

A. Gerunds, Participles, and Infinitives Identify each underlined verbal as a gerund, a participle, or an infinitive.

(1) Many animals seem <u>to be able</u> to sense natural disasters before they happen. (2) There are stories about bears <u>coming</u> out of hibernation early, just before an earthquake. (3) At other times, <u>frightened</u> animals have warned of tornadoes and floods. (4) One woman told of her cat's <u>stopping</u> a car accident. (5) The cat, Missey, usually didn't mind <u>riding</u> in the car. (6) But one day, she refused <u>to go</u>. (7) <u>Hiding</u> under the car was his way of avoiding the trip. (8) As the woman tried to coax Missey out, she saw a car <u>coming</u> around the corner. (9) <u>Crashing</u> through a row of mailboxes, it landed in the lake. (10) If the cat hadn't stopped his owner from leaving, they would have been in the path of the <u>sinking</u> car.

B. Verbal Phrases

Look at the cartoon on this page. Then write a sentence describing each of the seven "rescue animals" pictured. You can let your imagination run wild about what the animals are doing or are about to do. Use a variety of verbals and verbal phrases in your sentences.

The Far Side by Gary Larson

Some of our more common "rescue" animals

Examples:

Bringing a pepperoni pizza to the rescue, the rhinoceros rang the doorbell.

The cow delivered a box of cereal *to go with her milk.*

Choose the letter of the answer that correctly identifies each underlined item.

Bruno was a dog <u>living in Northern Ireland</u>. Having been injured
                       (1)
by an <u>exploding</u> car bomb, Bruno was frightened of explosives.
     (2)
<u>Seeing some thugs with firecrackers near his backyard</u>, Bruno
                 (3)
barked furiously. One day his owner, Brian McMullan, <u>was working</u>
                                  (4)
on his <u>damaged</u> car in the backyard. McMullan's one-year-old
      (5)
daughter, Anne Marie, sat playing nearby. The thugs threw a
firecracker into the yard. When Anne Marie started <u>to reach</u> for it,
                                       (6)
Bruno reacted by <u>jumping</u> in front of her. The firecracker exploded,
                (7)
<u>sending Bruno to the ground</u>. Fearing that Bruno was dead,
            (8)
McMullan rushed <u>to him</u>. Bruno was scarred, but he survived.
              (9)
<u>Saving Anne Marie</u> made Bruno a hero.
    (10)

1. A. gerund
   B. gerund phrase
   C. participle
   D. participial phrase

2. A. gerund
   B. present participle
   C. past participle
   D. infinitive

3. A. gerund
   B. gerund phrase
   C. participle
   D. participial phrase

4. A. gerund
   B. participle
   C. infinitive
   D. verb

5. A. gerund
   B. participle
   C. participial phrase
   D. infinitive

6. A. infinitive
   B. participle
   C. gerund
   D. gerund phrase

7. A. gerund
   B. participle
   C. infinitive
   D. verb

8. A. infinitive used as adjective
   B. infinitive phrase
   C. participial phrase
   D. verb

9. A. infinitive
   B. gerund phrase
   C. participle
   D. prepositional phrase

10. A. gerund phrase
    B. verb
    C. participial phrase
    D. infinitive phrase

Student Help Desk

Verbals and Verbal Phrases at a Glance

Kind of Verbal	Job	Example
Gerund Phrase	Noun	**Rescuing hikers** is the job of Saint Bernards.
Participial Phrase	Adjective	These dogs, carefully **trained,** brave storms.
Infinitive Phrase	Noun	They have been taught **to search** thoroughly.
	Adjective	They are the dogs **to trust.**
	Adverb	They are always quick **to respond.**

CHAPTER 7

Gerund, Participle, or Verb? Lending a Hand

	Example	Clue
Gerund	**Swimming** was Sue's only hope for survival.	Could be replaced by a noun
Participle	Her **swimming** movements attracted a sea turtle.	Could be replaced by an adjective
Verb	The turtle that **was swimming** next to her helped her stay afloat.	Always preceded by a helping verb

HERO

To Build a Fire

Infinitive or Prepositional Phrase?

	Example	Clue
Infinitive	Hal built a fire **to keep** warm. VERB	A verb follows *to.*
Prepositional phrase	Hal's dog snuggled up **to him.** PRONOUN	A noun or pronoun follows *to.*

HERO

To Serve and Protect

Infinitive Phrases

Noun

SUBJECT
To own a parrot was Joan's dream.

PREDICATE NOUN
The parrot's favorite activity was **to talk.**

DIRECT OBJECT
Soon, the parrot began **to imitate voices heard on television.**

Adjective

Once, an intruder thought the bird was something **to fear.**

Adverb

For the burglar, the bird's sounds became too strange **to bear.**

VERBALS

The Bottom Line

Checklist for Verbals and Verbal Phrases

Have I . . .

____ used gerund phrases to express actions?

____ used participial phrases to modify nouns and pronouns?

____ understood the functions of different kinds of words that end in *ing?*

____ understood the difference between infinitives and prepositional phrases beginning with *to?*

____ used infinitive phrases as nouns, adjectives, and adverbs?

____ used verbals and verbal phrases to add fluency and excitement to my writing?

Sentence Structure

Mei and Sarah,
Here are your jobs for the
Service Club project. Thanks
for your help.
✓ Water the shrubs.
   Plant flowers.
   Also the bulbs.
   Paint the jungle gym.
✓ To protect the wood.

Theme: Get Involved

Give It a Try

Have you ever gotten incomplete or confusing directions? Then you might understand why these volunteers were frustrated by their "to do" list. Often you can use compound and complex sentences to communicate clearly. What clear directions can you build from the sentences and fragments in the list?

Write Away: No Big Deal
It's not always a big deal to help other people or improve the environment. However, little things can mean a lot. Write about a time when someone did a small thing that helped you. Put your writing in your 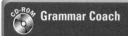 **Working Portfolio.**

Grammar Coach

Choose the letter that correctly identifies each underlined section.

There are many ways to volunteer, <u>since there are so many</u>
<u>worthy causes.</u> <u>Right now young people are feeding the homeless.</u>
(1)
They are also working as assistant camp counselors for needy
(2)
children, <u>and they are restoring the environment.</u> <u>Although</u> these
(3)   (4)
ways of volunteering sound very different, <u>each reflects a desire to</u>
<u>serve others.</u> People <u>who volunteer</u> not only help those in need, but
(5)
<u>they help themselves as well.</u> <u>Whatever these people choose to do,</u>
(6)
<u>volunteering can make them feel good, and it can change their</u>
(7)
<u>outlook on life.</u> It can give them exciting experiences <u>that they</u>
(8)
<u>would not have otherwise.</u> <u>Because volunteering can be a lot of</u>
(9)   (10)
<u>fun</u>, many people work long and hard for their favorite causes.

1. A. independent clause
   B. dependent clause
   C. compound sentence
   D. simple sentence

2. A. independent clause
   B. dependent clause
   C. compound sentence
   D. complex sentence

3. A. part of a compound sentence
   B. sentence fragment
   C. part of a complex sentence
   D. simple sentence

4. A. coordinating conjunction
   B. subordinating conjunction
   C. adverb clause
   D. relative pronoun

5. A. independent clause
   B. dependent clause
   C. compound sentence
   D. simple sentence

6. A. noun clause
   B. adjective clause
   C. adverb clause
   D. independent clause

7. A. coordinating conjunction
   B. subordinating conjunction
   C. relative pronoun
   D. independent clause

8. A. simple sentence
   B. compound sentence
   C. complex sentence
   D. compound-complex sentence

9. A. noun clause
   B. adjective clause
   C. adverb clause
   D. independent clause

10. A. noun clause
    B. adjective clause
    C. adverb clause
    D. independent clause

SENTENCES

LESSON 1

What Is a Clause?

1 Here's the Idea

▶ **A clause is a group of words that contains a subject and a verb.** For example, the following sentence contains two clauses.

SUBJECT ↓ ↓ VERB

Some students work in the food pantry because they care about helping hungry people.

SUBJECT ↑ ↑ VERB

There are two kinds of clauses, independent and dependent.

Independent and Dependent Clauses

▶ **An independent clause expresses a complete thought and can stand alone as a sentence.**

Some students work in the food pantry

INDEPENDENT CLAUSE

▶ **A dependent clause does not express a complete thought and cannot stand alone as a sentence.** Most dependent clauses are introduced by words like *because, when, if, while,* and *that.*

because they care about helping hungry people

DEPENDENT CLAUSE

A dependent clause can be joined to an independent clause to add to the complete thought that the independent clause expresses.

Some students work in the food pantry because they care about helping hungry people.

Students also make bag lunches that are distributed at a shelter.

CHAPTER 8

Dependent clauses are also known as **subordinate clauses.**
These clauses cannot stand alone and are dependent on the
main clause.

❷ Why It Matters in Writing

By itself, a dependent clause is a sentence fragment. Notice
how connecting the dependent clause to the preceding
sentence in the model below makes a sentence that
expresses a complete thought.

> **STUDENT MODEL**
>
> Students will organize a coat-and-hat drive
> this winter. Because homeless people
> often do not have warm clothes.

INDEPENDENT CLAUSE

DEPENDENT CLAUSE

❸ Practice and Apply

A. CONCEPT CHECK: What Is a Clause?

Identify each underlined group of words as an independent
clause or a dependent clause.

Helping People Who Are Homeless
1. When Amber Lynn Coffman was only nine years old, she
wrote a book report about a biography of Mother Teresa.
2. The book inspired her to volunteer at a shelter for the
homeless when she was ten years old.
3. Because Amber wanted to do more, she started an
organization.
4. Amber and 14 other student volunteers prepared 600
bag lunches each week.
5. They did this so that homeless people in their town of
Glen Burnie, Maryland, could have a good meal.

6. <u>While Amber prepared lunches each week</u>, she thought about doing something special for the holiday season.
7. <u>She organized a huge gift drive</u>, which was very successful.
8. People donated small, useful gifts <u>that were wrapped by volunteers</u>.
9. <u>Amber's work inspired other students around the country</u> because they saw the power of one student to help others.
10. <u>Now Amber's organization exists in about 30 states</u>, and her efforts have been recognized nationally.

➡ **For a SELF-CHECK and more practice, see the EXERCISE BANK, p. 609.**

B. EDITING: Fixing Fragments

Read the following first draft of a student's paragraph. Rewrite the paragraph to eliminate sentence fragments. Combine dependent clauses with independent clauses.

STUDENT MODEL

My friend Cara had a great idea for her last birthday party. She made it a "wish list" party. So that homeless people could get some of the items they needed. Cara called a shelter to get a wish list. When she sent out her invitations. She sent along copies of the list. Cara asked her friends to bring things from the list instead of gifts. While we had fun at her party. We were also helping others.

C. WRITING: Creating a Caption

This photograph shows Amber Lynn Coffman and some of her fellow volunteers at work. On a separate sheet of paper, write

a caption for the photo, describing what is happening. Use at least one independent clause and one dependent clause.

Simple and Compound Sentences

LESSON 2

① Here's the Idea

Simple Sentences

▶ **A simple sentence contains one independent clause and no dependent clauses.** Remember that even a simple sentence can be quite elaborate. Each of the following sentences has only a single independent clause.

> Shawn tutors.

INDEPENDENT CLAUSE

> Benita teaches young children acrobatics after school.

Compound Sentences

▶ **A compound sentence contains two or more independent clauses and no dependent clauses.** The clauses in a compound sentence must be closely related in thought.

> Shawn tutors, and he helps students learn math.

INDEPENDENT CLAUSE   INDEPENDENT CLAUSE

Independent clauses can be joined by a comma and a coordinating conjunction or by a semicolon.

> **Some children have no books, and volunteers can hold book drives for them.**

> **Some children have no toys; volunteers can collect donated toys for them.**

Coordinating Conjunctions
for   and   nor   or   but   so   yet

Don't mistake a simple sentence with a compound predicate for a compound sentence. No punctuation should separate the parts of a compound predicate.

> **The Newcomers' Club wrote a clever script, and then filmed it.**

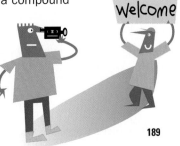

Welcome

189

❷ Why It Matters in Writing

You can avoid short, choppy sentences in your writing by using compound sentences. Notice how the writer of the model below combined related ideas to form compound sentences.

STUDENT MODEL

The park in my neighborhood has a lot of garbage all over the place. My friends and I want to clean it up. *so* We wrote to the park district for permission. We just got the OK. *and* We can start this weekend.

> Related thoughts combined

❸ Practice and Apply

A. CONCEPT CHECK: Simple and Compound Sentences

Identify each sentence as simple or compound.

Help for a Little Girl

1. The vice-principal of Alex Moore's school had a 16-month-old daughter with leukemia.
2. Alex wanted to help; he started making arrangements for a benefit auction to raise money for the girl's treatment.
3. Alex's younger brother, Cameron, and two other friends also became interested in the benefit.
4. They would charge people for a dinner and hold the auction at the dinner.
5. The group continued planning the benefit, but not many people would buy the $25 tickets for the dinner.
6. Cameron, a fifth grader, had an idea.
7. They should get Mark Eaton of the Utah Jazz basketball team at the dinner.
8. Mark Eaton lived in their hometown—Park City, Utah—and he was happy to help them out.
9. The boys called 80 sponsors, and all contributed goods.

10. More than 200 people bought tickets to the benefit, so the group raised several thousand dollars.

➡ **For a SELF-CHECK and more practice, see the EXERCISE BANK, p. 610.**

B. REVISING: Combining Sentences

Combine each pair of sentences to form a compound sentence, using one of the coordinating conjunctions *and, but, for, or, nor, so,* or *yet.* Remember to use a comma before the coordinating conjunction.

Helping Out During a Hurricane
1. Tropical storms often hit Florida. People from this state know how to prepare.
2. Windows are easily broken by fierce winds. The people cover them with plywood.
3. Not only do they board up windows in their own homes. They volunteer to help their neighbors board up too.
4. Volunteers also put sandbags around buildings near the shore. The bags help prevent damage from high waves.
5. Schools are shut down. County and state offices are closed.
6. People on low-lying islands near the shore may need to evacuate. They can go to emergency shelters.
7. Volunteers at the shelters help prepare food. They organize games and other activities for children.
8. After a hurricane there may be a lot of damage to homes. Fallen trees and other debris may be scattered about.
9. Volunteers repair buildings. They also clean up.
10. A hurricane is a great trial for a community. It can awaken the community's volunteer spirit.

🗂 **Working Portfolio** Reread what you wrote for the **Write Away** on page 184. Check to see if any short sentences can be combined to form compound sentences.

LESSON 3

Complex Sentences

❶ Here's the Idea

▶ **A complex sentence contains one independent clause and one or more dependent clauses.**

Most dependent clauses start with words like *when, until, who, where, because,* and *so that.* Such a clause might tell when something happened, which person was involved, or where the event took place.

DEPENDENT CLAUSE   INDEPENDENT CLAUSE

When we visited, Mrs. Brodsky shared her memories of working in a shipyard during World War II.

Mr. Ruiz was a photographer until he was drafted.

Mr. Liuzzo, who is a retired pilot, talked to us about his experiences in enemy territory, where he was a prisoner of war.

❷ Why It Matters in Writing

You can use complex sentences to clarify relationships between ideas. First read the passage below without the changes. Then read it as it has been revised. Notice how the revisions clarify why Nick does what he does.

STUDENT MODEL

My friend Nick really enjoys visiting
people at the Pines Nursing Home. *because* They
have many moving stories of life in our
town during World War II. Nick records
their memories. *so that he can share* He shares them with his
social studies class.

> Tells why Nick enjoys visiting

> Tells why he records memories

❸ Practice and Apply

A. CONCEPT CHECK: Complex Sentences

Write these sentences on a sheet of paper. Underline each independent clause once and each dependent clause twice.

Foster Grandparents

1. Although the Foster Grandparent Program is more than 30 years old, many people do not know about it.
2. This program was established so that hospitalized and institutionalized children could get special attention.
3. Anyone can volunteer who is at least 60 years old and meets other requirements.
4. After a volunteer is trained, he or she is assigned two children.
5. Because foster grandparents need to get to know their "grandchildren," they visit the children each day.
6. These daily visits last for two hours so that the children can get careful attention from their foster grandparents.
7. Although foster grandparents are volunteers, they are paid.
8. They also receive travel expenses while they serve.
9. Since this government program was founded in 1965, there have been foster grandparent projects in all 50 states.
10. Because more than 16,000 volunteers have been involved, more than 30,000 children have benefited.

➡ For a SELF-CHECK and more practice, see the EXERCISE BANK, p. 610.

B. REVISING: Varying Sentence Structure

Rewrite the following paragraph to make the ideas clearer. Combine simple sentences 1 and 2 to make a complex sentence. Do the same with sentences 4 and 5.

STUDENT MODEL

(1) Some retired people enjoy tutoring students in reading or math. (2) Retired people contribute their talents to their community. (3) Volunteers run homework centers after school. (4) They also maintain homework hot lines. (5) Students can get help with questions they have.

Kinds of Dependent Clauses

LESSON 4

❶ Here's the Idea

Adjective Clauses

▶ **An adjective clause is a dependent clause used as an adjective.** An adjective clause modifies a noun or a pronoun. It tells what kind, which one, how many, or how much.

> **Student volunteers read stories to the**
> MODIFIES NOUN
>
> **children who were in the daycare center.**
> ADJECTIVE CLAUSE

Adjective clauses are usually introduced by relative pronouns.

> **Relative Pronouns**
> who   whom   whose   that   which

> **The story, which made them laugh, is about a monkey.**

Notice that a clause that begins with *which* is set off with commas.

Adverb Clauses

▶ **An adverb clause is a dependent clause used as an adverb.** It modifies a verb, an adjective, or an adverb. An adverb clause might tell where, when, how, why, to what extent, or under what conditions.

Adverb clauses are introduced by subordinating conjunctions such as *if, because, even though, than, so that, while, where, when, as if,* and *since.*

> MODIFIES ADJECTIVE
>
> **They were happy because they were going to the zoo.**
> ADVERB CLAUSE

MODIFIES ADVERB

The zoo closed earlier than they expected.

An adverb clause should be followed by a comma when it comes before an independent clause. When an adverb clause comes after an independent clause, a comma may or may not be needed before it.

> **When the field trip ended, the volunteers took the children back to the daycare center.**

> **The volunteers took the children back to the daycare center when the field trip ended.**

For more about adjectives and adverbs, see Chapter 5, pp. 124–149.

Noun Clauses

▶ **A noun clause is a dependent clause used as a noun.** Like a noun, a noun clause can serve as a subject, a direct object, an indirect object, an object of a preposition, or a predicate noun. In the caption below, the noun clause is the subject of the sentence.

NOUN CLAUSE SERVING AS SUBJECT

What frustrates many physically challenged people is the problem of getting around.

SENTENCES

Volunteers know that physically challenged people do not want special treatment.

NOUN CLAUSE SERVING AS DIRECT OBJECT

NOUN CLAUSE SERVING AS INDIRECT OBJECT

Christopher will tell whoever is volunteering **the locations of the elevators.**

Noun clauses are introduced by words such as those shown in the following chart.

Words That Introduce Noun Clauses				
that	how	when	where	whether
why	what	whatever	who	whom
whoever	whomever	which	whichever	

If you can substitute the word *something* or *someone* for a clause in a sentence, it is a noun clause. (Volunteers know *something*. Christopher will tell *someone*.)

For more about nouns, see Chapter 2, pp. 34–55.

❷ Why It Matters in Writing

You can use dependent clauses to add detail to your writing. They allow you to express important ideas in a few words.

LITERARY MODEL

One of the young men who worked at the group home—a college student named Jack—grew a large garden in the back of the house. . . .

Jack tried to explain to Ernie that the seeds would grow into vegetables, but Ernie could not believe this until he saw it come true.

—Cynthia Rylant, "A Crush"

Adjective clause
tells which young men.

Noun clause
tells what Jack tried to explain.

Adverb clause
tells when Ernie could believe.

A. CONCEPT CHECK: Kinds of Dependent Clauses

Write these sentences on a sheet of paper. Underline each dependent clause, and identify it as an adjective clause, an adverb clause, or a noun clause.

Raising a Guide Dog
1. Some people who are visually challenged have guide dogs.
2. These dogs are important because they help the people get around in daily life.
3. A guide dog that completes its training can lead a visually challenged person across busy streets.
4. In fact, a visually challenged person can handle most traveling situations if a guide dog is with him or her.
5. There are organizations that raise puppies to be guide dogs.
6. Each puppy is given to a family who cares for it for a year.
7. They treat the puppy as if it were their own.
8. When the year is over, they give the dog back for special training.
9. All family members know why the dog must leave.
10. They realize that the dog will become a visually challenged person's constant companion.

➡ For a SELF-CHECK and more practice, see the EXERCISE BANK, p. 611.

B. WRITING: Using Clauses

Complete the sentence below by adding clauses of the types indicated in parentheses.

(1) Some students (adjective clause) volunteer at animal shelters. **(2)** They help take care of dogs and cats (adverb clause). **(3)** (noun clause) is appreciated by animal lovers everywhere.

Compound-Complex Sentences

LESSON 5

CHAPTER 8

❶ Here's the Idea

▶ **A compound-complex sentence contains two or more independent clauses and one or more dependent clauses.**

DEPENDENT CLAUSE   INDEPENDENT CLAUSE

When our school celebrates Earth Day, we sign up for environmental projects, and we try to complete them all in one day.
         INDEPENDENT CLAUSE

Students have cleaned up the beaches, and they have planted flowers in the parks so that the shore looks inviting to visitors.

❷ Why It Matters in Writing

You can use compound-complex sentences in your writing to show complicated relationships between events and ideas. Notice how Joan Aiken used such sentences in a detailed description of what a boy sees in a magical garden.

LITERARY MODEL

The gate grew again above him, and when he opened it and ran across the lawn through the yew arch, he found himself in a flagged garden full of flowers like huge blue cabbages. . . .

    The orchard was most wonderful, for instead of mere apples its trees bore oranges, lemons, limes and all sorts of tropical fruits whose names he did not know, and there were melons and pineapples growing, and plantains and avocados.

— Joan Aiken, "The Serial Garden"

INDEPENDENT CLAUSES

DEPENDENT CLAUSES

❸ Practice and Apply

A. CONCEPT CHECK: Compound-Complex Sentences

Identify each sentence as compound, complex, or compound-complex.

Helping Disaster Victims

1. In 1998 a hurricane swept through Central America, where it hit Honduras and Nicaragua especially hard.
2. Hurricane Mitch was one of the strongest storms ever in this region; it caused great destruction.
3. People on the coast tried to flee to higher ground, but flooding and mudslides made escape difficult.
4. More than 9,000 people were killed, and crops and roads were wiped out.
5. TV images of homeless and hungry people touched many Americans, who responded generously.
6. They donated money and supplies, which were flown to the region.
7. Volunteers helped clear roads so that supplies could get to villages that needed them.
8. Charity groups distributed food and safe drinking water, and they handed out sleeping bags and mosquito nets, which were needed in the tropical climate.
9. Medical volunteers treated people who desperately needed care.
10. Other volunteers rebuilt homes, and they helped restore the farm economy so that people could earn a living again.

➡ For a SELF-CHECK and more practice, see the EXERCISE BANK, p. 611.

B. WRITING: Creating Compound-Complex Sentences

Combine the following sentences to create a compound-complex sentence. Use *when* and *and* in your new sentence.

It rains. Rivers overflow. Neighborhoods near the rivers flood.

SENTENCES

Grammar in Literature

Using Compound and Complex Sentences

How do you write a description that allows you to create a vivid picture of a person? In the following excerpt, author William Jay Jacobs brings Eleanor Roosevelt to life by using compound and complex sentences. Such sentences allow him to vary the sentence structure and to add important details about Mrs. Roosevelt.

from

Eleanor Roosevelt
by William Jay Jacobs

UPI/Bettmann

After becoming interested in the problems of working women, she [Eleanor] gave time to the Women's Trade Union League (WTUL)....It was through the WTUL that she met a group of remarkable women....They awakened her hopes that something could be done to improve the condition of the poor....

> **COMPLEX SENTENCE**
> with adjective clause explaining Eleanor's hopes.

Eleanor helped the Red Cross raise money. She gave blood, sold war bonds....In 1943, for example, she visited barracks and hospitals on islands throughout the South Pacific. When she visited a hospital, she stopped at every bed....Often, after she left, even battle-hardened men had tears in their eyes....

> **COMPLEX SENTENCE**
> with adverb clauses explains how Eleanor acted and how she was affected by her visits to the hospitals.

In December 1945 President Harry S. Truman invited her to be one of the American delegates going to London to begin the work of the United Nations. Eleanor hesitated, but the president insisted. He said that the nation needed her; it was her duty.

> **COMPOUND SENTENCE**
> with coordinating conjunction explains how Eleanor came to her position at the United Nations.

Practice and Apply

Using Clauses to Create Interesting Sentences

Follow the instructions below to revise this passage by creating compound and complex sentences that add variety and interest to the writing.

> **(1)** Eleanor Roosevelt had a very unhappy childhood. **(2)** She did enjoy visits to see her uncle, Theodore Roosevelt. **(3)** Uncle Ted would read to the children. **(4)** The children had a day of romping outside and swimming. **(5)** Hearing his stories was very comforting to Eleanor and the other children. **(6)** Today volunteers often read to children to comfort them. **(7)** Who are hospitalized. **(8)** The volunteers make sure they choose books that each child will understand. **(9)** They also choose books that are funny. **(10)** They leave the book with the sick child. Until the next time they come.

1. Combine sentences 1 and 2 to make a compound sentence. Use the conjunction **but** to join the sentences.
2. Combine sentences 3 and 4 into a complex sentence. Begin sentence 4 with the subordinating conjunction *after.*
3. Combine sentence 6 with fragment 7, which is an adjective clause, to make a complex sentence.
4. Combine sentences 8 and 9 to make a compound-complex sentence.
5. Combine sentence 10 with the adverb clause after it to make a complex sentence.

You write it. Explain how your revisions affect the quality of the draft. Which version explains more about Eleanor's actions? Which version is easier to read? Put your paragraph in your 🗀 **Working Portfolio.**

Mixed Review

A. Sentence Structure Read the model about a student volunteer. Then write the answers to the questions below it.

PROFESSIONAL MODEL

(1) Rebecca is a seventh-grader who volunteers in a tutoring program for first-graders at her school. (2) The tutors in the program help the younger students with their reading. (3) They read stories to the students, and then the younger students read to the tutors. (4) Rebecca teaches her student Megan. (5) She herself struggled when she was in first grade, and she is thrilled that she can help teach someone else.

—Martin McNamara

1. Is sentence 1 simple or complex?
2. Does sentence 1 have an adjective, adverb, or noun clause?
3. Is sentence 2 simple or complex?
4. Is sentence 3 compound or complex?
5. What is the coordinating conjunction in sentence 3?
6. Is sentence 4 simple or complex?
7. Is sentence 5 compound or compound-complex?
8. Name the independent clauses in sentence 5.
9. Name the dependent clauses in sentence 5.
10. Does sentence 5 have an adjective, adverb, or noun clause?

B. Combining Clauses Rewrite the following paragraph, combining clauses to eliminate sentence fragments and to connect related ideas.

Reading Is Fundamental is a national organization. It promotes literacy. Students can participate. Who are interested. They can teach adults. Who may not have had a chance to learn. When they were young. After people learn to read. They lead more successful lives.

Choose the letter of the term that correctly identifies each underlined section.

Do you know <u>that free "volunteer vacations" are available</u>
<u>(1)</u>
<u>through national and state parks</u>? The parks have many types of

volunteer positions <u>that need to be filled</u>. <u>Although</u> some of the
(2)   (3)
positions require experience, others do not, <u>and</u> newcomers are
(4)
welcomed. <u>Volunteers have the chance to spend time in beautiful</u>
(5)
<u>natural settings, and they can combine work with pleasure.</u> Their

housing, <u>which</u> can be campsites, and their meals are usually
(6)
provided <u>while they are volunteering</u>. <u>What benefits are available</u>
(7)   (8)
depends on individual circumstances. <u>There is usually plenty of free</u>

<u>time for volunteers to explore the parks on their own, so a volunteer</u>
(9)
<u>vacation can be quite interesting.</u> Among the most popular parks

are those in Alaska and Hawaii, <u>which often have waiting lists</u>.
(10)

SENTENCES

1. A. independent clause
   B. dependent clause
   C. compound sentence
   D. simple sentence

2. A. adjective clause
   B. noun clause
   C. simple sentence
   D. adverb clause

3. A. subordinating conjunction
   B. coordinating conjunction
   C. relative pronoun
   D. noun clause

4. A. subordinating conjunction
   B. coordinating conjunction
   C. relative pronoun
   D. noun clause

5. A. simple sentence
   B. compound sentence
   C. complex sentence
   D. compound-complex sentence

6. A. relative pronoun
   B. adjective clause
   C. adverb clause
   D. independent clause

7. A. adjective clause
   B. adverb clause
   C. noun clause
   D. independent clause

8. A. noun clause
   B. adjective clause
   C. adverb clause
   D. independent clause

9. A. simple sentence
   B. compound sentence
   C. complex sentence
   D. sentence fragment

10. A. adjective clause
    B. adverb clause
    C. noun clause
    D. independent clause

Student Help Desk

Sentence Structure at a Glance

SIMPLE SENTENCE = independent clause
Olivia is running in a 5K race.

COMPOUND SENTENCE = independent clause + independent clause(s)
Nick is also running, but Greg isn't.

COMPLEX SENTENCE = independent clause + dependent clause(s)
Greg can't, because he is officiating.

COMPOUND–COMPLEX SENTENCE =
independent clauses + dependent clauses
Patti will find sponsors, and Jed will collect donations when we are ready.

Punctuating Compound and Complex Sentences

Join Up!

Use commas . . .	Example
to join independent clauses with coordinating conjunctions	She ran to the finish, **but** he dropped out.
after adverb clauses that begin sentences	After the race was over, they rested.
to set off adjective clauses that begin with *which*	His injury, **which was painful**, seemed rather severe.

Use semicolons . . .	
to join independent clauses without conjunctions	She was sympathetic; he was disappointed.

Help!

Avoiding Clause Confusion

Dependent Clause	Function	Example
Adjective clause	• modifies noun or pronoun • tells what kind, which one, how many, or how much	The **students** who participated enjoyed the race.
Adverb clause	• modifies verb, adjective, or adverb • tells where, when, how, why, to what extent, or under what conditions	They felt **proud** because they had done something worthwhile.
Noun clause	• acts as subject, direct object, indirect object, object of preposition, or predicate noun	What helps others can be rewarding for volunteers too.

The Bottom Line

Checklist for Sentence Structure

Can I improve my writing by . . .

____ eliminating sentence fragments?

____ creating compound sentences to link closely related ideas?

____ using dependent clauses to show how ideas are related?

____ using dependent clauses to add details?

____ punctuating compound and complex sentences correctly?

Subject-Verb Agreement

Theme: It's an Art

What's the Message?

What decisions do you think these artists had to make before beginning their mural? When working on a collaborative project, artists must discuss matters such as subject, style, and composition. If they fail to agree, they probably won't succeed in producing a harmonious artwork.

In the art of writing, subject-verb agreement is important for effective communication. Mistakes in agreement may confuse and frustrate readers. This chapter will help you use subjects and verbs correctly.

Write Away: Public Art

Draw a sketch of a public work of art, such as a statue or mural, in your town or neighborhood. Then write a description of the artwork and discuss why someone might have wanted to display it in public. Save your writing in your 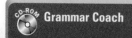 **Working Portfolio.**

CD-ROM **Grammar Coach**

Diagnostic Test: What Do You Know?

Choose the letter of the best revision for each underlined group of words.

> Diego Rivera were one of Mexico's greatest artists. His murals
> (1)
> and paintings have influenced artists around the world. Many
> (2)   (3)
> portrays historical subjects. For example, *The History of Mexico*
> (4)
> illustrates about 500 years of Mexican history. Within this mural
> is several groups of images. The first group show life in Mexico
> (5)   (6)
> before the arrival of the Spaniards. Others portrays the Spanish
> (7)
> conquest of Mexico and the cruelty of colonialism. The images
> reflects Rivera's deep concern for the suffering of common people.
> (8)

1. A. Diego Rivera are one of
      Mexico's greatest artists.
   B. Diego Rivera have been one
      of Mexico's greatest artists.
   C. Diego Rivera was one of
      Mexico's greatest artists.
   D. Correct as is

2. A. His murals and paintings
      has influenced
   B. His murals and paintings
      has been influencing
   C. His murals and paintings is
      influencing
   D. Correct as is

3. A. Many portray
   B. Many is portraying
   C. Many has portrayed
   D. Correct as is

4. A. *The History of Mexico*
      illustrate
   B. *The History of Mexico* do
      illustrate
   C. *The History of Mexico* have
      illustrated
   D. Correct as is

5. A. Within this mural was
      several groups
   B. Within this mural are
      several groups
   C. Within this mural appears
      several groups
   D. Correct as is

6. A. The first group shows
   B. The first group are showing
   C. The first group is showing
   D. Correct as is

7. A. Others portray
   B. Others does portray
   C. Others has portrayed
   D. Correct as is

8. A. The images was reflecting
      Rivera's deep concern
   B. The images reflect Rivera's
      deep concern
   C. The images has reflected
      Rivera's deep concern
   D. Correct as is

Agreement in Number

LESSON 1

CHAPTER 9

❶ Here's the Idea

▶ **A verb must agree with its subject in number.**

Number refers to whether a word is singular or plural. A word that refers to one person, place, thing, idea, action, or condition is singular. A word that refers to more than one is plural.

Singular and Plural Subjects

▶ **Singular subjects take singular verbs.**

AGREE

The new museum displays **works by local artists.**
SINGULAR SUBJECT   SINGULAR VERB

She enjoys **the towering sculptures at the art center.**

▶ **Plural subjects take plural verbs.**

AGREE

Chicago's art museums display **priceless paintings.**
PLURAL SUBJECT   PLURAL VERB

We enjoy **the peaceful outdoor sculpture garden.**

Most nouns that end in s or es are plural. For example, *artists* and *brushes* are plural nouns. However, most verbs that end in s are singular. *Paints* and *draws* are singular verb forms.

Verb Phrases

▶ **In a verb phrase, it is the first helping verb that agrees with the subject.** A verb phrase is made up of a main verb and one or more helping verbs.

AGREE

Theresa has collected **ceramic figurines.**
      SINGULAR HELPING VERB

She is building **a large collection.**

AGREE

Friends have admired **her interesting collection.**

⬆ PLURAL HELPING VERB

They have been finding **new figurines for her collection.**

Doesn't and *Don't*

Two common contractions are *doesn't* and *don't.* Use *doesn't* with all singular subjects except *I* and *you.* Use *don't* with all plural subjects and with the pronouns *I* and *you.*

Samuel doesn't use **computer clip art.**
SINGULAR VERB: does + not = doesn't

We don't like **slick and professional illustrations.**
PLURAL VERB: do + not = don't

I don't like **these pictures.**
WITH PRONOUN I: do + not = don't

❷ Why It Matters in Writing

Errors in subject-verb agreement can occur when you revise your work. If you change a subject from singular to plural or vice versa, be sure to change the verb as well.

> **STUDENT MODEL**
>
> *DRAFT*
> Three statues have been purchased for the park. Residents **want** to beautify the neighborhood.
>
> *REVISION*
> Three statues have been purchased for the park. An important resident **wants** to beautify the neighborhood.

❸ Practice and Apply

A. CONCEPT CHECK: Agreement in Number

For each sentence, write the verb form that agrees in number with the subject.

African *Kente* Cloth

1. The Ashanti people of Ghana (has, have) been making *kente* cloth for centuries.
2. *Kente* weavers (creates, create) complex designs with bright colors and geometric patterns.
3. The designs (doesn't, don't) just provide visual pleasure.
4. Each element (has, have) a precise meaning.
5. For example, the color gold (suggests, suggest) mineral wealth.
6. A shield pattern (suggests, suggest) a defense against hostile forces.
7. Weavers often (takes, take) months to complete *kente* garments.
8. The Ashanti people (wears, wear) *kente* cloth on important occasions.
9. Some designs (is, are) reserved for royalty.
10. *Kente* garments (appears, appear) in many museum collections.

➜ For a SELF-CHECK and more practice, see the EXERCISE BANK, p. 612.

B. WRITING: Completing a Caption

Choose the correct verb forms to complete the caption for the photograph.

The color gold in this piece of *kente* cloth (symbolizes, symbolize) mineral wealth. These fabrics (is, are) made by the Ashanti people of Ghana.

Compound Subjects

LESSON 2

❶ Here's the Idea

A **compound subject** is made up of two or more subjects joined by a conjunction such as *and, or,* or *nor.*

Subjects Containing *And*

▶ **A compound subject whose parts are joined by *and* usually takes a plural verb.**

Georgia and Louise paint **exceptionally well.**

Sometimes a subject containing *and* refers to a single thing or idea, so a singular verb is used.

War and peace is **the theme of the mural.**

Subjects Containing *Or* or *Nor*

▶ **When the parts of a compound subject are joined by *or* or *nor*, the verb should agree with the part closest to it.**

AGREE

Either ticket stubs or a photo completes **your collage.**

AGREE

Either a photo or ticket stubs complete **your collage.**

❷ Why It Matters in Writing

Writers sometimes reverse the order of compound subjects to make them sound more natural. If you do this, you may need to change the verb to make it agree with the new order.

The students or the teacher is attending **the show.**

The teacher or the students are attending **the show.**

S-V AGREEMENT

Subject-Verb Agreement **211**

❸ Practice and Apply

A. CONCEPT CHECK: Compound Subjects

Identify the sentences containing mistakes in subject-verb agreement, and rewrite them correctly. If a sentence contains no error, write *Correct.*

Crafty Arts

1. Arts and crafts are often hard to tell apart.
2. A basket or pot serve a practical function, such as food storage.
3. Yet collectors and museum curators prizes these objects for their beauty.
4. Many pots and jars display high levels of artistry.
5. Even forks and spoons appears in museum collections.
6. Arms and armor occupies special halls in some museums.
7. Neither dirt nor blood stains remains on their shiny surfaces.
8. Adults and children find these tools of warfare appealing.
9. Antique beds, couches, or a rug seem enticing to the weary museum patron.
10. Fortunately, signs and watchful guards reminds us not to rest on them.

➡ For a SELF-CHECK and more practice, see the EXERCISE BANK, p. 613.

B. REVISING: Making Verbs Agree with Compound Subjects

Rewrite this article for a school newspaper so that verbs agree with compound subjects. There are five errors.

In My Opinion . . .

Many ideas and opinions is expressed visually in editorial cartoons. Familiar symbols and caricatures communicate the cartoonists' messages. For example, a torn flag or a battered Uncle Sam suggest trouble in the nation. Politicians and celebrities are often criticized by exaggerating their physical appearance. Pompous leaders and corrupt people makes good targets. Sometimes neither caricatures nor a visual symbol bring across a cartoonist's point clearly. In such a case, a speech balloon or a caption help readers understand the cartoon.

Agreement Problems in Sentences

❶ Here's the Idea

Some sentences—ones with subjects in unusual positions, ones containing predicate nouns, ones in which prepositional phrases separate subjects and verbs—can be tricky. Here are some tips for choosing the correct verb forms in these situations.

Subjects in Unusual Positions

A subject can follow a verb or part of a verb phrase in a question, a sentence beginning with *here* or *there*, or a sentence in which an adjective, an adverb, or a phrase is placed first.

Subjects in Unusual Positions	
Type of Sentence	**Example**
Question	Does this **music video contain** interesting computer graphics?
Sentence beginning with *here* or *there*	Here **is** an on-air **announcer** with an enjoyable play list.
Sentence beginning with adverb, adjective, or phrase	Around the nation is **heard** the **sound**.

The following tips can help you to find the subject in one of these kinds of sentences.

> **Here's How** Choosing a Correct Verb Form
>
> **(Is, Are) the visual effects better than the song recording?**
>
> 1. Rephrase the sentence so that the subject precedes the verb.
>   The visual **effects** (is, are) better than the song recording.
>
> 2. Determine whether the subject is singular or plural.
>   **effects** (plural)
>
> 3. Choose the verb form that agrees with the subject.
>   The visual **effects are** better than the song recording.
>
> 4. Add correct verb to the original sentence.
>   **Are** the visual **effects** better than the song recording?

Predicate Nouns

In a sentence containing a predicate noun, the verb should agree with the subject, not the predicate noun.

AGREE

Nechita's works have been **a topic** of magazine articles.

Her inspiration is **abstract paintings** by Pablo Picasso.

Prepositional Phrases

The subject of a verb is never found in a prepositional phrase. Don't be fooled by words that come between a subject and a verb. Mentally block out those words. Then it will be easy to tell whether the subject is singular or plural.

AGREE

The colors ~~of a Javanese batik garment~~ indicate **where it came from.**

Traditionally, the pattern ~~of symbols~~ represents **things found in nature.**

❷ Why It Matters in Writing

Writers sometimes place verbs before subjects to make their writing more interesting. When you do this, make sure that the verbs agree with their subjects.

> **LITERARY MODEL**
>
> Between two pieces of cardboard were a **letter** and a large color **photograph.**
> The photograph showed John Wilson down on his right knee before a glistening dark wall. . . . Leaning against the wall to his right was Zebra's **drawing** of the helicopter and the zebra racing together across a facelike landscape.
>
> —Chaim Potok, "Zebra"

❸ Practice and Apply

A. CONCEPT CHECK: Agreement Problems in Sentences

Rewrite these sentences, correcting agreement errors. If a sentence contains no error, write *Correct*.

Poster Power

1. Does your classmates collect posters?
2. On the walls of many teenagers' rooms hang pictures of favorite singers, actors, and athletes.
3. An effective tool for advertising or announcing events is posters.
4. Vibrant colors in a poster attracts the public's attention.
5. Among the greatest of poster artists were Henri de Toulouse-Lautrec.
6. Has you ever seen Toulouse-Lautrec's bold, striking posters?
7. Japanese prints were the source of his inspiration.
8. There is few posters more famous than *I Want You!*
9. On that World War I recruitment poster is a portrait of Uncle Sam.
10. There is also patriotic posters from World War II.

➡ **For a SELF-CHECK and more practice, see the EXERCISE BANK, p. 613.**

B. MIXED REVIEW: Proofreading and Editing

Find the five errors in subject-verb agreement in this paragraph. In each case, write the correct verb form.

Roll the Videotape

Does you ever record family celebrations with a video camera? Then you probably has the basic skills to create a work of video art. Video artists combine technology with artistic expression. Just as painters apply paint to canvas, video artists record images for television monitors. There is works of video art that tell stories, just like feature films. Others are more like sculptures or paintings. For example, the artist Nam June Paik has created a pyramid out of 40 television sets. On all of the sets play a video of a dancing man. Paik are one of the most prominent artists working with video.

Indefinite Pronouns as Subjects

LESSON 4

1 Here's the Idea

▶ **When used as subjects, some indefinite pronouns are always singular, some are always plural, and some can be singular or plural, depending on how they're used.**
Remember, an indefinite pronoun is a pronoun that does not refer to a specific person, place, thing, or idea.

Indefinite Pronouns			
Singular	another	everybody	nothing
	anybody	everyone	one
	anyone	everything	somebody
	anything	neither	someone
	each	nobody	something
	either	no one	
Plural	both few	many	several
Singular or Plural	all any	most	none some

Singular indefinite pronouns take singular verbs.

Everyone enjoys Alexander Calder's mobiles.

Something about them reminds people of childhood.

Plural indefinite pronouns take plural verbs.

Few of the mobiles have electric motors.

Many consist of metal, wood, and wire.

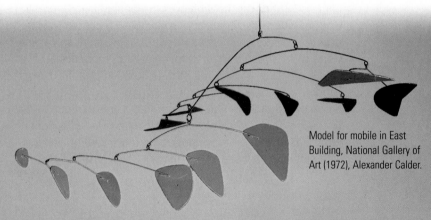

Model for mobile in East Building, National Gallery of Art (1972), Alexander Calder.

Singular or Plural?

The indefinite pronouns *all, any, most, none,* and *some* can be either singular or plural. When you use one of these words as a subject, think about the noun it refers to. If the noun is singular, use a singular verb; if it is plural, use a plural verb.

REFERS TO

All of the mobiles move in a breeze.

REFERS TO

Most of the design is ingenious.

Sometimes an indefinite pronoun refers to a noun in a previous sentence.

PLURAL NOUN

Many people attended the exhibition. Most were astonished.

INDEFINITE PRONOUN   PLURAL VERB

❷ Why It Matters in Writing

When you write about events for an assignment or a school newspaper, you will probably need to use indefinite pronouns as subjects. To help readers understand your writing, use correct subject-verb agreement.

> **PROFESSIONAL MODEL**
>
>   A fascinating art show has opened this weekend in Biloxi. Each of the paintings portrays a different blues musician. Many are painted in a realistic style. Some of the art depicts older musicians who play acoustic instruments.
>
> —Chris Bayard

❸ Practice and Apply

A. CONCEPT CHECK: Indefinite Pronouns as Subjects

Rewrite correctly each sentence in which the verb does not agree with the subject. If a sentence is correct, write *Correct*.

In Black and White

1. Many knows the saying "A picture's worth a thousand words."
2. One remembers the fascinating images in photo essays.
3. Few merely entertains people.
4. Most addresses important real-life issues.
5. For example, both *Let Us Now Praise Famous Men* and *How the Other Half Lives* tell powerful stories.
6. Some of the photographs reveals poverty.
7. Others portrays nature's fury.
8. Everyone are touched by pictures that capture human suffering.

Mother and two children on road at Tule Lake City, September 1939. Photo by Dorothea Lange.

9. No one ignores such strong evidence of problems in society.
10. All of this photography motivate people to take a stand.

➡ **For a SELF-CHECK and more practice, see the EXERCISE BANK, p. 614.**

B. WRITING: Agreement with Indefinite Pronouns

For each sentence, choose the verb form that agrees with the subject.

(1) Everybody (enjoys, enjoy) our school's art fairs. **(2)** Most of the artworks (is, are) quite good. **(3)** Something always (makes, make) the students smile because it is so ridiculous. **(4)** Yet one (has, have) no need to fear humiliation. **(5)** None of the artists (gets, get) upset. **(6)** None of the criticism (is, are) mean-spirited. **(7)** Everyone (understands, understand) that artists should be encouraged. **(8)** Some (takes, take) longer to develop their talent. **(9)** Each of us (has, have) the right to express himself or herself in art. **(10)** All of the fairs (is, are) conducted in this spirit.

LESSON 5 **Problem Subjects**

❶ Here's the Idea

When collective nouns, nouns ending in s, titles, and numerical expressions are used as subjects, it can be difficult to tell whether they take singular or plural verbs.

Collective Nouns

Collective nouns name groups of people or things.

Common Collective Nouns					
group	crew	flock	family	class	team
crowd	herd	public	club	faculty	choir

▶ **Many collective nouns can take singular or plural verbs, depending on how they are used.** When a collective noun refers to people or things acting as a group, it takes a singular verb.

  The faculty sponsors an art exhibit each year.
  (THE FACULTY MEMBERS ARE ACTING AS A GROUP.)

When a collective noun refers to people or things acting as individuals, it takes a plural verb.

  The faculty disagree on the rules of the exhibit.
  (THE FACULTY MEMBERS ARE ACTING AS INDIVIDUALS.)

Singular Nouns Ending in *S*

▶ **Some nouns that end in s or *ics* look plural but actually refer to singular concepts.** When used as subjects, they take singular verbs.

Singular Nouns with Plural Forms			
measles	linguistics	news	pediatrics
politics	forensics	civics	mathematics
genetics	mechanics	physics	economics
ceramics	molasses	mumps	

AGREE

Ceramics is the art of making objects from clay.

AGREE

The news includes information about several exhibits.

Titles

▶ **Titles of works of art, literature, and music are singular.**
Even a title consisting of a plural noun takes a singular verb.

Sunflowers is a famous painting by Vincent van Gogh.

Amounts and Time

▶ **Words and phrases that express weights, measures, numbers, and lengths of time are often treated as singular.** They take singular verbs when they refer to amounts rather than numbers of individual items.

Measures and Amounts		
Measures	seven pounds two cups	**Two hundred twenty-five tons is** the weight of the Statue of Liberty.
Amounts	three hours nine dollars	**Four years seems** a long time to work on a single portrait.

A fraction can take a singular or plural verb, depending on whether it refers to a single part or to a number of items.

Five-sixths of the canvas is blank.
(THE FRACTION REFERS TO ONE PART OF THE CANVAS.)

Two-thirds of the paintings are abstract.
(THE FRACTION REFERS TO A NUMBER OF PAINTINGS.)

❷ Why It Matters in Writing

When you write about science or math, you need to use numbers, weights, and measures. Show your readers that you know your stuff by using the correct verb forms with them.

Six-tenths of the human body is water.

❸ Practice and Apply

A. CONCEPT CHECK: Problem Subjects

Rewrite the underlined words in the following sentences to correct the mistake in subject-verb agreement. If a sentence contains no error, write *Correct*.

Memorial Wall
1. *In Country* <u>describe</u> a girl's effort to learn more about her father, who was killed in Vietnam.
2. Her family <u>travel</u> to Washington, D.C., to visit the Vietnam Veterans Memorial.
3. Many <u>spend</u> time at the wall designed by Maya Lin.
4. Each of the wall's halves <u>are</u> about 250 feet long.
5. Three days <u>are</u> how long it takes to read all 58,209 names of soldiers killed or missing in the war.
6. Mathematics <u>fails</u> to explain the wall's dramatic effect.
7. The public also <u>views</u> other sculptures at the memorial.
8. *Three Servicemen* by Frederick Hart <u>stand</u> near the wall.
9. Our class <u>have</u> looked at an exhibit of objects left at the wall.
10. A group of photos <u>show</u> a young man with family and friends.

➡ For a SELF-CHECK and more practice, see the EXERCISE BANK, p. 614.

B. WRITING: Using Fractions Correctly

Choose the correct verb form to complete each sentence about the bar graph. Then write a sentence explaining how you chose the correct form.

1. Two-thirds of the class (is, are) going on the trip to Washington, D.C.
2. One-half of the students (has, have) seen the Statue of Liberty.

Numbers of Students Who Have Visited Two Sites
(class size = 30)

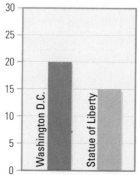

Grammar in Math

Word Problems

When you write and solve word problems, you need to pay attention to grammar. Subject-verb agreement can be tricky— especially if you're using fractions. In the following word problem, the subjects and the verbs that agree with them are highlighted.

42 **Theater** Northern Illinois University has a collection of scale models of stage sets. These models show sets that were built for Early American performances of operas. The models are built to a scale of 1/48 of the actual size. The model shown is a set representing a public square in nineteenth century Bohemia, a region of the Czech Republic.

Exploration:

A **door** on one of the buildings in the model **is** 11/16 in. wide and 1 3/4 in. tall. Explain how you would find the actual dimensions of the door on the stage set.

> The word *is* agrees with the subject *door,* not with the plural word *buildings.*

EXAMPLE

Describe how you would find the width of the actual door on the stage set.

ANSWER
11/16 in. is multiplied by 48 to find the width of the door on the stage set.

> Singular subject *11/16 in.* agrees with the singular verb *is.*

Practice and Apply

A. Use the information on the photograph of the model to write and answer a word problem. Figure out how many poles could be cut from a dowel that is 1 foot long.

$4\frac{5}{8}$ in.

$1\frac{3}{4}$ in.

$\frac{11}{16}$ in.

B. Write and solve a word problem in which you find the size of the pole on the actual stage set. Be sure you explain the proportion of the model to the set. Remember—if you are using fractions as subjects, you should use a singular verb.

S-V AGREEMENT

A. Agreement in Number, Compound Subjects, and Indefinite Pronouns
Write the verb form that agrees with the subject of each sentence.

1. Curators and conservators (is, are) important employees in museums.
2. Each of these people (has, have) specific responsibilities.
3. A curator (arranges, arrange) artworks in museum galleries.
4. Curators also (looks, look) for artworks to add to museums' collections.
5. Major museums (has, have) a curator for each department.
6. A conservator (cleans, clean) artworks.
7. Conservators also (performs, perform) scientific tests on them.
8. The tests (reveals, reveal) how old the artworks are and how they were made.
9. A conservator or a curator (needs, need) extensive training.
10. Most (has, have) advanced degrees in art history.

B. Additional Agreement Problems Rewrite the following advertisement, correcting six errors in subject-verb agreement.

Nightingale Art School

Why has the finest artists studied at the Nightingale Art School? Our excellent faculty and facilities is the source of our success. There is an excellent library stocked with art books.

In the drawing studio is live models. The faculty have expertise in all aspects of art. Ceramics are one of our specialties. The students in our school are well trained. Two-thirds of our graduates finds jobs within a year. Doesn't this school seem right for you?

CHAPTER 9

Choose the letter of the best revision for each underlined group of words.

> There are a remarkable example of folk art in Los Angeles,
> (1)
> called the Watts Towers. This group of sculptures were created by
> (2)
> Simon Rodia. The group contain nine sculptures. Some are nearly
> (3)   (4)
> 100 feet tall. Rodia gave them names such as *Ship of Marco Polo*
>
> and *Santa Maria Tower*. These names remind us of Rodia's Italian
> (5)
> heritage. Each of the sculptures are made of steel rods, wire mesh,
> (6)
> and mortar. Bottle caps, seashells, and other found objects is
> (7)
> imbedded in the mortar for decoration. Tourists from around the
>
> world comes to view the Watts Towers.
> (8)

1. A. There have been
   B. There is
   C. There were
   D. Correct as is

2. A. group of sculptures are
   B. group of sculpture is
   C. group of sculptures was
   D. Correct as is

3. A. The group contains
   B. The group have contained
   C. The group are containing
   D. Correct as is

4. A. Some is
   B. Some stands
   C. Some was
   D. Correct as is

5. A. names does remind
   B. names has reminded
   C. names is reminding
   D. Correct as is

6. A. Each of the sculptures were made
   B. Each of the sculptures have been made
   C. Each of the sculptures is made
   D. Correct as is

7. A. Bottle caps, seashells, and other found objects was imbedded
   B. Bottle caps, seashells, and other found objects are imbedded
   C. Bottle caps, seashells, and other found objects has been imbedded
   D. Correct as is

8. A. come
   B. has come
   C. is coming
   D. Correct as is

S-V AGREEMENT

Student Help Desk

Subject-Verb Agreement at a Glance

A singular subject takes a singular verb.

A plural subject takes a plural verb.

The artist paints dancers.

Dancers pose in her studio.

Subjects and Verbs	Tricky Cases
Verb phrase The first helping verb should agree with the subject.	**Folk art** is getting expensive. **Collectors** are raising prices.
Prepositional phrase between subject and verb Block out the phrase when deciding which verb form to use.	The **vases** ~~in this museum~~ are priceless.
Compound subject containing *and* Always use a plural verb.	The **artist and** his **work** arouse controversy.
Compound subject containing *or or nor* The verb should agree with the part of the subject closest to it.	Neither the **critics nor** the **average citizen** likes this exhibit.
Indefinite pronoun A singular pronoun takes a singular verb; a plural pronoun takes a plural verb. Some pronouns can be singular or plural.	**Everyone** admires this masterpiece. **Few** understand it. **Some** of the paint is peeling. **Some** of the critics want the museum to restore it.
Collective noun Use a singular verb if it refers to a whole, a plural verb if it refers to individuals.	The **staff** selects the paintings. The **staff** are arguing among themselves.
Singular noun ending in *s* Use a singular verb.	**Politics** is an art.
Title or expression of amount Use a singular verb.	**Three ounces** of gold was used in the sculpture.

Other Agreement Problems

Slippery Subjects

Predicate noun Make sure the verb agrees with the subject.	**Animals are** the subject of his photo series. The **subject** of his photo series **is** animals.
Question Change the question to a statement to find the subject.	(**Is, are**) the tapestries on the wall? The **tapestries are** on the wall.
Statement in which subject follows verb Turn the sentence parts around before deciding on a verb form.	Here (**is, are**) the expressionist paintings. The expressionist **paintings are** here. Beneath each painting (**is, are**) a title and a date. A **title** and a **date are** beneath each painting.

The Bottom Line

Checklist for Subject-Verb Agreement

Have I . . .

____ used singular verbs with singular subjects?

____ used plural verbs with plural subjects?

____ made the first helping verbs in verb phrases agree with the verbs' subjects?

____ used plural verbs with compound subjects containing *and*?

____ made verbs agree with the closest parts of compound subjects containing *or* or *nor*?

____ used correct verb forms with indefinite-pronoun subjects?

____ used singular verbs to agree with titles and some numerical expressions?

____ used verbs that agree with subjects in unusual positions?

Capitalization

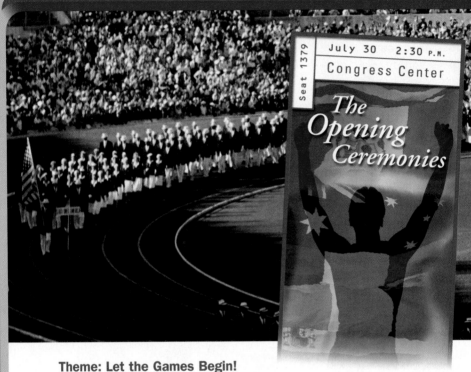

Seat 1379

July 30   2:30 P.M.
Congress Center

The
Opening
Ceremonies

Theme: Let the Games Begin!

Here's the Ticket

Congratulations! You are one of the lucky spectators who has a
ticket to the opening ceremony of the Olympic Games. What
is the date and the time of the ceremony? Where is it
scheduled to take place? On the ticket above, capitalized words
such as *July* and *Congress Center* provide you with the answers.
We use capitalization as a way to make certain words—such as
names, titles, and dates—stand out from others.

Write Away: Olympic Favorites
Write a paragraph describing your favorite Olympic event or
competitor. Save the paragraph in your ⬚ **Working Portfolio.**

CD-ROM **Grammar Coach**

For each underlined passage, choose the letter of the correct revision.

> Baron Pierre de coubertin, a french educator, was responsible
> <u>(1)</u>   <u>(2)</u>
> for creating the modern Olympic Games. He thought that an
> <u>(3)</u>
> International sports competition would promote World peace.
> <u>(4)</u>   <u>(5)</u>
> According to Dave Anderson in *The story of the Olympics,*
> <u>(6)</u>
> Coubertin said, "The revival of the Olympic Games will bring
>
> athletism to a high state of perfection."
>
> The first modern Olympic Games took place in 1896 in athens,
> <u>(7)</u>
> Greece. This site was East of the place where the ancient Olympics
> <u>(8)</u>
> had been held. The track-and-field events were held at the
>
> Panathenaic stadium. The Games were a huge success and set the
> <u>(9)</u>   <u>(10)</u>
> groundwork for many more Olympic competitions.

1. A. baron
   B. pierre
   C. Coubertin
   D. Correct as is

2. A. French
   B. Educator
   C. A
   D. Correct as is

3. A. olympic
   B. games
   C. he
   D. Correct as is

4. A. International Sports
   B. international sports
   C. international Sports
   D. Correct as is

5. A. World Peace
   B. world Peace
   C. world peace
   D. Correct as is

6. A. *the*
   B. *Story*
   C. *olympics*
   D. Correct as is

7. A. athens, greece
   B. Athens, Greece
   C. Athens, greece
   D. Correct as is

8. A. This site was east
   B. this site was east
   C. this site was East
   D. Correct as is

9. A. panathenaic stadium
   B. panathenaic Stadium
   C. Panathenaic Stadium
   D. Correct as is

10. A. the Games
    B. the games
    C. The games
    D. Correct as is

People and Cultures

❶ Here's the Idea

Names and Initials

▶ **Capitalize people's names and initials.**

Michelle **K**wan   **J**ackie **J**oyner-**K**ersee

Robert **D**. **B**allard   **W**. **P**. **K**insella

Personal Titles and Abbreviations

▶ **Capitalize titles and abbreviations of titles that are used before names or in direct address.**

Mr. Carl Lewis   **D**r. Dot Richardson

General Colin Powell   **M**s. Jenny Thompson

Did you write a book about the Olympics, **P**rofessor?

Capitalize abbreviations of some titles when they follow a name.

Todd Owens, **J**r.   Sylvester Fine, **D.D.S.**

Mary Mueller, **P**h.**D.**

▶ **Capitalize titles of heads of state, royalty, or nobility only when they are used before persons' names or in place of persons' names.**

Baron Pierre de Coubertin   **D**ame Judi Dench

Attorney **G**eneral Janet Reno   **E**mperor Hirohito

Do not capitalize these titles when they are used without proper names or after names.

We saw the **q**ueen sitting in the royal box.

Family Relationships

▶ **Capitalize words indicating family relationships only when they are used as names or before names.**

Aunt Carla   Cousin Maggie   Grandpa Johnson

Both Dad and Uncle Ray love to watch the Olympics on TV.

In general, do **not** capitalize a family-relationship word when it follows a person's name or is used without a proper name.

Lisa Fernandez, my cousin, will compete in the next Olympiad.

The Pronoun *I*

▶ **Always capitalize the pronoun *I*.**

Jo and I learned how to play softball from my cousin.

Religious Terms

▶ **Capitalize the names of religions, sacred days, sacred writings, and deities.**

Religious Terms	
Religions	Christianity, Buddhism, Islam
Sacred days	Ramadan, Easter, Yom Kippur
Sacred writings	Koran, Torah, Bible
Deities	God, Yahweh, Allah

Do not capitalize the words *god* and *goddess* when they refer to gods of ancient mythology.

The ancient Olympic Games honored the Greek god Zeus.

Nationalities, Languages, and Races

▶ **Capitalize the names of nationalities, languages, races, and most ethnic groups, as well as adjectives formed from these names.**

Kurds	Native American	French
Hispanic	African American	Korean

❷ Practice and Apply

CONCEPT CHECK: People and Cultures

Write the 15 words and abbreviations that should be capitalized but are not in the paragraph below. Capitalize each correctly.

An Olympic Legend
(1) When I was in sixth grade, my class studied the history of the ancient Olympic Games. **(2)** My teacher, mr. jones, assigned the books *The Olympic Games* by Theodore knight and *Olympic Games in Ancient Greece* by Shirley glubok and Alfred tamarin. **(3)** Knight tells of a legendary event that is considered the start of the first Olympics. **(4)** According to legend, king oenomaus offered princess hippodamia's hand in matrimony to the man who could find her and escape in a chariot while being pursued by the king. **(5)** After 13 men failed in their attempt to defeat oenomaus, prince pelops determined he would beat the king. **(6)** Somehow while pelops escaped with the princess, the axle in the king's chariot broke. **(7)** Pelops defeated the king and married hippodamia. **(8)** To celebrate his victory, the prince ordered a feast and gave thanks to the god zeus.

➡ For a SELF-CHECK and more practice, see the EXERCISE BANK, p. 615.

❶ Here's the Idea

Sentences and Poetry

▶ **Capitalize the first word of every sentence.**

Baseball comes from an English sport called rounders.

▶ **In traditional poetry capitalize the first word of every line.**

LITERARY MODEL

It looked extremely rocky for the Mudville nine that day;
The score stood two to four, with but an inning left to play.
—Ernest Lawrence Thayer, "Casey at the Bat"

HOT TIP Modern poets sometimes choose not to begin the lines of their poems with capital letters. If you make this choice in your own writing, make sure the meaning of your work is still clear.

Quotations

▶ **Capitalize the first word of a direct quotation presented as a complete sentence.**

Yogi Berra once asked a player, "How can you think and hit at the same time?"

Babe Ruth once stated that even if a team has "the greatest bunch of individual stars in the world," it won't succeed unless the players play as a team.

▶ **In a divided quotation, do not capitalize the first word of the second part unless it starts a new sentence.**

"Don't worry," said Nina. "There's always next season."

"Yes," said Fred, "but with us it's always spring training."

Outlines

▶ **Capitalize the first word of each entry in an outline and the letters that introduce major subsections.**

    I. Traditional games
        A. Games played in teams
            1. Baseball
            2. Football
            3. Soccer
    II. Extreme games
        A. Air games
            1. Skydiving
            2. Windsurfing

Parts of a Letter

▶ **Capitalize the first word in the greeting and in the closing of a letter.**

Dear Miss Ulasovich:

Yours truly,

Titles of Works

▶ **Capitalize the first word, the last word, and all other important words in a title. Don't capitalize articles, coordinating conjunctions, or prepositions of fewer than five letters.**

Type of Media	Examples
Books	*The Giver, The Call of the Wild*
Plays and musicals	*Bleacher Bums, Les Misérables*
Short stories	"The Noble Experiment," "Thank You, M'am"
Poems	"The Bat," "Ode to an Artichoke"
Periodicals	*Sports Illustrated, Teen People*
Musical compositions	"Take Me Out to the Ball Game," "La Bamba"
Movies	*Hoop Dreams, The Natural*
Television shows	*Weekend Sports, Boy Meets World*
Works of art	*American Gothic, Mona Lisa, The Thinker*

❷ Practice and Apply

A. CONCEPT CHECK: First Words and Titles

Write the words that should be capitalized but are not in these sentences. Capitalize each correctly.

> **Baseball—America's National Pastime**
>
> **1.** An outline for the game of baseball might begin like this:
> I. how the game is played
>   A. equipment
>   1. baseball
>   2. bat
> **2.** A famous scholar and educator, Jacques Barzun, once wrote, "whoever wants to know the heart and mind of America had better learn baseball."
> **3.** There are many movies about baseball, including *field of dreams.*
> **4.** This movie was based on W. P. Kinsella's book *shoeless joe.*
> **5.** Another enormously popular baseball film is *the natural.*
> **6.** The last line of the poem "casey at the bat" is familiar to many people.
> **7.** It runs, "but there is no joy in Mudville: Mighty Casey has struck out."
> **8.** A letter written by a child to his or her favorite home-run hitter might begin "dear mr. Sosa."
> **9.** The closing of the letter might consist of a phrase such as "sincerely yours."
> **10.** Finally, let us not forget this memorable quote by the New York Mets manager Yogi Berra: "it's never over till it's over."

→ For a SELF-CHECK and more practice, see the EXERCISE BANK, p. 615.

B. WRITING: The Name Game

Identify your favorite short story, magazine, song, movie, and television show. Then for each choice, write a sentence explaining why it's your favorite. Remember to capitalize titles.

Mixed Review

A. Capitalization in Outlining Rewrite the following portion of an outline, correcting the nine words that should be capitalized.

I. indoor games
   A. board games
   B. word and picture games
      1. charades
      2. twenty questions
II. outdoor games
   A. ball games
      1. baseball
      2. soccer

B. Capitalization in a Business Letter Rewrite the following business letter, correcting the 15 items that should be capitalized.

1399 Maple Street
Wilmette, Illinois 60091
January 2, 2000

Mr. Dominic d. Domenicas, sr.
The Domino Company
333 Congress Parkway
Highland Heights, Ohio 44143

dear mr. domenicas:
    I am writing about the set of dominoes made by your company that i recently purchased. unfortunately, my set is incomplete, containing only 27 dominoes rather than the usual 28. since your picture is shown on the box, with the words underneath it stating "your satisfaction is guaranteed or your money will be promptly refunded," i am writing directly to you.
    My uncle david and i are very eager to try out the new dominoes. Please let me know what your company can do to correct this matter.

sincerely yours,
Gabe Zaharias
Gabe zaharias

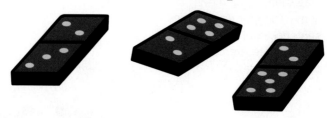

Places and Transportation

LESSON 3

1 Here's the Idea

Geographical Names

▶ In geographical names, capitalize each word except articles and prepositions.

Geographical Names	
Divisions of the world	Northern Hemisphere, Arctic Circle
Continents	Africa, North America, Australia
Bodies of water	Lake Erie, Pacific Ocean, Nile River
Islands	Oahu, Philippines, Aleutian Islands
Mountains	Rocky Mountains, Mount Hood, Andes
Other landforms	Niagara Falls, Cape Horn, Gobi Desert
Regions	Latin America, Southeast Asia, Gulf of Mexico
Nations	Monaco, Peru, Canada, Czech Republic
States	Texas, California, Florida
Cities and towns	Chicago, Providence, Olympia
Roads and streets	Pennsylvania Avenue, Interstate 55, Main Street

Bodies of the Universe

▶ Capitalize the names of planets and other specific objects in the universe.

Milky Way   Halley's Comet   Triton

Venus   Alpha Centauri   Pluto

Two moons of Mars were discovered—Phobos and Deimos.

Regions and Sections

▶ **Capitalize the words *north, south, east,* and *west* when they name particular regions of the United States or the world or are parts of proper names.**

In South Africa, children use small stones to play a game called *diteko.*

Children who live in the North might enjoy the snow game known as fox and geese.

Do not capitalize these words when they indicate general directions or locations.

If you go south on Main Street, you will find Mel's Video Rental.

Buildings, Bridges, and Other Landmarks

▶ **Capitalize the names of specific buildings, bridges, monuments, and other landmarks.**

World Trade Center   Statue of Liberty

Golden Gate Bridge   Vietnam Memorial

Did you know that Fort Sumter is a national monument?

Planes, Trains, and Other Vehicles

▶ **Capitalize the names of specific airplanes, trains, ships, cars, and spacecraft.**

Vehicle Names	
Airplanes	*Air Force One, Spirit of St. Louis*
Trains	*Southwest Chief, Orient Express*
Ships	U.S.S. *Arizona, Pinta*
Cars	*Mustang, Prelude, Pathfinder*
Spacecraft	*Challenger, Columbia, Apollo V*

❷ Practice and Apply

A. CONCEPT CHECK: Places and Transportation

Write the words that should be capitalized but are not in each sentence. Capitalize each correctly.

Just Playing Games

1. Dr. Jane J. Peabody's research for her book took her all over north america.
2. First, she boarded the train called the *cardinal.*
3. In the appalachian mountains she learned about homemade folk games, such as button on a string.
4. Later, in New Orleans, she saw the gulf of mexico for the first time.
5. She rented a Ford taurus for the next leg of her journey.
6. Heading west, she visited the grand canyon.
7. San luis, a town in northern mexico, provided a wealth of information about Native American games, such as *el coyote.*
8. Driving along the Pacific coastline, Dr. Peabody took some time to see the Redwood National forest.
9. She continued north to vancouver, british Columbia, where she observed Canadian children playing games.
10. Dr. Peabody eventually arrived back home in champaign, illinois, with stacks of information to use for her book.

➡ For a SELF-CHECK and more practice, see the EXERCISE BANK, p. 616.

B. REVISING: Correcting Map Titles

Look at this map of the eastern part of Australia, site of the games of the XXVII Olympiad. Find and correct five capitalization errors.

Organizations and Other Subjects

❶ Here's the Idea

Organizations and Institutions

▶ **Capitalize all important words in the names of organizations, institutions, stores, and companies.**

Library of Congress   Jefferson Middle School

Harry's Finer Foods   Babe Ruth Baseball League

Historical Events, Periods, and Documents

▶ **Capitalize the names of historical events, periods, and documents.**

Historical Events, Periods, and Documents	
Events	Civil War, Boston Tea Party, French Revolution
Periods	Great Depression, Bronze Age, Middle Ages
Documents	Bill of Rights, Gettysburg Address, Panama Canal Treaty

Do you have any relatives who were in the Gulf War?

Time Abbreviations and Calendar Items

▶ **Capitalize the abbreviations B.C., A.D., A.M., and P.M.**

The first recorded Olympic contest took place in 776 B.C.

The volleyball tryouts are at 5:00 P.M. sharp.

▶ **Capitalize the names of months, days, and holidays, but not the names of seasons (except when they are part of the names of festivals or celebrations).**

April   Saturday   Thanksgiving Day

May   Winter Formal   Fourth of July

This year my birthday, April 7, is on a Sunday.

Memorial Day is the unofficial start of summer.

Special Events, Awards, and Brand Names

▶ **Capitalize the names of special events and awards.**

Heisman Trophy   World Cup

Pulitzer Prize   Pan-American Games

The annual Harvest Festival is scheduled for next weekend.

▶ **Capitalize the brand name of a product but not a common noun that follows a brand name.**

Spiker volleyballs   Easy Over hurdles

❷ Practice and Apply

CONCEPT CHECK: Organizations and Other Subjects

Find and correct ten capitalization errors in the school-calendar page below.

north side junior high

september Events

Sunday, Sept. 1

Monday, Sept. 2:   Labor day

tuesday, Sept. 3:   3:30 P.m. girls' volleyball tryouts

Wednesday, Sept. 4:   Auditions for Thornton Wilder's *Our Town*

Thursday, Sept. 5:   Lions vs. vikings at home football game

Friday, Sept. 6:   District 112 Board of education meeting

Saturday, Sept. 7:   NSJH car wash

Grammar in Physical Education

Making the Most of Capitals

Writing is important in everything—even at sports meets. Although athletes may not write while they're throwing the shot put or sprinting the last 50 meters, they do need to share information about rules, schedules, and events.

The team manager for the Mae Jemison Jets has drafted a reminder memo for the members of his team. Because he was in a rush, he made a few errors in capitalization. Luckily, he had a friend proofread his draft.

Instructions for Round-Robin Track Meet

Where:

City is a proper noun.

South Village Recreation Area, Sauk (city)

Directions for carpool drivers:

Less-for-More is a brand name.

Take Onarga Street west to Route 42. Turn left and go three blocks. (You'll pass Martha's Cafe on the right and a (less-for-more) gas station on the left.) Park in the section marked with an orange banner.

When:

(wednesday)

October 13, 3:00 P.M.

Wednesday is a proper noun.

What to bring:

(bring) instruction sheet, track shoes, warm-up suit, and water bottle.

Capitalize the first word in a sentence.

What to do once you get there:

- Go to the area assigned to Mae Jemison (junior high.)
- Check the schedule.
- (do) your warm-up exercises.
- Be at the track at least 15 minutes before your race.
- *Relax and do your best!*

Proper noun

For more information, contact (michael) Warner, 555-3745.

Michael is a proper noun.

Practice and Apply

Writing: Reporting the Results Use the results in the diagram to write an article about the Jets for your school newspaper. Include the following information in your article:

• when and where the meet was held

• how each team did

• the name of the winning team (You decide.)

• any particularly exciting or unusual events during the meet

Be sure to check your capitalization. Save your paragraph in your ▭ **Working Portfolio.**

Track Tournament • October 13–15
South Village Recreation Area

Preliminary round	Semi-final play-off	Championship game

Horace Greeley Middle School

Marshall Junior High

Horace Greeley Junior High

?

Mae Jemison Junior High

Lincoln Middle School

Mae Jemison Junior High

A. Proofreading: Capitalization Identify and correct the 25 capitalization errors in the following paragraph.

STUDENT MODEL

It takes most people between 10 and 15 minutes to run a mile; only world-class runners can run the mile in less than 4 minutes. On may 6, 1954, in oxford, england, roger bannister broke the 4-minute-mile barrier that many people had failed to surpass. While bannister was a medical student at st. mary's hospital in london, he trained as a runner for britain's amateur athletic association (AAA) team. Bannister's world record of 3 minutes and 59.4 seconds stood for only seven weeks before john landy ran the mile in 3 minutes and 58 seconds in turku, finland. In july 1999 the moroccan runner hicham el guerrouj claimed the world record by running the mile in an astonishing 3 minutes 43:13 seconds in rome, italy.

B. Capitalization of Book Titles Capitalize the following titles of books correctly.

1. *board games round the world*
2. *children's games and rhymes*
3. *children's games from many lands*
4. *the cooperative sports and games book*
5. *games and sports the world around*

C. Revision: Capitalizing Important Words Fix the ten capitalization errors in the text below so that the tickets will be correct when they're printed.

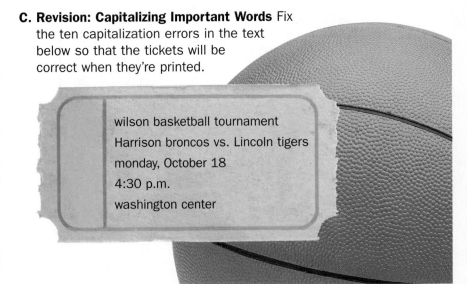

wilson basketball tournament
Harrison broncos vs. Lincoln tigers
monday, October 18
4:30 p.m.
washington center

CHAPTER 10

Mastery Test: What Did You Learn?

For each underlined passage, choose the letter of the correct revision.

I received an invitation to a <u>Memorial day party</u> at my friend
(1)
<u>David corny's house.</u> The party was to be on <u>monday, May</u> 27, at
(2)   (3)
<u>12:30 P.m. The</u> invitation stated that we would be going on a
(4)
scavenger hunt. I had never before been on a scavenger hunt.

When I got to David's house, <u>his mom, mrs. Corny,</u> handed each
(5)
of us partygoers a list of items that we needed to find during the
scavenger hunt. About 20 items were listed, including a <u>native</u>
<u>American belt,</u> the book <u>*to Kill a Mockingbird*,</u> a pink sock,
(6)   (7)
<u>Mr. Suds bubble bath,</u> and a roll of candy from <u>the Lions' club.</u>
(8)   (9)
Right then and there I knew that we would all be jumping into
Mrs. Corny's <u>SUV and driving all over Wisconsin</u> for the rest of
(10)
our lives to find all of that stuff.

CAPITALIZATION

1. A. Day
   B. memorial
   C. Party
   D. Correct as is

2. A. House
   B. david
   C. Corny's
   D. Correct as is

3. A. Monday, May
   B. monday, may
   C. Monday, may
   D. Correct as is

4. A. the
   B. p.m.
   C. P.M.
   D. Correct as is

5. A. Mom
   B. corny
   C. Mrs.
   D. Correct as is

6. A. american
   B. Native
   C. Belt
   D. Correct as is

7. A. *To*
   B. *kill*
   C. *mockingbird*
   D. Correct as is

8. A. mr.
   B. Bubble Bath
   C. suds
   D. Correct as is

9. A. lions'
   B. Club
   C. The
   D. Correct as is

10. A. wisconsin
    B. Suv
    C. suv
    D. Correct as is

Student Help Desk

Capitalization at a Glance

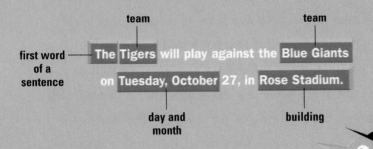

first word of a sentence — The **Tigers** will play against the **Blue Giants** on **Tuesday, October 27,** in **Rose Stadium.**

team

team

day and month

building

YOU'RE SAFE!

Do Capitalize

Proper nouns that name particular people, places, or things:
The **F**inn family will visit **S**ydney, **A**ustralia, for the **O**lympic **G**ames.

Family words used with names or in place of names:
Julia watched the hockey game with **U**ncle Tim.

First words of sentences:
Who will win this year's state championship?

First words in lines of traditional poetry:
And somewhere men are laughing, and somewhere children shout,
But there is no joy in Mudville: Mighty Casey has struck out.
　　　　　　　　　　　—Ernest Lawrence Thayer, "Casey at the Bat"

First words and important words in titles:
The House on Mango Street

Proper nouns that name particular dates, holidays, events, or awards.
On **J**uly 4, **I**ndependence **D**ay, Gus will compete in the **N**ewport **S**ummer **C**ook-**O**ff.

246 Grammar, Usage, and Mechanics

CHAPTER 10

Don't Capitalize

You're Out!

Common nouns referring to people, places, or things:
Our **t**eam is traveling **s**outh through the **d**esert for our next **m**eet.

Family words used as common nouns:
My **c**ousin is the fastest sprinter in the entire state.

First words in lines of some contemporary poems:
the world is not a pleasant place
to be without
someone to hold and be held by
  —Nikki Giovanni, "The World Is Not a Pleasant Place to Be"

Articles, conjunctions, and short prepositions in titles:
"Ode **t**o **a**n Artichoke"

Common nouns referring to times, events, or awards:
Jasmine is planning on running the **m**arathon in the **s**pring.

The Bottom Line

Checklist for Capitalization

Have I capitalized . . .

____ people's names and initials?

____ personal titles preceding names?

____ names of races, languages, and nationalities?

____ names of religions and other religious terms?

____ names of bodies of the universe?

____ names of monuments, bridges, and other landmarks?

____ names of particular planes, trains, and other vehicles?

____ names of historical events, eras, and documents?

____ names of special events, awards, and brands?

Punctuation

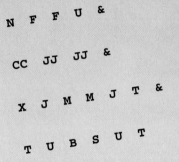

TOP SECRET

SECRET CODE: FOR YOUR EYES ONLY		
A=Z	J=I	S=R
B=A	K=J	T=S
C=B	L=K	U=T
D=C	M=L	V=U
E=D	N=M	W=V
F=E	O=N	X=W
G=F	P=O	Y=X
H=G	Q=P	Z=Y
I=H	R=Q	

& = letter space		
AA=1	EE=5	II=9
BB=2	FF=6	JJ=0
CC=3	GG=7	
DD=4	HH=8	

Theme: Secret Messages

What's It All About?

You may have figured out the words and numbers in the secret message above, but without punctuation, what do they mean? Are you to meet at 300 Willis Street? Or are you to meet at 3:00 and go to a movie called *Willis*? Maybe the movie starts at 3:00, so you'll need to meet earlier. By now, you see how important punctuation can be!

Write Away: I've Got a Secret

Write a short message to a friend in which you use a simple code of letters, numbers, or nonsense words. Be sure to use punctuation in your message. Keep your message and your code key in your 🗂 **Working Portfolio.**

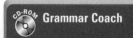

CD-ROM **Grammar Coach**

CHAPTER 11

Choose the letter of the best revision of each underlined item.

Not all secret messages are <u>codes, ciphers are used</u> for secret
(1)
communication too. A code is a group of <u>words symbols or numbers</u>
(2)
that has meaning to the receiver. For example, in World War II, the
message <u>It is hot in Suez</u> instructed <u>France's</u> resistance to attack
(3) (4)
railroad lines. <u>In a cipher, by contrast,</u> the letters of a message are
(5)
scrambled or replaced by other letters or numbers. You could write
"I <u>can;t</u> read <u>one half</u> of your cipher" by using a number for each
(6) (7)
alphabet letter. Would it surprise you that *cipher* comes from a
word meaning <u>"to number"</u> <u>Cryptology, the science of code breaking</u>
(8) (9)
comes from two Greek words meaning "secret wording." To learn
more, read <u>"The Secret Code Book"</u> by Helen Huckle.
(10)

1. A. codes; ciphers are
   B. codes? Ciphers are
   C. codes! Ciphers are
   D. Correct as is

2. A. words: symbols or numbers
   B. words, symbols or numbers
   C. words, symbols, or numbers
   D. Correct as is

3. A. It is hot in Suez"
   B. "It is hot in Suez"
   C. "It is hot in Suez
   D. Correct as is

4. A. Frances'
   B. Frances
   C. France"s
   D. Correct as is

5. A. In a cipher, by contrast;
   B. In a cipher by contrast,
   C. In a cipher, by contrast
   D. Correct as is

6. A. can,t
   B. can't
   C. cant
   D. Correct as is

7. A. one—half
   B. one-half
   C. one'half
   D. Correct as is

8. A. "to number."
   B. "to number?"
   C. "to number"?
   D. Correct as is

9. A. Cryptology, the science of
      code breaking,
   B. Cryptology the science of
      code breaking,
   C. Cryptology; the science of
      code breaking
   D. Correct as is

10. A. The Secret Code Book
    B. *"The Secret Code Book"*
    C. *The Secret Code Book*
    D. Correct as is

Periods and Other End Marks

❶ Here's the Idea

Periods, question marks, and exclamation points are known as **end marks** because they are used to indicate the end of a sentence. Periods have other uses as well.

Periods

▶ **Use a period at the end of a declarative sentence.**
A declarative sentence makes a statement.

Our team uses a code to make up plays.

The key is a carefully kept secret.

▶ **Use a period at the end of almost every imperative sentence.** An imperative sentence gives a command. Some imperative sentences express excitement or emotion and therefore end with exclamation points.

Do not ask me to reveal our code.

Stop! Don't tell the other team!

▶ **Use a period at the end of an indirect question.** An indirect question reports what a person asked without using the person's exact words.

INDIRECT QUESTION   The coach asked if our team code had been broken.

DIRECT QUESTION   The coach asked, "Has our team code been broken?"

Question Marks

▶ **Use a question mark at the end of an interrogative sentence.** An interrogative sentence asks a question.

Did the other team break the code?

Have they figured out all our plays?

Exclamation Points

▶ **Use an exclamation point to end an exclamatory sentence.** An exclamatory sentence expresses strong feeling.

What a terrible situation!

▶ **Use an exclamation point after an interjection or any other exclamatory expression.**

Oh! I have an idea!

Wow! Tell us!

Other Uses for Periods

▶ **Use a period at the end of most abbreviations or after an initial.**

Common Abbreviations and Initials

Abbreviations

sec. second	Thurs. Thursday	lb. pound	gal. gallon
min. minute	Pres. President	hr. hour	mo. month
St. Street	Feb. February	yr. year	in. inch

Initials

R.N. registered nurse	P.M. *post meridiem* (after noon)
B.A. bachelor of arts	M.D. doctor of medicine
P.O. post office	R.K.S. Rebecca Kate Simmons

Abbreviations Without Periods

CIA Central Intelligence Agency	mph miles per hour
VCR videocassette recorder	cm centimeter
CA California	mm millimeter

▶ **Use a period after each number or letter in an outline or a list.**

Outline

Uses for Codes
I. Use in wartime
  A. World War I
  B. World War II
II. Industrial uses
  A. To protect new methods
  B. To protect consumers' privacy

List

Communication Codes
1. Braille
2. American Sign Language
3. Egyptian hieroglyphics
4. Mayan hieroglyphics
5. Morse code
6. Semaphore

❷ Practice and Apply

A. CONCEPT CHECK: Periods and Other End Marks

Write the proper end mark for each numbered blank below.

Timely Messages

Do you think you are the only one interested in secret writing **1** Nonsense **2** For hundreds of years, people have used secret messages **3** Did you know that the great Roman general Julius Caesar invented a cipher **4** He used it to communicate with his staff in Rome **5** Consider also Mary Queen of Scots, who smuggled ciphers out of her household in England **6** One cipher told of a plot to kill England's queen, Elizabeth I. Poor Mary **7** Her note was intercepted and read, and she was put to death. During World War II, what do you think the Allies found in sunken German submarines **8** They found German codebooks. They used the books to decode messages about German naval operations **9** What do you think happened **10**

➡ For a SELF-CHECK and more practice, see the EXERCISE BANK, p. 617.

B. WRITING: Punctuating Abbreviations

The notes below were taken by a spy who had forgotten how to punctuate abbreviations. Write the notes, using correct punctuation.

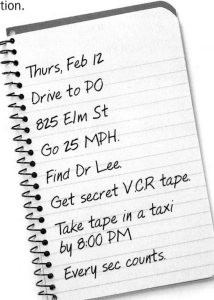

Thurs, Feb 12
Drive to PO
825 Elm St
Go 25 MPH.
Find Dr Lee.
Get secret VCR tape.
Take tape in a taxi
by 8:00 PM
Every sec counts.

Commas in Sentences

❶ Here's the Idea

Commas are used to make the meanings of sentences clear by separating certain elements of the sentences.

Commas in Compound Sentences

▶ **Use a comma before a conjunction that joins independent clauses in a compound sentence.**

The ancient Egyptians' written language was called hieroglyphics **,** **and** it was not decoded for many centuries.

In ancient times, scribes could read and write hieroglyphics **,** **but** most other Egyptians could not.

Scribes passed rigorous examinations **,** **or** they were rejected as scribes.

WATCH OUT Sometimes a sentence has a two-part compound verb but is not a compound sentence. Do not use a comma in this kind of sentence.

Scribes could **read** and **write hieroglyphics.**

Commas with Items in a Series

▶ **Use a comma after every item in a series except the last one.** A series consists of three or more items.

Symbols of **birds** **,** **lions** **,** and **snakes** appear in hieroglyphics.

Hieroglyphics could be read **from left to right** **,** **from right to left** **,** or **from top to bottom.**

Hieroglyphic writing was used for **business contracts** **,** **legal documents** **,** and other **important records.**

▶ **Use a comma between adjectives of equal rank that modify the same noun.**

> **Here's How** Adding Commas Between Adjectives

> To decide whether a comma is needed between two adjectives modifying the same noun, try one of the following tests.
>
> **Hieroglyphics used colorful decorative symbols.**
>
> **1.** Place the word *and* between the adjectives.
>
> **Hieroglyphics used colorful and decorative symbols.**
>
> **2.** If the sentence still makes sense, replace *and* with a comma.
>
> **Hieroglyphics used colorful , decorative symbols.**
>
> **1. Or** reverse the order of the adjectives.
>
> **Hieroglyphics used decorative and colorful symbols.**
>
> **2.** If the sentence still makes sense, replace *and* with a comma.
>
> **Hieroglyphics used decorative , colorful symbols.**

Do not use a comma between adjectives that express a single idea.

The symbols were often painted with brilliant gold paint.

Commas with Introductory Words and Phrases

▶ **Use a comma after an introductory phrase that contains a prepositional phrase. Use a comma after introductory words.**

Even after 2,000 years of study, no one could read hieroglyphics.

Finally, the Rosetta Stone was found in Egypt.

Commas with Interrupters

▶ **Use commas to set off a word or phrase that interrupts the flow of thought in a sentence.**

The stone provided, at long last, a key to hieroglyphics.

▶ **Use commas to set off nouns of direct address.** A noun of direct address names the person or group being spoken to.

Alex, your class would be thrilled with this discovery.

Your class, Alex, would be thrilled with this discovery.

Commas with Appositives

An **appositive** is a word or phrase that identifies or renames a noun or pronoun that comes right before it. Use commas when the appositive adds extra information; do not use commas when the appositive is needed to make the meaning clear.

Jean Champollion, **a French scholar,** deciphered the Rosetta stone. (The phrase *a French scholar* adds extra information.)

The French scholar **Jean Champollion** deciphered the Rosetta stone. (The phrase *Jean Champollion* tells which French scholar and makes the sentence clear and complete.)

Commas to Avoid Confusion

▶ **Use a comma whenever the reader might otherwise be confused.**

UNCLEAR	Before hieroglyphics records were not kept on stone or paper.
CLEAR	Before hieroglyphics , records were not kept on stone or paper.
UNCLEAR	After we studied hieroglyphics were less mysterious.
CLEAR	After we studied , hieroglyphics were less mysterious.

❷ Practice and Apply

CONCEPT CHECK: Commas in Sentences

Write the following paragraph, adding commas where they are needed.

A Hairy Story

Think of this readers when you have your next haircut. A Persian king had to get a message to his military leader a Persian general. The king shaved a man's head tattooed a message on his bare scalp and told the man to let the hair grow back. The man then traveled to find the general but no one knew he carried a message. When he reached the general however he delivered his message. Yes as you guessed it he had his head shaved again!

➡ For a SELF-CHECK and more practice, see the EXERCISE BANK, p. 618.

LESSON 3

Commas: Dates, Addresses, and Letters

❶ Here's the Idea

See these rules in action in the letter below.

Commas in Dates, Addresses, and Letters	
Commas in dates	In dates, use a comma between the day and the year. (Use a comma after the year if the sentence continues.)
Commas in addresses	Use a comma between the city or town and the state or country. (Use a comma after the state or country if the sentence continues.)
Commas in letters	Use a comma after the greeting of a casual letter and after the closing of a casual or business letter.

1   385 Webster Avenue

2   Hanover, MA 02339

3   March 26, 2000

> **Line 2:** comma between city and state

4 Dear Alanna,

5   Do you remember the code we used

6 to keep secrets from our nosy

7 brothers? Well, some animals have

8 codes too. They understand each

9 other. On February 12, 2000,

10 a scientist from Denver, Colorado,

11 spoke at my school. She told us

12 that bees communicate by the

13 way they move. A bee's dance

14 can tell other bees where to find

15 good flowers for making honey. Isn't

16 that incredible? Come and visit soon.

17   Your friend,

18   Regina

> **Line 3:** comma between day and year
>
> **Line 4:** comma after greeting
>
> **Line 9:** comma after year
>
> **Line 10:** comma after state
>
> **Line 17:** comma after closing

Do not use a comma between the state and the ZIP code.

CHAPTER 11

❷ Practice and Apply

A. CONCEPT CHECK: Commas in Dates, Addresses, and Letters

Write the following letter, adding any missing commas.

158 W. 23 Street
New York NY 10010
February 20 2000

Dear Hank

Do you know about Katy Payne? Payne studies elephants in countries like Kenya, Africa. She has found out that elephants' voices are below the human level of hearing! Payne proved this with a special tape recorder. Elephants can call to one another over hundreds of miles. What a terrific hidden code! You could call to me in New York City from Albany New York! Today Katy Payne lives in Ithaca New York where she writes and studies her elephant data. She will speak here on March 19 2000 and I can't wait to hear her.

Take care

Sammy

➡ For a SELF-CHECK and more practice, see the EXERCISE BANK, p. 618.

B. WRITING: Dear Friend

Put a letter together, using these parts. Don't forget to add commas where they belong.

210 Oak St.

Hinton IA 51104

May 3 2000

Dear Jon

I'm giving a surprise swimming party for Sara next Friday at the public pool in Moville Iowa. Keep it a secret.

Sincerely

Teresa

PUNCTUATION

Punctuating Quotations

❶ Here's the Idea

To punctuate quotations, you need to know where to put quotation marks, commas, and end marks.

Direct Quotations

A direct quotation is a report of a speaker's exact words.

▶ **Use quotation marks at the beginning and the ending of a direct quotation.**

"Flowers have meaning," said Sophie.

▶ **Use commas to set off explanatory words used with direct quotations (whether they occur at the beginning, in the middle, or at the end of the sentences).**

Sophie said, "Flowers have meaning."

"Flowers," said Sophie, "have meaning."

"Flowers have meaning," said Sophie.

▶ **If a quotation is a question or an exclamation, place the question mark or exclamation point inside the closing quotation marks.**

"What do flowers mean?" I asked.

▶ **If quoted words are part of a question or exclamation of your own, place the question mark or exclamation point outside the closing quotation marks.**

Do flowers tell "secret messages"?

Commas and periods always go inside closing quotation marks. They're too little to stay outside.

Indirect Quotations

▶ **Do not use quotation marks to set off an indirect quotation.** An indirect quotation is a restatement, in somewhat different words, of what someone said. An indirect quotation is often introduced by the word *that*. It does not require a comma.

INDIRECT   Shakespeare wrote **that** a rose would smell sweet regardless of its name.

DIRECT   Shakespeare wrote, "a rose by any other name would smell as sweet."

Divided Quotations

A divided quotation is a direct quotation that is separated into two parts, with explanatory words such as *he said* or *she said* between the parts.

▶ **Use quotation marks to enclose both parts of a divided quotation.**

"A rose," he said, "means love."

▶ **Do not capitalize the first word of the second part of a divided quotation unless it begins a new sentence.**

"A rose," he said, "sometimes means treachery."

"A rose usually means love," he said. "Sometimes it means treachery."

▶ **Use commas to set off the explanatory words used with a divided quotation.**

"A rose," he summed up, "can mean treachery or love."

Quotation Marks in Dialogue

▶ **In dialogue, a new paragraph and a new set of quotation marks show a change in speakers.**

A dialogue is a conversation between two or more speakers.

LITERARY MODEL

"Indeed. That is most interesting. Did the tune, perhaps, go like this?"

The princess hummed a few bars.

"That's it! How did you know?"

"Why, you foolish boy, it was I who put the spell on the garden, to make it come alive when the tune is played or sung."

—Joan Aiken, "The Serial Garden"

Using Quotation Marks

Use this model to review the punctuation in this lesson.

PROFESSIONAL MODEL

Did you know that some call flowers "secret messages"? Sophie told me that each kind of flower means something different.

> Question with quoted words

> Indirect quotation

"What does a rose mean?" I asked.

"It depends on the color," she explained. "In England, a red rose means true love, but a yellow rose suggests that a person has cheated."

> Dialogue

"That's a strong message!" I exclaimed. I asked what a man might do if he received a yellow rose from his girlfriend.

> Exclamation

"He might send her white violets," said Sophie, "to proclaim his innocence."

> Divided quotation

—J. Gallagher

---

❷ Practice and Apply

Write the following passage, correcting errors in the use and placement of quotation marks.

The Language of Flowers

"I want to send Megan flowers," Jay said.

"Are you nuts"? asked Dan. "She'll think you like her."

"I do," said Jay, and I want her to know it. Now help me look up in this book which flowers mean what."

Dan agreed that "he would help."

"Look!" said Jay. Irises mean faithfulness and courage."

Dan suggested that "he send pansies," which mean "I'm thinking of you."

"Good," Jay said.

"Geraniums," said Dan, "mean happiness".

Jay decided "he had enough ideas.

➡ **For a SELF-CHECK and more practice, see the EXERCISE BANK, p. 619.**

B. EDITING: Speaking Indirectly

Write as well as Shakespeare. Make these quotations your own by changing them into indirect quotations.

Example: We asked, "Did Shakespeare study flowers?"

Answer: We asked whether Shakespeare studied flowers.

1. Our teacher said, "Shakespeare knew the language of flowers."
2. In *Hamlet,* he has Ophelia say, "There's rosemary, that's for remembrance."
3. Oberon says "I know a bank where the wild thyme blows."
4. "Thyme meant sweetness," according to *The Book of Flowers and Herbs.*
5. A historian tells us, "Shakespeare's audience knew the meanings of the flowers he mentioned."

LESSON 5 — Semicolons and Colons

❶ Here's the Idea

A **semicolon** indicates a break in a sentence. It is stronger than a comma but not as strong as a period. A **colon** indicates an abrupt break. A colon indicates that a list follows. Colons are also used after greetings in business letters and in expressions of time.

Semicolons in Compound Sentences

▶ **Use a semicolon to join parts of a compound sentence without a coordinating conjunction.**

Enslaved people sang songs with secret messages; the songs told listeners how to escape.

▶ **Use a semicolon between the parts of a compound sentence when the clauses are long and complicated or when they contain commas.**

Runaways navigated by the stars; and they lived off the land, slept outdoors, and walked hundreds of miles to freedom.

Semicolons with Items in a Series

▶ **When there are commas within parts of a series, use semicolons to separate the parts.**

The travelers took clues from songs, such as a song about the stars; from quilts, which had special coded designs; and from other people along the way.

Colons

▶ **Use a colon to introduce a list of items.**

An escapee carried few items: a knife, a flint, and a warm cloak.

Avoid using a colon directly after a verb or a preposition.

INCORRECT   The recipients are: Joe, Sam, and Rita.
INCORRECT   Send this message to: Joe, Sam, and Rita.
CORRECT   Send this message to the following people: Joe, Sam, and Rita.

> **Use a colon after the formal greeting in a business letter.**

Dear Ms. Smith: Dear Sir:

For a model, see the business letter in the Model Bank p. 624.

> **Use a colon between numerals indicating hours and minutes in expressions of time.**

Meet me at 8:00 P.M. We'll send the message at 8:30.

❷ Practice and Apply

A. CONCEPT CHECK: Semicolons and Colons

Write the following paragraphs, correcting errors in the use of semicolons and colons.

Walking the Underground Railroad

    Here are two ways conductors on the Underground Railroad hid messages; in songs and in quilts. "The Drinking Gourd," for example, sounded like a folk song, however, it was a map to freedom. The "gourd" was actually the constellation known as the Big Dipper, it points to the North Star. The lyrics of the song told slaves how to head north; to the free states. The quilts were signal flags, travelers would see them and know where to go. The following quilt designs carried directions; the Bear's Paw, which told people to follow bear tracks in the mountains, the Crossroads, which said to head to Cleveland, Ohio; and the Flying Geese; which said to follow geese to water. Unlike real trains, which might leave at a specific time, say 730 P.M., the "freedom trains" left: anytime after dark.

→ For a SELF-CHECK and more practice, see the EXERCISE BANK, p. 619.

B. WRITING: All Business

Write a short business letter to the catalog company in this advertisement, ordering a list of items you would need to make a signal quilt. Choose from the items in the ad. Model your letter on the sample business letter in the Model Bank on page 624.

1999   Section

Quilter's xxxxx
xxxxxxxx **Corner**

LET US SUPPLY YOUR QUILTING NEEDS!

needles, patterns, fabric, padding, stencils

xxxxxxxxxxxxxxxxxxxxxxxxxxx

xxxxxxxxxxxxxxxx
2211 N. Lincoln Avenue
Chicago, IL 60614

Hyphens, Dashes, and Parentheses

LESSON 6

CHAPTER 11

❶ Here's the Idea

Hyphens, dashes, and parentheses help make your writing clear by separating or setting off words or parts of words.

Hyphens

▶ **Use a hyphen if part of a word must be carried over from one line to the next.**

1. The word must have at least two syllables to be broken.
RIGHT: num - ber   WRONG: co - de

2. Separate the word between syllables.
RIGHT: let - ter   WRONG: lette - r

3. You must leave at least two letters on each line.
RIGHT: twen - ty   WRONG: a - cross

▶ **Use hyphens in certain compound words.**

half - dollar   great - grandmother

▶ **Use hyphens in compound numbers from twenty-one through ninety-nine.**

sixty - three   twenty - six

▶ **Use hyphens in spelled-out fractions.**

two - thirds   three - fourths

Dashes

▶ **Use dashes to show an abrupt break in thought.**

Louis Braille — who lost his sight at age three — invented an alphabet for blind people.

Parentheses

▶ **Use parentheses to set off material that is loosely related to the rest of a sentence.**

Each six-dot cell stands for a character (a letter of the alphabet, a number, a punctuation mark, or a contraction).

264 Grammar, Usage, and Mechanics

❷ Practice and Apply

Read the following paragraph. Then indicate what punctuation mark—hyphen, dash, or parenthesis—is needed in each numbered blank. If no mark is needed, write *None.*

Braille's Brainstorm

Louis Braille was born in a small town in France nearly two hundred years ago. At age three, he was accidentally blinded. He learned to find his way around by tapping with a cane ___(1)___ the sound told him where it was safe to step. Ten ___(2)___year-old Louis went to the National Institute for Blind Youth in Paris. He had heard the school had a library full of books ___(3)___ he could read ___(4)___ but it had only a few. The letters in the books were embossed ___(5)___ so the books were large, bulky, and very expensive to produce).

A person reading braille.

As a student, Louis met Charles Barbier (a retired army captain ___(6)___. Barbier had invented a "night-writing" system ___(7)___ involving dots and dashes punched into cardboard—that let soldiers write and read orders in the dark. Louis spent the next several years simplifying Barbier's system and ___(8)___ another twenty ___(9)___ seven years fighting to get the Braille alphabet adopted. He died at the relatively young age of forty ___(10)___ three.

➡ **For a SELF-CHECK and more practice, see the EXERCISE BANK, p. 620.**

LESSON 7 Apostrophes

❶ Here's the Idea

Apostrophes are used in possessive nouns, contractions, and some plurals.

Apostrophes in Possessives

▶ **Use an apostrophe to form the possessive of any noun, whether singular or plural.**

For a singular noun, add 's even if the word ends in s.

    Becky**'s** bike   Louis**'s** alphabet

For plural nouns that end in s, add only an apostrophe.

    the girl**s'** code   the pioneer**s'** messages

For plural nouns that do not end in s, add 's.

    the children**'s** code   the people**'s** plan

Apostrophes in Contractions

▶ **Use apostrophes in contractions.**

In a contraction, words are joined and letters are left out. An apostrophe replaces the letter or letters that are missing.

Commonly Used Contractions		
I am → I'm	you are → you're	you will → you'll
she is → she's	they have → they've	it is → it's
cannot → can't	they are → they're	was not → wasn't

Don't confuse contractions with possessive pronouns, which do not contain apostrophes.

Contractions Versus Possessive Pronouns	
Contraction	**Possessive Pronoun**
it's (*it is* or *it has*)	its (belonging to it – *its tail*)
who's (*who is*)	whose (belonging to whom – *whose coat*)
you're (*you are*)	your (belonging to you – *your book*)
they're (*they are*)	their (belonging to them – *their house*)

CHAPTER 11

Apostrophes in Plurals

▶ **Use an apostrophe and _s_ to form the plural of a letter, a numeral, or a word referred to as a word.**

Cross your _t_'s.   The speaker used too many _um_'s.
How many 5's are in the answer?

❷ Practice and Apply

A. CONCEPT CHECK: Apostrophes

Write the paragraph, correcting the errors in the use of apostrophes.

> **Give Me an _E_**
>   One person's code is anothers challenge. Cryptanalyst's are people who break codes. They're most important clue is how often certain letters and word's appear. In English, _es_ and _ts_ occur most often, and _the_ is the most common word. Code breakers first goal is to identify these frequently occurring letters. Then theyll start to figure out the words the letters appear in. Once they know what the code uses to mean _e_ and _t_, theyre able to find the word _the_. Then they'll know what the code uses for _h_. Its a hard job, but it's rewards are many.

➡ **For a SELF-CHECK and more practice, see the EXERCISE BANK, p. 620.**

B. WRITING: Who or What Owns It?

Break the code by writing the correct possessive phrase for each "coded" message below.

Take the car that belongs to you.

Go to the house owned by Janus.

at the end of the day

for the party that belongs to Marty

Bring the gift belonging to the class.

Punctuating Titles

❶ Here's the Idea

Use quotation marks and italics correctly in titles to show what kind of work or selection you are writing about.

Quotation Marks

▶ **Use quotation marks to set off the titles of short works.**

Quotation Marks for Titles	
Book chapter	"Dirk the Protector" from *My Life in Dog Years*
Story	"The Richer, the Poorer"
Essay	"Names/ Nombres"
Article	"Primal Compassion"
Song	"Row, Row, Row Your Boat"
Poem	"I Might, I May, I Must"

Italics and Underlining

In handwriting, you show that something should be in italic type by **underlining** it.

▶ **Use italics for titles of longer works and for the names of ships, trains, spacecraft, and airplanes (but not for types of planes).** Show that they should be in italic type by underlining them.

Italics or Underlines for Titles			
Book	*The Phantom Tollbooth*	Epic poem (book length)	*Beowulf*
Play	*Rent*	Painting	*Mona Lisa*
Magazine	*Spin*	Ship	*Titanic*
Movie	*Star Wars*	Train	*Broadway Limited*
TV series	*60 Minutes*	Spacecraft	*Voyager 1*
Long musical composition or CD	*Surfacing*	Airplane (specific plane, not type)	*Spirit of St. Louis* (but not DC-10)

❷ Practice and Apply

A. CONCEPT CHECK: Punctuating Titles

Write the titles in the following paragraph correctly by using quotation marks or underlines.

Surrounded by Codes and Ciphers

The first book on secret writing, or cryptography, was Polygraphia, written in 1499. Today there are several magazines on the subject, including The Journal of Cryptology. An article titled New Directions in Cryptography was published not long ago. When Russians captured the German ship Magdeburg during World War I, they found a German naval codebook. To learn how to create and break codes, read the book Codes and Secret Writing by Herbert S. Zim. The hero of Edgar Allan Poe's short story The Gold Bug finds a cipher that directs him to pirate treasure. The old TV series The Avengers had plots dealing with secret codes; the recent movie The Avengers did not.

Garden Signs by Paul Klee

Even some songs, such as the 1970 single Knock Three Times, have referred to codes. Some paintings such as Paul Klee's *Garden Signs* have symbols that may seem to be codes.

➡ **For a SELF-CHECK and more practice, see the EXERCISE BANK, p. 621.**

B. WRITING: Favorite Titles

Write down the titles of your favorite book, poem, movie, TV show, and song. Then, with a partner, take turns giving clues about each other's favorite titles and write down your guesses. Be sure to use underlines and quotation marks correctly.

PUNCTUATION

Punctuation and Poetry

Without punctuation, poetry may seem like it's written in a secret code. The first word of every line is often capitalized and sentences may not end at the end of a line. For these reasons, punctuation marks are especially important in helping you understand and enjoy reading poetry—and writing it too.

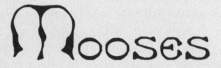

Mooses

by Ted Hughes

The goofy Moose, the walking house-frame
Is lost
In the forest. He bumps, he blunders, he stands.

> Missing periods indicate that sentences continue.

With massy bony thoughts sticking out near his ears—
Reaching out palm upwards, to catch whatever might be
    falling from heaven—
He tries to think,
Leaning their huge weight
On the lectern of his front legs.

He can't find the world!
Where did it go? What does a world look like?
The Moose
Crashes on, and crashes into a lake, and stares at the
    mountain and cries
"Where do I belong? This is no place!"

> Quotation marks indicate the moose's exact thoughts.

He turns and drags half the lake out after him
And charges the cackling underbrush—

> A dash tells you that the sentence runs into the next stanza.

He meets another Moose.
He stares, he thinks "It's only a mirror!"

"Where is the world?" he groans, "O my lost world!
And why am I so ugly?
And why am I so far away from my feet?"

He weeps.
Hopeless drops drip from his droopy lips.

The other Moose just stands there doing the same.

> Here, the author deliberately uses a sentence fragment.

Two dopes of the deep woods.

Practice and Apply

Using Punctuation in Poetry

Write your own poem about one of the strange animals in the pictures. Your poem can stress the humor of the animal's appearance as the model does. It could describe a viewer's response to the animal or the animal's response to the viewer. Even more exciting would be to present two animals reacting to one another. Be sure to use correct punctuation to help readers understand and appreciate your verse. Save your poem in your **Working Portfolio.**

Hedgehog

Macaw

Ladybugs

Frog

Chinese Water Dragon

Mixed Review

A. Proofreading Rewrite the passage below, adding any missing punctuation.

The Secret of the Navajo Code Talkers

During World War II the United States was looking for ways to ensure that its secret messages could not be decoded by the enemy. Philip Johnston who had grown up on the Navajo Indian Reservation and had become fluent in the Navajo language suggested recruiting Navajo soldiers to speak their native language. The language had no written form or alphabet very few people spoke it.

More than 400 Navajos went to the South Pacific. There they sent and received messages in an unbreakable code, their native tongue. They took part in all the Marines assaults on Pacific islands, from Guadalcanal in 1942 to Okinawa in 1945. Japans surrender occurred on August 14 1945.

"When I was going to boarding school, exclaimed code talker Teddy Draper Sr., "the U S government told us not to speak Navajo but during the war, they *wanted* us to speak it!

Navajo code talkers Preston Toledo and Frank Toledo

In 1969 nearly twenty five years after World War II had ended), the code talkers were nationally recognized. A book called *Warriors: Navajo Code Talkers* tells their story.

B. Revising Read the passage below. Then rewrite the passage, putting the punctuation marks where they belong. Add paragraph breaks. Then see if you can add one mark that is not given.

PROFESSIONAL MODEL

Punctuation 'R Easy

Hi Mr Johnson exclaimed Bob Where do you want me to put these punctuation marks Oh just stick them there at the end of the following sentence answered Mr Johnson OK said Bob ".!". ."?"","..".!".

—Dave Barry, *Dave Barry Is Not Making This Up*

Choose the letter of the best revision of each underlined item.

> People sometimes joke that the initials for the National Security Agency—NSA—stand for Never Say Anything. Its not
> (1)   (2)
> really a joke, though. The NSA is the largest; most hidden
> (3)
> intelligence organization in the United States. Those who work for it must learn to keep quiet about what they do, how they do it and
> (4)
> what they learn. The NSA constructs and oversees all the codes used by US intelligence services. Of course—the agency also is
> (5)   (6)
> involved in decoding other countries messages. I can hear you
> (7)
> saying, This is the job for me! But the NSA hires only one of every
> (8)
> six people who apply, competition is very tough. However, if you
> (9)
> study science or engineering, you could be considered. Do you still want a job as a code maker or a code breaker.
> (10)

1. A. Agency, NSA—
   B. Agency—NSA;
   C. Agency NSA—
   D. Correct as is

2. A. Its'
   B. It's
   C. It(s)
   D. Correct as is

3. A. largest: most hidden
   B. largest most hidden
   C. largest, most hidden
   D. Correct as is

4. A. do, how they do it, and
   B. do; how they do it; and
   C. do: how they do it, and
   D. Correct as is

5. A. U-S
   B. U,S,
   C. U.S.
   D. Correct as is

6. A. Of course;
   B. Of course
   C. Of course,
   D. Correct as is

7. A. countries'
   B. countrie's
   C. countries's
   D. Correct as is

8. A. This is the job for me!"
   B. "This is the job for me!"
   C. "This is the job for me!
   D. Correct as is

9. A. apply
   B. apply:
   C. apply;
   D. Correct as is

10. A. code breaker!
    B. code breaker?
    C. code breaker—
    D. Correct as is

Student Help Desk

Punctuation at a Glance

( ) **Parentheses**

○○ **Colon**

! **Exclamation Point**

⟩ **Apostrophe**

⊂⊃ **Hyphen**

⊂⊃ **Dash**

⟩ **Comma**

? **Question Mark**

○ **Period**

○ **Semicolon**

❝❞ **Quotation Marks**

Punctuating Titles

Italics Versus "Quotation Marks"

Italics (longer works)

Books, Movies, Magazines, Plays, TV series, Paintings, Long musical works, Epic poems

Quotation Marks (shorter works)

Stories, Essays, Songs, Poems, Book chapters, Episodes in a TV series, Magazine articles

Punctuation with Commas

	Use commas. . .	Examples
Items in a series	to separate items in a series	secrets , messages , and codes
Introductory words	after introductory words	Believe me , you must try.
Interrupters	to set off interrupters	It is , of course , your decision.
Nouns of direct address	to set off nouns of direct address	Are you , Jenny , prepared to try?

Punctuation with Quotation Marks The Inside Report

Always Inside (no matter what)

Period	Sly said, "We'll break their code**.**"
Comma	"We'll learn their secrets**,**" said Guy.

Sometimes Inside (if they punctuate the quoted words)

Question mark	"What's the secret word**?**" asked Jack.
Exclamation point	"What a horrible shock**!**" cried the spy.

Sometimes Outside (if they punctuate a sentence containing quoted words)

Question mark	Did you tell Jack to read "The Spy Who Cried**"?**
Exclamation point	I hated the story "Three Spies and Me**"!**

The Bottom Line

Checklist for Punctuation

Have I . . .

____ ended every sentence with an appropriate end mark?

____ used commas before the conjunctions in compound sentences?

____ used commas to separate items in a series?

____ used commas correctly in dates, addresses, and letters?

____ used quotation marks before and after a speaker's words?

____ used a semicolon instead of a conjunction in long compound sentences?

____ used apostrophes to form contractions and possessives?

____ used italics and quotation marks correctly for titles?

Diagramming: Sentence Parts

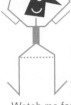

Mad Mapper

Here's the Idea

Diagramming is a way of showing the structure of a sentence. Drawing a diagram can help you see how the parts of a sentence work together to form a complete thought.

Watch me for diagramming tips!

Simple Subjects and Verbs

Write the simple subject and verb on one line. Separate them with a vertical line that crosses the main line.

Campers hiked.

Campers	hiked

Compound Subjects and Verbs

For a compound subject or verb, split the main line. Put the conjunction on a dotted line connecting the compound parts.

Compound Subject

Campers and counselors hiked.

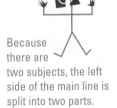

Because there are two subjects, the left side of the main line is split into two parts.

Compound Verb

Campers hiked and chatted.

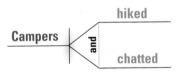

Compound Subject and Compound Verb

Campers and counselors hiked and chatted.

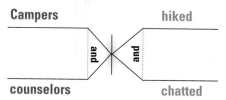

Because there are two subjects and two verbs, both sides of the main line are split into two parts.

A. CONCEPT CHECK: Subjects and Verbs

Diagram these sentences, using what you have learned.

1. Bears appeared.

2. Trees creaked and swayed.

3. Bees and butterflies fluttered and swarmed.

Adjectives and Adverbs

Write adjectives and adverbs on slanted lines below the words they modify.

A steep mountain suddenly loomed ahead.

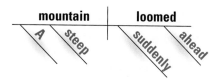

B. CONCEPT CHECK: Adjectives and Adverbs

Diagram these sentences, using what you have learned.

1. Dry, brown leaves rustled constantly.

2. Gloomy, gray clouds floated soundlessly overhead.

3. Sleepy campers rested peacefully.

Subject Complements

- Write a predicate noun or a predicate adjective on the main line after the verb.
- Separate the subject complement from the verb with a slanted line that does not cross the main line.

Predicate Noun

Cave explorers are spelunkers.

Predicate Adjective

Damp, dark caves can be scary.

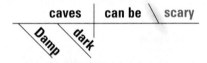

Direct Objects

A direct object follows the verb on the main line.

Brave spelunkers explore mysterious caves.

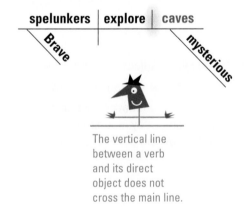

The vertical line between a verb and its direct object does not cross the main line.

Write compound direct objects on parallel lines that branch from the main line.

Cave explorers wear sturdy clothing and hard hats.

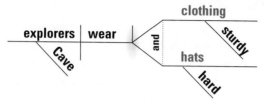

Indirect Objects

Write an indirect object below the verb, on a horizontal line connected to the verb with a slanted line.

Serious explorers give safety their careful consideration.

DIAGRAMMING

C. CONCEPT CHECK: Subject Complements and Objects

Diagram these sentences, using what you have learned.

1. Some caves are gigantic.
2. Spelunkers are courageous people.
3. Caves often contain long stalactites and tall stalagmites.

D. MIXED REVIEW: Diagramming

Diagram the following sentences.

1. Jewel Cave is gigantic.
2. It is an unusual underground world.
3. Shiny calcite crystals line the walls.
4. Strange, colorful formations fill the underground rooms.
5. The underground temperature is cool.
6. Visitors wear sturdy shoes and light jackets.
7. Knowledgeable guides give the visitors a lengthy tour.
8. Tourists and guides see shiny crystals and dark pools.
9. Brave visitors can take a candlelight tour.
10. They may encounter many bats!

Diagramming: Phrases and Clauses

Prepositional Phrases

- Write the preposition on a slanted line below the word the prepositional phrase modifies.
- Write the object of the preposition on a horizontal line attached to the slanted line and parallel to the main line.
- Write words that modify the object of the preposition on slanted lines below it.

Adjective Prepositional Phrase

Natural forces may cause cracks in solid rocks.

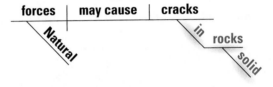

This adjective phrase modifies a noun. Adjective phrases can also modify pronouns and other prepositional phrases.

Adverb Prepositional Phrase

Glaciers move loose rocks down the valley.

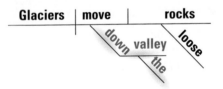

This adverb phrase modifies a verb. Adverb phrases can also modify adjectives and adverbs.

E. CONCEPT CHECK: Prepositional Phrases

Diagram these sentences, using what you have learned.

1. A glacier is a river of ice.
2. The flow of a heavy glacier carves a valley in a mountainside.
3. Inside their houses, people hear the eerie sounds of the ice outside.

Compound Sentences

- Diagram the independent clauses on parallel horizontal lines.
- Connect the verbs in the two clauses by a dotted line with a step in it.
- Write the coordinating conjunction on the step.

Birds fly naturally, but humans fly in balloons.

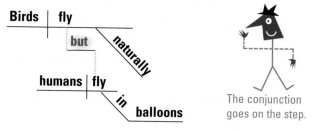

The conjunction goes on the step.

F. CONCEPT CHECK: Compound Sentences

Diagram these sentences, using what you have learned.

1. Balloons travel slowly, and they are blown by the wind.
2. Many have tried around-the-world flights, but few have succeeded.

Complex Sentences

Adjective and Adverb Clauses

- Diagram the main clause first. Diagram the subordinate clause on its own horizontal line below the main line.
- Use a dotted line to connect the word introducing the clause to the word it modifies.

Adjective Clause

The pilot is the person who controls a hot-air balloon.

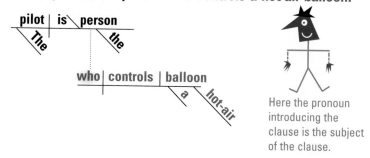

Here the pronoun introducing the clause is the subject of the clause.

Adverb Clause

After the balloon lands, the pilot releases the air.

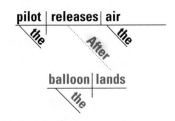

The conjunction goes on the dotted line, which connects the verbs in the two clauses.

Noun Clause

- Diagram the main clause first.
- Figure out what role the subordinate clause plays in the sentence.
- Diagram the subordinate clause on a separate line that is attached to the main line with a vertical forked line.
- Place the forked line in the diagram according to the role of the noun clause in the sentence.
- Diagram the word introducing the noun clause according to its function in the clause.

You may wonder how balloons come down.

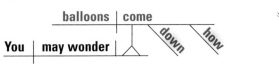

The noun clause functions as the direct object in this sentence.

Diagram these sentences, using what you have learned.

1. Someone who plans trips is a navigator.
2. While the trip continues, the navigator gives directions.
3. The navigator may tell the driver where he should turn.

H. MIXED REVIEW: Diagramming

Diagram the following sentences.

1. The campers planned a canoe trip, and they packed their duffels.
2. They drove for three hours before they put their canoes in the water.
3. When they reached their destination, they were very tired.
4. Some of the campers pitched their tents where they could find shelter.
5. They frowned at the other campers who did not help.
6. They asked why the others had come.
7. The campers who had been resting soon got busy.
8. They unpacked pots and pans, and they searched the duffels for food.
9. Because they could not find the food, they looked for edible plants.
10. What they finally prepared was dandelion greens.

Quick-Fix Editing Machine

You've worked hard on your assignment. Don't let misplaced commas, sentence fragments, and missing details lower your grade. Use this Quick-Fix Editing Guide to help you detect grammatical errors and make your writing more precise.

QUICK FIX

1 Sentence Fragments

What's the problem? Part of a sentence has been left out.

Why does it matter? A fragment can be confusing because it does not express a complete thought.

What should you do about it? Find out what is missing and add it.

What's the Problem?

Quick Fix

A. A subject is missing.

Feature four wheels in a row.

Add a subject.

In-line skates feature four wheels in a row.

B. A predicate is missing.

In-line skates first in the 1700s.

Add a predicate.

In-line skates first **appeared** in the 1700s.

C. Both a subject and a predicate are missing.

Probably the world's first roller skates.

Add a subject and a predicate to make an independent clause.

They were probably the world's first roller skates.

D. A dependent clause is treated as if it were a sentence.

Because they were much faster than traditional roller skates.

Combine the fragment with an independent clause.

They became popular because they were much faster than traditional roller skates.

OR

Delete the conjunction.

~~Because~~ they were much faster than traditional roller skates.

For more help, see Chapter 1, pp. 25–27.

Run-On Sentences

What's the problem? Two or more sentences have been written as though they were a single sentence.

Why does it matter? A run-on sentence doesn't show where one idea ends and another begins.

What should you do about it? Find the best way to separate the ideas or to show the proper relationship between them.

What's the Problem?

Quick Fix

A. The end mark separating two sentences is missing.

The computer store is a popular spot many kids visit it.

Add an end mark and start a new sentence.

The computer store is a popular spot. Many kids visit it.

B. Two sentences are separated only by a comma.

My sister wanted an inexpensive game, she rummaged through the sale bins.

Add a coordinating conjunction.

My sister wanted an inexpensive game, **so** she rummaged through the sale bins.

OR

Change the comma to a semicolon.

My sister wanted an inexpensive game**;** she rummaged through the sale bins.

OR

Replace the comma with an end mark and start a new sentence.

My sister wanted an inexpensive game. **S**he rummaged through the sale bins.

OR

Change one of the independent clauses to a dependent clause.

Because my sister wanted an inexpensive game, she rummaged through the sale bins.

For more help, see Chapter 1, pp. 25–27.

QUICK FIX

3 Subject-Verb Agreement

What's the problem? A verb does not agree with its subject in number.

Why does it matter? Readers may think your work is careless.

What should you do about it? Identify the subject and use a verb that matches it in number.

What's the Problem?	Quick Fix
A. The first helping verb in a verb phrase does not agree with the subject. **We has** been practicing our strokes for several weeks.	Decide whether the subject is singular or plural, and make the helping verb agree with it. We **have** been practicing our strokes for several weeks.
B. The contraction doesn't agree with its subject. The other **students doesn't** know how scared I am.	Use a contraction that agrees with the subject. The other **students don't** know how scared I am.
C. A singular verb is used with a compound subject containing *and.* **Reina and the instructor plunges** into the water first.	Use a plural verb with a compound subject joined by *and.* **Reina and the instructor plunge** into the water first.
D. A verb doesn't agree with the nearer part of a compound subject containing *or* or *nor.* Neither the instructor nor the **students uses** the diving board.	Make the verb agree with the nearer part of the compound subject. Neither the instructor nor the **students use** the diving board.
E. A verb doesn't agree with an indefinite-pronoun subject. **Each** of my friends **hope** to pass this class.	Decide whether the pronoun is singular or plural, and make the verb agree with it. **Each** of my friends **hopes** to pass this class.

For more help, see Chapter 9, pp. 206–227.

What's the Problem?

Quick Fix

F. A collective noun referring to a single unit is treated as plural.

The **class are** using this time to practice.

If the collective noun refers to a single unit, use a singular verb.

The **class is** using this time to practice.

G. A singular subject ending in *s* or *ics* is mistaken for a plural.

Like swimming, **mathematics are** fun.

Watch out for these nouns and use singular verbs with them.

Like swimming, mathematics is fun.

H. A verb doesn't agree with the true subject of a sentence beginning with *here* or *there*.

There is encouraging words from my classmates.

Mentally turn the sentence around so that the subject comes first, and make the verb agree with it.

There are encouraging words from my classmates.

I. A verb agrees with the object of a preposition rather than with its subject.

The sound of their **voices give** me confidence.

Mentally block out the prepositional phrase and make the verb agree with the subject.

The sound of their voices gives me confidence.

J. A plural verb is used with a period of time or an amount.

Four weeks are all it took for me to pass the test!

Thirty dollars are what it cost!

Use a singular verb.

Four weeks is all it took for me to pass the test!

Thirty dollars is what it cost.

For more help, see Chapter 9, pp. 206–227.

QUICK FIX

4 Pronoun Reference Problems

What's the problem? A pronoun does not agree in number, person, or gender with its antecedent, or an antecedent is unclear.

Why does it matter? Lack of agreement or unclear antecedents can confuse your reader.

What should you do about it? Find the antecedent and make the pronoun agree with it, or rewrite the sentence to make the antecedent clear.

What's the Problem?

Quick Fix

What's the Problem?	Quick Fix
A. A pronoun doesn't agree in number with its antecedent. Every **town** has **their** deserted house.	Make the pronoun agree in number with the antecedent. Every **town** has **its** deserted house.
B. A pronoun doesn't agree in person or in gender with its antecedent. **Kids** know **you** should stay away from a deserted house.	Make the pronoun agree with the antecedent. **Kids** know **they** should stay away from a deserted house.
C. A pronoun doesn't agree with an indefinite-pronoun antecedent. **Anyone** can claim that **they** saw something extraordinary.	Decide whether the indefinite pronoun is singular or plural, and make the pronoun agree with it. **Anyone** can claim that **he or she** saw something extraordinary.
D. A pronoun could refer to more than one noun. **Roberto** and **Ishi** went into a deserted house. **He** saw something strange.	Substitute a noun for the pronoun to make the reference clear. Roberto and Ishi went into a deserted house. **Ishi** saw something strange.
E. A pronoun agrees with a noun in a phrase rather than with its antecedent. Ishi, like many **people,** let **their** imagination run wild.	Mentally block out the phrase and make the pronoun agree with its antecedent. Ishi, ~~like many people,~~ let **his** imagination run wild.

For more help, see Chapter 3, pp. 76–83.

⑤ Incorrect Pronoun Case

What's the problem? A pronoun is in the wrong case.

Why does it matter? Readers may think your work is careless, especially if you are writing a school paper or formal letter.

What should you do about it? Identify how the pronoun is being used, and replace it with the correct form.

What's the Problem?

Quick Fix

What's the Problem?	Quick Fix
A. A pronoun that follows a linking verb is not in the subject case. The best all-around player **is her**.	Always use the subject case after a linking verb. The best all-around player **is she**.
B. A pronoun used as an object is not in the objective case. Andrea **asked** Inez and **I** to practice.	A pronoun takes the objective case when it is used as an indirect object, a direct object, or the object of a preposition. Andrea **asked** Inez and **me** to practice.
C. A pronoun in a compound subject is in the wrong case. **Ben and me** will start the game.	Always use the subject case when a pronoun is part of a compound subject. **Ben and I** will start the game.
D. A pronoun followed by an identifying noun is in the wrong case. **Us players** are ready to play. They told **we fans** to yell louder.	Mentally drop the noun and decide whether the pronoun is a subject or an object. We ~~players~~ are ready to play. They told **us** ~~fans~~ to yell louder.
E. A contraction is used instead of a possessive pronoun. **You're game** has really improved!	A possessive pronoun never has an apostrophe. **Your game** has really improved!

For more help, see Chapter 3, pp. 61–64.

QUICK FIX

Who and *Whom*

What's the problem? The pronoun *who* or *whom* is used incorrectly.

Why does it matter? When writers use *who* and *whom* correctly, readers are more likely to take their ideas seriously.

What should you do about it? Decide how the pronoun functions in the sentence, and then choose the correct form.

QUICK FIX

What's the Problem?

Quick Fix

What's the Problem?	Quick Fix
A. *Whom* is incorrectly used as the subject pronoun. **Whom is knocking** at our door?	Use *who* as the subject pronoun. **Who is knocking** at the door?
B. *Whom* is incorrectly used as a predicate pronoun. The visitor **is whom?**	Use *who* as the predicate pronoun. The visitor **is who?**
C. *Who* is incorrectly used as a direct object. **Who can** we **send** to answer the door?	Use *whom* as a direct object. **Whom can** we **send** to answer the door?
D. *Who* is incorrectly used as the object of a preposition. A basket was left **by who?**	Use *whom* as the object of a preposition. A basket was left **by whom?**
E. *Who* is incorrectly used as an indirect object. You **gave who** our address?	Use *whom* as an indirect object. You **gave whom** our address?
F. *Who's* is confused with the possessive pronoun *whose*. **Who's puppy** is in this basket?	Always use *whose* to show possession. **Whose puppy** is in this basket?

For more help, see Chapter 3, pp. 70–71.

Confusing Comparisons

What's the problem? The wrong form of an adjective or adverb is used when making a comparison.

Why does it matter? Comparisons that are not worded correctly can be confusing.

What should you do about it? Use a form that makes the comparison clear.

What's the Problem?

Quick Fix

A. Both *-er* and *more* or *-est* and *most* are used in making a comparison.

In the 1920s, cosmetics manufacturers used some of the **most strangest** ingredients in lipstick.

Delete one of the forms from the sentence.

In the 1920s, cosmetics manufacturers used some of the ~~most~~ **strangest** ingredients in lipstick.

B. A comparative form is used where a superlative form is needed.

In fact, dangerous ingredients made lipstick one of the **more** unhealthy cosmetics of that time.

When comparing more than two things, use the superlative form.

In fact, dangerous ingredients made lipstick one of the **most** unhealthy cosmetics of that time.

C. A superlative form is used where a comparative form is needed.

I'm not sure which ingredient was **worst**—spoiled olive oil or dried and crushed insects.

When comparing two things, use the comparative form.

I'm not sure which ingredient was **worse**—spoiled olive oil or dried and crushed insects.

For more help, see Chapter 5, pp. 137–139.

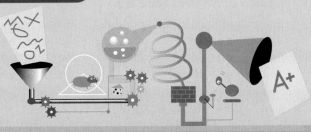

Verb Forms and Tenses

What's the problem? The wrong form or tense of a verb is used.

Why does it matter? Readers may regard your work as careless or find it confusing.

What should you do about it? Change the verb to the correct form or tense.

What's the Problem?

Quick Fix

What's the Problem?	Quick Fix
A. The wrong form of a verb is used with a helping verb. Soft drinks **have rose** in popularity over the past several decades.	Always use a participle form with a helping verb. Soft drinks **have risen** in popularity over the past several decades.
B. A helping verb is missing. One consumer group **spoken** out against this trend.	Add a helping verb. One consumer group **has spoken** out against this trend.
C. A past participle is used incorrectly. Several decades ago, teens **drunk** twice as much milk as soda pop.	To write about the past, use the past form of a verb. Several decades ago, teens **drank** twice as much milk as soda pop. **OR** Change the verb to the past perfect form by adding a helping verb. Several decades ago, teens **had drunk** twice as much milk as soda pop.
D. Different tenses are used in the same sentence even though no change in time has occurred. Some heavy soda drinkers **drink** as many as five cans a day and **got** one fourth of their calories from these beverages.	Use the same tense throughout the sentence. Some heavy soda drinkers **drink** as many as five cans a day and **get** one fourth of their calories from these beverages.

For more help, see Chapter 4, pp. 100–114.

What's the problem? Commas are missing or are used incorrectly.

Why does it matter? The incorrect use of commas can make sentences hard to follow.

What should you do about it? Figure out where commas are needed, and add them as necessary.

What's the Problem?

Quick Fix

A. A comma is missing from a compound sentence.

Certain plants capture insects and they use them for food.

Add a comma before the coordinating conjunction.

Certain plants capture insects, and they use them for food.

B. A comma is incorrectly placed after a closing quotation mark.

"One such plant is a Venus flytrap", remarked our teacher.

Always put a comma before a closing quotation mark.

"One such plant is a Venus flytrap," remarked our teacher.

C. A comma is missing before the conjunction in a series.

Reggie, Shayna and I hurriedly took notes on the exhibit.

Add a comma.

Reggie, Shayna, and I hurriedly took notes on the exhibit.

D. A comma is missing after an introductory word, phrase, or clause.

After an insect touches the sensitive hairs on a leaf the plant closes like a jaw.

Add a comma after the introductory word, phrase, or clause.

After an insect touches the sensitive hairs on a leaf, the plant closes like a jaw.

E. Commas are missing around an appositive or a clause that is not essential to the meaning of the sentence.

The Venus flytrap which is a fascinating plant takes ten days to digest its prey.

Add commas to set off the nonessential appositive or clause. Remember that a clause beginning with *which* is preceded by a comma.

The Venus flytrap, which is a fascinating plant, takes ten days to digest its prey.

For more help, see Chapter 11, pp. 253–255.

QUICK FIX

⑩ Improving Weak Sentences

What's the problem? A sentence repeats ideas or contains too many ideas.

Why does it matter? Repetitive or overloaded sentences can bore readers and weaken the message.

What should you do about it? Make sure that every sentence contains a clearly focused idea.

QUICK FIX

What's the Problem?	Quick Fix
A. An idea is repeated. We recently read a news story about bugs **that was in the newspaper.**	**Eliminate the repeated idea.** We recently read a news story about bugs, ~~that was in the newspaper.~~ ⊙
B. A single sentence contains too many loosely connected ideas. Radioactive flies and gnats were discovered at a nuclear site in Washington, and officials insisted there was no danger to the public, and one spokesperson said that these insects won't leave the area and they don't fly very far.	**Divide the sentence into two or more sentences, using conjunctions such as *and, but, when,* and *because* to show relationships between ideas.** **When** radioactive flies and gnats were discovered at a nuclear site in Washington, officials insisted there was no danger to the public. **One** spokesperson said that these insects won't ever leave the area **because** they don't fly very far.
C. Too much information about a topic is crammed into one sentence. The nuclear plant is working to get rid of the insects, but authorities insist that the bugs are no threat to people since according to one expert, a person would have to stand on a contaminated spot for an hour to get exposure equal to a dental x-ray.	**Divide the sentence into two or more sentences, using conjunctions such as *and, but, when,* and *although* to show relationships between ideas.** **Although** the nuclear plant is working to get rid of the insects, authorities insist that the bugs are no threat to people. **According** to one expert, a person would have to stand on a contaminated spot for an hour to get exposure equal to a dental x-ray.

For more help, see Chapter 18, pp. 388–391.

11 Avoiding Wordiness

What's the problem? A sentence contains unnecessary words.

Why does it matter? The meaning of wordy sentences can be unclear to readers.

What should you do about it? Use words that are precise and eliminate extra words.

What's the Problem?

	Quick Fix
A. A single idea is unnecessarily expressed in two ways. At 7:30 A.M. **in the morning,** Marissa has to walk two miles to her summer job. She has a job that doesn't pay well, **and she doesn't make much money.**	**Delete the unnecessary words.** At 7:30 A.M. ~~in the morning~~ Marissa has to walk two miles to her summer job. She has a job that doesn't pay well ~~and she doesn't make much money.~~
B. A simple idea is expressed in too many words. I **am of the opinion** that Marissa needs a bike. She should ride a bike to work **on account of the fact** she can get there quickly.	**Simplify the expression.** I **think** that Marissa needs a bike. She should ride a bike to work **so** she can get there quickly.
C. A sentence contains words that do not add to its meaning. **What I mean to say is** Marissa should save her money to buy a bike. **I have to tell you that** Marissa could save the money in just three months.	**Delete the unnecessary words.** ~~What I mean to say is~~ Marissa should save her money to buy a bike. ~~I have to tell you that~~ Marissa could save the money in just three months.

For more help, see Chapter 18, pp. 388–389.

12 Varying Sentence Structure

What's the problem? Too many sentences begin the same way, or too many sentences of one kind are used.

Why does it matter? Lack of variety in sentences makes writing dull and choppy.

What should you do about it? Rearrange the phrases in some of your sentences, and use different types of sentences for variety and impact.

What's the Problem?

Quick Fix

A. Too many sentences in a paragraph begin the same way.

The fans crowded the sidewalks and waited for the stars to arrive at the premiere. **The fans** screamed and watched their favorite actors enter the theater. The stars waved to their adoring public.

Rearrange words or phrases in some of the sentences.

Crowding the sidewalks, the fans waited for the stars to arrive at the premiere. **As their favorite actors entered the theater,** the fans screamed. The stars waved to their adoring public.

B. Too many declarative sentences are used.

There's the camera crew. My friend waves frantically. The crew hardly notice, because they're searching only for famous faces. They don't find any, since all the stars are already inside the theater.

Add variety by rewriting one sentence as a command, question, or exclamation.

Is that the camera crew? My friend waves frantically. The crew hardly notice, because they're searching only for famous faces. They don't find any, since all the stars are already inside the theater.

For more help, see Chapter 18, pp. 392–393.

13 Varying Sentence Length

What's the problem? A piece of writing contains too many short, repetitive sentences.

Why does it matter? The use of too many short, repetitive sentences makes writing choppy and monotonous.

What should you do about it? Combine or reword sentences to create sentences of varying lengths.

What's the Problem?

Too many short, repetitive sentences are used.

The flea market promised many bargains. The flea market was huge. It was outdoors. Bargain hunters explored every table. They were cheerful. One teen sold used video games. A man sold floral arrangements. One group enjoyed the antics of a clown. At the same time others sampled many different foods. The flea market is held every year. People save their treasures all year long. They can sell them at the market.

Quick Fix

Eliminate repetitive sentences that add only one detail about the subject. Insert those details into other sentences.

The **huge outdoor** flea market promised many bargains. **Cheerful** bargain hunters explored every table.

OR

Use a conjunction such as *or, and,* or *but* to combine related sentences.

One teen sold used video games, **and** a man sold floral arrangements.

OR

Form a complex sentence, using a word such as *because, while,* or *although* to combine ideas.

While one group enjoyed the antics of a clown, others sampled many different foods.

OR

Combine the sentences to form a compound-complex sentence.

The flea market is held every year, **and** people save their treasures all year long **so** they can sell them at the market.

For more help, see Chapter 8, pp. 189–199, and Chapter 18, pp. 394–395.

QUICK FIX

14 Adding Supporting Details

What's the problem? Not enough details are given for readers to fully understand the topic.

Why does it matter? Questions that aren't answered or opinions that aren't supported weaken a piece of writing.

What should you do about it? Add information and details that will make words and statements clear.

What's the Problem?	Quick Fix
A. An important word is not explained.	Explain or define the word.
In 1925, **diphtheria** threatened the town of Nome, Alaska.	In 1925, diphtheria, **a serious and sometimes fatal disease,** threatened the town of Nome, Alaska.
B. No details are given.	Add details that would help readers understand the significance of an event.
Dog-sled teams delivered medical supplies.	**Twenty** dog-sled teams relayed **almost 700 miles from Anchorage, Alaska, in five days** to deliver **desperately needed** medical supplies.
C. No supporting facts are given.	Add supporting facts.
The Iditarod Sled Dog Race is held every year.	Every year, the Iditarod Sled Dog Race is held **to honor the people and dogs who participated in that rescue mission.**
D. No reason is given for an opinion.	Add a reason.
There is probably no competitive sport in the world more grueling than this one.	There is probably no competitive sport in the world more grueling than this one. **The drivers and dog teams race more than 1,000 miles in high winds and frigid temperatures. They take two to three weeks to reach the finish line.**

For more help, see Chapter 17, pp. 376–381.

15 Avoiding Clichés and Slang

What's the problem? A piece of formal writing contains clichés or slang expressions.

Why does it matter? Clichés do not convey fresh images to readers. Slang is not appropriate in formal writing.

What should you do about it? Reword sentences, replacing the clichés and slang with clear, fresh expressions.

What's the Problem?

Quick Fix

A. A sentence contains a cliché.

Replace the cliché with a fresh description or explanation.

The workers were **as busy as bees.**

The workers **bounced from one task to another.**

One person, though, was **as slow as molasses.**

One person, though, was **as slow as leaves falling from a tree.**

B. A sentence contains inappropriate slang.

Replace the slang with more appropriate language.

The new gymnastics equipment was **the bomb.**

The new gymnastics equipment **would help us prepare for the state meet.**

For more help, see Chapter 19, pp. 402–403 and 408–409.

QUICK FIX

16 Using Precise Words

What's the problem? Nouns, modifiers, and verbs are not precise.

Why does it matter? Writers who use vague or general words don't give readers an accurate picture of their topic.

What should you do about it? Replace vague words with precise and vivid ones.

What's the Problem?

Quick Fix

A. Nouns are too general.

The **people** strapped on their **equipment** and moved into the **street.**

Use specific nouns.

The **anxious skaters** strapped on their **helmets and protective pads** and moved to the **starting line.**

B. Modifiers are too general.

Soon they would be able to show off their **great** skills on **city** streets.

Use vivid adjectives and adverbs.

Immediately, they would show off their **impressive** skills on **winding** city streets.

C. Verbs tell about the action rather than showing it.

The wind **is** against the contestants as they **go** down a steep driveway. The racers **go** around the statue in the park. A barricade forces the skaters to **go** onto the grass.

Use vivid verbs to show the action.

The wind **slaps** the contestants as they **zoom** down a steep driveway. The racers **orbit** the statue in the park. An unexpected barricade forces the skaters to **swerve** onto the grass.

For more help, see Chapter 19, pp. 404–405.

QUICK FIX

⑰ Using Figurative Language

What's the problem? A piece of writing is dull or unimaginative.

Why does it matter? Dull writing bores readers because it doesn't help them form mental pictures of what is being described.

What should you do about it? Add figures of speech to make writing lively and to create pictures in readers' minds.

What's the Problem?

A description is dull and lifeless.

Hopelessly bored, we left the house in search of excitement. We trudged down a narrow path toward the park.

All around us the snow was gray.

We stopped at a yard with snow that looked like whipped cream. The gate was half open.

Quick Fix

Add a simile.

Hopelessly bored, we left the house in search of excitement. We trudged down a narrow path toward the park **like an army of defeated soldiers.**

OR

Add a metaphor.

All around us the snow was **a gray carpet in need of a cleaning.**

OR

Use personification.

We stopped at a yard with snow that looked like whipped cream. **The half-open gate invited us to enter.**

For more help, see Chapter 19, pp. 408–409.

(18) **Paragraphing**

What's the problem? A paragraph contains too many ideas.

Why does it matter? A long paragraph discourages readers from continuing.

What should you do about it? Break the paragraph into smaller paragraphs. Start a new paragraph whenever a new idea is presented or the time, place, or speaker changes.

What's the Problem?

Too many ideas are contained in one paragraph.

Although Aunt Leona isn't known for her cooking ability, she offered to help me bake a birthday cake for my mom's party. I accepted her offer because I'm not known for my cooking ability either. After spending the whole morning in the kitchen, we got something into the oven, but what a mess we had afterward. The kitchen looked like the scene of a science experiment gone awry. Then real disaster struck. The cake broke into chunks when we took it out of the oven. "Oh, Aunt Leona!" I groaned. "How can we fix this mess?" "I have an idea," she said. Later that day we served the cake chunks with strawberries and chocolate sauce. Mom and the guests were quite impressed. Aunt Leona had turned disaster into success.

Quick Fix

Although Aunt Leona isn't known for her cooking ability, she offered to help me bake a birthday cake for my mom's party. I accepted her offer because I'm not known for my cooking ability either.

Start a new paragraph to introduce a new idea.

After spending the whole morning in the kitchen, we got something into the oven, but what a mess we had afterward. The kitchen looked like the scene of a science experiment gone awry. Then real disaster struck. The cake broke into chunks when we took it out of the oven.

Start a new paragraph whenever the speaker changes.

"Oh, Aunt Leona!" I groaned. "How can we fix this mess?"

"I have an idea," she said.

Start a new paragraph when the time or place changes.

Later that day we served the cake chunks with strawberries and chocolate sauce. Mom and the guests were quite impressed. Aunt Leona had turned disaster into success.

For more help, see Chapter 16, pp. 368–370.

What's the Problem?

An essay is treated as one long paragraph.

Scary, gigantic beasts are often the subject of today's horror films. However, tales of scary monsters have been told for centuries. One monster that appears in many tales is the fire-breathing dragon. Is it possible that the storytellers were referring to the Komodo dragon? Although it's no monster, the Komodo dragon is the world's largest lizard. It lives on Komodo Island in Indonesia and was discovered in 1912. Before scientists visited the island, rumors about giant dragons persisted. Today we know many facts about this remarkable animal. The Komodo dragon can be as long as 12 feet and weigh as much as 300 pounds. This lizard has strong claws and sharp, sawlike teeth. It eats dead animals as well as live prey. The Komodo dragon does not breathe fire, but it is fearsome. Unlike the dragons in old tales, however, Komodo dragons are protected from hunters, who nearly caused the lizards' extinction.

For more help, see Chapter 16, pp. 368–370.

Quick Fix

Scary, gigantic beasts are often the subject of today's horror films. However, tales of scary monsters have been told for centuries.

Start a new paragraph to introduce the first main idea.

One monster that appears in many tales is the fire-breathing dragon. Is it possible that the storytellers were referring to the Komodo dragon? Although it's no monster, the Komodo dragon is the world's largest lizard. It lives on Komodo Island in Indonesia and was discovered in 1912. Before scientists visited the island, rumors about giant dragons persisted.

Start a new paragraph to introduce another main idea.

Today we know many facts about this remarkable animal. The Komodo dragon can be as long as 12 feet and weigh as much as 300 pounds. This lizard has strong claws and sharp, sawlike teeth. It eats dead animals as well as live prey.

Start a new paragraph to give the conclusion.

The Komodo dragon does not breathe fire, but it is fearsome. Unlike the dragons in old tales, however, Komodo dragons are protected from hunters, who nearly caused the lizards' extinction.

QUICK FIX

Essential Writing Skills

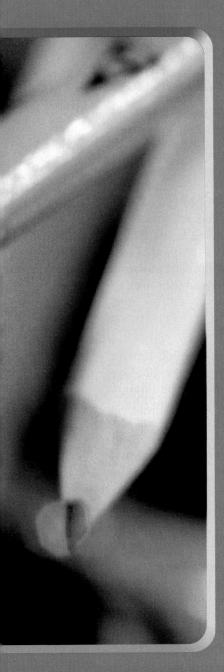

Ready, Set, Write!

Writing doesn't start with a sharpened pencil — it starts with ideas. When you write, you need to choose words carefully, put ideas in order, and include interesting details. Soon you'll be able to express your ideas in a style that's all your own.

Power Words
Vocabulary for Precise Writing

Thrilling or Scary?

The next time you face a challenge that scares you a little, use some of these words to express how you feel.

Ready to Go

Aren't you **excited** and **thrilled** when you play your favorite sport? You feel **energized, enthusiastic,** even **exhilarated.** You're **champing at the bit,** which means that you're **eager** to show what you can do. Whether you're playing soccer, baseball, or chess, sports and games can **focus** your mind and make you feel **invigorated.**

Afraid to Take the Plunge?

Some hobbies require a bit more **daring.** Jumping out of an airplane is a **terrifying** thing to do. Even with a parachute, it's **frightening,** maybe even **horrifying** if you don't like **alarming** heights. The plane climbs to a **fearsome** altitude that has you **petrified.** Then you take a deep breath and decide that this **daunting** challenge isn't going to **strike fear into** you anymore—and off you go, to a safe, soft landing.

▷ **Your Turn** A Web of Challenges

With a partner, think of an activity that would excite you and scare you at the same time, such as hang-gliding, climbing Mount Everest, or giving a speech in front of a big audience. Together, make a word web of all the emotions you both would feel.

Writing Process

Taking the Plunge

You've just been assigned to write a paper. You can probably think of 100 things you'd rather do—even organize your sock drawer. The answer may be just to plunge in and start writing. Think of writing as a roller-coaster ride. You may take some unexpected turns, go backwards, or even go in circles sometimes, but in the end you might find yourself saying, "That wasn't so bad after all."

Write Away: Jump Right In
Think of a time you had to do something that frightened you. Maybe you didn't want to try it at first, but you jumped right in anyway. Write a paragraph about one of these experiences that turned out better than you expected. Put your paragraph in your ⌐ **Working Portfolio.**

Prewriting: Finding a Topic

In the writing process, two things are certain. You begin with a blank page, and you end up with a final draft. Otherwise, each writer works through the writing process—prewriting, drafting, revising, editing, and publishing—in a different way. You may need to repeat steps or switch the order. But the first step is always finding something to write about. Taking a self-inventory, freewriting, and brainstorming are three helpful ways to begin the writing process and find a topic.

"Writing is an exploration.
You start from nothing and learn as you go."

—E.L. Doctorow

❶ Taking a Self-Inventory

Choosing a topic allows you to write about whatever interests you. You probably have a lot of interests, so how do you choose one? One way is to take a self-inventory. Ask yourself the following questions:

- What are some interesting, funny, weird, or annoying things that happened this week?
- What is my favorite way to spend my spare time?
- Who is the most interesting or unusual person I know? What makes that person unique?
- What community issues interest me? Why?
- What fascinates me? confuses me? troubles me? surprises me?
- What do I know a lot about?

Many writers explore ideas in a writer's journal. Throughout the day, try jotting down thoughts and ideas in your journal.

For more on finding ideas, see pg. 322.

❷ Freewriting

When you freewrite, put pencil to paper and write whatever comes to mind. Write without stopping for at least ten minutes, letting one idea flow into the next. After ten minutes, stop and circle any ideas you like. Then freewrite about one or two of those ideas until you hit on a topic that interests you.

STUDENT MODEL

What a great day! I wish I didn't have to be in (school.) At least I got to ride my (bike)—except for one thing that really bothered me when I rode past the (train station.) The (trash) can was totally gross & overflowing which made me mad because it was full of (newspapers) that could have been (recycled) except that they were all slimy from the garbage thrown on top of them.

❸ Brainstorming

Brainstorming is a way to come up with ideas in a group. For ten minutes or so, each member of the group offers ideas for topics while one person writes them down. Don't criticize suggestions or try to choose a topic while you brainstorm. When the time is up, read over the list and choose the idea you like best.

sharks
music
outer space
ballet

hot-air balloons
Grand Canyon
baseball
environmental issues

WATCH OUT

Decide on a topic early so you'll have time to research, draft, and edit your work long before your paper is due.

Prewriting: Narrowing and Exploring a Topic

Once you've decided on a topic, narrow it so that you won't be overwhelmed by information when you start to research it. It's easier to focus on only one aspect of a broad topic. Try narrowing your topic by making a cluster diagram and by considering audience and purpose.

❶ Focusing a Topic

Creating a Cluster Diagram

Suppose you decided to write about environmental issues in your community. You could narrow that topic by making a cluster diagram like the one below. The general topic is in a large oval, while different aspects of that topic are in smaller ovals. You could choose one aspect to focus on in your writing.

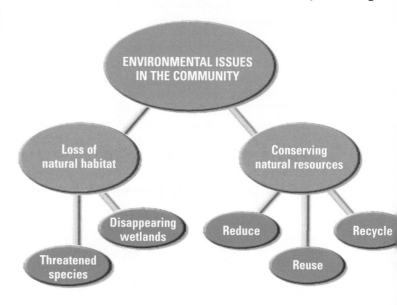

As a way of enlarging your cluster diagram, you can ask yourself questions. For example, ask yourself: What more do I already know about this topic? or What more do I want to know about this topic?

Identifying Audience and Purpose

After you've narrowed your topic, ask yourself two questions: "*Why* am I writing this?" and "To *whom* am I writing?" These questions will identify your purpose and your audience.

1. I want to persuade the student body to recycle.

2. I want to tell a story to my best friend about the day my grandmother and I rode in a hot-air balloon.

3. I want to describe for my classmates the geological formations in the Grand Canyon.

4. I want to explain to the community what happens to forest life when hundreds of trees are cut down.

Once you decide on a topic, think about what you want to say in your writing and who will be reading it. In order to focus your efforts, write your own "I want to . . ." sentence before you begin researching your topic.

❷ Developing a Topic

Asking Specific Questions

You can develop your topic by asking yourself specific questions. Ask **informative** questions to help yourself find out how much you already know and what more you'd like to know. Ask **imaginative** questions to help spark ideas about unusual aspects of your topic.

Informative
- How many households in the community recycle?
- How many different materials can be recycled?

Imaginative
- If every scrap of paper in the country were recycled, how many acres of forests would be saved?
- What would happen if we started fining people for not recycling?

Researching a Topic

Calvin and Hobbes by Bill Watterson

Calvin may have some trouble writing about bats if he doesn't know much about them. Before you begin writing a draft, do some fact-finding. Check the following sources at the library:

- books
- encyclopedias
- the Internet
- magazines

You could also interview an expert in the field.

Finding information can seem overwhelming. Try to stay focused on what you are looking for instead of getting sidetracked by interesting information that doesn't relate to your topic.

For more on finding information, see p. 493.

❸ Organizing Information

One simple way to organize your information is to list all the things you want to discuss in your report. Once you've made the list, you can experiment with rearranging the order.

STUDENT MODEL

- Why we should recycle
- Strengths and weaknesses of our recycling program
- How our recycling program can be improved
- How kids can get involved in our recycling program

Ways to organize writing include sequential order, spatial order, cause-and-effect order, and compare-and-contrast order.

For more on organizing, see pg. 351.

Drafting

It might surprise you, but there are no set guidelines for writing your first draft. Some writers start in the middle and add the introduction during a later draft. The important thing is to start writing! With each draft, your ideas will change, develop, and come into sharper focus.

PROFESSIONAL MODEL

> Start by getting something—anything—down on paper. A friend of mine says the first draft is the down draft—you just get it down. The second draft is the up draft—you fix it up. . . . And the third draft is the dental draft, where you check every tooth, to see if it's loose or cramped or even . . . healthy.
>
> —Anne Lamott, *Bird by Bird*

❶ Types of Drafting

You may find that different types of writing call for different types of drafting. To write a report or proposal, you may need to plan out the draft. Personal narratives and short stories may benefit from a discovery draft.

Drafting from a Plan

Suppose that at the organizing stage you made a list of the points you want to cover in your paper. Now you can go back to that list and add more specific details. You may want to think of your paper in terms of an introduction, body, and conclusion and list information that way. Refer to your plan as you write.

Drafting to Discover

Perhaps making an orderly list doesn't appeal to you, and you'd rather just start writing and see what happens. You may find that your discovery draft takes some unexpected twists and turns. These can actually help define the direction of your writing, or you may need to go back and reorganize.

Don't be surprised if, while you draft, you decide to drop some ideas, rearrange other ideas, or even add new ideas.

❷ Using Peer Response

After you finish a draft, it's often helpful to get some feedback from your peers, or classmates.

As the writer you should . . .	As the reader you should . . .
• ask the reader specific questions • use only those suggestions that make sense to you • encourage the reader to be honest • listen politely, and be open-minded	• offer specific feedback • give positive comments first • be sensitive to the writer's feelings • carefully consider the writer's questions

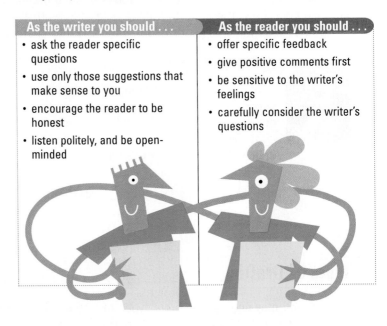

- **Group Response** With a group response, two or more readers review your work so that you get different points of view and suggestions. If several readers find a certain passage confusing, you may need to rethink that section.

- **One-on-One Response** A one-on-one response gives you and a classmate the chance to analyze your piece together. When you revise, it's important to keep in mind that your classmate's comments are only suggestions. As the writer, you are responsible for the final decisions.

- **E-mail Partner** If you e-mail a draft to a partner, you can include a list of questions or concerns you'd like your partner to think about as he or she reads your work. Your partner could insert comments and suggestions (in another color or typestyle) directly into your draft and e-mail it back to you.

LESSON 4 **Revising**

In the revising stage, you start making changes to your draft. As you begin revising, bear in mind the feedback you've gotten from peers. Also remember that revising often involves rewriting entire paragraphs or reorganizing information. You may have to revise several times before you are finished.

❶ Evaluating Your Draft

The following chart shows six traits of good writing. Use these six traits to help evaluate your writing and pinpoint areas that need revision.

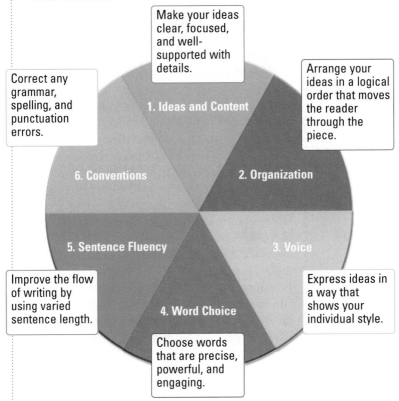

Make your ideas clear, focused, and well-supported with details.

1. Ideas and Content

Arrange your ideas in a logical order that moves the reader through the piece.

2. Organization

Correct any grammar, spelling, and punctuation errors.

6. Conventions

5. Sentence Fluency

3. Voice

Express ideas in a way that shows your individual style.

Improve the flow of writing by using varied sentence length.

4. Word Choice

Choose words that are precise, powerful, and engaging.

HOT TIP

After you've written a draft, let it "cool" for a few hours or days. Don't work on it for a while, and try not to think about it. This will give you a fresh view of your work when you return to revise it again.

WRITING PROCESS

❷ Traits in Action

The following is part of a student's draft. The student's purpose is to persuade members of her community (her audience) to make a stronger commitment to recycling. See how the six traits work throughout this draft.

STUDENT MODEL

Two weeks ago, I was cruising by the train station on my bike. But something just didn't fit in with the beautiful day and the flower-scented breezes I'd been enjoying. The station's trash cans were overflowing with newspapers, foam cups, Sportin' Life Donut bags, soda cans, and even a pair of smelly old running shoes! Bees and flies buzzed in a little cloud above the disgusting container.

Word Choice: Writer uses precise words to bring the scene to life.

Because I am concerned about the destruction of our nation's forests, I was upset that so many newspapers had been contaminated with coffee dregs, flat soda, and stale doughnut crumbs. Those newspapers could have been recycled.

Sentence Fluency: Writer uses varied sentence length and structure.

I decided to see what could be done about this problem. First I talked to Ms. Naomi Cohn, the coordinator of the Blue Hill Recycling Center. She told me that recycling a 4-foot stack of newspapers saves a 35-foot tree. Judging by how much newspaper was in the station can, I'd estimate that Blue Hill commuters "throw away" a tree a week. She also told me that placing cans for recyclables next to the trash could solve the problem.

Ideas and Content: Ideas are clear and supported with details.

Throughout the draft, notice that:

• the writer presents ideas in an **organized** way.

• the writer expresses ideas in her own **voice.**

• the writer has addressed the **conventions** of good writing.

LESSON 5

One way to edit your draft is to check it against the six traits of good writing. Revise your work until you feel it demonstrates those traits.

Proofreading will probably be the final step in your revision process. Read through your work line by line to correct errors in spelling, grammar, and punctuation. Finding errors can be tough!

Use these marks as you proofread.

Proofreading Marks

Using Proofreading Marks		
Symbol	**Explanation**	**Example**
∧	insert letters or words	I've never written a paper before. _research_
⊙	add a period	Writing can be fun⊙It's better to write about things you like.
∧	add a comma	Outer space dinosaurs and sports interest me.
#	add a space	The planet Pluto is farthest from the sun. #
ℒ	take out letters or words	The T. Rex was one of the largest big dinosaurs.
⌒	close up	I wonder how many points Michael Jordan scored dur ing his career.
¶	begin new paragraph	¶Muhammad Ali was a famous boxer.
≡	capitalize	Researching the origin of boxing in the united states might be interesting.
/	use lowercase	I think I'll do some more freewriting about sports in my Journal.
∾	switch the positions of letters or words	Once I decide which sport to focus no, I'll do a diagram cluster to narrow the topic.

 Computer spell check catches spelling mistakes, but it won't alert you to usage errors, such as _The slug tracked mud all over there rug._ Always proofread your work yourself before presenting it.

Publishing and Reflecting

Seeing your ideas appear in finished form (in print, on a computer screen, or in performance) will give you a sense of accomplishment. Knowing that others will see your work provides an extra motivation to make sure it is polished and mistake-free.

❶ Exploring Ways to Publish

Print Media
- Enclose a copy of your work in a letter to a friend.
- Get permission to post your work on a classroom bulletin board or in a public place in the school.
- Design and distribute a "zine" containing your writing and original artwork by you or a friend.
- Submit your work to your school or community newspaper.
- Enter a magazine contest.

Electronic Media
- E-mail your work to a friend or relative.
- Post your work on your school's Web site.
- Submit your work to an Internet journal or literary magazine that publishes student writing.

Performance
- Give a dramatic reading of your work to friends or family members.
- Make a radio or television "broadcast" by recording your work on audiotape or videotape.
- Dramatize your piece for an audience you choose. Add music or props to make it lively.

❷ Reflecting on Your Writing

After you've finished, look back and consider how well the writing process worked for you.

Questions for Reflection
- What part(s) of the process were easy or difficult?
- What would I do differently next time?
- What did I learn that will improve my writing skills?

Prewrite   **Draft**   **Revise**   **Edit**   **Publish**

You may need to repeat one or all of these steps to work the final draft into presentation form.

Portfolios

You can save all your writing in folders called portfolios.

🗀 Working Portfolio
This portfolio will probably contain the bulk of your work. Even if a piece didn't turn out as well as you had hoped, save it in your working portfolio. You may refer back to work in this portfolio to track your progress as a writer.

🗀 Presentation Portfolio
Reserve this portfolio for work that best demonstrates your writing skills. These pieces are ready for publication and may travel with you into next year. If you rework and improve a piece from your **Working Portfolio,** you can place the new version in your Presentation Portfolio.

Student Help Desk

Writing Process at a Glance

Prewriting Drafting

Revising and Proofreading

Publishing and Presenting

Finding a Topic Keep Ideas *Flowing*

A journal can serve as a valuable writing tool and a source of ideas.

- Carry your journal around with you.
- Jot down things you find funny, weird, sad, annoying, or frustrating.
- Keep a list of short story ideas.
- Write about things you want to do.
- Draw cartoons.
- Write jokes.
- Solve problems.

Editing Hints *Write* the **Right** Words

As you edit, look for these words. Check a dictionary to be sure you have used them correctly.

there, their, or they're?

who's or whose?

than or then?   affect or effect?

principle or principal?   it's or its?

sit or set?   farther or further?

Proofreading Tips

Let's Have ~~Some~~ proof

Some tips for spotting writing errors

Read backwards.	Start with the end and read sentence by sentence to the beginning.
Find more eyes.	Ask a peer or family member to review your work after you.
Speak up!	Listen and look for mistakes while you read the piece out loud.
Is there an echo in here? echo echo	Read each sentence twice, out loud or to yourself. Be sure to read slowly.

Getting Published

Submissions, Please!

Whether you are submitting to magazines, books, journals, on-line publications, or radio or TV programs, consider the following:

1. Write the publisher for submission guidelines.
2. Be sure your piece meets the publisher's specifications.
3. Proofread and edit your work one more time before you send it.
4. Include a cover letter and/or a tape of your oral reading, and a SASE (self-addressed stamped envelope).
5. Don't be discouraged if your piece isn't chosen after the first submission. Try, try again!

The Bottom Line

Checklist for Writing

Have I used the six traits of good writing and . . .

____ presented my ideas clearly and used supporting details?

____ logically organized my writing?

____ made my sentences flow smoothly?

____ used precise words?

____ expressed ideas in my own way?

____ spelled every word correctly?

Power Words
Vocabulary for Precise Writing

sarcastic

solemn

smirk

joyous

gloomy

melancholy

self-conscious

Face Talk

When you try to describe someone's expression, you will need more than just the words "smile" and "frown."

Smile, Simper, or Smirk?

When you look at the Mona Lisa on the facing page, you may wonder why she is smiling. Then you might ask, Is that really a smile? Perhaps it's her attempt at a smile, and it came out a **smirk** or a **simper.** Could it even be a **sneer?**

A smile can have all kinds of emotions behind it. A **pleased** or **joyous** smile is very different from a **sarcastic, scornful,** or **derisive** smile; a **brave** smile is different from a **self-conscious** smile or a **knowing** one.

A Change of Mood

Imagine that Mona becomes tired of sitting in one position for hours on end. Her smile disappears. She seems **solemn, somber,** even **grave.** As time passes, she might appear increasingly **gloomy, downcast,** and **melancholy.** As the days turn into weeks, her face twists into a **frown, scowl,** or **glower.**

▷ **Your Turn** All Over Your Face

Work in small groups. Each person in the group should choose one of the boldfaced words above and smile or frown in a way that reflects that word. (If you need to, you can look up the words in a dictionary.) Take turns sketching each other's facial expressions. Label each sketch with the word that reflects it.

pleased

sneer

brave

glower

Building Sentences

The woman is smiling.

Making Good Even Better

Any work of art begins with a mere sketch of an idea. Although the sketch is essential, it's not a finished work. The artist adds color and texture to the sketch and improves it.

"The woman is smiling" is a pretty sketchy sentence. Like the sketch above, it needs to be expanded and improved so it will give the reader a clearer picture.

As you write, add details to produce sentences that are richer and clearer—and you may create a masterpiece.

Write Away: *Do Sweat the Small Stuff!*
Write one or more sentences describing the finished painting above to someone who has never seen it. Choose your words carefully to make your writing both accurate and descriptive. Save your work in your 📁 **Working Portfolio.**

Improving Your Sentences

Have you ever written a sentence that seemed dull to you? Have you written one that your reader had trouble understanding? You can review your sentences to make sure they are clear, accurate, and interesting. The lessons in this chapter will show you a number of techniques that you can use.

❶ Checking for Completeness

A **complete sentence** is a group of words that expresses a complete thought. Which of the following is a complete sentence?

Ingrid prepared to climb the mountain.

Had all the required equipment.

Aware of the dangers.

To express a complete thought, a sentence needs both a **subject** and a **predicate.**

Complete thought

Ingrid	prepared to climb the mountain.
COMPLETE SUBJECT	COMPLETE PREDICATE

Complete thought

She had all the required equipment.

Complete thought

The experienced climber was aware of the dangers.

Check your sentences to be sure each one has a subject and a predicate. If you are missing the subject, the predicate, or both, you have created a **sentence fragment.** Sentence fragments are incomplete sentences and can confuse your reader.

For more on fragments, see p. 286.

❷ Using Precise Words

Your choice of words affects how well your reader understands your sentence. Unclear, general words give your reader a sketchy outline. Accurate, precise words give your reader a clear, detailed picture.

> **The woman breathed.**
>
> **The mountain climber breathed.**
>
> **The mountain climber gasped for air.**

❸ Expanding with Modifiers

Modifiers are words that modify, or make more specific, the meanings of other words. You can use modifiers to add detail to your sentences.

> **The mountain climber gasped for air.**
>
> **The exhausted mountain climber gasped for air.**
>
> **The exhausted mountain climber noisily gasped the thin, cold air.**

 Avoid overused modifiers such as *very, really,* and *totally.* Try using more precise words instead. For example, instead of writing "very cold," try "bitterly cold" or "below freezing."

For more on modifiers, see p. 124.

PRACTICE ▸ Make It Clear

Improve the sentences below by following the directions in parentheses.

1. The view was nice. *(Use precise words.)*
2. The clouds were thick. *(Add modifiers.)*
3. It was windy on the mountain. *(Add modifiers.)*
4. The climber wore layers of clothes. *(Add modifiers.)*
5. The tired climber was happy to reach the top. *(Use precise words.)*

Expanding Sentences

A sentence becomes more informative, more accurate, and more interesting when it is expanded. Think of everything you want your reader to know about your topic.

❶ Adding Sentence Openers

Introductory words and phrases add information and emphasis. They clarify the message that you want your sentence to deliver.

On the stage, Emil felt extremely nervous.

Shaking and perspiring, he searched the room for an exit.

In the end, Emil was much happier in the audience.

A sentence opener should make the reader want to continue reading. Choose words that will spark your reader's interest.

Although her opponent was tall and strong, Felicia was not afraid.

After four years of training, she was ready to earn her black belt.

> **PROFESSIONAL MODEL**
>
> With a powerful snap kick, Felicia sent her opponent crashing to the mat. Felicia is one of thousands of girls who are having fun, staying in shape, and learning to defend themselves through martial arts.
>
> —Elizabeth Gordon

❷ Adding to the Middle

A well-chosen word or phrase in the middle of the sentence will often "spice up" an otherwise ordinary statement. These words and phrases usually go between the subject and the predicate or after the first verb in a compound predicate.

Liz, forgetting her manners, hollered across the table.

The principal, offended, frowned at her.

Liz blushed, completely embarrassed, and quietly apologized.

❸ Adding Sentence Closers

You can also improve your sentences by adding a word or a phrase at the end, after the predicate. A sentence closer can provide more information for your reader.

Stan went to the beach every day last summer.

He swam a lot, becoming stronger and faster.

He plans to be a lifeguard when he turns 18.

PRACTICE Beginning, Middle, and End

Write an imitation of each sentence below. Change the words, but keep the same sentence structure.

1. Juanita planned the party carefully.
2. Some skaters, unhappy with their performance, did not want to see their scores.
3. The smell of pizza came through the air vents, making us hungry.
4. Victorious, the soccer team hurried back to its hotel.
5. Exhausted by two small children, Sandy told herself that she would never baby-sit again.

SENTENCES

Combining Complete Sentences

LESSON 3

Sometimes a short sentence says all that you need to say. However, a parade of short, choppy sentences is boring to write and boring to read. Combining short, *related* sentences makes your writing flow smoothly.

Combining with Conjunctions

When combining short sentences that have similar or contrasting ideas, use *and, but,* or *or.* This creates a compound sentence.

Draft

> **Nicholas usually dresses smartly. Today his socks did not match.**

Revised

> **Nicholas usually dresses smartly, but today his socks did not match.**

Draft

> **You should hurry. You will be late.**

Revised

> **You should hurry, or you will be late.**

When you join two complete ideas, be sure to add a comma before the conjunction.

> **Spike was looking for the Big Rock Candy Mountain, but it was taking him a long time to find it.**

> **He had been looking all day, and he was feeling tired.**

Peanuts by Charles M. Schulz

For more on compound sentences, see pp. 189–191.

Try using *although, because,* or *since* to connect ideas that are related. To connect similar ideas, use *because* or *since.* To connect contrasting ideas, use *although.* When you do this, you create a complex sentence.

Draft

> **Sheela and Shawna are best friends. They argue quite a bit.**

Revised

> **Although they argue quite a bit, Sheela and Shawna are best friends.**

Draft

> **Dan's lunch will be nothing special. He lost his wallet.**

Revised

> **Dan's lunch will be nothing special because he lost his wallet.**

Mix compound and complex sentences with shorter, simpler sentences to lend variety to your writing. Your reader will appreciate it!

For more on complex sentences, see pp. 192–193.

PRACTICE Get It Together

Combine each set of sentences using the conjunction given in parentheses. Don't forget the comma!

1. A tree fell on the tent. Nobody was hurt. *(although)*
2. Our talent show is Friday. Dell hasn't chosen a song yet. *(but)*
3. Ferrets are goofy creatures. They make terrific pets. *(and)*
4. I fell last winter. I am afraid of icy sidewalks. *(since)*
5. It snowed this morning. Jan was late for school. *(because)*
6. Becky baked a cake for her mother's birthday. She almost forgot to add the eggs. *(but)*
7. Are you going to the mall? Are you staying in the park? *(or)*
8. Marianne had trouble sleeping during the camping trip. She found a beetle in her sleeping bag. *(because)*
9. The bass drum was heavy. I didn't mind carrying it. *(although)*
10. Action movies are my favorites. I always watch them when they are on TV. *(and)*

SENTENCES

Combining Sentence Parts

Good writers know that they should cut out the fluff. If you write a sentence that offers little new information to the reader, delete that sentence and add the important information to a related sentence. Combining keeps your writing lean and direct.

❶ Creating Compound Parts

Sometimes two or more sentences can be combined by moving part of the second sentence to the first. The new sentence will have a compound part.

> **Norman was learning to search the Internet. Gayle was learning to search the Internet, too.**
>
> **Norman and Gayle were learning to search the Internet.**
> COMPOUND SUBJECT

> **Janek collects foreign coins. He sometimes acquires interesting medallions. He also collects old U.S. paper money.**
>
> **Janek collects foreign coins, interesting medallions, and old U.S. paper money.**
>   COMPOUND DIRECT OBJECT

In the passage below, the author describes a whole series of events in just two sentences.

LITERARY MODEL

The large woman simply turned around and kicked him right square in his blue jeaned sitter. Then she **reached down, picked the boy up by his shirt front, and shook him until his teeth rattled.**

COMPOUND VERB

—Langston Hughes, "Thank You, Ma'm"

Don't forget to use commas to separate words in a series!

In your 🗁 **Working Portfolio,** find your **Write Away** paragraph from page 325. Add words and phrases to describe the painting more precisely. You may want to combine related sentences to strengthen your writing.

❷ Adding Words that Change Form

Sometimes you must change the form of a word before adding it to another sentence. For example, you might need to add -y or -ly to some words, -ed or -ing to other words.

> **Ann produced the concert posters. She did** quick **work.**
>
> **Ann** quickly **produced the concert posters.**

> **The students cheered the football team. The team** had **returned.**
>
> **The students cheered the** returning **football team.**

PRACTICE B From One to the Other

Combine the sentences in each item below by adding a key word or phrase from one sentence to the other. If necessary, change the form of the word you add.

1. Clarice borrowed a jacket. The jacket had stripes.
2. Tamera had a burrito for dinner. She also had a taco.
3. You could bring some sunscreen to the beach. You could bring a volleyball. You could bring a towel, too.
4. The audience began to applaud. It was all very sudden.
5. Sara sighed. She stared into space. She wondered when the bus would arrive.

SENTENCES

LESSON 5 Using *Who, That,* and *Which*

Sometimes you will introduce a person, place, or thing in one sentence and give details about it in another sentence. You may be able to combine the sentences using *who, that,* or *which.*

❶ Adding Details About People

Use the word *who* when adding details about people. If the information you are adding is not essential to the meaning of the sentence, set it off with commas. If the information is essential, leave out the commas.

Essential detail

> **One monster scares me most. That monster is Frankenstein.**

> **The monster who scares me most is Frankenstein.**

Nonessential detail

> **The writer of *Frankenstein* was born in London in 1797. Her name was Mary Wollstonecraft Shelley.**

> **The writer of *Frankenstein*, Mary Wollstonecraft Shelley, was born in London in 1797.**

 Information is essential if you need it to understand the basic meaning of the sentence. Information is not essential if it adds extra information to a sentence in which the meaning is already clear.

PRACTICE A Who Is It?

Combine each pair of sentences below with the word *who.* Use commas if necessary.

1. Dr. Carter hoped one of his children would study medicine. He was a pediatrician.

2. The cheerleader has a megaphone. He is the loudest.

3. The camp counselor led the hike. That camp counselor had the most experience.

4. I baby-sit for my neighbor. She has lived next door to us for several years.

5. Cyclists follow traffic safety rules. Those cyclists are rarely in accidents.

❷ Adding Details About Places and Things

When combining sentences in which details about places or things are given, use *that* if the details are essential. Use *which* if the details are not essential. If the meaning of the sentence is complete without the detail, the detail is not essential.

Essential detail

> **We have a chameleon in our science classroom. That chameleon is the biggest one I have ever seen.**

> **The chameleon** that lives in our science classroom **is the biggest one I have ever seen.**

Nonessential detail

> **Rain forced cancellation of the three-legged sack race. Rain had been predicted yesterday.**

> **Rain,** which had been predicted yesterday, **forced cancellation of the three-legged sack race.**

HOT TIP

When you use *which* to add information, set off the information with commas. When you use *that*, no commas are needed.

PRACTICE B > Which Is It?

Combine each pair of sentences below using either *that* or *which*.

1. Diamond fields were first discovered in South Africa in 1867. They have also been found in Australia, Botswana, and Russia.
2. The rubies sold for a high price. They had no flaws.
3. Emeralds are highly valuable gemstones. They were once thought to cure certain diseases.
4. There were emerald mines in ancient Egypt. The mines provided gems for Egyptian rulers.
5. Garnets are more common gemstones. They are less valuable than diamonds.

Student Help Desk

Building Sentences at a Glance

Does It Make Sense? Be sure your sentence expresses a complete thought. Use precise words.

Is That All There Is? Decide whether you should add detail to the beginning, middle, or end of the sentence.

Can You Combine It? See if you can combine two sentences into one more sophisticated sentence.

Expanding Sentences   Cook up Something Interesting

Technique	Example
Adding a sentence opener	**Scratching her head,** Lucy wondered what she should have for lunch.
Adding to the middle	The cafeteria special, **lasagna,** was her favorite.
Adding a sentence closer	Lucy decided to have the lasagna, **even though she had brought her lunch.**

Add More Ingredients

Combining Sentences

Technique	Example
Combining complete sentences	Pizza is my favorite food. I don't eat it every day. Pizza is my favorite food, **but** I don't eat it every day.
Adding words and phrases	Joshua had cake for lunch. He had it for dinner, too. Joshua had cake for lunch **and for dinner.**
Adding words that change form	Dan gulped some soda. He was noisy. Dan **noisily** gulped some soda.
Adding details	The macaroni that my uncle makes is my friends' favorite. It is very cheesy. The macaroni that my uncle makes, **which is very cheesy,** is my friends' favorite.

Menu for Adding Details

	Rule	Example
Who	Use *who* when adding details about people.	The boy **who ate six hot dogs** feels ill.
	If the details are not essential, add commas.	His friends**, who can't believe how much he ate,** are taking him to the school nurse.
	If they are essential, don't use commas.	The girl **who dared him to eat that much** feels guilty.
That	Use *that* when adding essential details about places or things. Don't use commas.	The kind of carrot cake **that my mother bakes** is my favorite.
Which	Use *which* when adding nonessential details about places or things. Use commas.	Her carrot cake**, which has cream-cheese frosting,** always gets eaten quickly.

SENTENCES

The Bottom Line

Checklist for Stronger Sentences

Have I . . .

____ made sure that each sentence expresses a complete thought?

____ given enough detail about my subject?

____ combined similar sentences to eliminate unneeded repetition?

____ added words and phrases to make my sentences stronger?

____ added details about people, places, or things to my sentences?

Power Words
Vocabulary for Precise Writing

Food for Thought

Whether you're building a sandwich or a paragraph, it pays to be precise.

One Step at a Time

A good bacon, lettuce, and tomato sandwich should be **planned.** Your ingredients can be **organized** into **orderly** groups. Be **methodical** and **efficient:** slice the tomatoes, peel off the lettuce leaves, and broil the bacon in a **systematic** way. See that your utensils are **arranged** conveniently on the counter-top. Combine the ingredients smoothly at a **steady, measured** pace, in **logical** order—first the lettuce, then the tomato, then the bacon. When you are done, leave the kitchen **shipshape** and in **apple-pie order.**

Dig In!

How will you go about eating this great sandwich? If you're really hungry, you might **devour** it all at once, just **wolf, gobble,** or **scarf** it down. Then again, you might take your time, **savoring** each bite. Whether you **gulp** your sandwich all at once or **consume** it gradually, you'll be glad you took care in making it.

▷ **Your Turn** Recipe for Success

Write out the steps of a favorite recipe of yours. After you have described how to create it, write a paragraph describing what it's like to eat it.

Building Paragraphs

Putting It Together

Open up the average lunch bag and you'll find a sandwich—two pieces of bread with something in the middle. They're all built basically the same way, but you can use a seemingly endless number of ingredients to make your own unique sandwich.

Good paragraphs are also built with some basic "ingredients" and follow logical structural patterns. Once you master those elements and patterns, however, each paragraph can be as unique as the subject you're writing about.

Write Away: Starting from Scratch
Write a paragraph of five or six sentences about a time you put something together. Maybe you were doing a science project, building a model, or making a scrapbook. Save your paragraph in your ⬧ **Working Portfolio.**

Qualities of a Good Paragraph

Because paragraphs are the building blocks of most writing assignments, you'll need to know what it takes to craft a good one. Two basic qualities appear in any well-written paragraph—unity and coherence. Understanding these qualities means you'll have the tools to put together any type of paragraph, including descriptive, narrative, informative, and persuasive paragraphs.

What Makes a Good Paragraph?

Recipe for a Good Paragraph	
Unity	A **topic sentence** states the main idea of the paragraph. All sentences contain **related information** that supports the topic sentence.
Coherence	All sentences connect to one another smoothly and logically.

STUDENT MODEL

You may have seen a movie in which some unlucky character is slurped down into quicksand. But could that really happen? Quicksand exists, but it's not quite as scary as the movies make out. Quicksand is sand that has so much water in it that it acts like a fluid and cannot support as much weight as usual. If the trapped person tries to lift out one foot, the other foot sinks deeper. A person could even sink in to her waist. However, it's impossible to sink entirely below the surface. Thus, the main danger with quicksand is that it's hard to get out if someone isn't there to help.

Topic Sentence
Quicksand isn't what you might think.

Related Information
Each sentence tells more about quicksand.

Coherence
However and *thus* link ideas in sentences.

Unity
All sentences help support the topic sentence.

340 Essential Writing Skills

Unity and Coherence

You'll know a paragraph has **unity** if all its sentences help explain the main idea. You'll know a paragraph has **coherence** if all the sentences flow smoothly and logically. Achieving both unity and coherence is easier if you start with a good topic sentence.

❶ Unity: What's the Big Idea?

Stating the "big idea" of your paragraph in a **topic sentence** can help keep you on track as you write, as well as introduce the subject of the paragraph. A good topic sentence also hooks the audience into wanting to know more.

STUDENT MODEL

James Armisted

    No one suspected that James Armisted was a spy. During the American Revolution, the young African-American man was a waiter at the camp of the British commander general Cornwallis in Virginia. While he waited on the British officers, Armisted listened carefully for information that could help the American rebels. Then he smuggled information to the American commander general Lafayette. Armisted never was caught.

> Topic sentence introduces the subject of the paragraph and captures the reader's attention.

Here's How Writing a Topic Sentence

1. Decide what your main point will be.
2. Write a sentence that states your main point and gives information about the subject.
3. Look for ways to make the topic sentence interesting and engaging.

    WEAK: I'm going to tell you about James Armisted.
    (doesn't tell who he was or what the paragraph will say)

    BETTER: No one suspected that James Armisted was a spy.
    (interests the reader and tells what the paragraph will be about)

② Unity: Supporting the Big Idea

What if you found a salamander in your sandwich? The first thing you'd probably wonder is why this creature is in your lunch. You don't want odd things cluttering up your paragraphs either. **Unity** means that each sentence contains information that supports your topic sentence. As you write, try to stay focused on the topic sentence.

STUDENT MODEL

DRAFT

Early one morning, a bear came down out of the mountains into our yard. It was as big as a car. It snacked on food scraps from three cans of garbage in our shed. Last week we had a raccoon in our shed. Dad built that shed himself. Finally, it left.

| Topic Sentence |

| Unrelated information distracts from topic sentence. |

REVISION

Early one morning, a bear came down out of the mountains into our yard. The bear was as big as a car. It knocked our garbage shed over on its side. Then the bear sat down and rummaged for some breakfast. By the time the bear left about 30 minutes later, it had snacked on food scraps from all three of our garbage cans.

| Related information supports the main idea and creates unity. |

When you write a paragraph, test for unity by looking at each sentence and asking: How does this sentence develop or support the idea stated in the topic sentence?

PRACTICE A   Room for Improvement?

In your 🗂 **Working Portfolio,** find your **Write Away** paragraph from page 339. Check for a topic sentence, unity, and coherence. Revise the paragraph until there is no unrelated information, and the sentences connect in a way that is easy to understand.

❸ Coherence: Making Connections

To give your paragraphs coherence, use words that connect sentences to one another so your readers easily can see how one idea leads to the next.

DRAFT

Don't buy a backpack unless it fits you and will last a long time. The seams shouldn't be single row stitches. They should be zig-zag stitches. They are better. The zippers should be covered by flaps. The pack should rest on your hips. Your homework shouldn't get wet when it rains.

> Sentences do not connect to one another or flow smoothly.

REVISION

Before you buy a backpack, you should make sure it fits you and will last a long time. **First,** check the seams to be sure they are zig-zag stitched and not single-row stitched. This is because zig-zag stitches hold together longer. **Next,** check that the zippers are covered by flaps so your homework doesn't get wet when it rains. **Finally,** make sure the pack fits you. The bottom of the pack should rest comfortably on your hips.

> Using **before, first, next,** and **finally** helps the reader follow the process.

PARAGRAPHS 1

For more on connecting words, see p. 349.

PRACTICE B ❯ Smooth It Out

Rewrite this paragraph, adding words that logically connect sentences to each other. Choose from the following: *also, in addition, finally, second, first, in the end.*

Three inventions helped settlers survive on the Great Plains in the 1800s. The steel plow made it possible for farmers to till prairie sod and plant crops. Fences stopped cattle from trampling farmers' fields. Portable windmills pumped water from deep in the earth for irrigating crops and for drinking. These things all contributed to successful life on the prairie.

Paragraphs: Descriptive and Narrative

Use **descriptive** paragraphs to describe a person, place, thing, or experience. Use **narrative** paragraphs to relate a story or event.

❶ Paragraphs That Describe

Have you ever read a description so good that you could almost see the subject? You can write good descriptive paragraphs that give the reader an opportunity to re-create a scene. They bring a character to life and create a picture in your reader's mind.

LITERARY MODEL

Henrietta even looked submissive. She was **thin** and **pale**. She had enormous **sky-blue** eyes surrounded by a long fringe of totally **colorless** eyelashes. Her hair was a **dim beige** color without gradations of light or dark, and it hung **straight and lifeless** from two barrettes. Her fingers were **long and bony**, and she kept them folded in her lap, **motionless**, like a tired old lady.

—Budge Wilson, "Waiting"

> Carefully chosen adjectives and adverbs appeal to the sense of sight.

Here's How Planning a Descriptive Paragraph

- Use a cluster diagram to list sights, sounds, smells, tastes, and textures that describe the person, place, or thing.
- Choose specific and vivid nouns, verbs, adjectives, and adverbs.
- Arrange the details in an order that readers can follow, such as head to toe, side to side, front to back.

For more on sensory details, see pp. 378–379.

PRACTICE A As You See It

Using the model above as a guide, write a descriptive paragraph about a person you know well. Include vivid sensory details that you think will help this person spring to life for your reader.

② Paragraphs That Tell a Story

You can use narrative paragraphs to tell a story or report an event. Because most things you write about have a beginning, middle, and end, it's important that your paragraph does too. Add **connecting words** to help readers follow the narrative.

PROFESSIONAL MODEL

> Showing off for the bridesmaids at my sister's wedding reception **years ago,** I caught and ate a large black cricket. **Later** I mentioned the incident in a book I wrote. At a talk I gave **recently,** someone who had read the book asked if the story was true. My sister happened to be present, **so** I pointed her out and told the questioner he should ask her himself. All heads swiveled to look at her where she was sitting by the aisle in the back row. "He eats bugs," she explained shortly, her lip curled in understated disgust.
>
> —Ian Frazier, "It's Hard to Eat Just One"

Beginning

Middle

End

Here's How Planning a Narrative Paragraph

- Include details that will answer the questions *who, what, when, where, why,* and *how.*
- Use connecting words to help readers follow the sequence of events.
- Give your paragraph a clear beginning, middle, and end.

For more connecting words, see p. 349.

PRACTICE B What's Going On?

Write a narrative paragraph about the picture to the right. Use your imagination to invent details that help answer *who, what, when, where, why,* and *how.*

PARAGRAPHS 1

345

LESSON 4 Paragraphs: Informative and Persuasive

If you need to explain something or provide information on a subject, you can choose to write an **informative**, or expository, paragraph. If you want to offer information about your own ideas to persuade someone to see things your way, a **persuasive** paragraph is a good tool.

❶ Paragraphs That Inform

Informative paragraphs are used when you need to present facts and examples to explain how something works, give directions, define a term, or provide the origin or history of a person, place, or thing.

PROFESSIONAL MODEL

Venus is the solar system's most devastating example of the greenhouse effect. The great amounts of carbon dioxide and other greenhouse gases trap so much heat under the clouds that the temperature is about 875 Fahrenheit on the venusian plains. An unprotected person would burn up almost instantly. . . .

—*Odyssey* science magazine

Topic sentence presents the main idea.

Facts and examples help define "greenhouse effect."

Here's How Planning a Persuasive Paragraph

- Write a topic sentence introducing the subject in an interesting way.
- Explain your subject with definitions and other specific information.
- Illustrate your ideas with examples, facts, statistics, and definitions.

PRACTICE A Explain This!

Choose one of the three terms below. Define and explain the term in an informative paragraph of five to six sentences. Use an encyclopedia, dictionary, or the Internet to find information.

Supernova   *What is it? How did it get its name?*
Great Wall of China   *Why was it built? How long is it?*
Giant squid   *How is it different from other squid?*

CHAPTER 14

❷ Paragraphs That Persuade

In a persuasive paragraph, you present your point
of view and try to make readers agree with you,
or follow your suggestions. This writer argues
that dolphins that perform in shows, like the one
pictured, should be set free.

PROFESSIONAL MODEL

   **Keeping dolphins in marine parks is
harmful to the species.** Those who run
"dolphinariums" say the purpose of their
shows is to educate the public. Ask someone
who has been to a dolphin show what they
learned, and you'll hear, "They jump really
high!" and "They sure are cute!" How is that
educational? In addition, dolphins in "petting
pools" are touched by hundreds of people
everyday, exposing them to human diseases.
Dolphins in captivity live only 25 to 30 years,
but in the wild they can live up to 50 years.
Shouldn't they be given that chance?

—Becky Polivka

> Topic Sentence

> Writer presents
> an opposing
> argument, then
> responds to it.

> Writer provides
> facts and
> examples.

Here's How **Planning a Persuasive Paragraph**

- Clearly state your opinion or idea in the topic sentence.
- Use clear reasoning to sway readers to your point of view.
- Offer specific facts, examples, and statistics to support your opinion.

PRACTICE B **Be Convincing**

Community leaders are voting on the following issues:

- Banning in-line skating in public places.
- Banning jeans and jewelry in school.

Could you sway the voters? Pick one issue, and state in a
topic sentence whether you agree or disagree. Use the rest of
your persuasive paragraph to support your opinion.

PARAGRAPHS 1

Student Help Desk

Building Paragraphs at a Glance

Topic Sentence	Unity	Coherence
The "big idea"	All sentences support the "big idea."	All sentences are logically and smoothly connected.

Unity and Coherence — Pull it Together!

Take out what doesn't fit and connect what does.

Did you know that you don't actually have to touch poison ivy to be poisoned? *One time* My cousins went camping. At night they built a campfire to roast marshmallows. ~~They also brought brownies for dessert.~~ A little later, they had an itching sensation in their lungs. They had accidentally pushed a dried poison ivy leaf into the fire. ~~Did you know pine cones pop when they burn?~~ The oil that contains the "poison" is called urushiol, and when it burns, it goes airborne. *So* My cousins had inhaled urushiol! ~~They are my favorite cousins.~~ Next time you're camping, watch where you walk and what you throw onto the fire.

> Add connecting words and phrases between sentences.

> Delete unrelated information.

Calvin and Hobbes by Bill Watterson

I CAN'T BELIEVE IT! HOMEWORK ALREADY! I JUST GOT BACK TO SCHOOL!

I HAVE TO WRITE A PARAGRAPH ON WHAT I DID OVER THE SUMMER! *A WHOLE PARAGRAPH!!*

I'LL *NEVER* BE ABLE TO WRITE THAT MUCH! IT'S *NOT FAIR!!*

HOW'S IT COMING?

NOT SO GOOD. WHAT DID YOU DO BESIDES WATCH TV?

CHAPTER 14

Paragraph Types Decisions, Decisions

Type	Uses
Descriptive	Presents colorful, exact picture of a person, place, thing, or experience by appealing to the five senses
Narrative	Tells a story and often answers the questions *who, what, where, when, why,* and *how*
Informative	Defines terms, gives directions, or tells how things work by presenting or explaining facts or ideas
Persuasive	Uses facts and reasons to support a point of view and tries to persuade reader to agree

Connecting Words and Phrases A Few Coherence "Condiments"

on the other hand

although

because

besides

eventually

one time

for this reason

however

for example

but

in the same way

also

therefore

yet

in addition

The Bottom Line

Checklist for Building Paragraphs

Have I . . .

____ stated the main idea clearly in a topic sentence?

____ made sure all sentences support the topic sentence?

____ made a descriptive paragraph lively by using sensory details?

____ helped readers follow narrative events by using connecting words?

____ used facts and examples to explain my topic?

____ included logical reasoning in a way that is likely to persuade readers?

Power Words
Vocabulary for Precise Writing

guide

Getting from Here to There

It's especially important to be clear and precise when you are giving directions.

Giving Directions

The easiest way to get somewhere new—if you don't have access to the transporter room, that is—is if someone who knows the way **accompanies** you. He or she may **conduct** you to the exact spot and even **usher** you in the door. However, if you don't have a **navigator, pilot, guide,** or **shepherd,** use your map-reading skills and try to figure it out on your own.

Taking Control

Giving directions doesn't always mean going from one place to another. If you are the leader of a country, a photo safari, or a white-water rafting trip, you are the one in charge. You may have to **initiate** the planning, **marshal** the available resources, and **steer** things in the right direction. It's up to you to **assign, coordinate, supervise,** and **administer** to make sure that the project is a success.

ACCOMPANIES

coordinate

navigator

▷ **Your Turn** I'm in Charge Here!

Write a description of your ideal job. List the job's duties, location, hours, and needed abilities.

steer

USHER

Organizing Paragraphs

Alternate Routes

An adult is driving you to a party and you are giving him directions. Since he is famous for getting lost, you've got to be extra careful and clear. "Turn here," just won't do it. He'd probably respond, "What?" "Now?" "Left or right?" You've got to give him advance warning and be specific: "*After* you get to the *next* stoplight, *then* turn *left*."

You've probably noticed that it is also possible to get "lost" while you're reading. Good writers organize their paragraphs in logical patterns so readers can easily follow their ideas. In this chapter, you'll learn to recognize these patterns and use them yourself.

Write Away: Pointing the Way
A new student has to get to gym class on time. Write a set of detailed directions in paragraph form that will take her from your classroom to the girls' locker room. Save your paragraph in your 🗂 **Working Portfolio.**

Sequential Order

All writing must to be organized to be understood. Choose a method of organizing that is most appropriate for the purpose of your paragraph. In this chapter, you'll see how sequential, spatial, cause-and-effect, and compare-and-contrast order can help you organize paragraphs.

Paragraphs That Show Time and Sequence

Writers use **sequential order** to show how events follow one another in a certain order. A term for showing how events unfold over a certain period of time is **chronological order.**

LITERARY MODEL

At one-hour intervals the night guards paced past every room. Each time I heard the approaching footsteps, I jumped into bed and feigned sleep. And as soon as the guard passed, I got back out of bed onto the floor area of that light-glow, where I would read for another fifty-eight minutes—until the guard approached again. That went on until three or four every morning.

FIRST EVENT

SECOND EVENT

THIRD EVENT

FOURTH EVENT

—Malcolm X with Alex Haley,
The Autobiography of Malcolm X

In the cartoon below notice how Calvin uses sequential order to explain to Susie the process of his great idea in action.

Calvin and Hobbes by Bill Watterson

Connecting words, or **transition words,** link sentences and help readers relate one event in time to another.

Between 1100 and 1300 in England, the goal of many boys was to become a knight. The **first** step began at age seven when a boy went to live with a knight or nobleman and work for him as a page. **Next,** when he had reached age 15 or 16, the page became a squire and served the knight in battle. The **last** stage occurred at age 21, when the squire took vows to uphold the code of knighthood.

> **Transition words** link one step to another, adding unity and coherence to the paragraph.

For more transition words, see p. 361.

PRACTICE No Wrong Turns

Your friend has given you the map below to help you find the way to his party. In a paragraph that you will read to the driver, write directions in sequential order based on this map. Use the landmarks and street names as well as transition words to help get you to the party on time.

Then, in your 📁 **Working Portfolio,** find your **Write Away** paragraph, and add transition words to those directions.

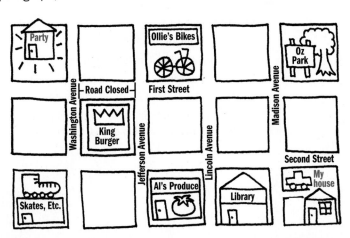

PARAGRAPHS 2

Spatial Order

Writers use **spatial** (space) **order** to show how people and objects appear. When you read a paragraph that uses spatial order, you might have the feeling of following a camera as it pans across a scene.

Paragraphs That Put Things in Their Place

You can use spatial order any time you want readers to picture a place as it really looks or as you imagine it. You can describe a space from top to bottom, left to right, front to back, faraway to close-up, or outside to inside.

LITERARY MODEL

Miss Pride's **shop window** was full of nasty, dingy old cardboard cartons with nothing inside them, and several empty display stands which had fallen down and never been propped up again. **Inside the shop** were a few small, tired-looking tins and jars, which had a worn and scratched appearance as if mice had tried them and given up.

—Joan Aiken, "The Serial Garden"

> The writer begins with the outside window of the store.

> Then the writer describes the inside of the store.

Here's How Using Spatial Order

- Look at or picture in your mind the place you want to show and the people and objects within it.
- Decide how much of the space you will describe.
- Present the description from top to bottom, left to right, front to back, faraway to close up, or outside to inside.
- As you write, move from object to object and use transition words to describe the relationship of one object to another.

Direction or location words within a paragraph can help you show where objects and people are in relation to each other.

STUDENT MODEL

As I stepped into Jewel Cave, I noticed that the walls sparkled as if they were wallpapered with diamonds. When I walked up **close to** the wall, I realized that it was covered with a thick layer of crystals. **At the base of** the wall, I saw a massive stalagmite jutting up toward the ceiling. A huge stalactite directly **above** it dripped steadily down onto the giant stalagmite.

> **Close to** lets us "zoom in" and see the wall's crystals.

> **At the base of** and **above** help us locate the formations within the cave.

For more direction words, see p. 361.

Avoid writing sentences such as "There was a book." Was it on a desk, inside a backpack, on someone's head? Be sure the objects in your sentences don't just float in space.

PRACTICE Picture This

Using spatial order, describe what is happening in this picture so that your readers would be able to imagine the picture without seeing it. You may want to give the dog a name and tell a brief story using the objects you see. Use direction and location words to help define where things are in relation to each other.

For more direction words, see p. 361.

PARAGRAPHS 2

Cause-and-Effect Order

Just about any time you explain why or how something occurs, you'll find yourself presenting causes and effects. A **cause** is something that brings about a result. An **effect** is the result of the cause.

Paragraphs That Explain Why or How

You can use cause-and-effect to explain a process or an event. Sometimes there is more than one cause for a given effect. At other times, a single cause can lead to several effects.

PROFESSIONAL MODEL

During the medieval period, travel across Europe became difficult and dangerous as many kingdoms fought among themselves for land and wealth. As a result, trading activities diminished and towns ... became depopulated. Many people had to move to the countryside to make their living as peasants on large estates called manors, owned by lords.

Across the Centuries, Houghton Mifflin

This chart shows the cause-and-effect chain described above.

Here's How Using Cause-and-Effect Order

- Use your topic sentence to introduce the cause or the effect.
- Explain each cause and each effect clearly.
- Use transition words or phrases to link causes and effects.

Often, transitions, such as **because, as a result,** and **consequently,** signal cause and effect. Notice how transition words make these relationships clear in the student model.

Because Maria Mitchell's father was an amateur astronomer, she learned how to use a telescope at an early age. As a girl, she studied hard, especially astronomy and the sciences. **As a result** of her hard work, she discovered a new comet in 1847. **Consequently,** she became the first American woman to be recognized as an astronomer.

Notice how these causes and effects relate to one another.

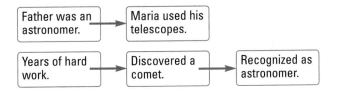

| Father was an astronomer. | → | Maria used his telescopes. |

| Years of hard work. | → | Discovered a comet. | → | Recognized as astronomer. |

For more transition words, see p. 361.

Make sure that you have chosen a true cause-and-effect relationship. Ask yourself this: "Is it clear to me how one event led to the next? Could I make it clear to a reader?"

PRACTICE What's Happening?

Create a chart like those in this lesson showing the cause-and-effect relationships in the following paragraph.

"Dust Bowl" is the term used to describe the severe conditions of the early 1930s that caused a migration westward. Farmers in the Great Plains region of the Southwest dug up prairie grass and planted crops with roots too shallow to hold soil. Drought conditions, combined with severe winds, caused great clouds of dust to rise and blow through the air. As a result, farmers lost their crops. Many families moved west in search of more fertile soil.

Compare-and-Contrast Order

When you tell how two things are alike, you are **comparing** them. When you tell how two things are different, you are **contrasting** them.

Using Compare-and-Contrast Order

Use compare-and-contrast order to show similarities and differences. Scientific and historical writing often use this order. A subject-by-subject approach is used below. This means that one subject is discussed completely before the second is introduced.

PROFESSIONAL MODEL

Eskimo clothing was extremely efficient. It was lightweight, comfortable, warm, and allowed the wearer to move around easily. A complete winter outfit weighed only about ten pounds. **By contrast,** an average Minnesota businessman wears twenty to thirty pounds of clothing on his way to work in winter; if caught in a sudden blizzard, he would be in danger of freezing to death.

—Charlotte and David Yue, "The Igloo"

Subject 1: Eskimo clothing

↓

Linked by transition

↓

Subject 2: modern clothing

In the model below, the two subjects are compared feature-by-feature.

STUDENT MODEL

Alligators and crocodiles look a lot alike. Both have long, thick bodies, strong tails, and powerful jaws with sharp teeth. **However,** crocodiles have snouts that come to a point. **In contrast,** alligators have round snouts. Crocodiles are lighter in weight than alligators and are more likely to attack humans than are alligators.

Similar features of alligators and crocodiles

↓

Linked by transitions

↓

Different features of alligators and crocodiles

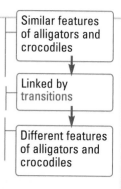

CHAPTER 15

Here's How) **Writing a Compare-and-Contrast Paragraph**

1. Find similarities and differences between the subjects.

2. Use a Venn diagram to help organize your thoughts.

Features of Subject A — Shared Features — Features of Subject B

3. State the main idea in a topic sentence.

4. Choose subject-by-subject or feature-by-feature organization. Use transition words where they are helpful or needed.

For more transition words, see p. 361.

When choosing your own subjects to compare and contrast, be sure the subjects have plenty of similarities as well as differences. If not, you will run out of things to discuss.

PRACTICE) **Jupiter Versus Saturn**

Use the comparison made in the Venn diagram below to write a paragraph comparing and contrasting Jupiter and Saturn. You may use a subject-by-subject approach, in which you discuss the features of Jupiter first, then the features of Saturn. Or, you may choose a feature-by-feature approach, in which you compare and contrast features of Jupiter to features of Mars.

PARAGRAPHS 2

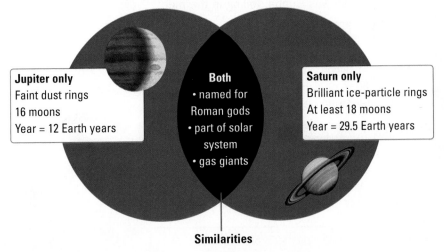

Jupiter only
Faint dust rings
16 moons
Year = 12 Earth years

Both
• named for Roman gods
• part of solar system
• gas giants

Saturn only
Brilliant ice-particle rings
At least 18 moons
Year = 29.5 Earth years

Similarities

For more on compare-and-contrast order, see pg. 446.

Student Help Desk

Organizing Paragraphs at a Glance

Sequential Order	Spatial Order	Cause-and-Effect Order	Compare-and-Contrast Order
	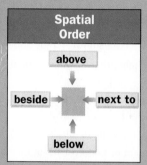	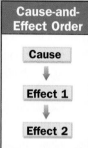	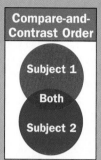

Organizing a Paragraph   Where to Find Order

Sequential

Used in how-to instructions and manuals, stories, science writing, directions
Example: First, we sprayed our dog Bubba with a hose. Next, we lathered him up until he was good and sudsy, rinsed, and repeated the process because he was still smelly.

Spatial

Used in eyewitness accounts, crime reports, stories
Example: To the left of the doghouse lay the hose. Next to it was a pile of soggy towels with an empty bottle of shampoo on top. To the right of the doghouse was Bubba, rolling in the mud.

Cause and Effect

Used in stories, science or history reports, news articles, editorials
Example: Giving a dog a bath frequently reduces the risk of the animal getting fleas or being infected by ticks. In a severe case, a dog could catch mange and end up losing all its fur.

Compare and Contrast

Used in consumer guides, reviews, descriptions
Example: Compared with giving a cat a bath, bathing a dog is easy. Dogs jump into ponds and run through puddles, but cats can't stand being wet.

Transition Tool Box

Sequential Order	Spatial Order	Cause-and-	Compare
during	(direction	Effect Order	also
eventually	words)	caused by	by comparison
last	around	as a result	either . . . or
later	center	so	neither . . . nor
meanwhile	in front of	thus	the same as
now	below	for this reason	
once	outside	affected by	Contrast
tomorrow	inside	owing to	instead
yesterday	to the left	accordingly	nevertheless
	to the right	in this way	on the contrary
	underneath	consequently	unlike
	on top of		yet

The Bottom Line

Checklist for Organizing Paragraphs

Have I . . .

____ made sure the method of organization fits the purpose?

____ written steps and ideas in an order that is easy to follow?

____ used the correct transition words and phrases?

____ included a beginning, middle, and end when writing sequentially?

____ allowed the reader to see the space I am describing when using spatial descriptions?

____ made sure causes and effects are correct and clear?

____ shown similarities and differences when using compare-and-contrast order?

Power Words
Vocabulary for Precise Writing

invincible

fixe

immutable

sturdiness

Brick by Brick

Sometimes "big and strong" just isn't descriptive enough.

A *Really* Great Wall

Like the castles of Europe, the Great Wall of China was designed to be **unassailable** and **unconquerable.** Invading armies found this **massive bulwark** of brick, granite, and earth to be an **impenetrable** barrier.

Protected by the Great Wall, the emperors of China may have felt **invincible.** The **stability** and **sturdiness** of the wall must have made the Chinese people feel **secure** as well. The wall is as much as 35 feet high in some places, making it a **forbidding obstacle** for anyone on the other side.

The Test of Time

Today the Great Wall is **timeworn, weathered,** even **crumbling** in places. Still, people come from all over the world to see it and to study it. At about 4,000 miles long, it is the longest structure anyone has ever built—and its sheer size, its **vastness,** makes it **fixed, unvarying,** and **immutable.**

▷ **Your Turn** Wish You Were Here

Write a postcard describing the Great Wall, the Grand Canyon, the Statue of Liberty, or another large-scale tourist attraction without mentioning its name. Read your postcard aloud. See if your classmates can guess what you are describing.

secure

vastne

impenetrable

unconquerab

Building Compositions

Medieval castles were enormous stone buildings built to protect a lord and lady, their family, and their servants. The ground level, also called the cellar, contained a granary, casks, and great boxes storing food and utensils.

Notes on medieval castles
- stone buildings, protected family and servants
- ground level (cellar): granary, casks, great boxes (food, utensils)

Piece by Piece

Think about the last time you built a puzzle. What do you remember being the most challenging about it? Perhaps you couldn't find all the pieces. Maybe you couldn't fit the pieces together right away. Writing a composition can seem very similar to putting together a puzzle. However, when you build a composition, by focusing on one part at a time, you will often find the right way to fit your ideas together, and the final product will take shape before your eyes.

Write Away: Built to Last
Human beings have built some pretty amazing structures: medieval castles, Egyptian pyramids, the Eiffel Tower. Write a paragraph describing a structure you've seen that seems as if it must have been impossible to build. What about it impresses you the most? Save your paragraph in your
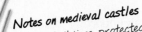 **Working Portfolio.**

COMPOSITIONS

Structuring a Composition

❶ What Makes a Composition?

A **composition** is made up of paragraphs. Each paragraph is a separate unit that helps develop, or build on, the main idea of the composition. Your understanding of how paragraphs work can help you to write a strong composition. Notice the similarities and differences between them shown in the chart below.

Paragraphs and Compositions	
A paragraph has	**A composition has**
a topic sentence	an introductory paragraph that states the topic of the composition
sentences that support the topic	body paragraphs that develop the topic, or "main idea"
	a concluding paragraph

Unity and coherence are just as important in compositions as they are in paragraphs. **Unity** means that the information in each paragraph supports the thesis statement. A composition has **coherence** when paragraphs are connected smoothly to one another with transition words and phrases.

❷ What Does a Composition Look Like?

A composition has three parts:

The **introduction** begins the composition and tells what it is about. The introduction includes a sentence stating the main idea of the composition, called a **thesis statement.**

The **body** is the central part of a composition, usually made up of three or more paragraphs. Each paragraph builds on and explains the thesis statement.

The **conclusion** finishes a composition by restating the main idea, offering a summary, and giving a final comment or opinion.

As you read the model, notice how the parts build on one another to create a finished composition.

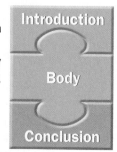

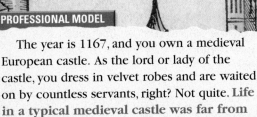

The year is 1167, and you own a medieval European castle. As the lord or lady of the castle, you dress in velvet robes and are waited on by countless servants, right? Not quite. **Life in a typical medieval castle was far from luxurious.**

At the first light of dawn, it's time to get up. After a quick sponge bath with icy cold water, you put on your woolen undergarments and hurry off to a short religious service. After church you eat breakfast, which is nothing more than a bland slice of bread.

After several hours of carrying out your morning duties, you must be hungry. On today's menu: stewed pigeon, boiled starling, and roasted sea gull. Sorry, there's no lark's tongue today—you only get that on special occasions. Be sure to wash your hands; you have to eat everything with your fingers.

Once your midday meal is over, afternoon activities begin. The lord of the castle goes hunting to make sure there is something on tomorrow's dinner table. The lady of the castle oversees household chores, including keeping the castle warm—there is no central heating!

As the sun sets, it's time for the last meal of the day and some entertainment. While you eat, a lady acrobat does a handstand while balancing on the tips of two swords. Then it's off to your bed—a hard rope mattress covered by feather pillows and animal fur.

Perhaps your day in a medieval castle wasn't as luxurious as you expected. Was one day enough? You probably want to race back to the hot showers and soft beds of the 21st century.

—Elizabeth Laskey

The **introduction** states the main idea and gives the **thesis statement**.

Body paragraphs support the thesis statement.

COMPOSITIONS

The **conclusion** restates the thesis and offers an opinion.

Writing an Introduction

An **introduction** tells readers what your topic is, lets them know how you plan to discuss that topic, and captures their attention so they'll want to read more of your composition.

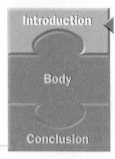

Introduction

Body

Conclusion

❶ Thesis Statement

Your introduction should always include a **thesis statement,** a sentence that clearly presents your main idea and your purpose for writing.

Thesis Statement	
A thesis statement SHOULD	A thesis statement SHOULD NOT
tell the subject of your composition	be an incomplete thought: "Battles in the 1300s."
give your view on the subject and your purpose for writing	be a simple statement of fact: "Battles in the 1300s were bloody."
be a statement supported by fact	be merely an opinion: "Battles in the 1300s were cool!"
be stated in an interesting way	be an announcement: "In this paper I will write about . . ."

DRAFT

I'm going to tell you about how battles were fought in the 1300s.

(too general)

REVISION

Warfare in medieval times was fairly simple and included unusual strategies.

(more specific and effective)

❷ Types of Introductions

Capture your readers' imagination at the earliest opportunity— in the introduction. Use one or more of these attention-getting techniques in the first sentence to grab readers' attention.

- include an interesting fact
- use a vivid description
- ask a question
- use a quotation

Wooden catapult used in siege warfare

STUDENT MODEL

Have you ever seen a flying horse? Many soldiers in medieval times did. Attackers would sometimes catapult the rotting corpse of a horse over the castle wall in hopes of spreading disease among the enemy. In the heat of battle, any available object would do—rocks, branches, and, of course, flaming arrows. Today, warfare is strategically planned and weapons are carefully crafted. **Warfare in medieval times, however, was fairly simple and included many unusual strategies.**

> The writer addresses the reader with a question.

> Thesis statement appears at the end of the paragraph.

STUDENT MODEL

"Send to us forty of the fattest pigs of the sort least good for eating to bring fire beneath the tower," commanded King Alfred while preparing to burn his way into an enemy castle. **As strange as this plan might seem, it was just one of the many unusual strategies used by warriors in medieval times.** Since medieval warfare was not sophisticated, attackers had to take advantage of any weakness in the enemy's fortress. The king who demanded the pigs knew that lard burned well and that the tower's foundation was weak. Believe it or not, burning pigs under castle walls wasn't even the most bizarre strategy used during that time.

> Writer begins with a quotation to spark the reader's interest.

> Thesis statement

> Last line introduces the next paragraph.

COMPOSITIONS

The thesis statement doesn't have to be the first sentence of your introduction. It can come anywhere within the opening paragraph.

Writing the Body

The **body** of a composition is made up of three or more paragraphs that support the thesis statement. Each paragraph in a composition should be organized logically and should have unity and coherence.

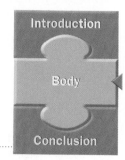

Introduction

Body

Conclusion

❶ Unity in a Composition

Unity in a composition means that all of the paragraphs relate to and support the thesis statement. Writing an informal outline is one way to see whether your plan for the composition has unity. First, jot down the main idea of each paragraph to be sure it relates to the thesis statement. Then develop each main idea into a topic sentence.

Informal Outline: Warfare in the Middle Ages

Introduction, Thesis Statement:
Warfare in medieval times was unsophisticated and included unusual strategies.

Body:
1st paragraph: entering a fortress (ladders, trickery)
2nd paragraph: hand-held weapons (crossbows, longbows)
3rd paragraph: siege engines (catapults, mobile towers)
4th paragraph: use of fire (flying "Greek fire")
~~**5th paragraph:** castle treasures (gold and jewelry)~~

> Unrelated topic is deleted.

Conclusion:
Today it is hard to imagine a battle in which things like ladders, bows, and catapults play a role.

Paragraphing also helps keep the body unified. Each paragraph should focus on one main idea—the idea presented in the topic sentence. You should start a new paragraph when:

• you present a new idea

• there is a change in time or place

• the dialogue shifts to a new speaker

The following model shows how one writer broke his composition into paragraphs and then rearranged his ideas as necessary.

Crossbow

Attackers used several strategies to storm an enemy stronghold. One was scurrying up long ladders placed against the outside walls. A second strategy was trickery. Enemies would disguise themselves as peasants and walk right through a castle gate undetected. Crossbows and longbows were important weapons used when attacking a castle. Arrows shot from a crossbow could be fired long distances. Longbows had a shorter range and were good on the battlefield. However, castle soldiers would sometimes see attackers climbing the ladders and simply push them away from the wall.

> This is the **topic sentence** of the first paragraph.

> This becomes the **topic sentence** of the second paragraph.

> This sentence belongs in the first paragraph.

❷ Organization and Coherence

In addition to supporting the thesis statement, paragraphs should be organized logically. Your method of organization should be based on what your composition is trying to achieve.

Types of Organizations

If you need to . . .	Use this . . .
explain events in chronological order or explain a process	sequential order
describe how something happens	cause-and-effect order
show likenesses or differences	compare-and-contrast order

A composition that has **coherence** flows logically from one paragraph to the next. **Transition words and phrases** help connect ideas both within paragraphs and between paragraphs, as shown in the model on the next page.

COMPOSITIONS

In contrast to hand-held weapons, "siege engines" like catapults and mobile towers did wide-scale damage. Soldiers loaded huge boulders onto catapults and flung them at foes. **In addition,** mobile towers could protect many archers while being wheeled toward an enemy castle.

However, one of the deadliest strategies was the use of fire. A certain explosive called "Greek fire" actually ignited when moistened. Attackers would load it onto catapults, ignite it, and fling it over fortress walls. It blazed fiercely, and the flame was difficult to put out.

PRACTICE   Unity and Coherence

Rewrite the following and break it into two paragraphs. Add transitions where necessary. Delete unrelated sentences.

In the Middle Ages, a "bathtub" was a small wooden tub with a padded lining. The wooden tub was placed in a chamber near the fireplace for warmth. In warm weather the tub was moved to an outside garden for bathing. Jesters seldom lived in castles. Members of royalty often had permanent bathrooms in their quarters. My parents have a bathroom in their bedroom. Henry III had hot and cold running water for bathing and drinking. Edward II even had a tiled floor in his bathroom.

Writing the Conclusion

In the **conclusion,** you can end your composition by restating your thesis statement and leaving your reader with a final thought about your topic.

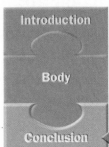

Introduction

Body

Conclusion

Types of Conclusions

A good conclusion is interesting as well as useful to a reader. The conclusion gives you an opportunity to sum up your message and leave the reader with your final thoughts.

Here's How Writing the Conclusion

- Restate your thesis statement.
- Sum up your composition in an interesting way.
- Offer your opinion on the subject, leaving readers with something to think about.

STUDENT MODEL

Today it is hard for us to imagine ladders, bows, and catapults being used in battle. Yet such "primitive" strategies accomplished the attackers' main goal—to get a castle's inhabitants to surrender. While these strategies seem strange and even funny to us, they were taken very seriously in medieval times. Warfare is serious and deadly business, no matter what century you are in!

Writer sums up the composition.

Writer offers a personal opinion on the subject.

WATCH OUT

Be careful not to introduce any new information in the conclusion. Stick to the topic of your composition.

COMPOSITIONS

Student Help Desk

Building Compositions at a Glance

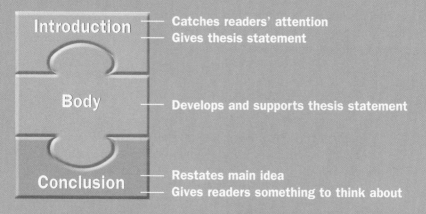

Introduction — Catches readers' attention
— Gives thesis statement

Body — Develops and supports thesis statement

Conclusion — Restates main idea
— Gives readers something to think about

Getting a Reader's Attention   Reeling Them In

Types of Introductions	Examples
Use vivid or sensory descriptions	The marketplace echoed with the sounds of geese honking, cows mooing, pigs oinking, and shoppers arguing heatedly with merchants.
Include startling or interesting facts	Pepper was so expensive that a medieval housewife sometimes could afford only a single peppercorn. Even then she would have to inspect it to be sure it wasn't a fake made of clay, oil, and mustard.
Ask questions	How would you like to catch and roast a seagull over an open fire for dinner every night? That's what you would have had to do back in the 1300s.
Use quotations	Erasmus once said that on castle floors lay "an ancient collection of grease, fragments, bones, spittle, . . . and everything that is nasty."

Ways to Conclude · A Final Thought on the Subject . . .

Types of Endings	Examples
Restate the thesis statement	Most people today don't realize they live in the lap of luxury compared with people in the Middle Ages.
Make a recommendation	If you could choose to live in the 1300s or now, I'd suggest staying in the 21st century.
State an opinion	We should all be grateful we don't have to hunt for our food like the lord of a medieval castle did.

Coherence Connection · Putting Things in Order

Types of Order	Transitional Words and Phrases
Sequential	finally, during, while, last, soon, at the beginning, at the same time, before, after
Cause and effect	so, consequently, for this reason, because, resulting from, accordingly, thus, therefore
Comparison	either . . . or, neither . . . nor, by comparison, also, likewise, just as, in addition
Contrast	yet, still, unlike, instead, nevertheless, on the contrary, in spite of, regardless, although

The Bottom Line

Checklist for Building Compositions

Have I . . .

____ written a thesis statement that describes my subject and purpose for writing?

____ used an attention-getting technique in my introduction?

____ organized my composition logically and checked for unity?

____ made sure my topic sentences support my main idea?

____ used transitions to create coherence?

____ checked my paragraph breaks?

____ restated my main idea in the conclusion?

Power Words
Vocabulary for Precise Writing

GRUB

sustenance

chow

eats

CHAPTER 17

tidbits

meal

On the Menu

We cannot live without food. Perhaps that's why we have so many words for it.

Formal and Fancy

We have many fancy words for food: **nourishment, refreshment, edibles,** and **sustenance. Rations** are the food of a soldier at war, and people stock up on **provisions** when they are about to go camping. **Nutriment, aliment,** and **alimentation** are words that doctors and scientists use to describe digestion. **Comestibles, victuals,** and **viands** are very old-fashioned ways of describing food, but you'll want to recognize them when you read them.

Time for Some Grub!

Instead of saying, "Would you join me for a **meal?**" you might ask, "Want some **chow?**" Other informal or slang words for food are **eats, grub,** and **vittles.** For snacks we have the delicious words **munchies, tidbits,** and **treats.**

The **board** in "room and board," **keep** in "earn your keep," **chuck** in "chuck wagon," and **fare** in "hearty fare" are yet other ways to say *food.*

▷ Your Turn Eat Up and Chow Down

Create three dinner invitations: a formal one to someone you don't know very well, an informal one to some friends, and an old-fashioned one that might have been sent 200 years ago.

treats

vittle

Elaboration

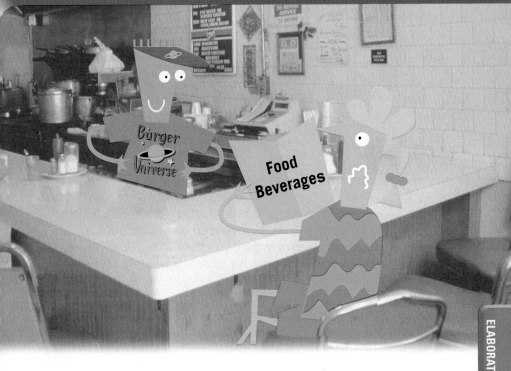

Tell Me More!

What's wrong with this customer's menu? If you were ordering lunch at this restaurant, wouldn't you want to know a few more details? For example, you'd probably be just a little curious about what kinds of food and drinks the restaurant had and how much each cost! This menu needs elaboration to answer all of those questions.

   Elaboration means adding supporting details and explanations to your writing. Elaboration enriches descriptions, narrations, arguments, and just about any other kind of writing.

Write Away: Food, Glorious Food
Write a paragraph about the best or worst meal you have ever had. Make sure you add enough supporting details for your readers to understand why this meal was the best or the worst. Save your work in your **Working Portfolio.**

ELABORATION

Uses of Elaboration

❶ What Is Elaboration?

FoxTrot by Bill Amend

Elaboration provides details that help your reader fully understand your topic. It's a lot easier to picture a log ride with "three stomach-wrenching corkscrews" than just "the log ride." Use elaboration to make a story more exciting, strengthen a persuasive essay, or improve a report like the one below.

> **STUDENT MODEL**
>
> **DRAFT**
>
> In 1892, George Ferris designed an observation wheel. The wheel was very big. It was expensive to build.
>
> > Information on how the wheel was designed helps the reader "see" it.
>
> > Details help the reader understand how big and expensive the wheel was.
>
> **REVISION**
>
> In 1892, George Ferris designed an observation wheel for the Columbian Exposition in Chicago. The wheel was made of steel, with two inner and two outer rings connected by steel spokes. The seats were attached to the outer rings. The two support towers were 140 feet high. Ferris's wheel was 250 feet in diameter and could carry 1,440 riders. It cost $300,000 to build.

② Why Use Elaboration?

Elaboration makes your writing clearer, stronger, and more effective. You can use elaboration for these purposes:

TO EXPLAIN Give your reader facts, statistics, and definitions.

TO DESCRIBE Use sensory details that show how the subject looks, sounds, tastes, feels, or smells.

TO ANSWER QUESTIONS Think about questions your reader might ask, and then answer them in your writing.

TO SUPPORT OPINIONS Give reasons for your opinions. You may need to do research to support them.

TO SHOW, NOT TELL Instead of just *telling* your reader that a roller coaster is scary, *show* how scary it is by describing its effects.

ELABORATION

PRACTICE Let's Go!

You want to spend the day at a local amusement park, but your friend isn't sure about going. Write a paragraph persuading your friend. Use sensory details to describe the park. Answer questions your friend might have. Give reasons for any opinions you state.

Sensory Details

Using the Senses

Sensory details are bits of information that you collect by using your five senses: sight, sound, touch, taste, and smell. When you elaborate with sensory details, you give the reader a much clearer idea of what you are describing. The models below show how sensory details can enrich both fiction and nonfiction.

LITERARY MODEL

At the first step upon the cold surface, Buck's feet sank into a white mushy something very much like mud. He sprang back with a snort. More of this white stuff was falling through the air. He shook himself, but more of it fell upon him. He sniffed it curiously, then licked some up on his tongue. It bit like fire, and the next instant was gone. This puzzled him. He tried it again, with the same result. The onlookers laughed uproariously and he felt ashamed, he knew not why, for it was his first snow.

TOUCH

SIGHT

SOUND

TASTE

—Jack London, *The Call of the Wild*

PROFESSIONAL MODEL

The [Arctic] air was filled with a thundering, grinding, rumbling roar, a very frightening sound, one we had not heard before.... What I saw amazed me. A wall of ice, 20 feet tall and as long as a football field, was moving our way as if being pushed by the blade of a giant bulldozer.

SOUND

SIGHT

—Will Steger and Jon Bowermaster,
Over the Top of the World

You can use a word web to help you add sensory details to your writing.

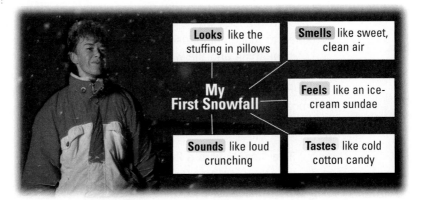

Looks like the stuffing in pillows

Smells like sweet, clean air

My First Snowfall

Feels like an ice-cream sundae

Sounds like loud crunching

Tastes like cold cotton candy

STUDENT MODEL

I saw snow for the first time when I was ten. I was visiting my grandparents in Wisconsin. When I looked out the window early one morning, it seemed like someone was shaking the stuffing out of pillows and letting it drift downward. I put on my new boots and ran outside. I was surprised by the noise of my boots crunching on the hard surface of the packed snow. It sounded the way hard pretzels sound in my head when I am chewing them. The air smelled clean and sweet. I grabbed a handful of snow. It felt like I was putting my hand into an ice-cream sundae! The snow tasted like cold cotton candy as it melted on my tongue.

To gather details about a person or object, make careful observations. Keep a small notebook or journal with you and jot them down. If you are writing about something that has happened, close your eyes and try to visualize the event.

PRACTICE A Meal to Remember

In your 📁 **Working Portfolio,** find your **Write Away** paragraph from page 375. Add sensory details to show your reader exactly what made this meal so delicious or so horrible. Then trade papers with a partner. Discuss whether your descriptions are clear enough to "taste" the meal.

Elaboration **379**

Using Proven Information

Facts are statements that can be proved. **Statistics** are facts expressed with one or more numbers. Statistics can be used to make comparisons between things or between a part of something and the whole. When you elaborate with facts and statistics, you help your readers understand your ideas.

Read the sentence below and then look at the literary model. In what ways does the literary model give you a better understanding of the size of the *Titanic*?

The *Titanic* was a large ship.

> **LITERARY MODEL**
>
> The final size and richness of this new ship was astounding. She was **882 feet long**, almost the length of four city blocks. With **nine decks**, she was as high as an **eleven-story building**....
>
> As her name boasted, the *Titanic* was indeed the biggest ship in the world.
>
> —Robert D. Ballard, *Exploring the* Titanic

HOT TIP

Give your reader comparisons, not just numbers. Knowing that the *Titanic* was 882 feet long is interesting, but knowing that it was nearly the length of four city blocks gives the reader a much better understanding of its size. This bar graph compares the *Titanic* with other famous ships.

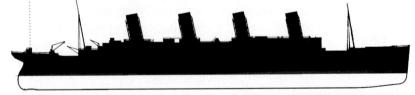

882 feet
length of the *Titanic*

117 feet   length of the *Santa María*, one of Christopher Columbus's ships

90 feet length of the *Mayflower*, the ship that took the Pilgrims to Plymouth, Mass.

Using facts and statistics can improve your essays, stories, lab reports, and research papers.

DRAFT

Wolverines are medium-sized animals. They are good hunters and can be very fierce.

REVISION

Adult wolverines are about three feet long and can weigh more than 55 pounds. They are known for their strength and will attack reindeer or even bears.

Here's How Using Facts and Statistics

1. Ask yourself: What does my reader need to know? Use facts and statistics to make your topic clearer, not just longer.

2. Look for facts and statistics in reference books, in newspapers, in magazines, and on the Internet. Gather them from your own interviews and observations.

3. Tell your reader exactly where the information is from and how old it is by citing the source and the date it was written.

For more on finding facts, see p. 502.

PRACTICE Prove It!

Choose from the facts and statistics below to write a paragraph about a lost ship. Put the items in a logical order. Don't use items that are unrelated to the topic.

Topic Sentence

In 1865, a ship called *Sultana* sank in the Mississippi River.

- ship was rediscovered in 1982
- Civil War lasted from 1861 until 1865
- ship found two miles away from the river under 21 feet of earth
- Mississippi River is 2,350 miles long
- river changed its course over many decades
- between 1,500 and 1,900 people died when ship sank
- a farmer was growing crops on top of the buried ship

ELABORATION

Visuals

Using visuals to elaborate is a great way to show rather than tell. Your reader can see at a glance what information you are giving and how it all fits together.

❶ Making a Point with Diagrams

Diagrams are drawings that give information about an object or a process. Time lines, flow charts, and labeled drawings are all types of diagrams. You can make a definition clearer by adding a labeled drawing like the one below.

A **volcano** is an opening in the crust of the earth where lava, ashes, and gases are released.

Inside a Volcano

Ash cloud
full of bits of magma (hot, liquid rock) and rock

Cone
layers of hardened, cooled lava and other materials ejected from the volcano

Magma chamber
volcanic eruption happens when magma travels upward and breaks through the earth's crust

Central vent and *side vent*
magma flows from the chamber through here

Sources: Jon Erickson, *Volcanoes and Earthquakes*, 1988; *World Book Encyclopedia*

❷ Showing Information with Other Visuals

Charts and **graphs** present facts and statistics in a visual format. They let your reader see and compare information easily. The writer of the student model on the next page added a bar graph, which she created with the graphing function of a word-processing program, to support her statements.

Volcanoes have caused some of the worst natural disasters in history. Lava flows have destroyed whole towns, and people have starved to death because their farmland got covered with ashes and nothing could grow. Over the past 200 years, more than 250,000 people have died because of volcano eruptions. Four huge eruptions caused about 70 percent of those deaths.

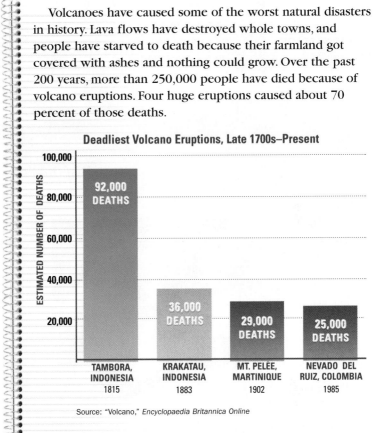

Deadliest Volcano Eruptions, Late 1700s–Present

Source: "Volcano," *Encyclopaedia Britannica Online*

For more examples of visual displays of information, see pp. 510–511.

PRACTICE Be a Statistician

Work with three or four classmates to take a survey of your class's preferences. Pick a topic to ask about, such as favorite foods, hobbies, sports, or video games. Combine your group's results and present them as a chart or graph. For example, you might find out that 12 of your classmates say that pizza is their favorite food, 10 prefer hamburgers, and 7 like hot dogs best.

ELABORATION

Student Help Desk

Elaboration at a Glance

What is it?
Supporting details, reasons, and explanations that enrich your writing

Why should I use it?
To give your reader enough details to understand your topic

What kinds can I use?
- sensory details
- facts and statistics
- graphs, charts, and other visuals

Adding Sensory Details Just the Right Word

These words may spark an idea for adding your own sensory details.

SIGHT
shiny, pale, furry, sparkling

SMELL
fishy, sweet-smelling, fragrant

TASTE
bitter, salty

SOUND
growling, gurgling, fluttering, crunching

TOUCH
slippery, smooth, bumpy, cold, wet, scaly

Finding Facts Where to Go, Whom to Ask

Here are some good places to dig up facts and statistics.

 Almanacs, atlases, encyclopedias, and other reference books

 Online databases of newspaper and magazine articles

 Interviews you conduct, either in person, by telephone, or by e-mail

 Web sites of publishers, museums, or other reliable sources

Kinds of Visuals   Get the Picture?

Maps, charts, and graphs give your reader information at a glance.

Pie Graph: shows how one or more parts relate to the whole

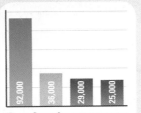

Bar Graph: compares numbers or sets of numbers

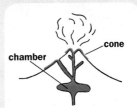

Diagram: shows information about an object or process

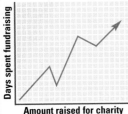

Line Graph: shows change over time

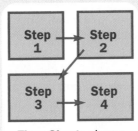

Flow Chart: shows steps in a process

Map: shows physical location

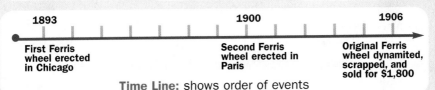

Time Line: shows order of events

The Bottom Line

Checklist for Elaboration

Have I . . .

____ told my reader enough about my topic?

____ explained, described, answered questions, and supported opinions where needed?

____ used sensory details to give my reader a clear picture?

____ used facts and statistics to give more information?

burly

brawny

SCRAPPY

wea

courageous

muscular

Tough Guys

How do you describe strength?

Getting Ready for the Title Bout

A professional wrestler is nothing if not **husky** and **muscular.** To be a good wrestler, you need to be **brawny** and **burly.** (If you are **beefy,** maybe you've put on too much weight.) You have to be **gutsy, scrappy,** and ready for a brawl. What you don't want to be is **muscle-bound,** because then you'd have difficulty moving.

The Power of Persuasion

You might prefer to take part in a battle of words. If you do, make sure that your reasoning isn't **weak** or **unsupported.** You can't afford to be **indecisive** or **wishy-washy.** When you stand up to speak, be **bold** and **courageous.** Your opponent will be quick to take advantage of a **feeble** or **puny** defense!

CHAPTER 18

beefy

▷ **Your Turn**
Get Stronger

Create an advertisement for a gym. Use some of the boldfaced words above in your ad. Include a sketch of what the gym or the people who go there might look like.

GUTSY

wishy-washy

bold

Revising Sentences

Making Sentences Stronger

The writer on the left knows he has a problem—he hasn't learned how to revise his sentences to make them more interesting and sophisticated. You can learn to be like the writer on the right. The techniques found in this chapter will help you make your sentences stronger and more energetic.

Write Away: How Strong Is He?

On a separate piece of paper, write the sentence *Charles is strong*. Add details, examples, descriptions, or other information, and write a sentence that is 10 to 12 words long. Save your work in your ☐ **Working Portfolio.**

Padded and Empty Sentences

LESSON 1

❶ Refining Padded Sentences

A **padded sentence** has more words than are needed to communicate an idea. Sometimes padded sentences have long phrases that can be replaced with shorter ones. At other times, padded sentences bore your reader by needlessly repeating an idea.

STUDENT MODEL

DRAFT

I was upset because **of the fact that** my friend wouldn't ride the roller coasters with me. The reason is he **is of the opinion that** roller coasters look **like they could be full of danger.**

REVISION

I was upset because my friend wouldn't ride the roller coasters with me. He thinks they look dangerous.

> Does the writer really need all these words to make his point?

Here's How **Filling Empty Sentences**

1. Think about what you really want to say.
2. Look for words and phrases that could be deleted and never missed.
3. Look for places where one or two words could replace many words.

Unnecessary Phrase	Replacement
on account of the fact that	because *or* since
is of the opinion that	thinks *or* believes
what I really want to say is	(Just say it!)

Peanuts by Charles M. Schulz

PEANUTS reprinted by permission of United Feature Syndicate, Inc.

❷ Improving Empty Sentences

Some sentences say nothing or repeat an idea that has already been stated. Other sentences make statements that are not supported by facts.

DRAFT

I like bike riding because it is fun and enjoyable. It is good transportation. Mountain bikes are the best. They are my favorite bikes because they are the best ones.

> This sentence says the same thing three times.

> Tell *why* they are the best.

REVISION

I like bike riding. It's a fun way to get somewhere quickly. Mountain bikes are my favorite kind of bike because you can ride them almost anywhere, even over hills and through mud.

> Here the writer supports her opinion and eliminates repetition.

REVISING

Here's How Filling Empty Sentences

1. Eliminate words and phrases that needlessly repeat an idea.
2. Don't leave your reader asking, "Why?" Add reasons, examples, and facts to support your opinions.

PRACTICE Tell More, Repeat Less

Follow the instructions in parentheses to revise these sentences.

1. A pickup truck is better than a car. (Add a reason or fact.)
2. What I really mean is that I hope your team wins. (Eliminate unnecessary words.)
3. Science fiction rules! (Add a reason or fact.)
4. I don't like scary movies because they are frightening. (Eliminate the repeated idea; then add a reason or fact.)

Stringy and Overloaded Sentences

Both stringy and overloaded sentences confuse the reader by forcing too many ideas into one sentence. Often, the reader can't tell how the ideas in the sentence are related.

Fixing Stringy and Overloaded Sentences

A **stringy sentence** contains too many ideas loosely connected by the word *and*. Stringy sentences seem to go on and on. To fix stringy sentences, make each complete thought a separate sentence. Write the sentences in a logical order.

HOT TIP

You can use conjunctions such as *first, then, when, next, after that,* and *because* to show the relationship between ideas.

STUDENT MODEL

DRAFT

My class visited Washington, D.C., and we went to the National Air and Space Museum, and we saw the Wright 1903 Flyer, which was the first successful airplane, and we saw Viking 1, the first spacecraft to operate on the surface of Mars, and I thought seeing Viking 1 was the best part of the tour, and I would really like to go to Mars someday.

REVISION

When my class visited Washington, D.C., we went to the National Air and Space Museum. **First,** we saw the Wright 1903 Flyer, which was the first successful airplane. **After that,** we saw Viking 1, the first spacecraft to operate on the surface of Mars. I thought seeing Viking 1 was the best part of the tour **because** I would really like to go to Mars someday.

PRACTICE A Blast Off!

Rewrite this stringy sentence.

Viking 1 landed on Mars on July 20, 1976, and it was designed to search for life on Mars, and scientists couldn't prove that there is life on that planet, but the information Viking 1 collected gave them a better understanding of Martian weather and the Martian landscape.

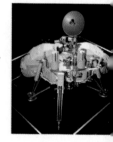

An overloaded sentence contains too much information about a single topic. You may know what you want to say, but your reader won't understand you.

DRAFT

    Even though most people think that pterodactyls, flying reptiles that lived more than 65 million years ago in Europe and East Africa, were huge animals, not all of them were, and some of them were about the same size as a sparrow.

> There are too many facts and details here for one sentence.

REVISION

    Pterodactyls were flying reptiles that lived more than 65 million years ago in Europe and East Africa. Most people think that pterodactyls were huge animals, **but** not all of them were. **Some** pterodactyls were about the same size as a sparrow.

> This version is easier to understand because it has been broken into three sentences.

Here's How   **Revising Stringy and Overloaded Sentences**

1. Break down your sentence into separate ideas.

2. Combine related ideas, using conjunctions such as *and, but, or, so, then,* and *when.*

3. Rewrite your sentence as two or more sentences, making sure that you have not packed too many ideas into any one sentence.

PRACTICE B   Sentence Checkup

In your ⬒ **Working Portfolio,** find your **Write Away** sentence from page 387. Make sure it is not padded, empty, stringy, or overloaded. Revise your work to make it even stronger. If your revisions make your sentence longer, you may want to break it into two or more sentences.

Varying Sentence Structure

❶ Rearranging Phrases

Try rearranging the phrases in your sentences for more impact. Words that give the most important information often have the greatest effect at the start or end of a sentence.

Minerva opened her front door, and fifteen of her friends spilled out, **wishing her a happy birthday.**

Fifteen of Minerva's friends spilled out **her front door as she opened it, wishing her a happy birthday.**

Wishing her a happy birthday, fifteen of Minerva's friends spilled out **her front door as she opened it.**

HOT TIP

There are no precise rules about the "most important" words in a sentence. You can put interesting details up front to grab your reader's attention or at the end to go out with a bang.

PRACTICE A Order, Order!

Rewrite each sentence two ways, as shown in the examples above.

1. Matala checked the controls and gazed out the window as her rocket blasted off.
2. She switched on the rocket boosters and began planning her return while the ship gathered speed.

❷ Varying Sentence Types

You can make your writing livelier by including questions, exclamations, and commands.

PROFESSIONAL MODEL

What can kids do about pollution in their communities? Students at Bellamy Middle School in Chicopee, Massachusetts, found out. Chicopee had a problem storing sludge from factories and sewers. In winter the sludge froze before it could be taken to landfills. Some Bellamy students toured the sludge plant to see the problem for themselves—and smell it too! The town used the students' idea of building a greenhouse to keep the sludge from freezing. Look around your community for environmental problems you can help solve.

—Greg Hess

> The writer uses a question to draw readers into the topic.

> An exclamation adds emphasis.

> A command urges readers to apply the example to their own lives.

 Don't overuse exclamations. Too many can make your writing seem breathless or overexcited.

For more on questions, exclamations, and commands, see p. 16.

PRACTICE B Question? Exclaim! Command.

Add some variety to the letter below. Rewrite at least three sentences as questions, exclamations, or commands.

Dear Jennifer,

I'm not sure if you heard that I won first place in the science fair. I bet you can imagine how surprised I was to win. It was thrilling. The science-fair judges asked me lots of questions. I hope you will tell your aunt about it the next time she is in town. The information she gave me helped a lot. I wonder what I should do for next year's science project.

Write back soon!

Trish

REVISING

Varying Sentence Length

❶ Changing Sentence Length and Rhythm

Professional writers know that using sentences of varying lengths is an important way to keep reader interest.

LITERARY MODEL

People who live on hills sleep so close to the stars they forget those of us who live too much on earth. They don't look down at all except to be content to live on hills. They have nothing to do with last week's garbage or fear of rats. Night comes. Nothing wakes them but the wind.

—Sandra Cisneros, *The House on Mango Street*

> Cisneros's long sentences give information.

> Her short sentences add drama.

As you write and revise, think about the length and rhythm of your sentences. Do they keep the reader interested?

Don't mistake short sentences for sentence fragments. "Night comes" is a complete sentence—the subject is *night* and the predicate is *comes*.

❷ Combining Choppy Sentences

Choppy sentences are a series of short sentences that often lack detail. When read in a group, choppy sentences seem boring and immature. Your writing falls into the same rhythm for sentence after sentence, and pretty soon . . . zzzzzzzzz. This writer fell asleep reading his own essay!

I have many chores to do. My least favorite chore is mowing the lawn. It is hard work. It takes a long time. It is boring. I am tired when I finish.

DRAFT

Guide dogs were first trained in Germany. They were trained to help blind veterans. Doberman pinschers have been trained as guide dogs. Golden retrievers have also been trained as guide dogs. German shepherds are the most commonly used breed of guide dog.

REVISION

Guide dogs were first trained in Germany **to help blind veterans.** Doberman pinschers **and** golden retrievers have been trained as guide dogs**, but** German shepherds are the most commonly used breed.

> This version gives the same information with less repetition.

Here's How Smoothing Choppy Sentences

1. Use conjunctions such as *but, and,* and *or* to combine related sentences.

2. Get rid of repetitive sentences that add only one or two details about your subject. Insert those details into other sentences.

Don't create run-ons as you combine sentences.

, and

My dog got loose‸she ran all over the neighborhood.

For more on sentence combining, see p. 26.

PRACTICE Smooth It Out

Rewrite this choppy paragraph. Add conjunctions where they are needed. Vary the length and rhythm of the sentences.

> We took a field trip. We went to the aquarium. It was interesting. There were guides. One of them showed us around. There were tanks of fish. There was a huge shark tank. I thought the best part was the tank full of horseshoe crabs. We could touch them. Their shells felt bumpy.

REVISING

Student Help Desk

Revising Sentences at a Glance

Trim excess words from padded and empty sentences.

Reorganize stringy and overloaded sentences to make your ideas clearer.

Vary the length and structure of your sentences to keep your reader interested.

Phrases to Avoid — Get to the Point!

These words and phrases bog down your writing. Get rid of them or replace them with shorter, simpler words or phrases.

Unnecessary Word or Phrase	Replacement
on account of the fact that	because or since
being that	because
the reason is the reason why is that the reason is because	
is of the opinion that	thinks or believes
at this point in time at the present time at the current time presently	now
in spite of the fact that	although
what I mean is the point is the fact is	(Just say it!)

Conjunctions

Connect **Your Ideas.**

Use these conjunctions to show how your ideas are related.

To connect ideas that are . . .	. . . try using these conjunctions:
similar	and, plus, also
different	not, but, however
related in time	first, then, next, later, finally
related in space	beside, over, under, between

Rephrasing Sentences

Say It a **Different** Way.

Strengthen your writing by changing some of your statements into questions, commands, and exclamations.

Type of sentence	Can be used to . . .	Example
Question	• draw your reader into your subject • help your reader think about how your topic relates to his or her life	Have you ever wanted to be stronger and faster?
Command	• ask your reader to consider a point you have made • urge your reader to take action	Think about adding more exercise to your routine.
Exclamation	• emphasize a point • add feeling to your writing	Being in shape is really fun!

The Bottom Line

Checklist for Revising Sentences

Can I improve my sentences by . . .

____ cutting unneeded words from padded sentences?

____ deleting empty sentences?

____ breaking up stringy sentences to make them clearer?

____ reworking overloaded sentences to make my ideas more understandable?

____ changing sentence structure and length to add variety?

Power Words
Vocabulary for Precise Writing

Miles of Style

You can describe anyone's personal style if you know the right words.

Formal Finery

At a party attended by the rich and famous, all the guests wear formal **garb,** their **finery.** There are no ordinary **garments** at this party; no everyday, off-the-rack **apparel.** Everyone is in rich **attire,** in full **regalia,** in glittering **raiment.**

The men wear **custom-tailored** suits, **tuxedoes,** or **tie and tails.** Some women are in **classic, elegant** gowns. Others are more **daring,** dressed in the latest **modish** creations. All are glamorous; each is more of a fashion plate than the next. This is the world of **high style** and **fashion,** the world of **haute couture.**

The Rest of Us

The rest of us, the not-so-rich-and-famous, have also put on our fancy **getups;** we're wearing our finest **duds** or **threads.** Our **gear** is all the rage, and we're stepping out. The food may not be as fancy, but we'll have as much fun!

▷ **Your Turn** Dressed to the Nines

Make a sketch that shows you wearing a special outfit or your everyday clothes. Add labels to your sketch that give details on your personal style. Use at least one of the boldfaced words above.

Style and Effective Language

Which hat might have an owner who would say . . .

"Them's fightin' words, pardner!"

"You have been most ungracious, sir."

"Say that again and I'll throw you in the brig!"

Which Style Suits You Best?

Which of these hats would you like to wear? Would you rather wear a different kind altogether, or maybe no hat at all? Your choice was probably affected by your own personal style—the way you look, dress, talk . . . and write. Clothes help show your fashion style. Your choice of words, the length and complexity of your sentences, and the expressions you use combine to make up your **writing style.** Just about everything you write lets a little of your personality show through.

Write Away: Who's That in the Hat?
Choose one of the hats in the photograph. Imagine a person who might wear the hat, and write a paragraph about him or her. Save your work in your 🗁 **Working Portfolio.**

The Elements of Style

Style means the way you express yourself in writing. The words you choose and the way you use them affect how your reader reacts to your writing.

❶ Exploring Style

Read the two passages below. The first model, from an encyclopedia article, is meant to inform. The second, from a story about a mongoose named Rikki-tikki-tavi and a snake named Nagaina, is intended to entertain.

PROFESSIONAL MODEL

The mongoose is best known for its ability to kill snakes. It is not immune to poison, but its swiftness allows it to seize and kill poisonous snakes such as the cobra. The mongoose also kills mice, rats, poultry, wild birds, and other small animals.

—*World Book Encyclopedia*, "Mongoose"

> Details are made up of facts and concrete words.

> Tone is very matter-of-fact.

LITERARY MODEL

Rikki-tikki was bounding all round Nagaina, keeping just out of reach of her stroke, his little eyes like hot coals. Nagaina gathered herself together and flung out at him. Rikki-tikki jumped up and backwards. Again and again and again she struck, and each time her head came with a whack on the matting of the veranda, and she gathered herself together like a watch spring.

—Rudyard Kipling, "Rikki-tikki-tavi"

> Writer uses strong images and figures of speech.

> Tone is one of excitement.

❷ Recognizing Elements of Style

As you read, look for these elements of style. You will learn more about them in the rest of the chapter.

Levels of Language

Writers use formal or informal language, depending on their audience and purpose.

Formal The mongoose is a carnivorous creature.

Informal A mongoose eats just about anything it can catch.

Precise Words

Writers choose words carefully to create just the right effect.

Vague wording Rikki-tikki **moved** toward the **snake.**

Precise wording Rikki-tikki **leaped** toward the **hissing cobra.**

Connotation and Denotation

Denotation is the dictionary definition of a word. **Connotation** is all the thoughts and feelings the word brings into the reader's mind.

What's the best way to describe a mongoose?

Positive Connotation   **Negative Connotation**

| brave | aggressive | vicious |
| hunter | meat-eater | killer |

Other Elements of Style

- **Figures of speech** describe something by comparing it to something else, as in "Nagaina gathered herself together like a watch spring."

- **Imagery** refers to the "pictures" a writer creates for the reader.

- **Tone** is the writer's attitude toward the subject, as shown in the words and images he or she chooses.

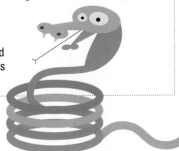

STYLE

Choosing Language Levels

Formal and Informal Language

You may not realize it, but you speak and write differently depending on the situation. Knowing when to use formal and informal language can make you a more confident and successful writer.

Formal language is serious and polite. It often uses sophisticated words and longer sentences. **Informal language** is more like conversation. It uses simpler words, shorter sentences, and more contractions.

For example, an informal E-mail to a friend is very different from a formal letter of complaint to a manufacturer.

STUDENT MODEL

INFORMAL

Hey Dani,

    I am so **steamed!** You know that new **bike** I bought? Well, **it's a piece of junk.** Even my **bike shop guy can't** fix it. I'm **gonna** write to the manufacturer.

> Uses informal language, contractions, and slang

                          Meg

FORMAL

Dear Madam or Sir:

    The Mountain Express **bicycle** I **purchased** last week has already broken down. Some of the plastic parts have cracked, and my local repair shop tells me that they **cannot** be repaired. I am enclosing a copy of the shop's diagnosis for your reference. **Please let me know how I can receive a refund or a new bicycle.**

> Uses more sophisticated vocabulary and precise language

               Yours truly,
               Megan Briggs

HOT TIP As you choose what level of language to use, think about your audience—the person or people who will read your writing. Also, think about why you are writing—your purpose.

Choosing Formal or Informal Language	
Formal	**Informal**
Audience: teacher or someone you don't know well	**Audience:** friends or family
When to use: speeches, essays, reports, or formal letters	**When to use:** friendly letters and E-mails, casual conversation
Formal writing has . . . • few or no contractions (such as *you're* or *I'll*) • no slang (or very informal language, such as *goofing off* or *did a number on us*) • longer, more sophisticated sentences • exact words • a serious, impersonal tone (attitude toward the topic)	**Informal writing has . . .** • contractions where they are needed • slang (if the audience understands it) • shorter, simpler words and sentences • a friendly, personal tone

Some writers think that using difficult, impressive-sounding words makes their writing seem more important. However, using too many of these words can confuse your reader. Your goal is to communicate clearly, whether you're using formal or informal language.

Expressions such as *ain't got none* and *them thing*s are not considered Standard English. Nonstandard English often violates accepted rules of spelling and grammar. If you use nonstandard English in formal writing or speaking, people tend to focus not on *what* you are saying but on *how* you say it. Use Standard English in school and business situations.

PRACTICE **A Number-One Hit?**

With a partner, change these song titles into formal language.

1. "You Stomped on My Heart, You Nasty Toad"
2. "I Ain't Gonna Listen to You No More"
3. "I Am Such a Cool Dude"
4. "Why Are Ya Freaking Me Out Like This?"
5. "My Love for You Has Totally Croaked, Baby"

Choosing Precise Words

The Best Way to Say It

Precise words give your reader a better idea of your message. Notice how the second passage gives a clearer picture of the scene.

I was **angry.** I remember the **sadness** of Colin's face in the **light.**

LITERARY MODEL

I was **stricken** and **furious.** I remember the **misery** of Colin's face in the **lamplight.**

—Paul Annixter, "Last Cover"

Many times, one very precise word can give your reader a more accurate picture than a long string of words.

Draft

The audience **made a lot of noise to show** its approval.

Revision

The audience **roared** its approval.

You can make your own writing stronger by using strong nouns and verbs instead of a series of weak modifiers.

STUDENT MODEL

DRAFT	REVISION
The **small brown birds quickly ate** the crumbs and flew away. The **little child** who had been feeding them **said in a loud voice** that she wanted to keep them as pets.	The **sparrows gobbled** the crumbs and flew away. The **toddler** who had been feeding them **screamed** that she wanted to keep them as pets.

Try using strong verbs instead of *is* or *was.* "The sun blazed in the sky" is stronger than "The sun was very bright in the sky."

404 Essential Writing Skills

How to Be Specific		
Nouns	**General: a dog**	
	Specific: a poodle	
Verbs	**General: went** home	
	Specific: dashed home	
Adverbs	**General: really** excited	
	Specific: wildly excited	
Adjectives	**General: old** book	
	Specific: battered, dusty book	

As you write and revise, ask yourself whether the words you have chosen give an accurate picture of your topic. A friend, relative, or classmate can help you by asking questions about parts of your writing that seem unclear.

Revising with Exact Words		
First Draft	**Peer Reader's Comments**	**Revised Version**
When I was young, I traveled by airplane for the first time. It was really scary. There was a lot of noise when the plane took off.	How old were you? Why was it scary? What were the noises like?	When I was **four and a half**, I traveled by airplane for the first time. I was **terrified** by the **whining, buzzing, and thumping** when the plane took off.

For more on powerful words, see p. 410.

For more on powerful words, see p. 410.

PRACTICE As You See It

Revise these boring sentences with precise words. Use the information in the picture to help you.

The girl danced. Her costume was pretty. The audience cheered for all the dancers.

STYLE

Connotation and Denotation

LESSON 4

Two Kinds of Meaning

Almost every word you use has two kinds of meanings. A word's **denotation** is the straightforward dictionary definition. The **connotation** of a word includes all the thoughts and feelings that word may bring to people's minds. When you choose a word, make sure that you have considered its possible connotations.

What's the Connotation?	
When you write . . .	**Your reader may think . . .**
Phil is **conceited**.	Phil has a very high opinion of himself and his abilities—probably too high. He thinks he can't do anything wrong. *(negative connotation)*
Phil is **confident**.	Phil is certain of himself and his abilities. *(positive connotation)*

Words can have positive, negative, or neutral connotations. Use words with neutral connotations when you don't want to show strong positive or negative feelings in your writing.

POSITIVE

Aunt Callie is always interested in what other people are doing.

NEUTRAL

Aunt Callie is always curious about others.

NEGATIVE

Aunt Callie is nosy. What a snoop!

Connotations can depend on your audience. If you say, "Gee, Uncle Ted, what an unusual tie," your uncle may be pleased. However, if you tell your mother, "That dinner was, uh . . . unusual, Mom," she may be insulted. Ask someone else to review your writing to be sure that your message gets across.

CHAPTER 19

Decoding Connotations		
Positive	**Neutral**	**Negative**
That's a **glamorous** necklace.	That's an **attractive** necklace.	That necklace is **gaudy.**
The racehorse was **slender.**	The racehorse was **thin.**	The racehorse was **scrawny.**

If you're not sure what connotations a word may have, check a dictionary for the uses of the word. If you need to find a word with a similar meaning but a different connotation, use a thesaurus.

PRACTICE Can You Picture It?

For each phrase, write "positive" for positive connotations and "negative" for negative connotations. Use a dictionary if you are uncertain of a word's meaning. Then use each phrase in a sentence that reflects the connotation.

Example:
an **imaginative** sculpture—positive
a **crazy** sculpture—negative

The imaginative sculpture drew a crowd of admirers.

The crazy sculpture made the children giggle.

1. an unusual stench; an unusual fragrance
2. a brave explorer; a reckless explorer
3. an inexpensive present; a cheap present
4. a decisive camp counselor; a bossy camp counselor
5. hoarded the supplies; preserved the supplies

A garish shirt?
A colorful shirt?

How would you describe this shirt? Write two sentences, one with a positive connotation and one with a negative connotation.

Using Figurative Language

LESSON 5

❶ Figures of Speech

Figures of speech are expressions that go beyond the dictionary definitions of the words being used. Figures of speech and other kinds of descriptive language are often easy to remember because they appeal to the senses. They have strong **imagery**—in other words, they bring clear pictures to your reader's mind.

One figure of speech, a **simile,** is a comparison using the word *like* or *as.*

Bizarro by Dan Piraro

"HAVE A SEAT" IS A FIGURE OF SPEECH AROUND THESE PARTS, MR. GREESON.

LITERARY MODEL

Dolores was the assistant manager at Stan's and had worked there for twenty years, since high school. **She knew the store like a mother knows her baby....**

—Cynthia Rylant, "A Crush"

A **metaphor,** which is a comparison that does not use the word *like* or *as,* can contribute even stronger imagery to your writing. Which of the following sentences paints a more vivid picture?

SIMILE

Mr. Patel knew so much sports trivia that he was like an encyclopedia.

METAPHOR

Mr. Patel was an encyclopedia of sports trivia.

Another type of figurative language, **personification,** gives human qualities to animals or objects.

The light danced on the surface of the water.

As I stumbled around the forest carrying 40 pounds of camping equipment, I could hear an owl laughing at me.

❷ Avoiding Clichés

Many figures of speech have been overused. These tired phrases are called **clichés.** Instead of relying on clichés, try to think of fresher ways to say what you mean.

Cliché Alert!

Stale Imagery	Fresh Replacement
free as a bird	free as a student on the first day of summer vacation
raining cats and dogs	thousands of stinging raindrops
big as a house	enormous, gigantic, *or* vast
stubborn as a mule	stubborn as a toddler who hasn't had his nap
quick as a flash	a human lightning bolt

DANGER
Clichés
Ahead

PRACTICE A Away with Clichés

Revise this dull paragraph. Replace the clichés with fresh figurative language of your own.

My first week at camp was as dull as dishwater. I just sat around like a bump on a log. Then I made some friends, and the difference in my attitude was like night and day. Spending time with them made me as happy as a clam. I can't wait to go back next year!

PRACTICE B Making It All Work

In your 🗐 **Working Portfolio,** locate your **Write Away** paragraph from page 399. Use what you have learned about style and effective language to revise your paragraph. Add some figurative language, but don't include any clichés!

Student Help Desk

Style and Effective Language at a Glance

Keep It on the Level	Precisely Right	Brave or Foolhardy?	Light as a *What?*
Select formal or informal language to match audience and purpose.	Get rid of vague words.	Weigh the connotations of your words.	Use fresh figurative language.

Language Levels

Dressing Up or Down

Extremely Formal	Somewhat Formal	Somewhat Informal	Extremely Informal
displeased	angry	mad	blowing a gasket
dine		eat	munch
funds	money	cash	dough

Powerful Words

Pack a *Genuine* Punch

Nifty Nouns	Vivid Verbs	Appealing Adjectives	Admirable Adverbs
redwood, cloak	sweep, flutter	plush, wrinkled	freshly, gloomily
otter, rubbish	float, polish	cautious	recently, speedi
toddler, mare	soothe, whisper	handsome	gracefully
chimes	demolish, shriek	scaly, hushed	suspiciously
quilt, desert	scrape, perspire	costly, crowded	violently, warmly

Spot the Connotation

What I *Mean* Is . . .

The words you choose can bring positive, negative, or neutral feelings to your reader's mind.

Positive	Marcia's new dog is **lively**.
Neutral	Marcia's new dog is **active**.
Negative	Marcia's new dog is **wild**.

Phrases to Avoid: Cliché Display

How many clichés can you find?

As quick as a wink, Trent rose to the occasion. With a mind like a steel trap, he saw that the sink was not clean as a whistle, the way Dad liked it. In the blink of an eye, he put a little elbow grease into his chore. Soon, Trent was working like a house afire. A man's home is his castle, he reasoned, and Dad should be home any minute. You could set your watch by him.

Trent was right as rain. When Dad saw the sparkling kitchen, he was pleased as punch.

"Let's eat at Pizza Heaven!" he said. "You've worked like a dog today, and this money is burning a hole in my pocket!"

The Bottom Line

Checklist for Style and Effective Language

Have I . . .

____ chosen the right language level?

____ used precise, effective words?

____ considered the connotation and denotation of my words?

____ enriched my writing with figurative language?

Writing Workshops

Turn It On!

So you want to spark your imagination? Shock your friends and family? By using different forms of writing, you can really turn the juice on in your writing.

Personal Narrative

Learn What It Is

Stories about events in people's lives fascinate us. They are the focus of many television programs and articles in newspapers and magazines. You may have an interesting story to tell about your own life. Writing your own **personal narrative** may help you understand better why certain events in your life are so important to you.

Basics in a Box

PERSONAL NARRATIVE AT A GLANCE

Middle
- Describes the event using descriptive details and dialogue
- Makes the importance clear

Beginning

Introduces the incident, including the people and place involved

End
- Tells the outcome or result of the event
- Presents the writer's feelings about the experience

RUBRIC

Standards for Writing

A successful personal narrative should

- focus on one well-defined experience
- begin with an image or idea that makes readers want to find out more
- make the importance of the event clear
- show clearly the order in which events occurred
- use details that appeal to the senses to describe characters and setting
- use dialogue to develop characters
- provide a strong conclusion

See How It's Done: *Personal Narrative*

Student Model
Dan Walsh
Hauser Junior High

RUBRIC
IN ACTION

Tackle Football

On a warm Friday in early October my friend asked me if I wanted to play tackle football after school.

"Someone's really going to get hurt one of these days," I said in my usual cautious way. "I bet one of us is going to break an arm or a leg."

"No one's going to get hurt," said Tom. "How many times have we played tackle football without getting more than a scrape or a bruise?"

"About a million times," I said, sort of agreeing with him. "Fine," I said, "I'll go."

Later that day, after we had been playing football for no longer than 15 minutes, it happened. Larry was tackled. I heard a loud snap and then screaming and crying, and not only from Larry. About three kids who were huddling around him were saying, "Oh, man! Oh, man!" over and over. Larry was on the ground, but I thought he had just a cut or a scrape. Then I saw it. His arm was snapped to the side just below his elbow. You could see the bone sticking through his skin!

Tom and I started running to find help. I ran faster than I ever had or probably ever will. When I got to a house, I started banging and pressing the doorbell as hard as I could. Finally the door opened.

"There's a kid over there who's really badly hurt!" I said, panting. "I really need to use your phone!"

"Settle down, young fella," the old man said. "The phone's in back." After about 40 seconds I was able to dial 911. My hands were shaking so hard!

A policewoman answered the phone and I said, "There's a kid over here and he's really badly hurt! He's at Herrington Park, right near the baseball field."

① Begins with a scene that makes readers want to find out what will happen

② Uses details that appeal to the senses

③ Clearly shows the order in which events occurred

NARRATIVE

"An ambulance is on its way," she said.

Slam! I hung up the phone and ran all the way back to Larry. A bunch of my friends were sitting near him with wide eyes and teary faces. I lay down near Larry and told him that an ambulance was coming.

"I'm going to die!" said Larry. "It hurts so much! I want you to give all my money to my mom and dad when I die!" he said, panting for air.

> ❹ Uses dialogue to develop the characters

By the time a police officer got there, Larry was beginning to curse. "What did I just hear you say?" asked the police officer. He was just like the ones in the movies, a little chubby, dark sunglasses, and it looked like he had just eaten a powdered doughnut.

"Sir," I said, "the kid just broke his arm. See it?"

"I'll ask for your opinion when I want it, young man."

> ❺ Uses details to make the importance of the event clear

The police officer then started to talk to Larry until the ambulance came. Larry said that the pain had stopped. When the paramedics got him onto the stretcher, Larry screamed again. "Oww! The pain started again!"

> ❻ Includes sensory words to show the drama of events

Then the ambulance screeched away with sirens blasting and everything. We could hear it for a long time, and all of us just stood or sat there without saying anything.

On my way home, I started running as fast as I could for no reason. I was really thirsty, but when I got there, I just went to bed and tried to stop shivering.

> ❼ Provides a strong conclusion by telling the effect the event had on the writer

I had nightmares for about a week after that.

Do It Yourself

Writing Prompt Select an event from your own experience, and write a personal narrative about it.

Purpose To entertain and inform

Audience Friends, classmates

❶ Prewriting

Brainstorm topics. Think of subjects to write about by recalling what you remember most about a vacation, a school event, or a favorite place.

For more topic ideas, see the Idea Bank, p. 420.

Freewrite about one event. How did things look, smell, feel, taste, sound? Who was there? What was the most interesting part? Circle the idea that interests you the most. You may be able to use that idea as your focus.

Analyze why you care. Think about why this event sticks in your mind. Did you learn something important? Did it change your life in any way?

❷ Drafting

Consider the organization. Every narrative must have a beginning, middle, and end. Can you fit the key elements of your narrative into the chart below?

Organization of a Personal Narrative		
Beginning	**Middle**	**End**
• Who was involved? • What happened? • What will grab a reader's attention?	• How did the event progress? • What caused each part to happen?	• What changed after the event? • Why is this event meaningful to you?

Think about descriptive details. What words or images can you use to make readers see, hear, and feel what is happening?

Wrap it up. Make sure that by the end of your story, readers will understand what happened and why it was important to you.

For information about getting feedback from your peers, see p. 421.

NARRATIVE

❸ Revising

TARGET SKILL ▶ **Using Dialogue** Quoting people directly can make your essay lively and easy to read. For more help with revising, review the rubric on page 414.

> *"Sir,"*
> ∧ I said, ~~that~~ the kid just broke his arm, ~~and I pointed to it.~~ *see it?"*
> ¶ ~~The officer told me he would~~ *"I'll* ask for ~~my~~ *your* opinion when ~~he~~ I
> wanted it. *young man."*

❹ Editing and Proofreading

TARGET SKILL ▶ **Punctuating Dialogue** Put quotation marks around the speaker's exact words. Put end punctuation inside the quotation marks.

> When the paramedics got him onto the stretcher, Larry
> screamed again. "Oww! The pain has started again"!

For more about quotation marks, see pp. 258–260.

❺ Sharing and Reflecting

You can **share** your personal narrative with others by making copies for friends and classmates. You might want to put the work of several classmates together into booklets.

For Your Working Portfolio It can be helpful to read others' work to help you **reflect** on your own writing. Read published writers as well as peers and identify the strategies they used to write their personal narratives. How can these other writers help you learn to write better? Attach your reflections to your finished work. Save your narrative in your 🗀 **Working Portfolio.**

Speak for Yourself: *Telling an Anecdote*

"I'll never forget the time Larry broke his arm when we were playing football. . . ."

When you share a story like this, recalling a funny or interesting incident, you are telling an anecdote. Turning your **personal narrative** into an anecdote is a way to present your story orally in an entertaining and informal way.

Here's How) Creating an Anecdote

- Choose a specific part of your narrative to share. Pick the section that has the most action or the most interesting characters.

- Think about what you could add to the story, or places where you could condense what you wrote.

- Change your more formal written language to everyday, conversational language.

- Act out the parts. Use different voices for each character.

- Memorize your anecdote so you are free to add gestures and voices.

- Ask a friend to listen as you practice telling the story.

For more information on speaking skills, see p. 545–47.

NARRATIVE

Student Help Desk

Personal Narrative at a Glance

Beginning

Introduces the incident, including the people and place involved

Middle

• Describes the event using descriptive details and dialogue
• Makes the importance clear

End

• Tells the outcome or result of the event
• Presents the writer's feelings about the experience

Idea Bank

Need a topic for a personal narrative?

Write about when a special pet did something funny.

Choose an event that helped you deal with anger or disappointment.

Think of someone who surprised you by being different from what you expected.

Remember a time when you were really scared.

Recall how you felt when you walked into a group of people and you didn't know any of them.

Read a personal narrative by someone else to give you ideas. Try a narrative such as Ernesto Galarza's *Barrio Boy* (*Language of Literature*, Grade 7).

Sensory Details

Add details like these to your personal narrative.

Sense	Details
Sight	*bright, green, dark*
Sound	*loud, buzzing*
Touch	*cold, rough*
Smell	*lemony, smoky*
Taste	*sour, sweet*

Friendly Feedback

Questions for Your Peer Reader

- What is the subject of my narrative?
- What did you like best about my narrative?
- How do I show that the subject is important to me?
- What details are most memorable?
- How could I make what happened more clear?
- What could I do to make either the beginning or the ending more interesting?

Publishing Options

Print	Begin a scrapbook that will contain essays about interesting events in your life.
Oral Communication	Form a circle of friends who will read or tell personal narratives to one another. Practice using gestures and tone of voice to communicate actions and feelings. Ask your audience to give you feedback on the effectiveness of your presentation.
Online	Check out **mcdougallittell.com** for more publishing options.

The Bottom Line

Checklist for Personal Narrative

Have I . . .

___ focused on one particular experience?

___ used an interesting beginning?

___ made the importance of the event clear?

___ made the order of events clear?

___ included details that appeal to the senses?

___ used dialogue when appropriate?

___ written a strong ending?

Character Description

Learn What It Is

An artist draws a sketch to give a quick impression of a person. A writer can accomplish the same goal with words. Like a sketch, a **character description** includes details about how the person looks and feels and what the person does and says, for example, that give readers a quick impression.

Basics in a Box

CHARACTER DESCRIPTION AT A GLANCE

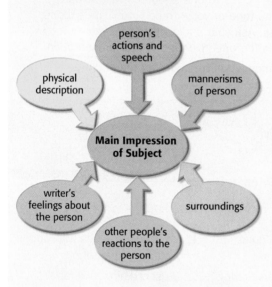

- person's actions and speech
- physical description
- mannerisms of person
- **Main Impression of Subject**
- writer's feelings about the person
- surroundings
- other people's reactions to the person

RUBRIC

Standards for Writing

A successful character description should

- describe the personality and physical appearance of the person
- give a main impression of the person
- include dialogue, descriptions, and other devices that show, rather than tell, what the character is like
- reveal the writer's response to the person
- place the person in surroundings that will help readers understand him or her
- have a clearly organized structure, an effective beginning, and a strong conclusion

See How It's Done: *Character Description*

Student Model
Britney Chilcote
Fort Morgan Middle
School

RUBRIC
IN ACTION

Fallen Ballerina

Shannon's hands were like a baby's, so soft and pudgy. Her skin was fair and soft. Her hair was like black velvet. She smelled of medicine and flowers. Shannon's speech was mumbled and hard to understand because of the tubes that went down her nose and throat. At the time I thought that she was lucky to have an oxygen tank and I wanted one badly. Now, I realize that her oxygen tank was only prolonging her death. . . .

❶ Presents details about the person's physical appearance

I remember carrying Shannon's oxygen tank around because she was so little that she couldn't support the weight. We met in first grade, and Shannon's oxygen tank was very small. At that time she could go outside and play like all of the other kids. As the year went on, her tank got bigger and bigger, and her playing time got smaller. It seemed as Shannon's tank grew, so did our friendship. Later in the year, Shannon missed more and more school, because she spent her time home sick, or in the hospital. When she was in school, she had to sit in a soft chair, and toward the end, she couldn't move very much at all. That is when I started to read to her. . . .

❷ Places the person in a setting that enables readers to understand more about her situation

I can remember reading to her during recess, because she could not go outside for fear of getting holes in her oxygen tubes. When I read to Shannon, I would hold her soft, puffy hand. Every now and again, I would make a mistake, and Shannon would correct me. Some days, she would read to me. We would read books about princesses or ponies, because those were the things she loved most. . . .

❸ Describes the writer's interaction with the character

DESCRIPTION

Other than her tubes and tanks, Shannon was just like all the other girls at school. She thought boys had cooties and Barbies were the best thing next to chocolate chip cookies. Shannon's black hair was always up in pretty braids or in a cute little bun. She wanted to be a ballerina when she grew up. She even used to bring a tutu to school. Shannon and I would dance and play dolls during free time.

Shannon will never get the chance to be a ballerina. I often wonder why Shannon, who wanted something so badly, can never have it and why I, who never really wanted to be a dancer, have a chance to be one. . . .

Shannon's funeral was beautiful. There were pink and white flowers everywhere. Pictures of her favorite items, stuffed animals and dolls, filled the room. Shannon was a very loving person, and many people came to her funeral.

When I saw Shannon lying in her casket, she looked like she was asleep, with her pretty blue dress and her favorite doll in her arms. With all the tubes and the oxygen bottle gone, I remember thinking that for the first time Shannon looked peaceful. She looked very beautiful. . . .

I live close to the cemetery where Shannon is buried. Every time I go there, I stop and talk to her. I only wish that she could be talking with me, but I know that she's listening. I believe that Shannon's short time with me has made me richer.

❹ This writer includes descriptions that show, rather than tell, what the character is like.
Another option: Include dialogue that reveals the character's personality.

❺ Gives a main impression of the character

❻ Ends with a strong statement expressing the impact that the character had on the writer's life

Do It Yourself

Writing Prompt   Write a character description of someone you find fascinating.

Purpose To show why the person is especially interesting

Audience Classmates or anyone else who might be interested

❶ Prewriting

First, choose a person. Make a list of people whom you really like, admire, or find interesting.

For more ideas, see the Idea Bank, p. 428.

Freewrite. Make a list of words and phrases that come to mind about the person—*grows the tallest sunflowers, has the silliest laugh, taught me to ride a bike.*

Focus on your strongest image of the person. When you think of your subject, what is the first thing you see that person doing? Where is the person? What is he or she wearing? Record your thoughts in a chart like the one below.

Observations of a Person	
Physical appearance	*dirty uniform, wispy hair*
Voice	*high, silly laugh*
Mannerisms	*pulls ear*
Personality	*friendly, laughs often*

Choose a main idea. Focus only on memories of your subject or select just one that will give your readers a strong impression of the person.

❷ Drafting

Use vivid details. Try to visualize your subject as you write. Refer to your lists of words and phrases and your chart of observations to help you choose details. For example, don't just say that your subject wore a dirty uniform. Help readers picture the stain: "Ice cream, catsup, and specks of sand formed an almost planned pattern on the front of her uniform."

For information about getting feedback from your peers, see p. 429.

DESCRIPTION

③ Revising

TARGET SKILL ▶ Making Effective Word Choices Choosing the right words can make the difference between a description that is adequate and one that is fascinating. For instance, saying that someone is messy is not nearly as descriptive as saying that mounds of clothes covered almost every inch of the person's room. Effective words will give readers more to see. For more help with revising, review the rubric on page 422.

> Shannon's hands were like a baby's, so soft and ~~fat.~~ *pudgy.* Her skin was ~~smooth.~~ *fair and soft.* Her hair was like a black ~~crayon.~~ *velvet.* She smelled ~~both strong~~ *of medicine* and ~~sweet.~~ *flowers.*

④ Editing and Proofreading

TARGET SKILL ▶ Correcting Pronoun Case If a pronoun is used as the subject of a sentence, use *I, she,* or *he.* If a pronoun is used as an object, use *me, her,* or *him.*

> Shannon and ~~me~~ *I* would dance and play dolls during free time.

For more help with pronoun case, see pp. 56–89.

⑤ Sharing and Reflecting

After you have organized and edited your character description, **share** it with another person or a group, either by handing out copies or by reading it to them. Have them give you feedback on the effectiveness of your character description.

For Your Working Portfolio Use the readers' reactions and comments to **reflect** on how effective your description is. Can the audience picture the person clearly? Does the person's personality come through? Make notes on what you might do to make the character sketch even more effective. Save your notes and your description in your 🗀 **Working Portfolio.**

Speak for Yourself: *Roleplaying a Character*

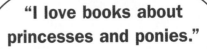

"I love books about princesses and ponies."

History lessons can be much more interesting when guest speakers assume the roles of historical figures. Sometimes comedians have great success in entertaining when they assume the role of another person. They speak to the audience as that person—the bus driver, the worried parent, the rebellious child. You can make your **character description** especially memorable by turning it into a roleplay in which you become the character you wrote about.

Give Women the VOTE

Here's How) Creating a Character

• Decide what aspects of your character to focus on. What parts of your character's life would be most interesting to your audience?

• Create a script in which you present yourself as the character, telling the audience about yourself. Use the pronoun "I" when referring to the character.

• Use costumes, props, or anything else to make you look like your character.

• Include some dialogue so your character has a chance to speak rather than simply tell about an event or another person.

For more information on speaking skills, see p. 545–47.

DESCRIPTION

Student Help Desk

Character Description at a Glance

```
                         person's
                         actions and
                         speech
     physical                              mannerisms
     description                           of person

                    Main Impression
                      of Subject

     writer's                             surroundings
     feelings about
     the person          other people's
                         reactions to the
                         person
```

Idea Bank

Tips for finding a subject

Make a list of people who have been important in your life since your childhood.

Recall the most unusual person you ever knew.

Think of a person who is not famous but should be.

Look through a magazine or a newspaper for a well-known person you admire or one who puzzles you.

Choose a beloved pet or a neighbor's pet that has been terrorizing you.

Read literature featuring a character description to see the strategies a published author uses. Try "An Hour with Abuelo" by Judith Ortiz Cofer (*The Language of Literature*, Grade 7).

Adding Details

Don't Tell	Show
Her knee hurt.	She winced when she bent her knee to sit down.
He felt cold.	The wind whistled through his thin jacket and made him shiver.
She yelled at her younger brother.	"Stop it! Can't you do anything right?" she roared as the boy tried to look away from her.

Friendly Feedback

Questions for Your Peer Reader

- How would you describe my character?
- How do you think I feel about this character?
- What was the most interesting part of the character description?
- How could I have done a better job of showing instead of telling?
- Where should I have added more details?

Publishing Options

Print	With your classmates, gather each other's written character descriptions. Write a foreword about what the people have in common. Make a booklet and add a title that shows how these descriptions tell similar stories.
Oral Communication	Read your character description aloud to someone who would like to know about the person you have chosen. Let the tone of your voice show how you feel about the person.
Online	Check out **mcdougallittell.com** for more publishing options.

The Bottom Line

Checklist for Character Description

Have I . . .

- ____ given vivid details about the physical appearance and the personality of the character?
- ____ given a main impression of the person?
- ____ included dialogue and mannerisms to show, rather than tell, what the character is like?

- ____ made the time and place obvious?
- ____ let readers know my reaction to the person?
- ____ used an effective beginning, a clearly organized middle, and a strong ending?

Interpreting a Poem

Learn What It Is

You probably have had strong reactions to a poem, whether you liked or disliked it. You may have loved a poem that tells a story, or perhaps a poem helped you explore feelings that puzzled you. When you read a poem more than once, you often discover new meanings. Writing to **interpret a poem** means going below the surface to find the deeper meanings waiting for you.

Basics in a Box

INTERPRETING A POEM AT A GLANCE

Introduction
Introduces the title, author, and a clear statement of your response

Body
Supports the response with evidence from the work

Evidence
examples from the poem
quotations
specific reactions

Conclusion
Summarizes the response

RUBRIC

Standards for Writing

A successful interpretation of a poem should

- state the title and author of the poem
- give a clearly stated interpretation of the poem's message
- present examples from the poem to support the interpretation
- use transitions to guide the reader
- summarize the interpretation in the conclusion

CHAPTER 22

See How It's Done: *Interpreting a Poem*

The Rider

A boy told me
if he rollerskated fast enough
his loneliness couldn't catch up to him,

the best reason I ever heard
for trying to be a champion.

What I wonder tonight
pedaling hard down King William Street
is if it translates to bicycles.

A victory! To leave your loneliness
panting behind you on some
   street corner
while you float free into a cloud
  of sudden azaleas,
luminous pink petals that have
   never felt loneliness,
no matter how slowly they fell.

               —Naomi Shihab Nye

Student Model
Elizabeth Albertson
Chute Middle School

RUBRIC
IN ACTION

POEM

Response to "The Rider"

When I read the poem "The Rider" by Naomi Shihab Nye, I noticed that there didn't seem to be a hidden message that required a lot of interpretation. However, that's not to say that the idea expressed in the poem is unimportant. I think the speaker of this poem is trying to describe how certain events or activities have the power to remove fears and worries.

A boy has told the speaker that "if he rollerskated fast enough his loneliness couldn't catch up to him." The speaker seems to be lonely when she thinks about this because she tries to apply it to herself. She wonders whether this idea will apply to bicycling, which is what she herself is doing. For

❶ Names the poem and author

❷ Clearly states the interpretation of the poem

❸ Tells enough about the poem so that readers who are not familiar with it can understand this response her, to bike is to "float free into a cloud of sudden azaleas," which I have taken to mean that she is so focused on going faster that her mind forgets all worries and concentrates on that one goal.

I love the way the poet uses personification to describe the loneliness. When the speaker says, "A victory! To leave your loneliness panting behind you on some street corner," it almost seems that the loneliness is a person, trying to catch up with her as she rides and trying to take her focus away from the wonderful feeling of bicycling.

When I read this poem, I couldn't help thinking about my own experiences taking part in sports and different activities. During some activities my mind is incapable of thinking about anything other than doing my best, and all of my other thoughts and worries seem to disappear. However, I have found that this incredible feeling cannot happen unless I'm doing something that I love to do. For example, when I play softball, if I'm into the game, I don't worry about having to do something great. My worries leave me and I can think of nothing but having fun.

I think this poem is very well written. Naomi Shihab Nye's strength is her ability to convey an important message simply. She believes that loneliness can be left behind when you are doing something you enjoy and are "trying to be a champion."

❹ Supports statements with quotations and details

❺ This writer gives her personal reactions and responses to the poem.

Another option: Intersperse references to or quotations from the poem along with personal experiences.

❻ Summarizes the interpretation of the poem in the conclusion

Do It Yourself

Write a personal response to a poem.

Purpose To share your reaction

Audience Classmates, teacher, others who would be interested

❶ Prewriting

Select a poem. You might choose a poem that you already know well and love. You can use your essay to share your enthusiasm. You might choose a poem that puzzles you and use your essay to either figure out why it puzzles you or to explain why you don't understand it.

For more topic ideas, see the Idea Bank, p. 436.

- **Read and reread.** Go through the poem line by line. Make notes as you read. Write down anything that comes to mind. Don't worry about whether your ideas are good or bad.

- **Think about your reactions.** Ask yourself how the poem relates to your own life, as well as your own thoughts and feelings.

- **Think about your audience.** What will readers need to know in order to understand your essay?

❷ Drafting

Start writing. Write down your thoughts in as much detail as possible. Keep in mind that there are no right or wrong ideas when you are responding to a poem. What is important is to express your own response as honestly and as clearly as you can. After you have written your ideas down, revise them, as needed, to make sure that you have an introduction, a body, and a conclusion.

- **Introduction:** Include the title, the author's name, and your response to the poem.

- **Body:** Support your response with quotations and details.

- **Conclusion:** Summarize your response.

For information on getting feedback from your peers, see p. 437.

POEM

③ Revising

TARGET SKILL ►**Elaborating with Examples** When responding to a poem, you should give specific examples to help your readers understand your reactions. For more help with revising, review the rubric on page 430.

> For her, to bike is to "float free into a cloud of sudden azaleas," which I have taken to mean
>
> ~~I think~~ that ~~when she bikes~~ she is so focused on going
>
> faster that her mind forgets all worries and concentrates
>
> on that one goal.

④ Editing and Proofreading

TARGET SKILL ►**Using Correct Punctuation and Spelling** For your ideas to be clear to your reader, you must use correct punctuation and spelling. Use a dictionary or a word processing program to check your spelling.

> The speaker
>
> ~~She~~ seems to be ~~lonly~~ lonely when she thinks about this
>
> because she tries to apply it to herself she wonders whether
>
> ~~or not~~ this idea will apply to bicycling. Which is what she herself
>
> is doing.

For more about punctuation and spelling, see pp. 250–69 and 628–35.

⑤ Sharing and Reflecting

Share your response with others who wrote about the same poem. Hold a discussion about the varied interpretations.

For Your Working Portfolio After you have shared your response, **reflect** on the experience of writing it. Did it help you understand the poem better? Did it help you understand something about yourself? Attach your answers to your interpretation and save them both in your 🗀 **Working Portfolio.**

Speak for Yourself: *Oral Interpretation*

"A *victory*! To leave your loneliness . . . *panting* behind you. . . ."

A poem you have found difficult to understand may become clear when you hear it read aloud with expression and gestures. You can take the **interpretation of a poem** you wrote and express your ideas by interpreting the poem orally.

A boy told me *(slowly)*
if he rollerskated fast enough *(faster)*
his loneliness couldn't *(slow with emphasis)*

catch up to him. *(pause)*

Here's How **Oral Interpretation**

- Plan how you will communicate your interpretation. Where will you make your voice loud? soft? On what lines will you speed up or slow down? Where will you pause? What tone of voice will you use? angry? sad? amused? thoughtful?

- Practice reading the poem out loud. Make notes on the poem for pauses, gestures, tone of voice, and rhythm.

- Read the poem in front of an audience. Act it out enough so that the meaning of each word is communicated.

- You might follow your reading with a brief explanation of your interpretation.

- Invite questions and discussion from your audience.

For more information on speaking skills, see p. 545–49.

POEM

Student Help Desk

Interpreting a Poem at a Glance

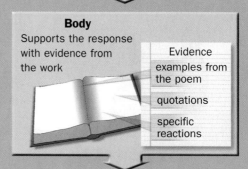

Introduction
Introduces the title, author, and a clear statement of your response

Body
Supports the response with evidence from the work

Evidence

examples from the poem

quotations

specific reactions

Conclusion
Summarizes the response

Idea Bank

Tips for choosing a poem to interpret

Make a list of the poems you have studied in class to help you choose a poem.

Note your reactions. Make a list of things you might say about several poems: how each poem makes you feel, what you don't understand, what you find particularly interesting. Then choose the one that inspires you the most to talk about.

Ask other people to talk about their favorite poems.

Including Quotations

Quoting directly from the poem at key points will

- support your opinions
- help give your readers a feel for the work
- help give vigor to your own words

However, do not use too many quotes. After all, the interpretation is supposed to show your own ideas.

CHAPTER 22

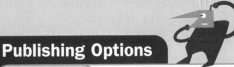

Friendly Feedback

Questions for Your Peer Reader

- What did I seem to feel most strongly about?
- What was my main point?
- What could have been stated more clearly?
- What seemed to be unnecessary?

Publishing Options

Print	Submit your response to a student literary magazine.
Oral Communication	Present the poem as an oral interpretation. Use your voice and gestures to convey the emotional content of your interpretation. Follow the presentation with a discussion about your presentation.
Online	Check out **mcdougallittell.com** for more publishing options.

The Bottom Line

Checklist for Interpreting a Poem

Have I . . .

- ____ named the title and the author in the introduction?
- ____ clearly stated how I feel about the poem in the introduction?
- ____ told enough about the poem so that readers who are unfamiliar with it can understand my response?
- ____ given my specific reactions and responses to the work?
- ____ supported my statements with quotations and details from the poem?
- ____ summarized my response to the poem in the conclusion?

Cause-and-Effect Essay

Learn What It Is

Why do athletes exercise and eat balanced diets? It's so that they can keep their bodies in tiptop shape. They see a relationship between diet and exercise and physical fitness. Writing a **cause-and-effect essay** can help you examine the causes leading up to an effect as well as the effects of an event or action.

Basics in a Box

CAUSE-AND-EFFECT ESSAY AT A GLANCE

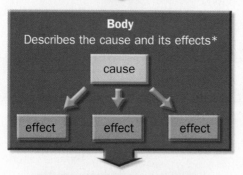

Introduction
Introduces the subject

Body
Describes the cause and its effects*

cause

effect   effect   effect

Conclusion
Summary

*or presents an effect and then analyzes the causes

RUBRIC

Standards for Writing

A successful cause-and-effect essay should

- clearly identify the cause-and-effect relationship
- provide any necessary background information
- make clear the relationship between causes and effects
- arrange details logically and include transitions to show relationships between causes and effects
- summarize the cause-and-effect relationship in the conclusion

CHAPTER 23

See How It's Done: *Cause-and-Effect Essay*

Student Model
Aaron Vinson
Northbrook Junior High

RUBRIC
IN ACTION

Pinned Up over the Summer

On June 11, 1999, I was hit by a pick-up truck while I was riding my bike. I was thrown several feet and fractured my left femur, or thigh bone. I needed four pins to hold my broken bone in place. After ten days in the hospital, I was told I could go home. The doctor gave me some rules to follow. He told me not to put any weight on my leg, and that I would need therapy.

❶ Strong opening includes needed background information

When I got home, I began to realize that because of the accident, I was going to have to change my lifestyle. I was going to have to slow down. I was also going to try not to concentrate on the pain in my leg.

❷ Clearly identifies the cause-and-effect relationship being discussed

Now that my leg is broken, I need help doing things that are ordinarily easy, like carrying a package and walking at the same time! I can't carry anything while walking with crutches. I can't even leave the house on my own. I can't play baseball or basketball or go swimming with my friends and family.

Because of the accident I can't go to camp. I have to go to therapy instead, to learn how to walk again. Sometimes therapy is okay. Sometimes it isn't, and it hurts.

❸ Arranges details logically by listing bad effects, and then listing good effects

One thing that has helped me, though, is the support that I received from friends and family. My mom used all her sick days at work so she could take care of me in the hospital. After that, I got to see my grandmas, who took care of me when my mom had to go back to work. I got many calls and visits from family and friends. I also got presents!

CAUSE-EFFECT

It's strange that seeing so many people and having a good time with them is the result of being hit by a truck.

Some other good things that came out of the accident are not having to do my chores and not having to practice my viola. These can be overshadowed, though, by bad things like losing my summer job. Since I broke my leg, I had to give up my lawn-mowing job, and I may not get it back next year. I can always look on the bright side, though; I don't have to cut their lawns or mine!

So, all in all, getting hit by a truck doesn't make summer fun, but it doesn't ruin it, either. It has the effect of making the summer very different. Normally I would have gone to camp and gone on hikes and climbed mountains, but instead I get to watch really good movies I probably never would have seen. And instead of playing baseball with my team this year, I watched and got to keep score. I can now score better than ever before!

❹ This writer summarizes the cause-and-effect relationship by first giving an overview, and then repeating key items.

Another option: Repeat key items, and then conclude with the overview statement.

Do It Yourself

❶ Prewriting

Choose a topic. Think about an important past event. What
caused the event? What effects did it have? Think about the
future. Do you need to make a decision about something?
What effect will your decision have on others?

For more topic ideas, see the Idea Bank, p. 444.

Decide what you need. Can you draw on your own thoughts and
observations for the necessary background information? Or will
you need to do research?

Do a reality check. Did one event really cause another or did
one event simply follow another? Use a map like the one
below to organize your ideas.

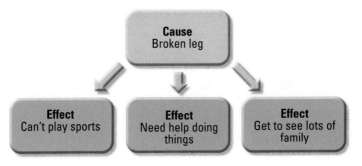

❷ Drafting

State your cause-effect relationship. Try to sum up the cause-
and-effect relationship in a sentence or two. Refer to this
statement as you write to keep yourself on track. Be sure to
include your statement in your draft.

Organize your ideas. Keeping your statement in mind, decide
how to organize your ideas. Here are two possibilities:

• Describe how one cause can have many effects.

• Show how many causes can lead to one effect.

For information about getting feedback from your peers, see p. 445.

CAUSE-EFFECT

❸ Revising

TARGET SKILL ▶**Transitions** Use transitions to show how your ideas are related. Some words and phrases that show cause-and-effect relationships are *because, since, as a result.* For more help with revising, review the rubric on page 438.

> because of the accident,
> When I got home, I began to realize that I was going to
> ⋀
>
> have to change my lifestyle.

❹ Editing and Proofreading

TARGET SKILL ▶**Fragments** If you don't use complete sentences, readers may have trouble following your ideas. Make sure every group of words you have put together as a sentence has a subject and predicate.

> are
> Some other good things that came out of the accident. ⋁
> ⋀
> ~~N~~ot having to do my chores and not having to practice my
>
> viola.

For more on sentence fragments, see pp. 25–27.

❺ Sharing and Reflecting

Did your cause-and-effect essay help you learn something about yourself that would be worth **sharing** with others? Did you make a scientific discovery that could be formally presented in science class or at a science fair?

For Your Working Portfolio After you have shared your essay, **reflect** on the way you wrote it. Did you leave out any good points you could have made or include material you didn't need? Were there parts that you particularly liked? Attach your answers to your essay and save them both in your 🗂 **Working Portfolio.**

Speak for Yourself: *Demonstration*

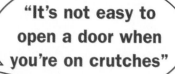

"It's not easy to open a door when you're on crutches"

When you say this, most people will understand what you mean. However, if you actually get a pair of crutches and try to open a door, everyone will see exactly what you mean. By giving a demonstration, you can show an audience your ideas in action. The ideas in your **cause-effect essay** may make a good basis for a demonstration. You can act out some of the causes or effects or stage a demonstration with objects.

Here's How Creating a Demonstration

- Choose specific causes or effects from your essay that would be easy to demonstrate in a classroom. Is it something you could act out? If it's a more scientific cause-effect, can you perform an experiment before your audience?

- Get whatever props or materials you will need. What materials do you need to perform your experiment? What props do you need to act it out?

- Practice your demonstration and memorize the explanations you will give.

For more information on speaking skills, see p. 545–47.

CAUSE-EFFECT

Student Help Desk

Cause-and-Effect Essay at a Glance

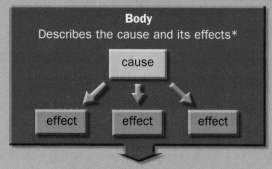

Introduction
Introduces the subject

Body
Describes the cause and its effects*

cause

effect   effect   effect

*or presents an effect and then analyzes the causes

Conclusion
Summary

Idea Bank

How do you find a topic?

Discuss how a recent change at school affected the students.

Consider what effects might result if you take up a new activity.

Write about how a change in your family's life has affected family members.

Research how a certain historical event affected your town or state.

Imagine what the effects would be if cars or television or computers were suddenly removed from our lives.

Read literature such as *The Autobiography of Malcolm X* by Malcolm X with Alex Haley to see how other writers handle causes and effects (*The Language of Literature*, Grade 7).

Friendly Feedback

Questions for Your Peer Reader

- What is the main cause that I named? What is the major overall effect?
- What flaws in my logic could you find?
- What parts did you have trouble understanding?
- What did you need to know more about?

Publishing Options

Print	Submit your essay to the school newspaper or literary magazine. Use a desktop publishing program to produce a booklet of essays from your class.
Oral Communication	Present your essay to your classmates, to an appropriate school club, or to a local speech club. Use charts to illustrate your points.
Online	Check out **mcdougallittell.com** for more publishing options.

The Bottom Line

Checklist for Cause-and-Effect Essay

Have I . . .

____ clearly identified the cause-and-effect relationship that I was discussing?

____ given any background information that was needed?

____ made the relationship between causes and effects clear?

____ arranged details logically?

____ used transitions to show relationships between causes and effects?

____ used language and details appropriate to my audience?

____ summarized the cause and effect relationship in the conclusion?

Comparison-Contrast Essay

Learn What It Is

Maybe you need to decide between two brands of athletic shoes. Perhaps you're considering whether to join the marching band or the chorus. One way to make decisions is to study the similarities and differences of two subjects. Writing a **comparison-contrast essay** can help you see the subjects clearly and make a decision if that is your purpose.

Basics in a Box

COMPARISON-CONTRAST ESSAY AT A GLANCE

Introduction	Body	Conclusion
• introduces the **subjects** being compared • tells the **reason** for the comparison	explains similarities and differences Subject A only — Both subjects — Subject B only	• summarizes the comparison • explains new understanding

RUBRIC

Standards for Writing

A successful comparison-contrast essay should

- introduce the subjects being compared
- state a clear purpose for the comparison
- include transitional words and phrases to make similarities and differences clear
- follow a clear organizational pattern
- include both similarities and differences and support them with specific examples and details
- summarize the comparison in the conclusion

See How It's Done: *Comparison-Contrast Essay*

Student Model
Caroline Watkins
Lake Forest Country Day
School

RUBRIC
IN ACTION

Culture Shock!

Culture shock! Before I moved to Japan, I never really knew what the meaning of those words was. Now I do. I thought that Japan and America couldn't be that different. But with 6,300 miles and the largest ocean in the world separating us, cultural differences really do exist. The biggest shock for me was how different the teenagers were.

One example of how Japanese and American teenagers differ is their school backgrounds. From kindergarten, Japanese are taught discipline and obedience. There are many more rules and regulations in Japanese schools than in American schools. Children have to follow these rules and they always do. Students in Japan never disobey their teachers. They have about three more hours of school every day than Americans do, and they have school every other Saturday. They also have less than a month of summer break.

Another difference is that they honor their elders much more than most American teenagers do. They don't ever question their parents. Obedience, instead of creativity and independence, is what's taught.

Many Japanese teenagers are very superstitious and are devoted to tradition. For example, a Japanese person would never stand in the doorway of a temple because the person would worry about that causing years and years of bad luck. If American teenagers break a mirror, they jokingly say that they will have bad luck for seven years. Japanese teenagers actually believe it.

Another difference between the teenagers is their views on fashion. While teens in America were wearing jeans, overalls, and pea coats, teens in

❶ Establishes the purpose for the comparison

❷ Identifies the subjects being compared

❸ This writer uses a feature-by-feature organization, first discussing school backgrounds for both sets of teens.
Another option: Use a subject-by-subject organization, discussing all the characteristics of each group separately.

❹ Lists differences and supports them with specific examples and details

❺ Uses transitional phrases to make relationships between ideas clear

COMPARISON

Japan were wearing camouflage; really, really short skirts or incredibly baggy or flair jeans; and knee-high boots. Also, a lot of Japanese teens, once they get out of high school, think it is cool to dye their hair. Some of the colors they use are blond, red, brown, purple, silver, gold, pretty much anything.

There are also interesting similarities between Japanese and American teens, such as how Japanese teens like American "things" and American teens like Japanese "things" so much. Whenever I would go shopping in Tokyo, I would see countless teens with shirts that bore American writing. I always wondered if they knew what it said on their shirts because often there were pretty strange phrases that an American teenager would never wear. In Tokyo I saw a 15-year-old girl wearing a shirt that said, "The flowers in the garden of heaven smell tasty." Somehow, I don't think an American would wear that shirt. Back in the U.S., I have seen my friends wearing T-shirts that bear Japanese characters; my Japanese friends would never wear these shirts.

❻ Includes similarities and supports them with specific examples and details

My Japanese friends loved my American items, such as movies, food, and magazines. I didn't think of them as anything special, but my Japanese friends thought they were the coolest things in the world. And my American friends loved my Japanese things like pens, pencils, and diaries.

I learned a lot in my four years in Japan. I learned that even though American and Japanese teens grow up differently and learn to like different things, it doesn't make them completely different.

❼ Summarizes the comparison in the conclusion

Do It Yourself

Writing Prompt Choose two subjects and write a comparison-contrast essay to show how they are alike and how they are different

Purpose To explain or to clarify

Audience Anyone interested in your subjects

❶ Prewriting

Choose a topic. You might start by making a list of decisions you've made recently that involved making a choice between two things.

For more topic ideas, see the Idea Bank, p. 452.

Make a list of the similarities and differences in your topics.

Decide on an organizational pattern. Use a chart like the one below to help you decide how to present the similarities and differences of your subjects.

Subject-by-Subject		Feature-by-Feature	
Subject A	*Japanese teens*	**Feature 1**	*Rules, obedience*
Feature 1	*Rules, obedience*	Subject A	*Japanese teens*
Feature 2	*Dress*	Subject B	*American teens*
Subject B	*American teens*	**Feature 2**	*Dress*
Feature 1	*Rules, obedience*	Subject A	*Japanese teens*
Feature 2	*Dress*	Subject B	*American teens*

❷ Drafting

Get started. Start writing in the organizational pattern you choose, which you can always change when you revise. For either pattern, you will need an **introduction, body,** and **conclusion.**

- **Introduction.** Identify the subjects you are comparing and tell your purpose for making the comparison.
- **Body.** In the body, explore each subject or feature in turn. Use examples and details for support.
- **Conclusion.** Here is where you sum up the comparison and tell your decision if that was your purpose.

For information about getting feedback from your peers, see p. 453.

❸ Revising

TARGET SKILL ▶Varying Sentence Structure To engage your readers' interest and to show the relationship between ideas, vary the structure of some of your sentences. Use a variety of simple, compound, and complex sentences. For more help with revising, review the rubric on page 446.

> I thought that Japan and America couldn't be that
> different. ~~There are~~ *But with* 6,300 miles ~~between Japan and America.~~ *and*
> ~~The Pacific Ocean is~~ the largest ocean in the world. ~~It~~
> *separating us,*
> ~~separates Japan and America.~~ Cultural differences really
> do exist.

❹ Editing and Proofreading

TARGET SKILL ▶Making Comparisons When you use adjectives and adverbs to make comparisons, use only one form of comparison at a time. Do not use *more* and *-er* together or *most* and *-est* together.

> I didn't think of them as anything special, but my
> Japanese friends thought they were the ~~most~~ coolest things
> in the world.

For more on comparisons, see pp. 137–138.

❺ Sharing and Reflecting

Share your essay with classmates who are interested in your subjects. After reading, ask what similarities and/or differences were more important to them.

For Your Working Portfolio As you **reflect** on your writing, think about how effective it was. Did your audience find it convincing? Were there other points you could have made? Attach your answers to your finished work. Save your essay in your ▭ **Working Portfolio.**

Speak for Yourself: *Multimedia Presentation*

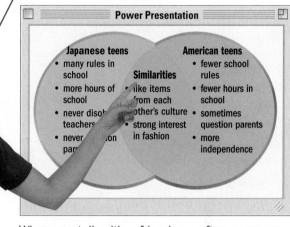

"How are Japanese and American teens similar? How are they different?"

Power Presentation

Japanese teens
- many rules in school
- more hours of school
- never disob... teache...
- never ...on par...

Similarities
- like items from each other's culture
- strong interest in fashion

American teens
- fewer school rules
- fewer hours in school
- sometimes question parents
- more independence

When you talk with a friend you often compare things. You might tell each other about your summer vacations and compare the experiences. Or you might discuss the advantages and disadvantages of playing certain sports. To make the ideas in your **comparison-contrast essay** clear to an audience, you might give a multimedia presentation to show clearly the similarities and differences in the two items.

Here's How **Creating a Multimedia Presentation**

- Choose items from your essay that you can show to an audience either through actual objects or through media like photographs, videos, or computer presentations.

- If you're comparing two products, bring them in. If you are comparing two cultures, use items from the cultures in your presentation.

- Don't forget low-tech media like overhead projectors and flip charts. Graphs, tables, and charts can effectively demonstrate the differences in two items.

- Practice with your visuals before you give your presentation.

For more information on speaking skills, see p.545–47.

COMPARISON

Student Help Desk

Comparison-Contrast Essay at a Glance

Introduction
- introduces the **subjects** being compared
- tells the **reason** for the comparison

Body
explains similarities and differences

Subject A only   Both subjects   Subject B only

Conclusion
- summarizes the comparison
- explains new understanding

Idea Bank

Tips for finding a topic

- **Debate** who the greatest athlete of all time was.
- **Consider** the best computers for a computer lab.
- **Decide** how to spend the money in the science club treasury.
- **Recommend** a video to rent for a quiet night at home.
- **Pick** the most appropriate television program for the family to watch together.

Transition Words and Phrases Glue It Together

Comparison Words	Contrast Words
Use these words to show similarities.	**Use these words to show differences.**
like	instead
also	unlike
too	however
the same as	on the other hand
in the same way	yet

Friendly Feedback

Questions for Your Peer Reader

- What was the purpose of my essay?
- What is the most important similarity?
- What is the most important difference?
- What other points could I have made to strengthen the comparison?
- What did I explain that you didn't already know?

Publishing Options

Print	Look for a publication that deals with the subject you have written about, and submit your essay for an article or guest editorial.
Oral Communication	As a class, choose two subjects to compare and contrast. Then form small groups to create a list of similarities and differences between the two subjects. Share and discuss your list with the other groups in class.
Online	Check out **mcdougallittell.com** for more publishing options.

The Bottom Line

Checklist for Comparison-Contrast Essay

Have I . . .

____ identified the subjects being compared?

____ made the purpose for comparison clear?

____ included both similarities and differences?

____ provided support with specific examples and details?

____ followed a clear organizational pattern?

____ used transition words and phrases appropriately?

____ summarized the comparison in the conclusion?

COMPARISON

Proposal

Learn What It Is

Have you ever seen a problem or a situation that you would like to change? Perhaps you have some ideas for solutions or improvements. If so, you could write a **proposal,** a document or speech that offers solutions to a problem or ideas about how to change a situation.

Basics in a Box

PROPOSAL AT A GLANCE

Summary of Proposal

Briefly states the purpose of the proposal

Need

- Defines the problem or need
- States why addressing it is important

Proposed Solution

- Presents a detailed solution
- Explains its benefits
- Restates the problem or need and the benefits of the solution

RUBRIC

Standards for Writing

A successful proposal should

- target a specific audience
- clearly define a problem or state a need
- present a clear solution, using evidence to demonstrate that the plan is workable

- show how the plan will be implemented and what resources will be required
- show that the advantages of the plan outweigh possible objections to it

See How It's Done: *Proposal*

Student Model
Andy Sturgeon
Thomas Middle School

RUBRIC
IN ACTION

Cheer on Thomas

You are at a Thomas Middle School home basketball game, and the score is tied at 32 with only five seconds left until the final buzzer will sound. The star player is hurt, and it looks like Thomas has no chance. The crowd is starting to doubt their own team. To boost the fans' excitement and team spirit, a newly introduced pep band plays a roaring rouser that gets the fans into it. That one rouser may give our Timber Wolves the edge they need to defeat their opponent.

❶ Targets a specific audience—fans of the Thomas basketball team

Nothing creates school spirit like a winning team, and a team needs the energy of the crowd to keep winning. Therefore, I propose a Thomas pep band, which would give our musicians another outlet for their talents and would keep our school spirit high.

❷ Clearly states a need

❸ Presents a clear solution

To begin with, Thomas has a lot of talent in music, and not everyone gets to show it off. For instance, a tuba or flute player may not want to play in a jazz or rock band in addition to the concert music they already play. There's not really any room for a tuba in a jazz band, but it's perfect for a pep band. The pep band would let musicians play the kind of music they want to, without making them change their instruments.

❹ Uses evidence to demonstrate that the plan is workable

Also, having a pep band would increase school spirit. How many students know the Thomas school song? Almost no one does, and that shouldn't be. A pep band could learn the music for the school song and teach it to the basketball crowd with the help of the cheerleaders. At the pep rallies the school holds, the pep band would play some of their prepared songs. Having them

PROPOSAL

play would get the students into the team spirit and the school spirit.

<u>In addition</u>, a pep band would make games more interesting. At some games where there is no band, spectators may get restless and not watch or cheer their own team on. A band will cause the crowd to stay involved and actually participate. Cheering is what gives a team a home court advantage. A band would increase this advantage and give Thomas a better chance at winning home games.

<u>Finally</u>, to get a pep band organized would be simple. Talented musicians are already available in the concert band, waiting to get started on something like this. In fact, nine out of ten Thomas band performers said they would want to be in a pep band. All that would be required would be some rehearsal time for the band members.

As you can see, a Thomas pep band would be a great addition to the Thomas band program. It would let talented musical performers play music they enjoy. A pep band would keep school spirit high at Thomas and give the basketball team an edge over their opponents. Can't you just hear the band, with the crowd roaring in the stands and cheering the Thomas team to victory?

❺ Uses transitions to tie paragraphs together smoothly

❻ Shows how the plan can be implemented and what resources are available

❼ This writer shows the advantages of the plan.
Another option: Include possible objections and show how the advantages outweigh the objections.

Do It Yourself

Writing Prompt   Write a proposal to change or improve a situation.

Purpose To inform and to convince others to follow your proposal

Audience People who can make the change you recommend

❶ Prewriting

Identify a problem or a need. Talk to friends and neighbors about issues that bother them. Or you may already know about a situation that could be improved. Jot down several ideas, and brainstorm possible solutions for each one.

For more topic ideas, see the Idea Bank, p. 460.

Explore your issue. One way to plan your proposal is to make a chart listing support for your proposal and answers to possible objections.

Need: Video yearbook	
Proposal: Video Yearbook Club	
Support	• collection of memories • hear students as well as see them • generate funds for the school
Possible Objections	• finding equipment and members—A/V room has both • cost to produce—less than print yearbook

❷ Drafting

State the need early. Start by writing a clear statement of what is needed and your proposal for meeting that need. Explain why the need or problem is important.

Support your proposal. Include facts, statistics, or examples that support your plan, and show how it will work. If you propose a solution that requires money, you'll need to figure out where the money will come from.

Answer the critics. Include what your opponents might say. Then tell how the advantages of your plan will outweigh their objections to it.

For information about getting feedback from your peers, see p. 461.

PROPOSAL

❸ Revising

TARGET SKILL ▶ **Making Sequence Clear** Your plan won't win any support if it's not easy to follow. Read the following sentences in the order indicated by the numbers. How does the new order improve the paragraph? For more help with revising, review the rubric on page 454.

(4) All that would be required would be to schedule some rehearsal time for the band members. (3) In fact, nine out of ten Thomas band performers said they would want to be in a pep band. (2) Talented musicians are already there in the concert band, waiting to get started on something like this. (1) Finally, to get a pep band organized would be simple.

❹ Editing and Proofreading

TARGET SKILL ▶ **Correcting Run-ons** A run-on sentence, two or more sentences written as a single sentence, can make your proposal confusing. One way to correct this error is to write the sentence as two separate sentences.

How many students know the Thomas school song ?
almost no one does, and that shouldn't be.

For more on run-on sentences, see pp. 25-27.

❺ Sharing and Reflecting

Share your proposal with an audience. Ask both supporters and critics of your ideas if you made a convincing case.

For Your Working Portfolio As you talked with others about your proposal, what changes did you think of? Was the proposal still important to you? As you **reflect** on your work, think of how you might have made an even stronger case. Save your answers along with your finished proposal in your 🗁 **Working Portfolio.**

Speak for Yourself: *Persuasive Speech*

Thomas Pep Band
a pep band will . . .
1. Add school spirit
2. Increase wins for Timber Wolves
3. Make more interesting games
   Give musicians more
   ~~~
   easy to organize

"Can't you hear it now? The Thomas Pep Band *roaring* in the stands!"

GO Timber Wolves

Persuading your family to set a later curfew time or persuading your friend to see the movie you like is a form of persuasive speech. On television you've seen politicians make formal speeches to persuade people to support their ideas and plans. Turning your proposal into a persuasive speech will give you the chance to look your audience in the eye, present your **proposal**, and convince them face-to-face that your ideas are good ones.

Here's How Creating a Persuasive Speech

- Choose specific parts of your proposal to emphasize. Don't simply plan to read your proposal aloud. A speech needs brief, clearly stated ideas, plenty of emphasis, and a clear call to action.

- Consider your audience. Do you need to define terms? give background explanations? Or can you get right to your proposed idea?

- Present yourself in a way that will make the audience pay attention. If you appear sloppy, for instance, you won't be taken as seriously as if you are dressed neatly.

- Use a flip chart as a point-by-point map of your proposal showing why your ideas are good and how they will work.

- Write out your speech. You may speak from notes, but you should write out the speech and practice your tone of voice, the pacing (how quickly or slowly you will speak), and gestures before you give the speech.

For more information on speaking skills, see pp. 545–547.

Student Help Desk

Proposal at a Glance

Summary of Proposal
Briefly states the purpose of the proposal

Need
• Defines the problem or need
• States why addressing it is important

Proposed Solution
• Presents a detailed solution
• Explains its benefits
• Restates the problem or need and the benefits of the solution

Idea Bank

Finding an Idea

Look in a newspaper for current concerns and issues.

Read about volunteer projects.

Think about how you might change one thing in the world. What would it be, and how would you do it?

Check out your school. Are there ways to reduce crowding in the halls or lunchroom? How could cafeteria food be improved? Should a particular sport be added to after-school activities?

Look at situations close to home. Maybe you want more responsibility at home to show that you can also handle a few more activities after school.

Make a list of things that bother you, as Calvin is doing in the cartoon below.

Calvin and Hobbes by Bill Watterson

Friendly Feedback

Questions for Your Peer Reader

- What problem or need did I address?
- What other points should I add to support my plan?
- How did I address possible objections to my plan?
- What problems do you see in carrying out my plan?

Publishing Options

Print	If your proposal is to correct a problem, you might print it as a leaflet and hand it out to support the change you recommend.
Oral Communication	Invite interested people to hear you present your proposal as a speech.
Online	Check out **mcdougallittell.com** for more publishing options.

The Bottom Line

Checklist for Proposal

Have I . . .

____ written in an appropriate way for a specific audience?

____ clearly stated a need or defined a problem?

____ presented a clear solution?

____ used evidence to show that the plan will work?

____ shown how to implement the plan?

____ shown what resources will be required?

____ demonstrated clearly that the advantages of the plan outweigh possible objections to it?

Short Story and Poem

Learn What It Is: *Short Story*

When you want to capture an event or a feeling in words, you can try your hand at writing a story or a poem. In this workshop, you will have the opportunity to try both.

Writing a **short story** is a way to share an experience or to explore an interesting idea. In writing a short story, you use the same elements you use in telling your friends about something amazing that just happened: the people, the event, and the place. Your story might be about a real event or an imagined one.

Basics in a Box

SHORT STORY AT A GLANCE

Introduction

Sets the stage by
- introducing the **characters**
- describing the **setting**

Body

Develops the plot by
- introducing the conflict
- telling a sequence of **events**
- developing **characters** through words and actions
- building towards a **climax**

Conclusion

Finishes the story by
- resolving the **conflict**
- telling the **last event**

RUBRIC

Standards for Writing

A successful short story should
- have a strong beginning and ending
- have a central conflict
- present a clear sequence of events
- maintain a consistent point of view
- use techniques such as vivid sensory language, concrete details, and dialogue to create believable characters and setting
- use the elements of character, setting, and plot to create a convincing world

See How It's Done: *Short Story*

Student Model
Rachel Smith
King Philip Middle School

RUBRIC
IN ACTION

The Floodgates of the Sky

Flood. The word scared her—she tried to dismiss it, but it just kept repeating in her mind. Flood . . . flood . . . flood . . . No. It was impossible, impossible and ridiculous. Nothing like that could ever happen to her family, she was sure of that, and nothing ever would. But then what would you call the mountains of water swallowing everything in their path? . . .

❶ Has a strong, tense beginning

She felt nauseous. The sickening smell of garbage mixed with water and dead fish choked her and seemed to hang limply in the air. There was a terrible knot in her stomach, tightening until she could hardly breathe. She looked over at her siblings, Peter, four years old, and baby Jane. If only she could be sleeping as peacefully as they. Her mother was white-faced and tense, and her father kept pacing back and forth across the tiny attic. Trying to distract herself from the pain and fright, she scrubbed at the dusty attic window with her fist. The clouds were still dark and the rain continued to beat down in a steady deluge. She could make out the shapes of familiar household items being swept away. Even the house across the street was gone. "Please don't let that happen to us!" she prayed. She looked away quickly. Better to hurt than to see others hurt.

❷ Includes vivid, sensory language and concrete details

❸ Provides details that make the scene convincing and vivid

Suddenly an ear-splitting *crack*! broke the silence. The family rushed to the window just in time to see the garage swept away by the great torrent of water.

"My car . . . Leo's wood business . . . gone!" her mother whispered in disbelief. . . .

"No warning. None." That was her father, sounding broken and far away. She had never heard

❹ Uses dialogue to increase the tension and make the characters believable

SHORT STORY

him cry before. Somehow that scared her more than a flood ever could. She pinched herself so hard she thought it might bleed. A nightmare. In a few minutes she would wake up, have some cornflakes, and tell her mom all about the horrible dream. Her mom would say "tsk-tsk" and it would all be over.

She woke up suddenly, shaking. It was a dream! she thought excitedly. It was! But if it was a dream, why wasn't she in her bed? Why were they in the attic? Why was it so damp and cold? Remembrance almost knocked her over. She'd fallen asleep, but in the middle of a flood, not in her bedroom.

"Oh, thank God!" her mother whispered unexpectedly. "Finally!" Variations of this comment moved throughout the room. She wondered why, until finally she glanced out the window and saw a rowboat heading toward them. Two men were in it, wearing bright red jackets saying Coast Guard. Relief flooded her like the water that had so quickly ruined her life on Scoville Street, Torrington, Connecticut. She was saved. She knew she would remember this day, August 18, 1955, forever.

"Come on, Elaine," said her father, standing up. "We're starting over."

This is a true story. The event happened to my mother's family in 1955. The story is written from the perspective of the oldest child in the family, my aunt.

5 This writer adds a paragraph to explain the point of view.

Another option: Tell the whole story in the first person from her aunt's point of view.

Do It Yourself

Write a short story about something that happened to you or something that might have happened.

Purpose To entertain

Audience Family, friends, others who might be interested

❶ Prewriting

Find a story idea. Recall stories you have heard in your family, or make up something that might have happened. Can you create a story around something you saw at a shopping mall or a story you heard from a friend?

For more topic ideas, see the Idea Bank, p. 472.

Think about story elements. Your story will need characters, a plot, and a setting.

Story Elements

Characters	Plot	Setting
• Who tells the story?	• What happens?	• Where does the story take place?
• Who is the main character?	• What is the central conflict?	• When does it happen?
• What are the other characters like?		

❷ Drafting

Make a plot outline. List all the events, and work out how to develop the conflict. Decide how to begin and end your story. Remember, you can change your plot at any time.

Begin writing. Start writing at any place in the story. As you write, you can see where the story takes you. You can go back later to make changes.

Use dialogue. Look for places to add dialogue so that your characters can speak for themselves.

Use description. Use as many details as possible. For example, a crack of lightning may show a person in danger, or hurried footsteps may reveal fright.

For information about getting feedback from your peers, see p. 473.

SHORT STORY

❸ Revising

TARGET SKILL ▶Show, Don't Tell Using words that show action rather than telling about the action is the way to keep your story moving. For more help with revising, review the rubric on page 462.

> *white-faced and* *kept pacing back and forth across the*
> Her mother was ̲tense, and her father ̲~~was nervous.~~ *tiny attic*
>
> Trying to distract herself from the pain and fright, she
> *dusty*
> ~~dusted~~ the ̲attic window with her fist.
> *scrubbed at*

❹ Editing and Proofreading

TARGET SKILL ▶Subject-Verb Agreement If the subject of a sentence or clause is singular, the verb that goes with it must also be singular. If the subject is plural, the verb must also be plural. Check to see that you have correct subject-verb agreement throughout your story.

> *were*
> The clouds ~~was~~ still dark and the rain continued to beat
>
> down in a steady deluge.

❺ Sharing and Reflecting

To **share** your story with your family or with friends, give it a dramatic reading, or get some friends and act out the characters. Ask your audience to give you feedback on your presentation.

For Your Working Portfolio Make notes on how you developed your story. As you **reflect** on the process, recall what was the most enjoyable part and what was the most challenging. Save your comments and your completed story in your 🗀 **Working Portfolio.**

Learn What It Is: *Poem*

Poems express ideas and feelings in a way that uses every word for a certain effect. Poems can be about anything and can take almost any form. Your poem can tell a story, express an emotion, or describe an experience. It can rhyme or not. Your poem will be most successful when it is about something that matters to you.

Basics in a Box

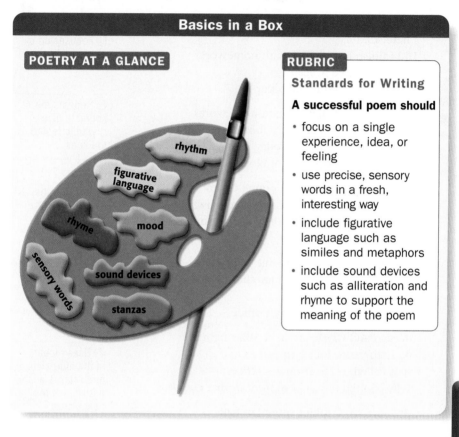

POETRY AT A GLANCE

- rhythm
- figurative language
- rhyme
- mood
- sensory words
- sound devices
- stanzas

RUBRIC

Standards for Writing

A successful poem should

- focus on a single experience, idea, or feeling
- use precise, sensory words in a fresh, interesting way
- include figurative language such as similes and metaphors
- include sound devices such as alliteration and rhyme to support the meaning of the poem

POEM

See How It's Done: *Poem*

Middle School Blues
I hate school.
Did I finish last night's math homework?
I forgot my lunch, again!
Act 1 scene 3 rehearsal today.

❶ Focuses on a single feeling

Did I finish last night's math homework?
Someone just spilled red punch on my Adidas.
Act 1 scene 3 rehearsal today.
What do you mean it's not block scheduling?

❷ Repeats the *s* sound to give a rhythmic feel to the lines

Someone just spilled red punch on my Adidas.
5 poems with a cover all due tomorrow.
What do you mean it's not block scheduling?
The health test is today?

❸ Repeats the second line of each stanza as the first line of the next stanza to create the feeling of sameness and boredom

5 poems with a cover all due tomorrow.
Morgan and Carrie are in another fight.
The health test is today?
I got called to Ms. Tormey's office.

Morgan and Carrie are in another fight.
My homework folder ripped in half.
I got called to Ms. Tormey's office.
Kelly tripped me right in front of that cute boy.

❹ Uses repetition of the fourth line of each stanza as the third line of the next stanza

My homework folder ripped in half.
Have you seen my science text book?
Kelly tripped me right in front of that cute boy.
There are no seats left at my lunch table.

❺ This writer mixes the topics of school work and personal interests throughout.
Other options: Stick to one topic.

Have you seen my science text book?
My mother just kissed me in front of that cute boy.
There are no seats left at my lunch table.
Oh no! I didn't make honor roll.

My mother just kissed me in front of that cute boy.
I got lunch detention for talking during a fire drill.
Oh, no! I didn't make honor roll.
I hate school.

❻ Last line repeats the first line and ties the poem together

Do It Yourself

❶ Prewriting

Seeing again for the first time. Look at all the ordinary things around you—but try to see them for the first time. How would the rain taste? What is the most significant yellow thing you see? Make some notes.

For more topic ideas, see the Idea Bank, p. 472.

Make an observation chart. Begin with your topic, and think of all the ways your senses can give more details about the topic. Record your ideas in a chart like the one below.

Observation Chart: Cafeteria	
Sight	kids in line at the cafeteria, cafeteria staff in white uniforms, kids at tables eating lunches brought from home
Sound	the clank of silverware on metal trays, boys yelling at each other across the room
Touch	warm, wet dishes, cold milk carton
Taste	spicy pizza sauce, apple cobbler
Smell	soapy steam from the kitchen, garlic, fresh-baked peanut butter cookies

❷ Drafting

Explore associations. Pick one or more of your most vivid observations, such as "fresh-baked peanut butter cookies," and list words, feelings, or ideas that come to mind when you think of it.

Put your observations together. Try various ways of stringing your observations together into a poem about a single moment, experience, or idea. As you experiment with different order and arrangements, think about whether you want to make your lines rhyme.

For information about getting feedback from your peers, see p. 473.

POEM

❸ Revising

TARGET SKILL ▶Using Precise Words Make every word in your poem say exactly what you mean. Substitute specific, colorful nouns, adjectives, and verbs for more general ones. For more help with revising, review the rubric on page 467.

> ⁀just⁀
> My mother kissed me in front of ~~everyone~~ ⁀that cute boy.⁀
> ⁀lunch detention⁀
> I got ~~punished~~ for talking *during a fire drill.*
> ⁀I didn't make the honor roll.
> *Oh, no!*

❹ Editing and Proofreading

TARGET SKILL ▶Punctuating Poetry Punctuation in a poem helps readers put ideas together and also understand when to pause. Poets can make their own decisions about how to punctuate their poems, but in general it is best to use standard rules for punctuating your poetry. Use end marks after full sentences, and use commas in the correct way.

> The health test is today*?*
> I got called to Ms. Tormey's office⊙

❺ Sharing and Reflecting

After you have revised and edited your poem, **share** it with an audience. You might have a poetry reading in your class where you and your classmates read your poems aloud. Remember to read your poem with expression. Ask your classmates to provide feedback on your delivery.

For Your Working Portfolio As you **reflect** on your writing process, make some notes about what you enjoyed most and least about writing a poem. Keep your notes along with your finished poem in your ⬑ **Working Portfolio.**

Speak for Yourself: *Drama*

If you've ever seen a movie based on a book you've read, you know that books and movies tell stories very differently. When you adapt your **short story** into a drama, you will be able to show your story in action. You will also have to consider how things that work in a story will need to be done differently when they are acted out.

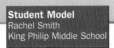

Student Model
Rachel Smith
King Philip Middle School

The family rushed to the window just in time to see the garage swept away by the great torrent of water. "My car . . . Leo's wood business . . . gone!" her mother whispered in disbelief. . . .

The family rushes to the window
ELAINE: The garage! It's being swept away!
Mother is stunned
MOTHER: My car . . . Leo's wood business . . . gone!

"I wish this were all just a nightmare!"

Here's How Creating a Drama

- Write the dialogue from your story on a separate page. Label all the dialogue with the names of the characters who say it.

- Add any background information, unspoken feelings, or thoughts from your story to your dialogue so the audience will understand everything. It could be as simple as a character saying, "I'm scared," or, "I haven't seen you since last summer."

- Write some stage directions so the actors will not only know what to say, but also what to do. Mention if a character is yelling or whispering a line, or standing in a certain place.

- Bring in props, music, and costumes to add some realism and mood to your drama.

- Assign roles to your friends and act out your drama in front of the class.

For more information on speaking skills, see p. 545–47.

SHORT STORY

Student Help Desk

Short Story and Poem at a Glance

SHORT STORY

POEM

Introduction
Sets the stage by
- introducing the **characters**
- describing the **setting**

Body
Develops the plot by
- introducing the conflict
- telling a sequence of **events**
- developing **characters** through words and actions
- building towards a **climax**

Conclusion
Finishes the story by
- resolving the **conflict**
- telling the **last event**

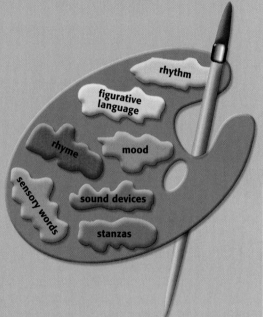

rhythm

figurative language

rhyme

mood

sensory words

sound devices

stanzas

Idea Bank

Finding a topic for a short story or poem

Talk with older family members about their experiences.

Play "remember when . . ." with other family members.

Imagine how your great-great-grandchild will see your life.

Recall an event or person that was especially important to you.

Make up a tall tale about something that might have happened years ago.

Look hard at the world around you. What sounds or textures do you like best?

CHAPTER 26

Friendly Feedback

Questions for Your Peer Reader

- What surprised you about my story or poem?
- What effect did my writing have on you?
- What was the part you liked best?
- How could I have improved my story or poem?
- What parts should I keep and make better?

Publishing Options

Print	Submit your writing to your school's literary magazine.
Oral Communication	Read your story or poem aloud to a small group, or turn it into a dramatic reading using props and music to enhance the mood.
Online	Check out **mcdougallittell.com** for more publishing options.

The Bottom Line

Checklist for Short Story

Have I . . .

____ provided a strong beginning and ending?

____ used story elements of character, setting, and plot to create a convincing world?

____ included sensory language and concrete details?

____ used dialogue effectively?

____ developed a main conflict?

____ made the sequence of events clear?

____ maintained a consistent point of view?

Checklist for Poem

Have I . . .

____ focused on one idea or feeling?

____ used precise words in an interesting way?

____ included fresh sensory words?

____ used figurative language, such as similes and metaphors?

____ included sound devices, such as alliteration and rhyme?

SHORT STORY

Research Report

Learn What It Is

Did you ever hear about something and think, "I'd like to know more about this?" If you went on to talk to people about the subject, or to look it up in books or on the Internet, you were doing research. A **research report** is a formal written report on a given subject. Here is how you write such a report.

Basics in a Box

RESEARCH REPORT AT A GLANCE

Thesis

Introduction — Body — Conclusion — Works Cited

Research

RUBRIC

Standards for Writing

A successful research report should

- include a strong introduction with a clear thesis statement
- use evidence from several sources to develop and support ideas
- credit the sources of information

- follow a logical pattern of organization, using transitions between ideas
- summarize ideas in the conclusion
- include a Works Cited list at the end

See How It's Done: *Research Report*

Clark 1

Joe Clark

Mrs. Williams

English

16 April 2000

Tsunamis

You probably know something about tornadoes, hurricanes, earthquakes, floods, and forest fires. You may not know much about tsunamis, or giant ocean waves. However, the deadly waves of a tsunami can be a serious natural disaster, striking with almost no warning. As Kathy A. Svitil has written, "If you can see the wave coming, it's too late to escape."

According to Robert E. Wilson, tsunamis are started by landslides, earthquakes, or volcanoes. The Handy Science Answer Book says that the ocean floor must shift upward. A horizontal, or sideways, shift will not cause the waves ("What" 82). Such a wave travels very fast, but it gets dangerous when it gets close to shore. There the wave slows down in shallow water, and it gets higher ("Physics"). In fact, the name *tsunami* means "harbor wave." Frank I. González thinks that the name may come from the fact that you can't really see a tsunami until it gets close to shore. Yet the earthquake that causes the tsunami can occur thousands of miles away.

One of the worst tsunamis in the last century hit Papua, New Guinea, on July 17, 1998. As described by Svitil, the first event was an earthquake, only about 15 miles offshore, that measured 7.1 on the Richter scale. Within ten minutes, a wall of water about 40 feet high slammed into four small villages. The villages of Arop and Warapu were wiped out.

RUBRIC IN ACTION

❶ This writer begins with a strong introduction that involves the reader.

Another option: Begin with a description of what happened when an actual tsunami struck land.

❷ Clear thesis statement

❸ Credits source of information. No page number is provided for an Internet source.

❹ This paragraph supports the thesis statement's claim that a tsunami is a serious natural disaster.

REPORT

Clark 2

Two-thirds of the village of Sissano and half of the village of Malol were also ruined. More than 2,100 people died.

Although records show that about 57 tsunamis happen every ten years (González), between 1990 and May 1999—slightly less than 10 years—82 had been reported. This "increase" is probably due to better communication. There may not be more killer waves, but we know about almost every one that happens.

Can anything be done to reduce the damage of tsunamis? Yes. The good news is that there would have been many more deaths in the last ten years if countries had not started warning systems and

⑤ Credits source of information

Clark 4

Works Cited

González, Frank I. "Tsunami!" <u>Scientific American</u> May 1999. 5 Jan. 2000 <http://www.scientificamerican.com/1999/0599issue/0599gonzalez.html>.

"Physics of Tsunamis." <u>West Coast and Alaska Tsunami Warning Center Home Page</u>. 6 Sept. 1999. West Coast and Alaska Tsunami Warning Center. 7 Mar. 2000 <http://wcatwc.gov/physics.htm>.

Svitil, Kathy A. "A Deadly Wave." <u>Discover</u> Jan. 1999: 68.

"What Is a Tsunami?" <u>The Handy Science Answer Book</u>. Detroit: Visible Ink, 1994.

Wilson, Robert E. "Tsunami." <u>Grolier Multimedia Encyclopedia</u>. CD-ROM. Deluxe ed. Danbury: Grolier, 1998.

Works Cited
- Identifies all sources credited in the report
- Presents entries in alphabetical order
- Gives complete publication information
- Contains correctly punctuated entries
- Is double-spaced throughout
- Follows an accepted style, such as MLA style

Do It Yourself

Write a research report about a topic that interests you.

Purpose To share information about the topic

Audience Your teacher, your classmates, and anyone else interested in the topic

❶ Developing a Research Plan

When you write a research report, you need to gather information from several sources. At first, your topic will probably be too broad. Your first job will therefore be to use information to narrow your topic to a size you can manage.

Narrowing Your Topic

Use several sources to learn more about your broad topic. Look for one aspect that interests you and that you could cover in the number of pages you have been assigned to write. To narrow your topic you might

- browse the Internet
- skim books on your broad topic. Check each book's introduction, table of contents, and picture captions
- ask questions of other people

Developing Research Questions

Once you have narrowed your topic, develop a set of questions to direct further research. For example, the writer of the report on tsunamis was assigned the subject of natural disasters. He wanted to explore a kind of natural disaster that was not well-known to most of his classmates. His research questions included the following:

- Just what is a tsunami?
- What does the name *tsunami* mean?
- How big a danger are tsunamis?

As you discover ideas and information during your research, you may decide to change the direction of your topic.

REPORT

❷ Finding Information

Locating Sources

It is important to use information from several sources in writing your report. Reading multiple sources will give you a deeper understanding of your subject and more ideas about it.

For in-depth information on finding useful sources, read Chapter 28, "Finding Information," on pages 493–505. Below are some of the many sources you should consider.

Information Resources		
Books	Dictionaries	CD-ROM encyclopedias
Newspapers	Atlases	Statistical abstracts
Magazines	Thesauri	Online databases
Encyclopedias	Almanacs	Internet sites

Evaluating Sources

Once you have located sources, you must make sure they are good ones. Ask yourself these questions for each source you consider.

- Is the author an expert? What qualifications does he or she have?
- Is the author fair?
- Is the source up-to-date?

For more on choosing and evaluating sources, see p. 502.

Making Source Cards

When you find a good source, write down its author, title, and publication information on an index card. This becomes your **source card.** See the chart and sample cards on the next page for guidelines on documenting each kind of source.

Number each of your source cards. Numbered source cards can help you in two ways. First, when you take notes, you can refer to the source by number instead of writing down the title and author again and again. Second, your source cards will help you create your Works Cited list, an alphabetized list of the sources actually used in writing the report. You will learn more about the Works Cited list on page 485.

- **Book** Write the author's name, the title, the location and name of the publisher, the copyright date, and the library call number.
- **Magazine or newspaper article** Write the author's name if the name is given, the title of the article, the name and date of the publication, and page numbers of the article.
- **Encyclopedia article** Write the author's name if given, the title of the article, and the name and copyright date of the encyclopedia.
- **Internet** Write the author's name if given, the title of the document, the publication name of any print version, the date you accessed the article, and the electronic address <in angle brackets>.

Sample Source Cards

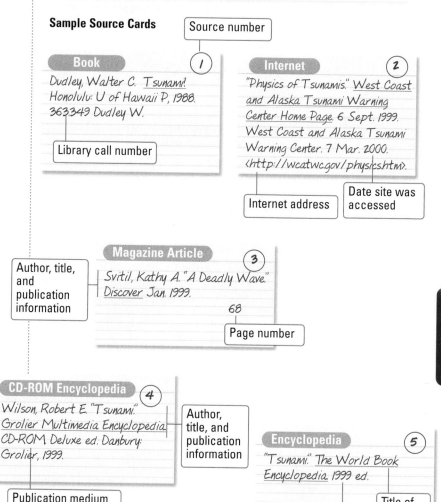

Source number

Book *1*

Dudley, Walter C. *Tsunami!*
Honolulu: U of Hawaii P, 1988.
363.349 Dudley W.

Library call number

Internet *2*

"Physics of Tsunamis." *West Coast and Alaska Tsunami Warning Center Home Page.* 6 Sept. 1999.
West Coast and Alaska Tsunami Warning Center. 7 Mar. 2000.
<http://wcatwc.gov/physicshtm>.

Internet address

Date site was accessed

Author, title, and publication information

Magazine Article *3*

Svitil, Kathy A. "A Deadly Wave."
Discover. Jan. 1999.

68

Page number

CD-ROM Encyclopedia *4*

Wilson, Robert E. "Tsunami."
Grolier Multimedia Encyclopedia.
CD-ROM. Deluxe ed. Danbury:
Grolier, 1999.

Author, title, and publication information

Publication medium

Encyclopedia *5*

"Tsunami." *The World Book Encyclopedia.* 1999 ed.

Edition

Title of source

REPORT

❸ Taking Notes

Take notes on any information you find that will be useful in writing your paper. Write each note on a separate index card. Most of your notes will paraphrase the author's words.

Here's How Taking Notes

- **Use a separate index card** for each piece of information.
- **Give each card a heading** to show the subject of the note.
- **Write the number of the matching source card** on each note card.
- **Write the number of the page** where you found the information.
- **Put quotation marks around anything** you copy word for word from the source.

For more on taking notes, see pp. 512–514.

Paraphrasing

When you paraphrase, you rewrite what the text says in your own words. Your words will usually be simpler. Here is a paragraph from a magazine article, followed by a note card with a paraphrase of the same paragraph.

PROFESSIONAL MODEL

Five or ten minutes later a wall of water 40 feet high at some points slammed into the spit, engulfing the villages. Almost instantly, Arop and Warapu, each home to 2,500 people, were gone; half of Malol and two-thirds of Sissano were also destroyed.

—Kathy A. Svitil, "A Deadly Wave"

Note Card

| Paraphrase | ③ | Source number |

What tsunami did in Papua, New Guinea — Heading showing subject
40-foot-high wall of water hit 4 small villages 5 or 10 minutes after quake. Arop and Warapu wiped out. Two-thirds of Sissano and half of Malol ruined.   68 — Page number

Quoting

Although most of your notes will paraphrase the source material, sometimes you will want to copy the author's words exactly. When you do, be sure to use quotation marks. You should save quotations for times like these:

- The author's words make the point in especially vivid language.
- The author's point is so important that it needs to be reported exactly.

Avoiding Plagiarism

If you use an author's words without giving credit, you are committing plagiarism. You are stealing words from the author and passing off his or her work as your own. Sometimes it is easy to let paraphrasing slip into plagiarism by accident.

ORIGINAL

In fact, the Japanese word *tsunami* translates literally as "harbor wave," perhaps because a tsunami can speed silently and undetected across the ocean, then unexpectedly arise as destructively high waves in shallow coastal waters.

—Frank I. González, "Tsunami!"

PLAGIARIZED VERSION

The Japanese word *tsunami* translates as "harbor wave," perhaps because a tsunami can speed unseen across the ocean, then unexpectedly arise as destructively high waves in coastal waters.

The writer did make changes. He left out some words ("literally," "shallow") and changed some words ("silently and undetected" became "unseen"), but that is not enough. The writer has plagiarized the source. Following is a version in which the source has been noted, and plagiarism is avoided.

STUDENT MODEL

In fact, the name *tsunami* means "harbor wave." Frank I. González thinks that the name may come from the fact that you can't really see a tsunami until it gets close to shore.

Source is credited.

REPORT

❹ Organizing and Outlining

Planning Your Report

Your research report will have three parts: the **introduction,** the **body,** and the **conclusion.**

Introduction Here is where you tell what your report is about. The introduction should have a lively opening and should include your **thesis statement,** or your statement of the main idea. A good thesis statement

• tells the subject of the report

• can be supported with facts

Body The body of your research report gives the information that supports your thesis statement. Good body paragraphs have the following characteristics:

• The topic sentences support the thesis statement.

• The paragraphs are logically organized, so that ideas flow smoothly.

Conclusion The end of your research paper should sum up your ideas and restate your thesis statement in different words.

Making an Outline

To ensure that your report will be well organized, prepare an outline before you write. To make an outline, begin by grouping your note cards according to key ideas. Then you can put them into an order that supports your thesis statement and flows logically. Here is the beginning of the outline for the research report on tsunamis.

> *Tsunamis*
>
> **Thesis statement:** *A tsunami can be a deadly natural disaster, striking with almost no warning.*
>
> I Introduction
> II What a tsunami is
> III The kinds of damage it can cause
> IV How often tsunamis happen

For more about creating outlines, see p. 515.

⑤ Drafting

Use your outline and notes to begin your draft. You don't have to begin at the beginning and work straight through to the end. If you want to, you can start with the section you have the strongest ideas about. As you work, follow these guidelines.

Follow your outline. Write one or more paragraphs for every major part of your outline. (If you don't have enough material to make a paragraph, either frame new questions and do further research or revise your plan.)

Put paragraphs in order. Make sure your paragraphs are in order before you begin your revision.

Support your thesis. Remember that everything in your paper should support your main idea.

Integrating Your Notes into Your Report

The writer of the report on tsunamis found a lot of material in several sources, so he took a lot of notes. When it was time to write his report, he grouped note cards into sections. Here are two notes he took about early-warning systems. Following the notes is a paragraph from his report that uses the information from the notes. Note that the writer gives credit to his source.

Early-Warning Systems (6)
Over a fourth of Pacific tsunamis reported since 1895 began near Japan. The Japanese have developed programs to reduce hazards, including warning systems, education, and coastal barriers.

Early-Warning Systems (6)
Japan has done better with cutting deaths than other countries, such as Indonesia. There most people did not know that an earthquake could be followed by a tsunami. In Papua, New Guinea, some actually went to the beach to see what was going on.

STUDENT MODEL

The good news is that there would have been many more deaths in the last ten years if scientists had not started educational programs and warning systems. The bad news is that in many places warning systems are not in place, and people have not been trained to recognize warning signals (González).

⑥ Documenting Information

You do not have to document, or give a source for, information that your readers could be expected to know. An example of such information is that the United States experiences tornadoes, hurricanes, floods, and forest fires.

For less well-known material, the most common way to document is to refer to its source in parentheses within the report. This is called **parenthetical documentation.** The reference in parentheses directs your reader to the Works Cited list at the end of your report. You should supply parenthetical documentation for each quotation, paraphrase, or summary that you use.

Here's How **Guidelines for Parenthetical Documentation**

Work by One Author Give the author's last name and the page number (unless it is a nonprint work) in parentheses.

> Records show that about 57 tsunamis happen every ten years (González).

If you mention the author's name in the sentence, give only the page number if the source is more than one page.

> As Dudley reports, tsunami waves in the open ocean are many hundreds of feet long but only a few feet high. In deep water, the wave usually passes unnoticed. In shallow water, however, the wave can become as high as a 10-story building (76).

Work with No Author Given Give the title (or a shortened version of the title) and the page number if it is a print work.

> A horizontal shift will not cause the waves ("What" 82).

Electronic Source Give the author's last name. If no author is given, list the title.

> Such a wave travels very fast, but it gets dangerous when it gets close to shore. There the wave slows down in shallow water, and it gets higher ("Physics").

Preparing a Works Cited List

- First, gather your source cards.
- Next, read your report.
- Whenever you come to a reference, put a check on the card for that source.
- If when you finish reading, you find that any source card remains unchecked, put it aside. Your Works Cited list will include only those sources you actually used in writing your paper.
- Place your checked source cards in alphabetical order by the last name of the author. If a card names more than one author, use the first author. If no author is named, use the first word of the title. Don't count *A, An,* or *The* as a title word. Use the format shown here.

Clark 4

Center the title, "Works Cited."

Works Cited

Indent the second and subsequent lines of each entry one-half inch or five spaces.

González, Frank I. "Tsunami!" <u>Scientific American</u> May 1999. 5 Jan. 2000 <http://www.scientificamerican.com/1999/0599issue/0599gonzalez.html>.

Double-space the whole list.

"Physics of Tsunamis." <u>West Coast and Alaska Tsunami Warning Center Home Page</u>. 6 Sept. 1999. West Coast and Alaska Tsunami Warning Center. 7 Mar. 2000 <http://wcatwc.gov/physics.htm>.

Svitil, Kathy A. "A Deadly Wave." <u>Discover</u> Jan. 1999: 68.

"What Is a Tsunami?" <u>The Handy Science Answer Book</u>. Detroit: Visible Ink, 1994.

Wilson, Robert E. "Tsunami." <u>Grolier Multimedia Encyclopedia</u>. CD-ROM. Deluxe ed. Danbury: Grolier, 1999.

For more about documenting sources, see MLA Citation Guidelines pp. 642–649.

REPORT

❼ Revising

TARGET SKILL ▶Paragraphing Start a new paragraph every time you begin a new subject. For more help with revising review the rubric on page 474.

> As Kathy A. Svitil has written, "If you can see the wave coming, it's too late to escape.¶According to Robert E. Wilson, tsunamis are started by landslides, earthquakes, or volcanoes.

❽ Editing and Proofreading

TARGET SKILL ▶Pronoun-Antecedent Agreement A pronoun needs to agree in number and person with its antecedent, the word it refers to.

> Such a wave travels very fast, but it gets dangerous
> *it gets*
> when ~~they get~~ close to shore, because the wave slows down in shallow water, and it gets higher.

For more on pronoun-antecedent agreement, see pp. 73–75.

❾ Sharing and Reflecting

When you are satisfied with your report, **share** it with others by giving an oral presentation. You may want to use photos or possibly a videotape or an interactive Web site to add excitement to your presentation. Ask for feedback regarding the content, purpose, and message of your report.

For Your Working Portfolio After sharing, **reflect** on what you learned by writing your report. Did you learn more about your topic? Are there still things you would like to know about it? Evaluate your own research and frame new questions for further investigation. Attach your reflections to your finished report and save them in your ▱ **Working Portfolio.**

Speak for Yourself: *Oral Report*

> "A wall of water 40-feet high and traveling at tremendous speed smashed into the villages."

TSUNAMI

What force could create such a wave? Because you have researched and written about tsunamis, often called tidal waves, you can tell others about them. Presenting your report to an audience offers many opportunities. You will have the chance to use charts, graphs, photographs, and multimedia to illustrate the information in your essay. Your report may get others so interested in your subject that they want to research another aspect of your topic.

Here's How) Creating an Oral Report

- Use your written report to plan the points of your presentation, but don't read the report to your audience.
- Gather charts, graphs, photographs, and anything else that will help make the facts you are presenting clear.
- Make an outline of the information you will present. Note when and where you will introduce the visuals.
- Make sure the visuals can be seen clearly from the back of the room.
- Practice your presentation, including how you will handle the charts, photographs, and other visuals.

For more information on speaking skills,
see p. 545–47.

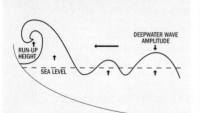

DEEPWATER WAVE
AMPLITUDE
RUN-UP HEIGHT
SEA LEVEL

REPORT

Student Help Desk

Research Report at a Glance

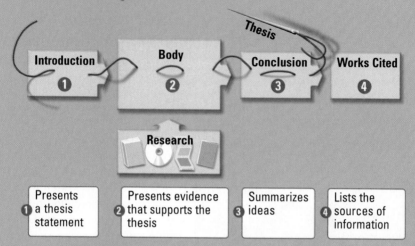

| Presents a thesis statement | Presents evidence that supports the thesis | Summarizes ideas | Lists the sources of information |

Idea Bank

Tips for Finding a Topic

Freewrite. List subjects like food or weather. Then list smaller parts of each subject. For example, you could begin with sports, then move to basketball, and then to women's college basketball. Finally, you might focus on the history of one women's college basketball team.

Listen to the news. As you listen, list any subject that appeals to you as a possible topic.

Think of people. Make a list of people you admire or wonder about. Review your list to see if one of them would make a good subject for a research report.

Think of places. Make a list of landmarks or historic places in your area. Include places that may be famous only in your area. Plan to write a research report about a place on your list.

Read literature. Think about authors you have been studying, such as Ray Bradbury and Virginia Hamilton. What topics did they write about that you might like to explore further? What more would you like to know about their lives?

Friendly Feedback

Questions for Your Peer Reader

- What did you like best about my report?
- What parts weren't clear?
- What did you learn from it?
- What further information should have been included?
- What information should have been left out?

Publishing Options

Print	Group your class's research reports by category, such as science, history, or popular culture. Make booklets compiling the reports in each category. Put the booklets in the classroom library.
Oral Communication	Work with another classmate to present your reports. One partner should tell the narrative of the report. The other partner should use visuals to illustrate key points, explaining what is being shown.
Online	Check out **mcdougallittell.com** for more publishing options.

The Bottom Line

Checklist for Research Report

Have I . . .

- ____ written a strong introduction?
- ____ stated my thesis clearly?
- ____ used evidence from reliable sources to support my ideas?
- ____ credited my sources of information?
- ____ used a logical pattern of organization?
- ____ used transitions?
- ____ written a strong summary for the conclusion?
- ____ included a correctly formatted Works Cited list at the end?

Communicating in the Information Age

Reading the Signs

To travel the information highway, you're going to need some special skills. By learning how to find, analyze, and use information, you can make the trip a lot less stressful and more enjoyable. So get ready to take a trip to knowledge! Who knows where you'll end up?

Power Words
Vocabulary for Precise Writing

seek *probe* *excavate* *exploring* *exhum* *quarry* *min* *unearth* *investigate*

Searching for Clues

Finding the answer to a difficult question can take you all sorts of places.

On the Lookout

People **seek** things in various ways. Archaeologists **excavate** ancient sites, hoping to **exhume** and **disinter** parts of the past that will **disclose** other ways of life. People also **prospect** for minerals and **pan** or **mine** for gold. They **quarry** marble and **probe** for oil. They do these things in hopes of **uncloaking** the secrets of history or **revealing** the earth's hidden riches.

Untouched for Centuries

Imagine **exploring** an ancient city. You **stumble into** a secret passageway leading to a hidden treasure room. Be sure to **investigate** every nook and cranny! You might find a goblet, **root out** a statue, or **unearth** some centuries-old jewelry. The deeper you **delve,** the more you will **uncover.**

▷ **Your Turn** Your Own Time Capsule

If you could make a time capsule to be opened in five hundred years, what five items would you put in it? Discuss this question with three or four classmates. Then list the five items the group agrees would be best to include. Be ready to explain why your group chose each item.

Finding Information

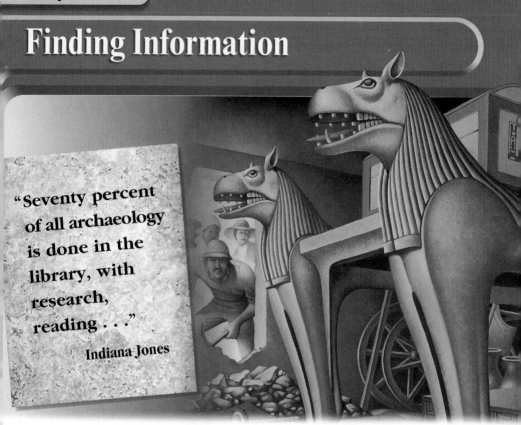

"Seventy percent of all archaeology is done in the library, with research, reading . . ."

Indiana Jones

Look in the Right Place

Can you imagine how much time archaeologists would waste if they simply wandered around looking for discoveries? Before they look for artifacts, scientists use books, journals, maps, and computers to figure out where rivers flowed and sediments were deposited millions of years ago. Then they dig.

Before you dig into a project, think about the research tools you can use—catalogs, indexes, reference books, periodicals, and on-line search engines. You may discover some new sources for the information you need.

Write Away: Finding a Place

Think of a topic that you know a lot about. How did you get your information? Write a brief paragraph about your source of knowledge on that topic. Then, as you work your way through this chapter, try using some of the resources suggested. See how much new knowledge you can dig up about your topic.

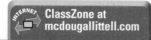

ClassZone at mcdougallittell.com

FINDING INFO.

The Library and Media Center

LESSON 1

The library and media center is a great place to find information on many topics. A number of different research sources are available, and the methods for finding and using them are easier than ever before.

❶ Using the Library Collection

Find out how your library is organized so you can easily get the material that you need. This diagram shows one common method of organization.

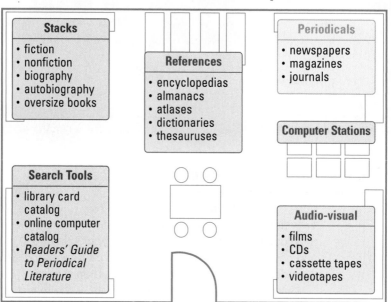

Sections of the Library

Stacks
- fiction
- nonfiction
- biography
- autobiography
- oversize books

References
- encyclopedias
- almanacs
- atlases
- dictionaries
- thesauruses

Periodicals
- newspapers
- magazines
- journals

Computer Stations

Search Tools
- library card catalog
- online computer catalog
- *Readers' Guide to Periodical Literature*

Audio-visual
- films
- CDs
- cassette tapes
- videotapes

❷ Using Special Services

Public libraries usually have special collections that might include rare books, public records, manuscripts, genealogical information, scrapbooks, maps, journals, and print or oral histories of a town, city, or region. Reference librarians, who are trained to find information about a wide variety of subjects, can help you to use these sources and others.

Locating Sources

Locating the right resources is an important step in preparing a report or completing an assignment that requires research.

❶ Using Catalogs

Head first to the library catalog. It lists all of the books, magazines, and other materials in the library.

Computer Catalog

Today, many libraries list all their materials in a computer catalog, which can be searched by author, title, subject, or keyword. A keyword search is unique to the computerized catalog. To develop a list of keywords, write down research questions and circle the most important words.

Example: How does (gravity) affect a (baseball) pitch?

Then, read the information on the computer screen to find out what commands to use for your keywords. The computer will search its index of the library's collection, and give you a list of all the materials that match your search request.

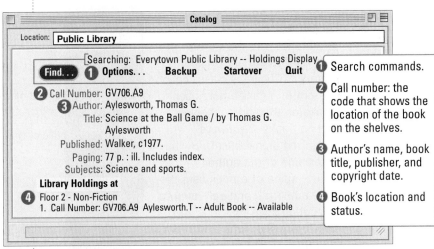

```
                              Catalog
 Location:  Public Library

        ┌─Searching: Everytown Public Library -- Holdings Display
  Find...  ❶ Options...   Backup   Startover   Quit
  ❷ Call Number: GV706.A9
     ❸ Author: Aylesworth, Thomas G.
        Title: Science at the Ball Game / by Thomas G.
               Aylesworth
    Published: Walker, c1977.
       Paging: 77 p. : ill. Includes index.
     Subjects: Science and sports.
  Library Holdings at
  ❹ Floor 2 - Non-Fiction
     1. Call Number: GV706.A9 Aylesworth.T -- Adult Book -- Available
```

❶ Search commands.

❷ Call number: the code that shows the location of the book on the shelves.

❸ Author's name, book title, publisher, and copyright date.

❹ Book's location and status.

FINDING INFO.

WATCH OUT

If your search turns up too many resources, you will need to narrow your topic. Try different research questions, or try different keywords.

Card Catalog

Card catalogs contain most of the same information that computer catalogs do. The information is listed on index cards in drawers, organized alphabetically. You can search by subject, author, or title, just as you could on the computer. Write down the title, call number, and author's last name to help you find the book. Here is a sample of a subject card.

❶ subject

❶ SPACE SHUTTLE

❷ TL795.5.J63 1982

❷ call number and year of publication

❸ Joels, Kerry Mark, 1931--

❸ author and date of birth

❹ The space shuttle operator's manual/Kerry Mark Joels, Gregory P. Kennedy; designed by David Larkin. 1st ed. --New York: Ballantine Books, c1982.
❺ ❻

❹ title

❺ publisher

❻ copyright date

❼ 154 p. : ill. ; 28 cm.--(A Del Rey book)
❽

❼ number of pages

❾ 1. Space shuttles. 2. Piloting. I. Title II. Author

❽ illustrated

❾ all the ways the book is listed

Classification Systems

All libraries use the Dewey decimal system and/or the Library of Congress classification system to organize nonfiction books on the library shelves. Fiction books are always organized alphabetically by the last name of the author.

The spine of a book lists the title, author(s), and **call number,** a location code that tells you the library shelf where you can find that particular book. The call number also is found on the card in the card catalog.

For more on the Dewey decimal system see p. 505.

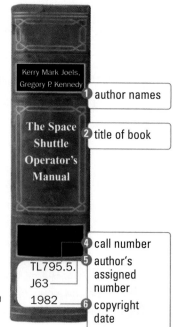

❶ author names

❷ title of book

❹ call number

❺ author's assigned number

❻ copyright date

❷ Using Periodical Indexes

Periodical indexes list, by subject, articles published in newspapers, magazines, and journals. Use periodical indexes to find information that is more up-to-date and focused than the information found in books.

The most widely used periodical index is the *Readers' Guide to Periodical Literature*, a monthly index. Here is a sample entry.

❶ **MUMMIES**
  ❷ *See also*
  ❸
    Mummy portraits
  ❹ Children of the ice [mummified remains of Incan sacrifices found by J. Reinhard]
  ❺ D. Schrieberg and S. Begley. il por maps
  ❻ *Newsweek* v126 p72-5 N 6 '95
       ❼   ❽

❶ subject heading
❷ cross-reference to other subject headings
❸ article about the subject
❹ article title
❺ authors
❻ periodical title
❼ volume and page numbers
❽ date of publication

You can find periodical indexes on CD-ROMs in your library's reference section or online in some libraries. You may also want to consult newspaper indexes, such as the *New York Times Index*, or electronic indexes, such as *Infonet*.

❸ Gathering Resources

Now that you have collected information on a number of possible resources, begin tracking them down. Books will be arranged on shelves that are marked with numbers or letters matching the information you found in the card catalog. Periodicals may be found in bound volumes, on microfilm, or sometimes in **vertical files:** a set of cabinets that contain current information in the form of pamphlets, handbooks, booklets, and clippings. Print out any good electronic sources you found on the computer.

Your library may not carry all the periodicals indexed by the *Readers' Guide*. You may be able to order copies of articles through an interlibrary loan program.

FINDING INFO.

Reference Works

LESSON 3

All libraries have a reference collection of material shelved together in a separate area or room. Most reference works cannot be checked out, but they can be photocopied. Some are even available on CD-ROM.

❶ Reference Books

Reference books give background information that might steer your research in a new direction. The chart below will give you an idea of the kind of research material available.

Library Reference Books	
If You Need...	**Try...**
general articles about a topic	• general encyclopedias *World Book* *Encyclopaedia Britannica* • specialized encyclopedias *Encyclopedia of Sports* *Baseball Encyclopedia*
information about specific people	• biographical indexes *Who's Who in America*
facts and statistics	• *Information Please Almanac* • *The World Almanac* • *Statistical Abstract of the United States*
maps	• *National Geographic Atlas*
word meanings, word origins, spellings, pronunciations, word choices	• dictionary • thesaurus
current information on a topic	• pamphlet files • periodical indexes • newspaper indexes

HOT TIP Your search for information should start, not end, with the encyclopedia. Use the encyclopedia to get background information and check facts, statistics, and dates. Then move on to other sources.

CHAPTER 28

❷ Electronic Reference Sources

Electronic reference sources put a huge amount of information at your fingertips. Here are some types of electronic reference sources and tips for using them.

Reference Sources on CD-ROM

Many classrooms and libraries have encyclopedias on CD-ROM. Some news magazines also prepare CD-ROMs that contain summaries of the year's news.

Tips:
- Use these CD-ROMs to find general information and to check facts from other sources.
- These CDs often are updated only once a year or less frequently, so check the copyright date to judge if the source is out of date.
- Don't rely on just one CD-ROM for an entire report—try books, newspapers, magazines, or the World Wide Web as well.

Online Databases

Libraries often have online databases that contain tens of thousands of articles from magazines and newspapers. These databases include both general interest and specialized articles.

Tips:
- Check the dates of articles you find on these databases. Is this information months or years old?
- Use these databases after you have done some general background research. Reading dozens of news articles on a topic can be a confusing way to start your research.

World Wide Web Sites

If you have access to the Web in your library, classroom, or home, you have access to Web pages.

Tips:
- Web pages aren't always fact checked and can disappear without notice. Look for the Web pages created by museums, government agencies, libraries, and other institutions.
- Make sure the Web site is up to date.

Using the Web

❶ Planning Your Search Strategy

The World Wide Web contains millions of pages of text as well as graphics, audio, and video. Here's a plan of attack for finding the information you need.

Step 1: Think ahead.

- Create research questions that summarize what you want to learn.
- Circle **keywords** in your questions—words that are likely to appear on pages that have the information you need.

Step 2: Try several search engines.

- No two search engines cover exactly the same pages. Use different search engines to expand your research.
- Most engines let you do advanced or expert searches. Use the "Help" buttons to learn about these searches.

Step 3: Choose sites wisely.

- Look for "best matches first"—that is, matches that include all your keywords early in the document.
- Many engines also tell you when each Web page was last updated and show the first few lines of text on the page.
- If you still have too many sites, narrow your search by adding more keywords.

Step 4: Explore and document.

- Open the site. Find the name of the person who created the page.
- Click on links that give other information.
- Print out useful pages or save them as text files. Note their Web addresses in case you need to go back to them.

❷ Analyzing Your Search Results

Take a look at the sample search results page below. Use the tips to make your own selection of sites more useful.

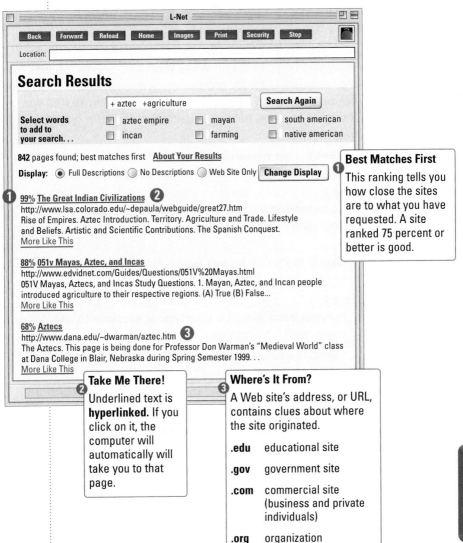

L-Net

Back | Forward | Reload | Home | Images | Print | Security | Stop

Location:

Search Results

+ aztec +agriculture   **Search Again**

Select words to add to your search...   ☐ aztec empire   ☐ mayan   ☐ south american
☐ incan   ☐ farming   ☐ native american

842 pages found; best matches first **About Your Results**

Display: ⦿ Full Descriptions ◯ No Descriptions ◯ Web Site Only **Change Display**

❶ 99% **The Great Indian Civilizations** ❷
http://www.lsa.colorado.edu/~depaula/webguide/great27.htm
Rise of Empires. Aztec Introduction. Territory. Agriculture and Trade. Lifestyle and Beliefs. Artistic and Scientific Contributions. The Spanish Conquest.
More Like This

88% **051v Mayas, Aztec, and Incas**
http://www.edvidnet.com/Guides/Questions/051V%20Mayas.html
051V Mayas, Aztecs, and Incas Study Questions. 1. Mayan, Aztec, and Incan people introduced agriculture to their respective regions. (A) True (B) False...
More Like This

68% **Aztecs**
http://www.dana.edu/~dwarman/aztec.htm ❸
The Aztecs. This page is being done for Professor Don Warman's "Medieval World" class at Dana College in Blair, Nebraska during Spring Semester 1999...
More Like This

Best Matches First ❶
This ranking tells you how close the sites are to what you have requested. A site ranked 75 percent or better is good.

Take Me There! ❷
Underlined text is **hyperlinked.** If you click on it, the computer will automatically will take you to that page.

Where's It From? ❸
A Web site's address, or URL, contains clues about where the site originated.

.edu   educational site

.gov   government site

.com   commercial site (business and private individuals)

.org   organization

FINDING INFO.

Choosing and Evaluating Sources

When you're doing research, too many sources can be a bigger problem than too few sources. To help narrow down your best sources, use the strategies in this lesson.

❶ Choosing Sources

After you have searched library catalogs, checked periodical indexes, and powered up World Wide Web search engines, you may feel as though you are swimming in information. Fortunately, not everything will be usable. Choose the sources that you think will be most helpful by using this five-step process.

Step 1:
Review your research questions. This will help remind you about the kind of information you really need.

Step 2:
Scan the table of contents to get an overview of a book or magazine. Identify chapters and articles that appear useful.

Step 3:
Check the index for key terms. Use the index to lead you to relevant information.

Step 4:
Preview each source's chapters or sections to see if they cover useful information.
- Skim titles, headlines, highlighted words or phrases, and topic sentences.
- Check maps, charts, and illustrations to see if the information applies to your topic.
- Read introductions, conclusions, and summaries.
- Scan for specific facts.
- If you need statistics, pay special attention to charts and graphs.

Step 5:
Return books that don't help you answer your research questions. Avoid books that oversimplify the subject, or that will be too difficult for you.

❷ Evaluating Sources

Now that you know which sources relate to your topic, evaluate each one for reliability. The questions and the scale below were used to judge sources for a research paper on immigration. The most reliable sources fell on the left side of the scale, and the least reliable fell on the right.

Most Reliable   **Least Reliable**

Topic: Immigration

1. Is the writer an expert on the subject?

a scholar who has studied immigration	a reporter writing a story on immigration	a tabloid story

Whether you need an expert depends on your topic. Sometimes a general interest book is the best source.

2. Does the source give a balanced point of view?

a scholarly paper that gives pros and cons	an autobiography telling one immigrant's experience	a political speech promoting changes to immigration laws

The best solution is to use more than one source.

3. Is the material current for the topic?

current immigration statistics	magazine article from 1950	immigration records from 1900

Information need not be current to be useful. But be sure to use current sources for information about science and technology.

4. Is the publisher trustworthy?

published by the Immigration and Naturalization Service	published by a national magazine	published on the Web by an unidentified person

Student Help Desk

Finding Information at a Glance

AAA Information Interchange

Ask Questions
- Prepare research questions.
- Identify keywords.

Access Library
- Find print and technological resources.

Analyze Source
- Scan table of contents, index, Web search page.
- Evaluate reliability.

Evaluating Web Sites

Does the Web site . . .

. . . present material issued by a reliable organization or expert?

. . . have a current date?

. . . publish a bibliography?

. . . link to other Web sites?

. . . provide information based on facts, not opinions?

"On the Internet, nobody knows you're a dog."

© The New Yorker Collection 1993 Peter Steiner from cartoonbank.com.

Information Sources

Consider the Possibilities!

- Books
- Magazine articles
- Web sites
- Newspapers
- Reference sources
- Special collections

Dewey decimal system

Find That Book!

Most libraries use the Dewey decimal system to classify all nonfiction books by number in ten major subject categories.

Numbers	Subject Areas	Examples
000–099	General Works	encyclopedias, handbooks
100–199	Philosophy	psychology, ethics, personality
200–299	Religion	Bibles, mythology, theology
300–399	Social Sciences	government, law, economics
400–499	Languages	dictionaries, grammars
500–599	Science	general science, mathematics
600–699	Technology	engineering, inventions
700–799	The Arts	music, theater, recreation
800–899	Literature	poetry, dramas, essays
900–999	History	biography, geography, travel

The Bottom Line

Checklist for Evaluating Information

Have I found sources that . . .

____ answer my research questions?

____ are easy to understand?

____ are up to date?

____ present both sides of my topic?

____ are written by experts?

____ are published by reliable sources?

focused

CALM

PANICKY   cool-headed

scared

tense

Calm or Panicked?

Have you ever felt jittery before an important test or a big game? Here is some helpful advice.

Uptight

You will do better in a high-pressure situation if you can avoid being **nervous, tense,** or **uptight.** If you feel **panicky,** try breathing deeply. Feeling a little **apprehensive,** as if you were **on pins and needles,** is okay. Don't let yourself become **scared** or **frantic!** In many situations, keeping calm is half the battle.

All Right

Imagine that you are in a basketball game and have a chance to score some points. You need to stay **calm, unrushed,** and **focused.** You need to be **cool-headed** enough to see where your team-mates are positioned and **collected** enough to perform well. On the other hand, if you don't give the game your all, your teammates may think that you are making a **half-hearted** effort. The coach might accuse you of being **indifferent, apathetic,** or **blasé.** To succeed, you should be relaxed, but not *too* relaxed!

nervou

apprehensive

FRANTIC

▷ **Your Turn** Then I Felt . . .

Choose one of the boldfaced words above. Tell a partner of a situation that made you feel that emotion. (You can look up the word in a dictionary to be certain of its meaning.) Then listen as your partner chooses a word and tells you about a situation he or she faced.

uptight

on pins and needle

Study and Test-Taking Skills

Perfect Papers and Terrific Tests

Do you panic when you open your assignment notebook? Are you feeling overloaded with papers and tests? Do you forget what you've read before you've even shut the book? Does writing an outline pose an overwhelming challenge?

Relax! There is a simple way to keep up with your schoolwork and handle almost any assignment or test: develop good study skills. Whether you're writing a paper or taking a test, it's important to focus on the task at hand and follow through on a plan.

Write Away: Scheduling Your Day
Are you an organized student? Make an outline of a typical school day. Remember to include meals, television viewing, and telephone conversations. Put your outline in your ▢ **Writing Portfolio.**

STUDY SKILLS

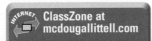
ClassZone at
mcdougallittell.com

Reading for Information

Reading Tips

Reading for information requires different skills than reading for pleasure does. Use these active reading strategies to stay on top of your material.

Preview
- Skim the pages.
- Read chapter title, introduction, and conclusion for overview.
- Note subheads, key words, pronunciation guides, and margin information.
- Read questions at the end of the chapter to give you an idea of the information you'll need to learn.
- Note maps, diagrams, and other graphics.

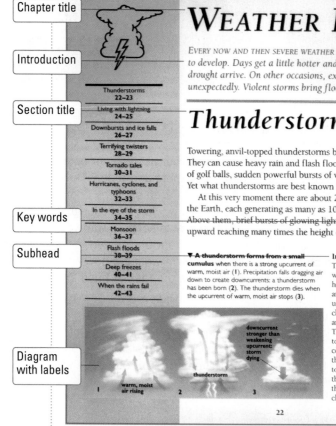

Chapter title

Introduction

Section title

Key words

Subhead

Diagram with labels

WEATHER EXTREME

EVERY NOW AND THEN SEVERE WEATHER OCCURS. SOMETIMES IT IS SLOW to develop. Days get a little hotter and drier until a heatwave and drought arrive. On other occasions, extremes arrive suddenly and unexpectedly. Violent storms bring floods and damaging winds.

Thunderstorms

Towering, anvil-topped thunderstorms bring many weather threats. They can cause heavy rain and flash floods, damaging hailstones the siz of golf balls, sudden powerful bursts of wind, and terrifying tornadoes. Yet what thunderstorms are best known for are lightning and thunder.

At this very moment there are about 2,000 thunderstorms raging acr the Earth, each generating as many as 100 flashes of lightning a minute. Above them, brief bursts of glowing lights called **jets and sprites** shoot upward reaching many times the height of the thunderstorms themselve

▼ A thunderstorm forms from a small **cumulus** when there is a strong upcurrent of warm, moist air (1). Precipitation falls dragging air down to create downcurrents: a thunderstorm has been born (2). The thunderstorm dies when the upcurrent of warm, moist air stops (3).

downcurrent stronger than weakening upcurrent: storm dying

thunderstorm

warm, moist air rising

Inside a thunderstorm
Thunderstorms can form on hot days when moist air close to the ground is heated and rises quickly. Strong upwa and downward rushes of air (called upcurrents and downcurrents) within cloud sweep ice crystals, water drople and ice pellets past and into one anoth This creates static electricity, which be to build up. Negative electrical charge collect in the middle and lower parts c the cloud and positive charges gather toward the top. The difference betwee the charges builds up until it is so grea that a massive spark is released as the charges even themselves out again.

22

CHAPTER 29

Read actively
- Read the text thoroughly.
- Read the first sentence of every paragraph for main ideas.
- Examine and answer all questions posed by the text.

Interpret maps and graphics
- Read the labels, captions, and explanations of graphics.
- Look through the text for reference to the graphic aids.
- Compare text information with graphic aids.

Review and take notes
- Reread difficult sections.
- Jot down important words, phrases, and facts.

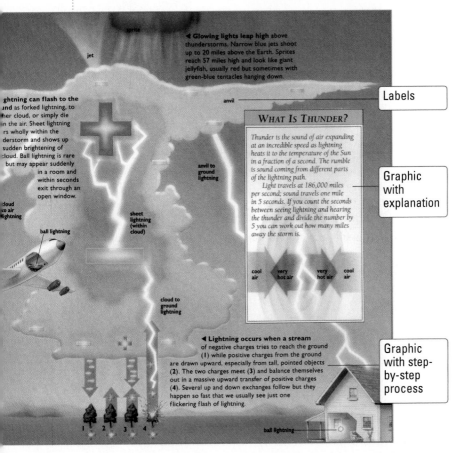

sprite

jet

◄ **Glowing lights leap high above** thunderstorms. Narrow blue jets shoot up to 20 miles above the Earth. Sprites reach 57 miles high and look like giant jellyfish, usually red but sometimes with green-blue tentacles hanging down.

anvil

Labels

ghtning can flash to the
und as forked lightning, to
her cloud, or simply die
in the air. Sheet lightning
rs wholly within the
derstorm and shows up
sudden brightening of
cloud. Ball lightning is rare
but may appear suddenly
in a room and
within seconds
exit through an
open window.

cloud
co air
lightning

ball lightning

anvil to
ground
lightning

sheet
lightning
(within
cloud)

cloud to
ground
lightning

WHAT IS THUNDER?

Thunder is the sound of air expanding at an incredible speed as lightning heats it to the temperature of the Sun in a fraction of a second. The rumble is sound coming from different parts of the lightning path.

Light travels at 186,000 miles per second; sound travels one mile in 5 seconds. If you count the seconds between seeing lightning and hearing the thunder and divide the number by 5 you can work out how many miles away the storm is.

cool
air

very
hot air

very
hot air

cool
air

Graphic
with
explanation

◄ **Lightning occurs when a stream** of negative charges tries to reach the ground (1) while positive charges from the ground are drawn upward, especially from tall, pointed objects (2). The two charges meet (3) and balance themselves out in a massive upward transfer of positive charges (4). Several up and down exchanges follow but they happen so fast that we usually see just one flickering flash of lightning.

ball lightning

Graphic
with step-
by-step
process

STUDY SKILLS

Understanding Graphic Aids

When you read for information, let built-in visual aids guide you through the material and increase your understanding.

Common Types of Graphic Aids

Diagrams

Diagrams are drawings that show how something works. Use these strategies to interpret diagrams.

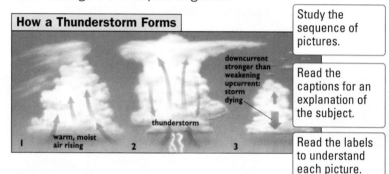

| How a Thunderstorm Forms |

Study the sequence of pictures.

Read the captions for an explanation of the subject.

Read the labels to understand each picture.

Maps

Maps are visual representations of an area. Consult the legend or key for help in understanding the symbols and colors on the map.

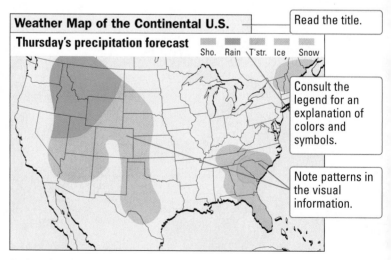

Read the title.

Consult the legend for an explanation of colors and symbols.

Note patterns in the visual information.

Tables and Scales

Tables allow you to compare facts. They are usually in column form. Tables often show numerical information. Read titles and column heads. A **scale** is a particular kind of table that shows information in order by size, degree, amount, or other ranking. The scale below shows one method of judging wind speed from the wind's effects.

Read the title.

Read the column heads.

The Beaufort Scale of Wind Strength

Wind	Wind Speed	Effect of Wind
Calm (0)	Less than 1 mph	Smoke rises straight up.
Light air (1)	1 to 5 mph	Smoke drifts.
Light breeze (2)	6 to 11 mph	Wind felt on face.
Gentle breeze (3)	12 to 19 mph	Leaves and twigs move.
Moderate breeze (4)	20 to 28 mph	Flags flap.
Fresh breeze (5)	29 to 38 mph	Small trees sway.
Strong breeze (6)	39 to 49 mph	Large branches move.
Moderate gale (7)	50 to 61 mph	Whole trees sway.
Fresh gale (8)	62 to 74 mph	Twigs break off trees.
Strong gale (9)	75 to 88 mph	Branches break off trees.
Whole gale (10)	89 to 102 mph	Trees uprooted.
Storm (11)	103 to 117 mph	Widespread damage.
Hurricane (12)	More than 117 mph	Destruction.

PRACTICE   Understanding Graphic Aids

Use the three graphics to answer the following questions.

1. Look at the diagram.
   - Does warm air rise or descend?
2. Look at the weather-map legend.
   - What color is used to show rain?
   - What is the forecast for Thursday on the Southeast coast?
3. Look at the Beaufort Scale.
   - When the wind is described as a fresh breeze, what effect does it have on trees?
   - How fast is a strong gale?

STUDY SKILLS

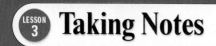

LESSON 3 **Taking Notes**

Taking notes helps you to remember what you read. You can take notes by paraphrasing or summarizing on note cards.

❶ Recognizing Key Information

When taking notes, focus on only the most important information. Pay attention to material presented in titles, topic sentences, and boldface type.

PROFESSIONAL MODEL

❶ **Inside a Thunderstorm**
❷ Thunderstorms can form on hot days when moist air close to the ground is heated and rises quickly. Strong upward and downward rushes of air (called ❸ **upcurrents** and **downcurrents**) within the cloud sweep ice crystals, water droplets, and ice pellets past and into one another. This creates static electricity, which begins to build up. Negative electrical charges collect in the middle and lower parts of the cloud and positive charges gather toward the top. The difference between the charges builds up ❹ until it is so great that a massive spark is released as the charges even themselves out again.

❹ —Derek Elsom, *Weather Explained*

❶ The subtitle gives a clue to the content.

❷ The topic sentence tells the main idea.

❸ Boldface type calls attention to key words and phrases.

❹ The source line tells where the information was found.

Formation of a Thunderstorm

- occurs on hot days
- upcurrents, downcurrents cause water and ice particles to collide
- static electricity builds
- energy releases in a massive spark

The page lists the main idea and supporting details.

❷ Paraphrasing

Paraphrasing is rewriting the text in your own words. A good paraphrase is about the same length as the original. It includes the main ideas and supporting details. It is often written in simpler language than the author used. If you use the author's exact words, put them in quotation marks. Using another person's words without giving credit to him or her is called **plagiarism** and is unlawful. Compare the two versions of the student model, each written from the following example.

Thunderstorms can form on hot days when moist air close to the ground is heated and rises quickly.

STUDENT MODEL

PLAGIARIZED VERSION

Thunderstorms form on hot days when moist air heats up and rises quickly.

PARAPHRASED VERSION

Hot, sticky days provide perfect conditions for thunderstorms. Thunderstorms form when moist air gets hot and rises fast.

❸ Summarizing

A summary is similar to a paraphrase, but it is shorter. In **summarizing** you make your own connections between ideas and details, and rewrite the main points in simple language. A summary is usually about one-third as long as the original. The following paragraph summarizes the model on page 512.

STUDENT MODEL

Thunderstorms happen on hot days when moist, hot air quickly rises. Upcurrents and downcurrents cause ice particles and raindrops to collide. This creates static electricity. As the charges build, negative ones sink to the bottoms of clouds, and positive ones rise to the tops. Finally, the difference between the charges becomes so great that it produces a giant spark.

❹ Using Note Cards

Using note cards is a practical way to take notes when you are doing research. When your information is on cards, you can sort and re-sort your material until you find an order that works well. Use a different card for each idea, quotation, or statistic. Be sure to give each card a heading that describes the note. Also remember to write the source of the information on the card.

Heading

How Thunderstorms Are Formed   2

air rushes up, upcurrent air
rushes down, downcurrent ice,
pellets, drops crash together static
electricity builds up negative charges in
middles and bottoms of clouds positive
charges in upper clouds

Elsom, Derek, _Weather Explained_ p. 99

Source

Thunderstorm Effect: Area   6

Most of the time, thunderstorms
cover an area of ten square miles.

"Storm." _World Book
Encyclopedia_, 1999 ed. p. 912

Page number
from source

Thunderstorm Formation: Squall Lines   4

"They are an unbroken line of black, ominous
clouds, towering 40,000 feet or more into
the sky, including thunderstorms of almost
incredible violence."

Lehr, Paul, _Weather_ p. 84

Quotation

Here's How) Using Note Cards to Organize

1. Sort your cards by topic.
2. Stack the cards into piles. This will help to identify the main ideas and bring together information from different sources.
3. Look for patterns of information in each stack and between stacks.
4. Reorder the piles until you are satisfied.

To avoid having to write source information on every note card, create source cards.

For more on source cards, see pp. 478–479.

Creating a Formal Outline

You can outline a chapter of your textbook to identify main ideas. In addition, you can use an outline to prepare a research paper. Use groups of note cards as the basis for this second kind of outline. Below is an outline for a research paper on thunderstorms using the note cards on page 514.

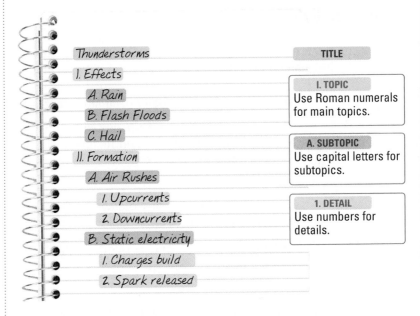

Thunderstorms — **TITLE**

I. Effects

  A. Rain

  B. Flash Floods

  C. Hail

II. Formation

  A. Air Rushes

    1. Upcurrents

    2. Downcurrents

  B. Static electricity

    1. Charges build

    2. Spark released

I. TOPIC
Use Roman numerals for main topics.

A. SUBTOPIC
Use capital letters for subtopics.

1. DETAIL
Use numbers for details.

When outlining, remember to keep all items of the same rank in parallel form. If subtopic *A* is expressed as a noun, then *B* and *C* should also be expressed as nouns. Also remember that when subtopics follow a topic or details follow a subtopic, there must be two or more of them: for every *I* there must be a *II*, for every *A* a *B*, and for every *1* a *2*. Finally, begin each item with a capital letter, and do not use end punctuation.

PRACTICE   Revising Your Schedule

Take a second look at the outline you made for the **Write Away** on page 507. Add or subtract details where necessary, then develop the outline into a paragraph.

STUDY SKILLS

LESSON 5 — Taking Objective Tests

Objective tests are designed to see how well you recall important facts and details. The key to success with such tests is to make sure you understand the test questions and what you are being asked to do. Objective questions come in several different forms: true-false, matching, multiple-choice, and short-answer. Before answering a question, be sure you know exactly what it is asking.

❶ True-False

A true-false question tests your ability to recognize what you've learned when that material is presented as a statement of fact.

> **Directions:** Indicate whether each statement is true or false.
>
> **1.** Sandra Day O'Connor, appointed to the Supreme Court by President Ronald Reagan in 1981, was the first woman to sit on the court.
> ❑ **True**   ❑ **False**

Answer: **True.** (All parts of the statement—including the date, and the name of the president—are correct)

> **2.** Thurgood Marshall was the first African-American member of the Senate.
> ❑ **True**   ❑ **False**

Answer: **False.** Thurgood Marshall was the first African-American member of the Supreme Court.

 Tips for Success

- Remember that for a statement to be true, every part of it must be true. If any part of it is false, the whole statement is false.
- Look for words like *all, always, never, only,* and *every.* Such words often signal a false statement.
- Look for words like *may, most, few, probably, usually, typically,* and *sometimes,* which often signal a true statement.

❷ Matching

Matching questions test your ability to recognize relationships between items in two columns and to pair items accordingly.

Directions: Match each item in the left-hand column with one item in the right-hand column.

Match the invention with the inventors. Use each answer only once.

_____ **1.** Thomas Edison   **a.** airplane
_____ **2.** Henry Ford   **b.** phonograph
_____ **3.** Orville and Wilbur Wright   **c.** assembly line
_____ **4.** Eli Whitney   **d.** cotton gin

Answers: **1-b, 2-c, 3-a, 4-d**

Tips for Success

• Determine from the directions whether you can use an item more than once.
• Check to see if there are extra items in the answer column.
• Match the items you are sure of first.

❸ Multiple-Choice

Multiple-choice questions test your ability to choose the correct answer from among several choices. In a well-written test, each of the wrong answers represents an error in thinking.

Directions: Write the letter of the correct answer.

1. What was the name of the Wright brothers' plane?

    a. *Spirit of St. Louis*
    b. *Concorde*
    c. *Enola Gay*
    d. *Flyer*

Answer: **d**

2. What did Thomas Edison invent?

    a. the electric light
    b. the telegraph
    c. the movie projector
    d. all of the above

Answer: **d**

- Read the question and try to answer it before you read the answer choices.
- Consider all the choices before selecting one.
- Cross out incorrect answers first.
- Look for words like *always, never,* and *only.* They often signal incorrect answers.

❹ Short-Answer

There are two kinds of short-answer questions. For one you supply missing information to fill in a blank. The other requires you to answer with one or two sentences.

Directions: Supply the missing word or phrase.

1. _____ invented the telephone.

Answer: Alexander Graham Bell

Directions: Write a brief response.

2. Name the inventor of the assembly line. Describe how this invention changed American factories.

_____

_____

_____

Answer: Henry Ford invented the assembly line. It allowed factories to produce more goods in less time.

The question above requires exactly two answers. Do not include unnecessary information.

 Tips for Success

- Make sure your answer to a fill-in-the-blank question fits grammatically into the sentence.
- If the question asks for more than one answer, be sure you provide all of them.
- When you are asked to reply in a sentence, make sure to avoid fragments. Also include phrases from the question in your answer.

Answering Essay Questions

Essay questions test your ability to reason, write persuasively, and communicate your ideas in a logical order. They require you to support your statements with appropriate facts.

❶ Understanding the Task

Before you start your essay, read the question carefully. Underline key words, and circle words that signal how to organize your answer.

Directions: Write an **essay** to answer the following question.

   1. **Discuss three** key factors that motivated early pioneers to settle the American West.

- Asks for essay.
- Asks you to **discuss,** or look at a topic from all sides.
- Asks for three reasons.

For more on essay questions, see the Student Help Desk, page 520.

❷ Writing the Response

Once you're sure you understand the question, you can draft your response. Organize your information into an informal outline before you begin to write.

> *Settling the American West*
>
> Motivating Factors
> - Cheap, available land
> - Get-rich-quick mentality
> - Better climate for farming

⭐ Tips for Success

- Read the question carefully.
- Underline key words.
- Make a quick outline.
- Jot down examples and details under each outline heading.
- State your main point clearly in the first sentence of the essay.
- Write and proofread your essay.

Student Help Desk

Study and Test-Taking Skills at a Glance

Read Carefully

There is a simple way to keep up with your schoolwork and handle almost any assignment or test: develop good study skills.

Use Assessment Skills

6. I The Cancel b...
7. I Pressing the ... box when en...
8. I When you en... in the cell.
9. E T...

Take Notes

Study Tips

- Take notes by listing, paraphrasing, summarizing, or outlining.
- List key terms, names, dates, and statistics.
- Briefly define or identify each term, name, or date.
- Review your notes regularly.
- Form a study group and split the work load among members.

Types of Essay Questions

If the question asks you to . . .	You should . . .
Compare/contrast	show similarities and differences between two or more topics
Describe	explain the most important aspects of a topic
Define	explain the basic meaning of a term
Discuss	look at a topic from all sides
Explain	tell how or why something happened or how something works
Analyze	examine the parts of a whole
Evaluate	examine and judge a topic carefully
Summarize/outline	give a brief overview of a topic

Before the Test

- Find out what the test will cover.
- Make a study plan.
- Allow yourself time to go over the material several times.
- Review your notes.
- Memorize key facts.
- Review sample tests or create your own.
- Give yourself a timed mock test.

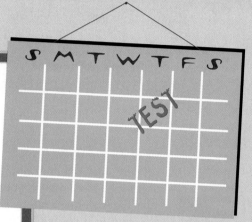

During the Test

- Skim the test.
- Read all of the instructions.
- Read each question carefully.
- If you don't know the answer to a question, skip it.
- Return to the hard questions after you've finished the others.
- Note the time limit and keep track of the time remaining.

The Bottom Line

Checklist for Developing Study and Test-Taking Skills

Have I . . .

____ read to obtain information?

____ created a formal outline?

____ taken and reviewed notes?

____ practiced my test skills?

Power Words
Vocabulary for Precise Writing

contemplate

ponderi

Brains Behind the Operation

What do you think of these words about thinking?

Train Your Brain

To be a great scientist or philosopher, you have to **think clearly** and **use your head** in the best possible way. A scientist will **reflect** on a problem and **mull over** a possible solution. A philosopher spends hours **meditating** and **cogitating.** Both like to **ruminate** on an interesting thought, and a difficult matter may cause them to **brood** unhappily. So as you **muse** about your future, if you **contemplate** being a scientist or philosopher, be prepared to **put on your thinking cap.**

Take a Brain Break

Spending hours **pondering** an idea can make you tired and irritable. Take a moment to gaze at some passing clouds and **imagine** what their shapes look like. Perhaps you can **visualize** an elephant or a herd of camels up there. At night, looking up at the sky, maybe you can **envision** yourself in a spaceship, speeding among the stars. It's fun to **daydream** and **woolgather** like this—to **build castles in the air.**

daydream

imagine

> ### Your Turn A Place to Think

Where and when do you think best? Do you prefer to do your homework alone or with friends, in silence or with music playing? Are you at your best in the morning, afternoon, or at night? Discuss these questions in a small group.

ruminate

mull ove

BROOD

visualize

Using Thinking Skills

What a Thought!

There's so much information coming at you from all directions these days that it's easy to get confused. How do you sort out facts from opinions? How do you know which opinions are reliable? How do you keep from thinking in circles? The good news is that learning some simple skills can help you answer these questions and think in a straight line from point A to point B. Read on in this chapter to find out how.

Write Away: Huh?
With a partner, discuss something you heard, saw, or read that didn't make sense to you. Then write a paragraph describing what you didn't understand and how talking with your partner helped—or didn't help—you understand it. Save your paragraph in your ☐ **Writing Portfolio.**

How Ideas Are Related

LESSON 1

How do you make sense of the information you hear, read, and see every day? You can start by deciding which ideas are important and which are not, and by figuring out how ideas are related.

❶ Main Ideas and Supporting Details

The first thing to do to make sense of new information is to find the **main idea,** or the important point expressed.

> **Here's How** **Identifying Main Ideas**
>
> Pay special attention to ideas
> - at the beginning or the end of a selection
> - at the beginning of paragraphs or following pauses in a speech
> - that are repeated several times
> - that follow statements such as "The point is" and "This is about"
> - that are underlined, bold-faced, or italicized in print, or that are spoken with emphasis or accompanied by forceful gestures

After you identify the main idea—or ideas—look for **supporting details.** These details often follow statements such as "For example" and "To illustrate the point."

> **PROFESSIONAL MODEL**
>
> What amazing device is spelled the same backwards and forwards? You guessed it— radar. Radar uses radio waves to determine how far away something is and how fast it's going. Our lives wouldn't be the same without it. Air traffic controllers, police officers, weather forecasters, and military personnel use it to guide planes, monitor car speeds, track tornadoes, and detect missiles.
>
> —Annette Ford

Main idea— Radar is an amazing device.

Supporting details.

WATCH OUT

If an idea has weak—or no—supporting details, ask yourself, Why should I believe this? Where's the proof?

CHAPTER 30

❷ Cause and Effect

One common way that ideas are related is by **cause and effect,**
a relationship that shows why something happens. Information
handouts and news reports often deal with causes and effects.

STUDENT MODEL

Due to budget cuts, the school band
may have to go without uniforms this
year. However, band members are
hoping that a car wash next
weekend will help them raise the
money they need. Strong support
by both the faculty and student
body could guarantee their success.

Cause—budget cuts➤
Effect—no band
uniforms

Cause—car wash➤
Effect—money to buy
uniforms

Cause—faculty and
student support➤
Effect—success

WATCH OUT In thinking about past events, look for solid evidence that
connects them. The fact that one event happened after another
does not necessarily mean the first event caused the second.

❸ Similarities and Differences

Another way that ideas are connected is by **similarities and
differences.** Science articles and movie reviews often compare
and contrast the similarities and differences among ideas.

PROFESSIONAL MODEL

[A Utah fossil bed]... held the bones of
two types of dinosaurs.... Both belonged
to a group called ankylosaurs. They were
plant eaters who were covered in thick,
armorlike plates. They could grow to more
than 30 feet long. [However] one... had a
long tail with a heavy club at the end....
The other... had spikes on its shoulders.

—*Time for Kids*

Dinosaur 1
long tail with
heavy club

Both Dinosaurs
ankylosaur, plant
eater, thick, armor-
like plates, more
than 30 feet
long

Dinosaur 2
spiky shoulders

THINKING SKILLS

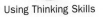

Separating Facts from Opinions

After you understand ideas and how they're related, you still need to figure out how reliable they are. To do this, you have to be able to separate facts from opinions.

❶ Identifying Facts

A **fact** is a statement that can be proved. Solid information is well supported by facts.

> ### Here's How Identifying and Proving Facts
>
> - **Make a personal observation.**
>   The weather report says the temperature is 80°.
>   **To prove:** Check an outdoor thermometer.
>
> - **Consult an authoritative source.**
>   A friend tells you the fastest animal is the cheetah.
>   **To prove:** Look up the information in an encyclopedia.
>
> - **Ask an expert.**
>   A cereal ad says that eating oatmeal can lower cholesterol.
>   **To prove:** Ask your doctor or the school nutritionist.

A statement is not necessarily a fact just because you agree with it. Be sure to check it out by one of the methods listed above.

❷ Identifying Opinions

An **opinion** is a statement of personal belief that cannot be proved. Words and phrases like those listed below signal opinions.

Signals of Opinion

believe	feel	think	would argue
doubt	don't see why	agree	don't agree
the best	excellent	the worst	useless

An opinion can be a good source of information, depending on whose opinion it is. Ask yourself: How much does this person know about the topic? How reliable is he or she?

Not All Opinions Are Created Equal

−	+	Why
"Lulu's is the best ice cream ever." **Jenny Landers** Seventh grader	*"Lulu's ice cream is better for you than other popular ice creams."* **Inez Molino** Nutritionist	The nutritionist has scientific knowledge about foods. The seventh grader just likes ice cream.
"Grass courts are the worst courts to play on." **Dr. Mark Cattel** Mathematician	*"Tennis matches are more challenging on clay than on grass courts."* **Nikita Pinsky** Eighth-grade tennis champion	The tennis champ plays hours of tennis every day. The mathematician probably plays tennis only on weekends.
"Terriers are not very friendly dogs." **Alvin Brown** College sophomore	*"Most terriers are easy to train."* **Leslie Chin** Dog trainer	The dog trainer has worked with many dogs. The college student probably hasn't.

PRACTICE   Identifying Facts and Opinions

Identify each of the following statements as a fact or an opinion. Write F for fact and O for opinion.

1. Mercury is the planet closest to the sun.
2. New York is the most exciting city in the United States.
3. Golf is a boring sport.
4. Rhode Island is the smallest state.
5. A vegetarian diet is the most healthy diet.

Explain what method you would use to prove each of the facts above.

Going Beyond the Facts

LESSON 3

Understanding and evaluating what you read or hear are important first steps in thinking. But you can't stop there. You have to go beyond the facts and think about how the new information affects what you already know. You can do this in three ways—by making inferences, drawing conclusions, and making generalizations.

❶ Making Inferences

An **inference** is a logical guess you make by "reading between the lines" of new information. You do this by combining what you learn with your prior knowledge. You make many inferences every day, probably without even knowing it. For example, if you walk into your classroom and see an answer sheet on each desk, you might infer that you're going to have a test.

New Information	+	Prior Knowledge	=	Inference
My sister came home from a date with a diamond ring on her finger.		My sister has been dating her boyfriend for three years. Women often get diamond rings when they get engaged.		My sister's engaged.

❷ Drawing Conclusions

A **conclusion** is a judgment or decision you arrive at by going "beyond the lines" of what you read or hear. A conclusion is based on a number of facts, inferences, and pieces of prior knowledge. It carries more weight than just a guess or inference.

CHAPTER 30

Drawing Conclusions

New Information	Prior Knowledge	Inferences
My friend Jess was hit by a car while riding his bike. He got a bad head injury.	Jess sometimes rides recklessly. He doesn't like to wear a helmet.	He wasn't wearing his helmet. He might not have hurt his head with a helmet on.

Conclusion

Jess's injuries were more severe than they had to be.

❸ Making Generalizations

A **generalization** is a broad idea or statement based on several specific examples. Generalizations help you group information, which makes it easier to understand and to remember.

Specific Examples

Food prices increased by 10%.
+
Housing costs have doubled.
+
Clothing is more expensive.
↓

Generalization

The cost of living has gone up.

Don't make generalizations that are too broad; for example, it would be wrong to conclude from the examples above that the economy is in ruin.

PRACTICE Making Inferences and Drawing Conclusions

List the inferences you can make and the conclusions you can draw about the person who lives in this room.

Avoiding Errors in Reasoning

Much of what you see, read, and hear is meant to persuade you to buy, believe, or do something. Before you make decisions or take action, use your thinking skills to look for reasoning errors. Becoming aware of these errors will help you avoid them in your own speaking and writing too.

❶ Overgeneralization

An **overgeneralization** is a statement that is too broad to be true. All it takes is one exception to make a statement false. Overgeneralizations often include words such as *always*, *never*, *all*, *none*, *everybody*, and *nobody*.

Overgeneralization
> **All tall people are good basketball players.**

True Statement
> **Some tall people are good basketball players.**

> That's not true. My science teacher's really tall, and he's a terrible basketball player.

An overgeneralization about a group of people, such as this one about tall people, is called a **stereotype.**

❷ Circular Reasoning

Circular reasoning is merely repeating an idea in different words instead of giving good reasons to support it.

> **I'm tired because I don't have any energy.**

Miss Peach by Mell Lazarus

THIS NEW TEXTBOOK CONFUSES ME...

HOW?

THERE'S STUFF IN IT THAT I DON'T KNOW...

MELL LAZARUS.

Creators Syndicate, Inc. ©1999 Mell Lazarus   E-MAIL - KPOP3@AOL.COM   www.creators.com   4-17

In the cartoon, the statement "There's stuff in it that I don't know" is an example of circular reasoning because it's just another way of saying that the textbook is confusing. Here are some statements the boy could have made that would give readers more information.

- "The book is written in Japanese."
- "It doesn't have any punctuation."
- "I'm reading it upside down."

❸ False Cause and Effect

False cause and effect is the mistaken idea that one event caused another. Be careful not to assume that Event A caused Event B just because Event A happened first. Consider other facts as well.

False Cause and Effect

> **I ate cold pizza this morning. That's why I got sick this afternoon.**

Correct Reasoning

> **The pizza probably had nothing to do with my getting sick. I just caught the flu that was going around.**

> That's not true. I've eaten cold pizza before with no problem. Also, two of my friends got sick, and neither of them ate any pizza.

PRACTICE Identifying Errors in Reasoning

For each sentence below, identify the error in reasoning. Then rewrite the statement to correct the error.

1. Mt. Everest is the supreme challenge for every mountain climber.
2. Because we were running late, we got a flat tire.
3. No one wants to be alone.
4. Sara is smart because she is so intelligent.
5. If I had bought those new running shoes, I would have won the race.

Recognizing Emotional Appeals

Emotional appeals are statements directed at people's emotions rather than at their sense of reason. There's nothing wrong with these kinds of appeals. But make sure you don't reach decisions without thinking about the information logically too.

❶ Loaded Language

Loaded language uses words that have strong positive or negative associations. The positive associations of words like *fresh, forceful,* and *fantastic* in this poster make you want to support Barbara. But remember who wrote the poster—people who want her to be elected. So before voting—or acting on any information that includes loaded language—think carefully about the issue and about the source of the information.

For more information on loaded language, see pp. 406–407.

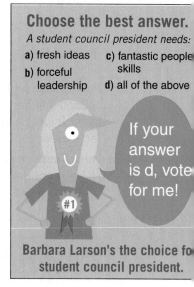

Choose the best answer.
A student council president needs:
a) fresh ideas   **c)** fantastic people skills
b) forceful leadership   **d)** all of the above

If your answer is d, vote for me!

#1

Barbara Larson's the choice for student council president.

If reading or hearing something makes you angry, enthusiastic, afraid, or sad, the message probably includes loaded language.

❷ Name Calling

Name calling is a way of getting people to reject someone's ideas by attacking the person rather than the ideas themselves. Even if the charges against a person aren't true, name calling can make you doubt the person. Politicians sometimes use this technique against their opponents.

Who do you want to represent you in Congress—a dinosaur who's stuck in the past or someone who's courageously facing the future? Why settle for Jill Jolsen, who hasn't lifted a finger to help this community? Invest in your children's futures. Vote for Velazquez!

NAME CALLING

LOADED LANGUAGE

❸ Bandwagon and Snob Appeal

Some people want to be just like everybody else. Others want to stand out from the crowd. Writers and speakers often appeal to these desires to help get their ideas across or sell a product. Be aware of these appeals and examine the ideas or products carefully and logically before taking action.

Bandwagon appeal is aimed at people's desire to be like everyone else.

Don't be left behind! Hop on the bike everyone's riding!

Snob appeal is aimed at people's opposite desire—to be seen as individuals.

Safari Tours—only for the wild at heart!

PRACTICE **Recognizing Emotional Appeals**

Identify the different types of emotional appeals in this advertisement.

What are you waiting for ?

Only the coolest people wear **Ray-Ons** – and that could be you! Don't hide your face behind those other boring brands. Put on a pair and have your day in the sun!

THINKING SKILLS

Student Help Desk

Using Thinking Skills at a Glance

Use your thinking skills to. . .

- identify main points
- discover relationships among ideas
- look for supporting evidence
- separate facts from opinions
- make inferences and generalizations
- draw conclusions
- find errors in reasoning
- recognize emotional appeals

Beware of

A   B

Fact or Opinion — Can You Prove It?

Statement	Fact	Opinion	Check It Out!
It's a rainy day today.	✓		**See for yourself.** Look outside.
The rafflesia is the world's largest flower.	✓		**Go to a reliable source.** Check an encyclopedia or guide to plants.
Too much vitamin A can be harmful.	✓		**Ask an expert.** Talk to a doctor or a nutritionist.
This is the best grammar book I've ever seen.		✓	**Consider all the options.** Ask, What grammar books has the person seen?
Talking to my father is useless.		✓	**Define terms.** Ask, What does *useless* mean?
That was an excellent meal.		✓	**Get the details.** Ask, What made the meal excellent?

CHAPTER 30

Give Me One Good Reason

Please, can I have a dog? All my friends have one.

I don't fall for that **bandwagon appeal**.

You never get me anything I want.

Now that's an **overgeneralization**, isn't it?

I'm the saddest and loneliest kid in the world.

If you're using **emotional appeals** to make me feel guilty, it's not working.

But a dog will keep me company and protect the house.

Ok, that sounds reasonable. What kind of dog should we get?

The Bottom Line

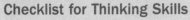

Checklist for Thinking Skills

Have I . . .

____ located main ideas and supporting details?

____ identified relationships among ideas?

____ separated facts from opinions?

____ gone beyond the facts to make inferences, drawn conclusions, and made generalizations?

____ recognized and avoided errors in reasoning?

____ recognized and evaluated emotional appeals?

THINKING SKILLS

Power Words
Vocabulary for Precise Writing

mimic

emula

jeers

sneers

praise

Compliments and Insults

Communication can be positive or negative, as these words show.

They're Singing Your Praises

We all like to get **compliments, accolades,** and **commendations,** especially when the **praise** comes from people we respect. "Imitation is the highest form of **flattery,**" they say. It's a compliment when you **imitate** a person's finest qualities, when you **emulate** his or her lifestyle and goals. On the other hand, it is an **insult** when you **mimic** someone's way of speaking or **ape** his or her walk or gestures.

What Did You Mean by *That*?

It may be difficult to distinguish between a sincere compliment and teasing **mockery** or veiled **sarcasm.** However, it isn't hard to recognize a **nasty, scornful, malicious,** or **contemptuous putdown.** We sure don't like it when someone **sneers, jeers,** or **scoffs** at us; **taunts** or **ridicules** us; **disparages** or **derides** us.

accolades

compliments

taunts

▷ **Your Turn** Introducing . . .

Get together with a partner and prepare introductions of each other. Include at least one interesting or little-known fact about the person you are introducing. Then try out your introduction on another classmate.

flattery

mockery

Listening and Speaking Skills

Read My Lips

How many times a day do you think you use the phrases shown in the picture above? How many times do you hear others say them? The problem might be as simple as a noisy room or clogged ears. However, it's more likely that you or your friends suffer from an acute case of poor listening skills!

Write Away: What's That Again?
Write about a time when poor listening led to a problem. The situation you write about can be real or imagined, serious or humorous. For example, what would happen if everybody were always plugged into an audiocassette player? Save your paragraph in your 🗀 **Working Portfolio.**

LISTEN/SPEAK

Listening Actively

When you have something important to say, you want to make sure that people are listening. But are *you* a good listener?

The fact that you hear sounds and words doesn't mean that you are really listening. To be a good listener, you must think about what you hear and actively try to remember it.

❶ Listening with a Purpose

People who listen effectively know why they're listening and what they're listening for. Whenever you're in a situation that requires you to listen to someone, try to match *how* you listen to *why* you're listening.

Reasons for Listening

Situation	Reason for Listening	How to Listen
Your friend tells a funny story about her pet iguana.	For enjoyment, to provide your friend with an audience	Maintain eye contact, nod to show you understand what he or she is saying, and make appropriate comments.
You're watching a TV show called "Wolves of the Tundra."	For enjoyment, to learn something new	Think about what you already know about the subject; listen for ideas that interest you or add to your own knowledge.
Your mother explains why you can't have an alligator as a pet.	To understand her point of view, to find opportunities to share your own ideas	Listen carefully to what she's saying, respond positively to the good points she makes, and listen for opportunities to state your own reasons.
You and your friends are trying to figure out how to arrange a trip to a concert.	To solve a problem	Identify goals and potential problems; listen closely to each other's ideas and build on them.

❷ Strategies for Active Listening

No matter what your purpose for listening is, using techniques like these can help you understand the speaker's message:

Look for signals indicating main ideas.

- Listen for ideas presented first or last or repeated several times.
- Note statements such as "My point is . . . ." Then listen carefully to what follows.
- Pay attention to ideas that the speaker says loudly or with forceful gestures.
- During a multimedia presentation, note the points the speaker has presented visually.

Block out distractions and focus on the speaker.

- Keep your eyes on the speaker.
- Rein in your mind if it starts to wander.

Look for relationships between ideas.

- Look for comparisons and contrasts.
  Signals: *similarly, but,* and *on the other hand.*
- Pay attention to causes and effects.
  Signals: *because, if . . . then,* and *as a result.*

Take notes, if appropriate.

- Don't worry about writing complete sentences.
- List questions that occur to you as you listen.
- Think about points you want to pursue.
- Read over your notes to help you remember what you heard.

Summarize and paraphrase.

- Identify the main ideas and the details that support them.
- Put information in your own words.

Ask questions for clarification.

- Ask for explanations of points that confuse you.
- Indicate if you don't agree with something or if you need more information.

❸ Evaluating What You Hear

Understanding a person's message is important, but good listening does not stop there. You also have to evaluate the information. This means deciding whether the information makes sense and is well supported by details, facts, and examples.

When evaluating what you hear, you should think about the **content,** or the information presented. Ask yourself questions like those in the box below.

Evaluating Content

- Does the information make sense?
- Does it contradict anything I already know?
- Are ideas presented in an interesting and logical way?
- Are points supported with facts and details?
- What is the purpose of the talk, and does the speaker achieve it?
- Do I still have any questions after hearing the talk?

Negative answers to several of these questions should alert you to think very carefully about the information you hear before believing it or acting on it.

The speaker's **delivery**—the way the information is presented—is also important. Thinking about the following points can help you evaluate the delivery of a message.

Evaluating Delivery

Does the speaker . . .
- speak clearly and understandably?
- seem confident about his or her knowledge of the topic?
- use helpful gestures and body language?
- make eye contact with the audience?
- stand up straight and not fidget?
- use appropriate presentation aids, such as charts and slides?

For more information on evaluating what you hear, see pp. 526–533.

A special situation that will put your listening skills to good use is conducting an interview. An **interview** is a formal question-and-answer session in which you tap into someone's special in-depth knowledge.

❶ Planning an Interview

Good planning can help to make an interview run smoothly. The important steps to consider are (1) identifying an appropriate, knowledgeable person to interview, (2) setting up the interview, and (3) preparing for the interview.

Identifying a Person to Interview

The quality of the information you get from an interview depends a great deal on the person you talk with, so pick that person carefully. Here are some steps to follow.

- **Identify** several people who are experts in your subject and who might be willing to speak with you. You also could contact an organization in that field and ask to be connected with an appropriate person.
- **Research** each person's background and experience to be sure the person actually has the kind of knowledge you are looking for.
- **Rank** the people whom you have researched and contact your first choice first. If that person is unavailable, try the next person on your list.

Setting Up an Interview

Telephone the first person on your list and ask for an interview. Be sure to cover the following points:

- identify who you are and why you want to interview the person
- arrange a time, date, and place that would be convenient for both of you to meet
- determine whether audiotaping or videotaping the interview is acceptable
- state where you can be contacted for a change of plans

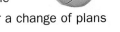

LISTEN/SPEAK

Preparing for an Interview

Be sure to prepare yourself carefully for an interview.

- Do background reading about the subject and make a list of questions to ask the interviewee.

- Create open-ended questions that can't be answered by a simple yes or no. Questions that begin with *How* or *Why,* for example, are particularly useful.

- Call the interviewee a day or two before the interview to remind him or her of your interview appointment.

❷ Conducting and Following Up on an Interview

To get the most useful information from the person you are interviewing, follow the tips and techniques listed below. Be sure to be punctual and polite and to bring all the supplies you'll need, such as a notebook, pens, and audio tape or video tape recorder.

> **Here's How** **Interviewing**
>
> **During the interview**
>
> - Ask your questions clearly and listen carefully. Give the person plenty of time to answer.
>
> - Be flexible with your plan and ask follow-up questions about anything that is especially interesting or confusing.
>
> - Even if you're recording the interview, take notes. Jot down the main ideas or interesting statements that can be used as quotes.
>
> - At the end of the interview, thank the person and offer to send him or her a copy of the final material.
>
> **After the interview**
>
> - While the interview is still fresh in your mind, review your notes and write a brief summary of the conversation.
>
> - If you recorded the interview, you may want to transcribe it or make a written version for your records.
>
> - Send a thank-you note to the person you interviewed.

Remember that your role as an interviewer is to ask questions and to listen. Show your interest in the person rather than in talking about yourself.

LESSON 3 — Speaking Informally

To speak informally means to speak "on the spot" without time to prepare beforehand. Most of the speaking you do every day—both inside and outside the classroom—is informal.

❶ Everyday Speaking

You speak informally many times a day. Here are some tips for clear communication:

- Speak clearly and don't mumble.
- Get to the point and don't ramble.
- Avoid using slang such as "like" and "you know."
- Make eye contact with the person you're speaking to.
- Let the other person speak without interrupting them.

It's always important that you listen carefully, think about what you're going to say *before* you say it, and speak confidently. Also, always be sure to use language and ideas that suit your audience.

❷ Participating in a Group Discussion

You also have to speak with others in school and elsewhere. Participating in a discussion requires all of your listening, speaking, and interpersonal skills.

The key to a successful group discussion is consideration for others. The best way to get your ideas across is to listen and think about others' ideas and feelings before speaking.

LISTEN/SPEAK

Group Skills

There are many reasons to have a group discussion—from just sharing ideas to solving problems. Following these simple rules can help you participate effectively in any group.

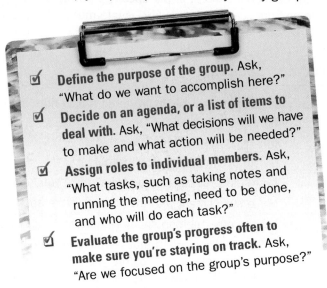

☑ **Define the purpose of the group.** Ask, "What do we want to accomplish here?"

☑ **Decide on an agenda, or a list of items to deal with.** Ask, "What decisions will we have to make and what action will be needed?"

☑ **Assign roles to individual members.** Ask, "What tasks, such as taking notes and running the meeting, need to be done, and who will do each task?"

☑ **Evaluate the group's progress often to make sure you're staying on track.** Ask, "Are we focused on the group's purpose?"

Discussion Skills

Good discussion participants both speak *and* listen effectively.

Here's How Taking Part in a Discussion

DO...
- Take turns speaking.
- Listen attentively to each speaker and take notes.
- Ask questions or comment on others' ideas.
- Speak clearly and confidently.

DON'T...
- Interrupt someone who is speaking.
- Think only about what you're going to say next.
- Use disrespectful language.
- Dismiss others' ideas without evaluating them.

Before you respond to a person in a group, ask yourself, "How would I feel if someone said that to me?"

Preparing an Oral Report

LESSON 4

An oral report or a speech is probably the most formal oral presentation you will have to make as a student. Making an oral presentation involves careful research, preparation, and practice. It can be based on a report you've already written or can be prepared originally as a speech.

① From Writing to Speaking

When preparing an oral report, you will often be working with material you have already written. You shouldn't just get up and read your report aloud, though. You have to think about your listeners, so that might mean making changes like these:

- creating an attention-grabbing opener
- shortening the material
- simplifying the language
- adding audio or visual aids or both
- using facial and hand gestures
- including humor

For information on writing reports, see pp. 474–489.

Adapting Different Types of Writing

The specific changes you must make to adapt a written report to an oral one can depend on the type of writing.

Adapting Different Types of Writing	
	Strategies to Consider
Informative	Using photographs, diagrams, and props to illustrate ideas
Persuasive	Using graphs and charts, body language, and differing tones of voice to emphasize your opinions and reasons
Interpretive	Using distinct voices and body language to portray individual characters
Research	Cutting unnecessary information, simplifying language, using visual aids whenever possible to make the important points clear

LISTEN/SPEAK

Choosing Presentation Aids

Think of an oral report as an opportunity to demonstrate, as well as talk about, your ideas. Using appropriate presentation aids can not only keep your audience awake but also can help to inform and entertain them. Here are some presentation aids you can use to turn a good report into a great one.

Presentation Aids		
	Advantages	**Special Considerations**
Slides	Show real people, places, and things	Require special projection equipment
Maps	Show specific locations and relations of events	Must be large, simple, and well-labeled
Drawings	Illustrate real or imaginary ideas or things	Need to be large, simple, and well-labeled
Photos	Show real people, places, and things	Probably should be passed around the room
CDs	Provide sound effects and music that help create an atmosphere or illustrate a point	Require special sound equipment
Web sites	Provide additional sources of information on your topic	A computer and a special projector may be too small to be seen if not projected on a large screen

Mark your note cards or report notes to remind you where and when to use your presentation aids. Make sure that all the equipment you need is available and working before you make plans to use it.

For more information on using presentation aids, see pp. 561–563.

CHAPTER 31

❷ Presentation Skills

When preparing to present an oral report, you have to consider not only the words you're going to say but also how you're going to say them and how you can best incorporate your presentation aids. Getting all of these elements to work together effectively requires practice, practice, and more practice.

Using Your Voice and Gestures

The success of an oral presentation often depends on how well you deliver it. Pay attention to the following points.

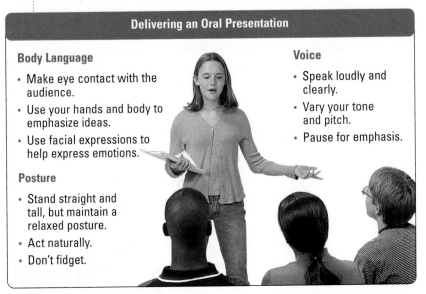

Delivering an Oral Presentation

Body Language
- Make eye contact with the audience.
- Use your hands and body to emphasize ideas.
- Use facial expressions to help express emotions.

Posture
- Stand straight and tall, but maintain a relaxed posture.
- Act naturally.
- Don't fidget.

Voice
- Speak loudly and clearly.
- Vary your tone and pitch.
- Pause for emphasis.

Dealing with Fear

Even the most experienced performers get stage fright. So if you feel butterflies in your stomach before giving an oral report, don't worry—you're in good company. Here are some symptoms many people experience and some ways to overcome them.

- **Dry mouth:** Drink plenty of water before speaking, or suck on a piece of hard candy or a mint. Stay away from milk—it can make your mouth sticky.
- **Shaky hands or voice:** Relax your muscles and breathe deeply. Speak slowly and pause or drink some water if you have to.
- **Queasy stomach:** Eat lightly before giving your report. Once you're on stage, relax and focus on a friendly face in the audience.

Presenting an Oral Interpretation

An oral interpretation is a way to show listeners what a story or a poem—whether it's yours or someone else's—means to you. By using appropriate vocal or facial expressions and gestures, you can create a special world for your audience.

❶ Choosing a Selection

When choosing a poem or a story for an oral interpretation, you should think about factors such as the assignment, your interests, your audience, and how much time you will have to make the presentation. The key, however, is to choose a selection that you enjoy and feel strongly about.

Once you have chosen a story or a poem, you may have to adapt or adjust it to fit your audience or the available time.

> **Here's How** Adapting a Selection for Oral Interpretation
>
> - Select your favorite part of the piece.
> - Identify a good place to begin and end your selection.
> - Make sure that the selection is complete in itself and that it allows you to express a number of emotions.
> - Cut out parts that are boring or are unrelated to the selection.
> - Cut out speakers' tags, such as *he said angrily* or *she sighed sadly.* You will express these emotions in your voice.

 WATCH OUT Avoid selections that include only description or only dialogue. Also avoid selections that have so many characters that listeners will be confused.

❷ Practicing Your Delivery

Once you have chosen and adapted your selection, prepare a reading script. A **reading script** is a typed or neatly handwritten copy of your selection, marked with cues that remind you when to express an emotion, emphasize something, pause, or use a visual aid.

As you practice, try out different voices and gestures. Also, think about sound effects, costumes, props, or other presentation aids that will make the characters and situations come alive. When you're comfortable with your delivery, present your interpretation with your friends and family as an audience. Ask them for their reactions and suggestions.

STUDENT MODEL

Use low and scary voice and spread hands and arms wide.

Play owl's cry on CD.

It was dark and gloomy as they entered the forest. An owl's cry shattered the eery silence. They had felt pretty brave starting out on their hike that morning. Now, they were beginning to wish they had stayed at home. Fear—true fear—descended on them in waves. Suddenly, Sara stumbled. She gripped Rachel's arm and cried out, "What's that?" Before Rachel could reply, a fierce gust of wind tore the flashlight from her hand. As she stooped down to pick it up, she and Sara became separated. They were then alone, each totally alone . . . in total darkness.

Emphasize with a pause and louder voice.

Use a high, frightened voice.

Pause dramatically.

Turn lights out.

Student Help Desk

Listening and Speaking Skills at a Glance

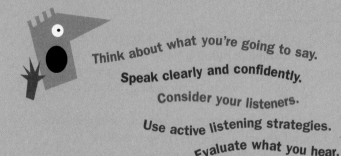

Think about what you're going to say.

Speak clearly and confidently.

Consider your listeners.

Use active listening strategies.

Evaluate what you hear.

Speaking Tips   You Don't Say?

Believe in yourself and in what you're saying.
If you don't, your audience won't.

Stand straight and tall.
Show your confidence and pride.

Act naturally.
If you're uncomfortable, your audience will be too.

Speak loudly and clearly.
Make sure the people at the back of the room
can hear you.

Make eye contact with people in the audience.
Pick several people in different parts of the
room to focus on.

Use your voice, hands, and face for emphasis.
Vary your pacing and gestures to express
emotion and create interest.

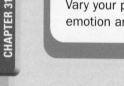

CHAPTER 31

Evaluating What You Hear   Ears the Deal

Is it . . .	Ask Yourself
factual?	What are the facts? How easy is it to tell facts from opinions?
well-supported?	Which details and examples are provided? How strong and convincing are they?
believable?	How much does the speaker know about the subject? Which experts are quoted?
persuasive?	Which techniques are being used to convince me? Are they directed at my emotions or at my mind?

Group Participation   Join the Club

- Define the purpose of the group.
- Assign roles.
- Stay on track.
- Be considerate and polite.

- Listen before you speak.
- Respond to others' ideas.
- Ask questions.
- Compromise to reach the group's goal.

The Bottom Line

Checklist for Listening and Speaking Skills

Have I . . .

____ paid careful attention to the speaker?

____ looked for main ideas and supporting details?

____ identified relationships between ideas?

____ asked questions if necessary?

____ evaluated the information?

____ waited for my turn to speak in a group?

____ spoken confidently and clearly?

____ varied my voice for emphasis and effect?

____ used appropriate gestures and facial expressions?

____ included presentation aids when possible?

LISTEN/SPEAK

Power Words
Vocabulary for Precise Writing

Ours Is the Best!

You may see some of these words in advertising—and you may want to use them if you are selling something.

You Won't Believe This Offer!

"Don't do a thing until you see our **stupendous** offer," says the advertisement you are reading. "We have the **finest, all-new** product on the market, with **breakthrough** advances in technology and **cutting-edge** design. On the **deluxe** model, **peak** performance is achieved through **superlative** engineering and **maximum** power output. Our sales force is **unmatched** in customer service and our company's reputation is **second to none.** This is a **once-in-a-lifetime** opportunity. Act now!"

Nothing But the Best

"Quality is the **hallmark** of our programming," you hear the announcer on the TV commercial say. "Our news programs have been a **benchmark** in responsible broadcasting, and every year our sports coverage reaches a new **high-water mark.** We represent the **gold standard,** the **acme** and **zenith** in the business, even if we do say so ourselves."

▷ **Your Turn** For Sale

Suppose you had to sell something of yours, such as a skateboard, an article of clothing, or a video game. Create an ad that convinces people of its worth. Be sure to include at least one of the boldfaced words above.

CHAPTER 32

Examining the Media

Media Circus

Just about everywhere you go these days, you're bombarded by the media—advertisements, newspapers, magazines, radio, and television. Different kinds of media are all competing for your attention, telling you, "Buy this product. Listen to this music. Read this story. Look at this image. Think about this opinion."

How can you make your way through this media circus? You need to know what media products are, who creates them, and what they mean. Then, you may just want to create some media products of your own.

Write Away: Life Without Media

How would your life be different if you had no access to media of any kind? That means no TV, no video games, no magazines, no books, and definitely no recorded music. What might be better in your life? What might be worse? Write a few sentences describing your thoughts and save them in your 📁 **Working Portfolio.**

MEDIA

**Media Wise
Media Literacy**

Comparing Media

LESSON 1

A **medium** is a system of communication. Forms of media that are designed to communicate with a large audience are called **mass media.** Newspapers, magazines, TV, and radio are considered mass media. So are books, movies, advertisements, billboards, junk mail, cartoons, and the Internet. Many media products get their message across using **verbal elements** (written or spoken words) plus **nonverbal elements** such as

- images (photos, art, and video or film footage)
- graphics (maps, charts, icons, and logos)
- design (use of color and placement of items)
- sound effects and music

You need to be able to understand these nonverbal elements of the media just as you understand the words you read or hear. The examples in this lesson have to do with tornadoes. As you look at the examples, think about how the coverage is similar and how it is different.

❶ Electronic and Film Media

The term **electronic media** refers to television, film, radio, and the Internet. This lesson concentrates on TV, Web sites, and documentaries.

Television Newscast

Television newscasts often show dramatic footage of news events. Nightly news programs include many close-ups of the news anchor. The program's producers want viewers to be comfortable with the anchor and to feel loyal to that person.

The anchor's facial expression and voice affect how viewers react to information.

On-screen graphics, such as this map, help viewers pinpoint the location.

Video footage from the scene gives a "you are there" feel.

Twister of Terror

Iowa

• Moline

Illinois

CHAPTER 32

Web Site

Like TV news, Web sites can provide a broad range of up-to-the-minute information. Sites can contain text, pictures, video and audio clips, and interactive features such as surveys.

Headlines identify written text, video, and audio that users can get to by clicking on <u>underlined</u> words or links.

Information is presented in short summaries that are easy to scan.

This site is updated as new information becomes available.

Documentary

Documentaries often provide more in-depth coverage of a subject than TV newscasts or Web sites, but the information they contain is often less current and more general. This documentary follows "stormchasers," people who observe tornadoes.

Dramatic footage shows what being close to a tornado is like.

Viewers receive detailed information on storms and the people who follow them.

Music and sound effects create a dramatic mood.

MEDIA

❷ Print Media

Print media include newspapers, magazines, newsletters, brochures, and junk mail. Print media are usually not as up to date as electronic media. However, print sources can provide a wealth of information in a format that is easy to understand. This article gives in-depth information and analysis.

Magazine Article

The design gives more space to the powerful photo than to the written text.

This big, sensational headline grabs readers' attention.

NATION

By DAVID VAN BIEMA

FUNNEL OF DEATH

In Oklahoma the wind came sweeping down the plains with record-breaking fury. And the tornado season has just begun

J. Pat Carter—AP

The brief summary of the article makes the reader want to read further.

A caption not only explains the photo but also gives interesting details.

PRACTICE ▸ Choose Your Coverage

Choose a current news item and compare the coverage of the same item in two different media, one electronic and one print. Then, create a chart or a Venn diagram highlighting the major differences between the two media. (For an example of a Venn diagram, see p. 359.)

Media Influence

LESSON 2

Anyone who creates a media product has a message that he or she wants heard. As you become more media savvy, you will notice how different media messages try to **influence** you, or affect how you think about something.

① Identifying Purposes

All media programs and products—from news reports to video games—are created by specific people for specific purposes. Whenever you read, watch, or listen to a form of media, ask yourself: "Why was this created? Who developed it? What is it trying to accomplish?" This chart can help you think about these questions.

Purposes of Media Products	
Purpose	**Examples**
Inform: to present information or to analyze an issue	news reports and articles; public service announcements; certain Web sites
Persuade: to sway the feelings, beliefs, or actions of an audience	advertisements; "infomercials" (program-length commercials); editorials; reviews; political cartoons
Entertain: to amuse or delight	most TV shows; recorded music; video and computer games; cartoons; most talk shows

HOT TIP

Most types of media have more than one purpose. For example, TV commercials are often entertaining, but their main purpose is to persuade you to buy something.

② Determining the Audience

Target audiences are portions of the population that have certain things in common. You are a member of several target audiences based on your age, whether you are male or female, your likes and dislikes, and many other factors.

MEDIA

Some companies spend millions of dollars to target a particular audience and get its support. For example, a cereal company targeting young children might advertise on Saturday-morning cartoon shows.

❸ Evaluating What You See and Hear

Most likely, you tune out media messages that don't target you. You probably grab the remote during commercials for minivans and life insurance, for instance. However, are you critical of media messages that do target you? To be a smart consumer of media, keep these questions in mind.

- **What sponsors are targeting you?** Pay attention to the products advertised on your favorite TV and radio shows and in your favorite magazines. The companies that make those products **sponsor,** or pay for, the programs and articles.

  Sponsors can affect what gets on the airwaves and in print. For example, if a TV show offends people, it may not attract many sponsors and will probably be canceled.

- **What messages are you getting?** A sponsor that is targeting you will try to tap into your hopes, fears, and desires. The sponsor may show people who look and sound like you. Think about whether the message is designed to inform, entertain, or persuade you.

- **Are the messages based on fact or opinion?** Some media messages are **biased,** or unfairly weighted toward one point of view. Others use **loaded language**—words that have strong positive or negative feelings attached to them. Watch out for messages that try to change your mind about something without giving you all the facts.

Loaded language

Are you done yet?

Super-sized for super taste!

Sponsor — **Hungry Boy Burgers**

Get 2 for 99¢ for a short time only.

Target audience: kids ages 11-14

Analyzing Media Messages

❶ What's Behind the Message?

You need to be able to analyze a media message so that you can develop a thoughtful opinion about it. On these two pages are messages about a band called the Gopher Brains. Notice what's behind the sometimes conflicting messages.

TV Commercial

This commercial tells viewers that *Gopher Broke,* the Gopher Brains' new album, is available now.

- **Purpose:** The recording company that sponsored Gopher Broke wants to inform viewers about the new album. It also wants to persuade them to buy it!
- **Target audience:** Teenagers with money to spend.
- **Methods:** The commercial uses footage of the band, graphics, music, and sound effects to attract viewers. It also uses loaded language, describing the album as "hot" and urging viewers not to miss it.

Evaluate: Do you think the claim in the commercial is an exaggeration? What do you think about when deciding whether to buy a product you see advertised?

Documentary

In a documentary, the Gopher Brains play four new songs and talk about the band's early years.

- **Purpose:** The music video network that created the documentary wants to inform viewers about the band's music. It also wants to entertain viewers and create interest in the band.
- **Target audience:** Fans of music and of the group.
- **Methods:** The documentary holds viewers' attention by combining footage, music, and sound effects.

Evaluate: The documentary might be interesting and informative, but it might also be a thinly disguised advertisement for the new album. Have you ever been persuaded to buy something without even realizing that you were being persuaded?

MEDIA

Music Review

This newspaper's music critic believes that *Gopher Broke* is a disappointment.

- **Purpose:** The newspaper that pays the critic wants its readers to be well-informed about new music. It wants readers to trust and depend on its critics.
- **Target audience:** Readers who buy albums regularly.
- **Methods:** An eye-catching image and clever headline draw readers in.

Evaluate: Does this critic support her opinion? When you are thinking about buying a product, whose opinions do you seek?

Music

Gopher Broke Goes Nowhere

The new Gopher Brains CD is getting a great deal of attention, though it's hard to see why. This bland collection of songs is the Gophers' lamest effort in years.

PRACTICE **You Be the Judge**

Now it's your turn. Analyze and evaluate this magazine ad.

- What is the purpose?
- Who is the sponsor?
- Who is the target audience?
- What methods are used to achieve the purpose?
- Do you think this ad is effective? Why or why not? Does it matter that the ad gives very little information?

CHOOSE THE JEANS THAT FIT YOUR ATTITUDE

Shop at TOTAL DENIM

CHAPTER 32

Using Media in Your Presentations

❶ Exploring Multimedia

You've already learned to be a smarter consumer of media. What about becoming a creator of media as well?

The next time you have a report or a project to do, consider doing a multimedia presentation. A **multimedia presentation** is a computer-enhanced report. It presents several kinds of media combined on a computer. Software programs such as PowerPoint and HyperStudio make multimedia presentations easier than ever to create.

You can combine some or all of the following media elements into an interesting, informative presentation.

Possible Components for Your Presentation	
Video	Video clips can add a "you are there" feel to your presentation. Use just a few, though—they can take a long time for your computer to load and play.
Sound	Recorded words, music, or sound effects can give your audience information or set a mood.
Graphs and charts	Visual aids give your audience lots of factual information at a glance.
Graphics and animation	These can make your presentation more attractive and lively. Many software programs provide graphics and animation for you to use.
Photographs and illustrations	Adding photographs and illustrations makes your presentation more informative and attractive.
Text	Don't forget the most important part of your presentation: writing the text that ties everything together!

HOT TIP

You can create a great presentation even if you don't have access to a computer. The next time you are assigned an oral report, consider creating posters and playing recorded words or music to go with your report.

MEDIA

❷ Planning Your Presentation

The planning stage of your multimedia presentation is essential. In fact, planning ahead for multimedia is just as important as for a written report because you have so many parts to track. Here are some steps that can help.

> **Here's How** Planning a Multimedia Presentation
>
> 1. Choose a topic that will work well in a multimedia format. Are there photos, illustrations, video clips, and audio clips available? Can you create them yourself?
> 2. Identify your audience and purpose.
> 3. Look for information as you would for a traditional report.
> 4. Create a flow chart or outline that shows what visuals, sounds, and information you will use.
> 5. Write a script of what you will say when each screen is displayed.

❸ Organizing Your Presentation

Organize your research in an outline, in a flow chart, or on note cards. Know exactly what kind of information you want to appear on each screen.

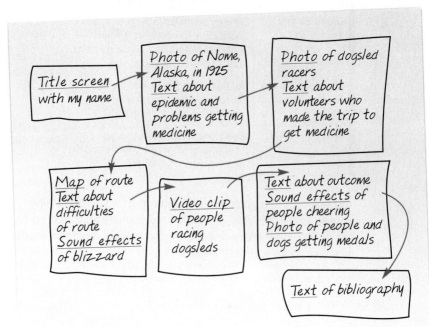

Title screen with my name

Photo of Nome, Alaska, in 1925
Text about epidemic and problems getting medicine

Photo of dogsled racers
Text about volunteers who made the trip to get medicine

Map of route
Text about difficulties of route
Sound effects of blizzard

Video clip of people racing dogsleds

Text about outcome
Sound effects of people cheering
Photo of people and dogs getting medals

Text of bibliography

❹ Creating a Script

It's a good idea to create a script to go with your presentation, so you'll know what you will talk about at each point. Here's how one student did it. Notice that the onscreen text gives only the main ideas.

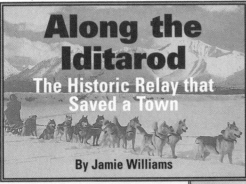

Along the Iditarod
The Historic Relay that Saved a Town

By Jamie Williams

Script
Have you ever faced a problem that seemed impossible to solve? Here's how the people of one town saved their children from an outbreak of a deadly disease.

Diphtheria, a deadly infection, broke out in Nome, Alaska, in January of 1925. Most of its victims were children. There was a serum that would prevent more children from getting sick, but it was more than 1,000 miles away. Planes could not carry the serum to Nome because the weather there was so severe.

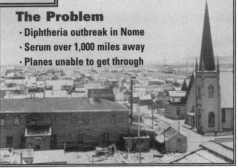

The Problem
· Diphtheria outbreak in Nome
· Serum over 1,000 miles away
· Planes unable to get through

Rehearse your presentation several times. Make sure all the parts are in the right order, the presentation flows smoothly, and all equipment works.

For more on giving presentations, see pp. 545–547

PRACTICE Multimedia About Media

Go back to your **Write Away** exercise from page 553. Using what you wrote then, plan a multimedia presentation on how media affect your life. How do TV, magazines, radios, and other forms of media make your life better? In what ways do they make your life worse? In your plan, explain what images and sounds you might use for each screen and make notes about the kind of text you would write.

MEDIA

Student Help Desk

Examining Media at a Glance

IDENTIFY

- What is the purpose: to inform, persuade, or entertain? Is there more than one purpose?
- Who is the target audience?

UNDERSTAND

- What is the written or spoken message?
- What does the overall design of images, colors, and/or sounds tell you?

ANALYZE

- Who sponsored the message?
- Why is the audience being targeted?
- Does the message use bias or loaded language?

Targeting Audiences

Out to Get Your Attention

Media creators choose target audiences—groups of people who have certain things in common. These magazines target very different audiences.

Ask yourself:

- Who is the target audience?
- What messages are being sent to that audience?
- Do the messages include bias or loaded language?
- Are the messages effective? Why or why not?

Persuasive Pitfalls

Bias means unfair preference.

"All our store owners agree—our products are the best!"

Loaded language is designed to give you strong positive or negative feelings.

"Vote for the brightest star in our school. Tran will take us to the top!"

Multimedia Presentations

- Don't use too many multimedia elements.
- Keep video and audio clips short.
- Make sure your text ties together all the multimedia elements.

Six Quick Tips

- Rehearse your presentation several times.
- Speak clearly and in a loud voice.
- Make eye contact with your audience.

FOXTROT by Bill Amend

The Bottom Line

Checklist for Examining the Media

Have I . . .

____ been aware of how media messages try to influence me?

____ identified the purpose and target audience?

____ thought about who sponsored the message and why?

____ planned and created a multimedia presentation?

Power Words
Vocabulary for Precise Writing

JOURNEY

tranqui

voyage

The Trip of a Lifetime

There are all kinds of trips to take, as these words show.

Choose an Adventure

Are you bored by the thought of a **trip** to Aunt Matilda's? Does the notion of a Saturday family **outing** or an afternoon's **jaunt** downtown leave you cold? Are you eager to escape the **excursion** to Lake Dullsville for Mom's company's annual picnic?

Let your imagination run loose. Would you care for a **cruise** in the Caribbean or a two-month **journey** to the tip of South America? What about a **sail** to the Seychelles in the Indian Ocean or a **voyage** to Vanuatu in the vast southern Pacific?

Would you like to go for an **odyssey** through Greece and its islands? Perhaps you would prefer an **expedition** to the Gobi Desert or a **trek** in the Himalayas.

Winter Weekend

Now imagine it's so cold and nasty out that you don't want to set foot outdoors. You want a **quiet, restful** weekend, one that is **tranquil** and **serene.** The only adventure you want is the one in the book in your lap.

odyssey

cruise

SAI

▷ **Your Turn** Travel the Globe

Working in small groups, create a travel brochure for a real or imaginary place. Use at least two of the boldfaced words above.

serene

expeditio

TREK

Developing Your Vocabulary

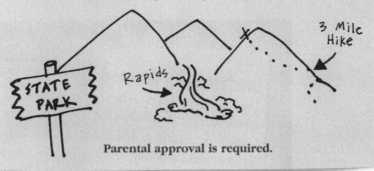

Weekend Adventure Trip
For Kids Ages 12 to 14

Do you have the endurance needed to hike an arduous trail and raft the state's most formidable river? If you've got the right stuff, this adventure will really test your mettle. Sign up in the principal's office.

Parental approval is required.

Is This Trip for You?

How can you tell if you've got "the right stuff" for this adventure if you don't know the meanings of key words in the poster? You'll have to figure out what *arduous, formidable,* and *mettle* mean. Expanding your vocabulary will improve your communication skills and help you to understand new concepts, like the ones in the poster above. When you build word power, you also build brain power!

Write Away: Figuring Out Meanings
Try rewriting the poster above using words that you think have the same meanings as *arduous, formidable,* and *mettle.* Then check the dictionary! Save your work in your 🗀 **Working Portfolio.**

VOCABULARY

ClassZone at
mcdougallittell.com

Building Vocabulary

❶ Strategies for Understanding New Words

Using a dictionary to learn the meaning of a new word is a good strategy for building your vocabulary. However, looking up a word means interrupting your reading. Three strategies—using context clues, analyzing word parts, and learning from related words—can help you guess the meanings of new words *while* you read. You can look up the definitions later if you still need help.

This poster contains words that you may not know. Use the clues given to figure out the meanings. You will learn more about each kind of clue later in the chapter.

Student Help Wanted

The main office needs after-school help with collating (assembling pages) of the Student Handbook and screenprinting of P.E. activity posters. If you are a reliable and conscientious worker, we need your energy! Pick up a work release form and an application from Mrs. Greene, fill them out with a parent's signature on each, and resubmit them to the main office. You will be called for an interview if you can work at least ten hours per week.

Collating is defined in parentheses.

Notice the two words that make up **screenprinting**.

Conscientious may be understood from the sentence in which it appears.

You may recognize a part of the word **resubmit**.

❷ Strategies for Remembering New Words

As you learn new words, you won't want to forget them. Use these strategies to help you remember.

> **Here's How** **Remembering New Words**
>
> • Keep a personal word list and add a new word to it right away. Review the list often to refresh your memory.
> • Begin to use the new word in conversations and in your writing as soon as possible.
> • Make up a memory cue, such as "a conscientious judge" or "collate, crease, and staple." Notice how rhyming can also be a helpful memory trick in the examples that follow.
>
> **evade** (to escape or avoid):   "**Evade** the raid!"
>
> **elude** (to hide from or lose):   "**Elude** the dude; he's too crude."
>
> **avert** (to ward off or prevent):   "**Avert** the hurt."
>
> **entice** (to attract or lure):   "**Entice** the mice with a little rice."

Add to your personal word list as you read textbooks, scan a newspaper or magazine, or hear an interesting word in conversation.

One new word a day adds up to 365 new words a year!

Jan.1
evade

FoxTrot by Bill Amend

VOCABULARY

LESSON 2 Using Context Clues

One way to understand an unfamiliar word is to look at its **context,** the words and sentences surrounding it. Context often provides clues to help you infer, or figure out, the general meaning of the word.

❶ General Context

General context refers to the several sentences or the whole paragraph surrounding an unfamiliar word. Photos, charts, and drawings can also be part of the general context. Notice how the details in this paragraph help you understand the meaning of the word *loathsome.*

> **LITERARY MODEL**
>
> But by far the most **loathsome** thing about Mrs. Pratchett was the **filth** that clung around her. Her apron was **grey** and **greasy.** Her blouse had **bits of breakfast** all over it, **toast crumbs and tea stains** and **splotches of dried egg-yolk.** It was her hands, however, that disturbed us most. They were **disgusting.** They were **black with dirt and grime.**
>
> —Roald Dahl, *Boy: Tales of Childhood*

Clues to the meaning of *loathsome.* How would you define this word?

❷ Definition and Restatement

Some texts define new words or restate their meanings in another way. Certain words and special punctuation (commas, dashes, and parentheses) may signal that a definition or restatement follows a new word.

Signal Words: Definition or Restatement			
which	that is	where	is called
in other words	or	this means	

Most household chemicals are **toxic, or poisonous.** Some chemicals are **corrosive, which means** they can eat away or damage skin, clothing, and other materials. Many other chemicals are **flammable**—very quick to burn—making all those containers under the kitchen sink extremely dangerous.

—Roberta Avakian

> Notice the **clue words, commas, and dashes** that signal definition or restatement of *toxic, corrosive,* and *flammable.*

❸ Examples

Writers often give examples of a word or term instead of the definition. These signal words sometimes introduce examples.

Signal Words: Examples

such as	for example	for instance
like	especially	including

It [the decade of the 1920s] was a **materialistic** age. People **concentrated on making money** and **buying things** for themselves. **Successful businesspeople became national heroes.** There were **more rich people than ever before** in American history.

—Joy Hakim, *War, Peace, and All That Jazz*

> **Examples** of being materialistic

WATCH OUT If you haven't learned the correct pronunciation of a word, you will sound misinformed when you use it in a conversation. Always check the pronunciation of a new word in the dictionary.

VOCABULARY

❹ Comparison and Contrast

Sometimes a sentence compares or contrasts a familiar word or phrase with a less familiar one. If you know one word, you can often figure out the other.

Signal Words: Comparison or Contrast

like	as	instead of	but
unlike	in contrast to	on the other hand	

STUDENT MODEL

Like the rest of my **frugal** family, I always save part of the money I earn. I wish I had more **ingenuity** in making money instead of simply relying on the same old baby-sitting jobs.

Clue words signal a comparison and a contrast. What do the words in red mean?

PRACTICE Use Those Clues!

Use context clues to define the following underlined words. Be ready to tell what clues you used.

1. Jane's <u>integrity</u>—the strict honesty with which she lived— made her the best candidate for class president.
2. We all hurried to vote, unlike Joe, who <u>lagged</u> behind.
3. At the gym, there was <u>turmoil</u>. Lemonade pitchers had been overturned, and we had to search for clean ballots.
4. Had someone <u>sabotaged</u> the election to keep us from voting?
5. The <u>conundrum</u> was solved when Joe discovered a squirrel's nest nearby with scraps of lemonade-stained ballots in it!
6. The election gave us an opportunity to exercise our <u>prerogative,</u> or right, to select our class leaders.
7. In contrast to the lower school, where students did not seem to care, the middle school showed an <u>ardent</u> enthusiasm.
8. The biggest <u>predicament</u> facing the new president—a very difficult problem—was how to unite the seventh grade.
9. Jane's <u>proposition</u> included regular open meetings, in contrast to her opponents, who proposed no plans at all.
10. No naughty squirrels could prevent us from <u>partaking</u> in the exciting election process!

Analyzing Word Parts

Breaking an unfamiliar word into its parts can often help you figure out its meaning. Words can be composed of prefixes, base words, word roots, and suffixes.

❶ Base Words

A **base word** can stand on its own or be combined with other words or word parts to form new words. The examples below show how adding word parts to a base word (shown in orange) can change its meaning.

violin + ist = violinist

inter + planet + ary = interplanetary

Two base words can be connected to make a **compound word,** which has a meaning that is different from but sometimes related to the original words.

BASE + BASE = COMPOUND WORD

grass + hopper = grasshopper

motor + cycle = motorcycle

quarter + master = quartermaster

❷ Prefixes and Suffixes

A **prefix** is a word part added to the beginning of a base word or root. Prefixes are powerful. They can turn a base word into its opposite or make the meaning more specific. Notice how the prefixes in this chart change the meanings of base words.

Common Prefixes		
Prefix	**Meaning**	**Examples**
auto-	self	autopilot, automobile
mal-, mis-	bad *or* wrong	malfunction, misplace
micro-	small *or* short	microphone, microscope
pre-	before	predawn, preschool
semi-	half	semicircle, semicolon

VOCABULARY

A **suffix** is a word part added to the end of a base word. Suffixes usually suggest a word's part of speech. For example, add suffixes to the adjective *popular* to get *popularly* (adverb), *popularity* (noun), and *popularize* (verb).

Prefixes and suffixes make it possible to expand one base word into several words. How many different words can be made by combining the following prefixes and suffixes with the base word?

Notice how the base words in the following chart change meanings as prefixes and suffixes are added to them.

PREFIX	+	BASE	+	SUFFIX	=	NEW WORD
re-	+	charge	+	-able	=	rechargeable
en-	+	courage	+	-ment	=	encouragement
pre-	+	history	+	-ic	=	prehistoric
semi-	+	week	+	-ly	=	semiweekly

Notice that you may have to change the spelling of the base word when adding a suffix:  **cycle + ist = cyclist.**

For more about spelling changes, see pp. 628–635.

❸ Word Roots

A **word root** is the part of a word that contains its basic meaning. A word root cannot stand on its own like a base word, but it may be combined with other word parts.

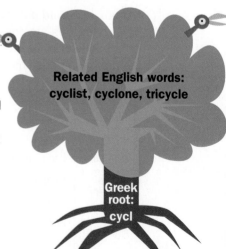

Related English words: cyclist, cyclone, tricycle

Greek root: cycl

The ancient Greek and Latin languages give English its most common roots. Knowing just some of these word roots can help you decode many complex English words.

Common Roots

Root	Meaning	Examples
bio	life	biology, biography
gram	something written	diagram, grammar
graph	write	autograph, photograph
phon	sound	symphony, telephone
photo	light	photography, photosynthesis
scop	see	microscope, telescope
therm	heat	thermal, thermometer

GREEK

Root	Meaning	Examples
aud	hear	auditorium, audience
cred	believe	credit, incredible
dict	speak	predict, diction
man	hand	manual, manufacture
mob, mot	move	mobile, motion, promote
rupt	break	rupture, bankrupt, interrupt
spec	see	inspect, suspect, respect

LATIN

Word roots are frequently combined with prefixes and suffixes in the same way that base words are.

re + **cycl** + able = recyclable

PRACTICE What Does It Say?

Analyze the following words to figure out their meanings.

1. photosensitive
2. semifinal
3. microcomputer
4. misstatement
5. autotimer

6. audition
7. spectacle
8. malformed
9. presuppose
10. mobilize

Understanding Related Words

LESSON 4

❶ Word Families

A **word family** is a group of words with a common root. Look for similarities in both meaning and spelling in the following words, whose roots come from the Latin words *vivere,* meaning "to live," and *vita,* meaning "life."

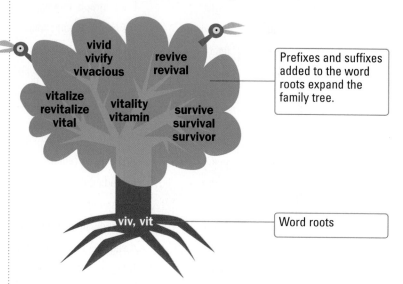

vivid
vivify
vivacious

revive
revival

vitalize
revitalize
vital

vitality
vitamin

survive
survival
survivor

Prefixes and suffixes added to the word roots expand the family tree.

viv, vit

Word roots

When you recognize the family resemblance between a word you know and one you don't know, you are on your way to learning the one you don't know.

> **Here's How** Using Word Families
>
> - To figure out the meaning of *vivacious,* first look for the root: *viv.*
> - Think of other words that have the same root, such as *survive, vivid,* and *revive.* Decide what common meaning they share.
> - Consider prefixes and suffixes that may change meaning: the suffix *–ous* makes *vivacious* an adjective.
> - From these clues, you can make a reasonable guess that *vivacious* means "full of life or lively."

Grouping words into families when studying them makes them easier to remember.

❷ Synonyms

Synonyms are words that have similar meanings. Building your vocabulary involves learning synonyms. Since synonyms do not always have identical meanings, learning to distinguish slight differences in meaning is important.

SYNONYMS

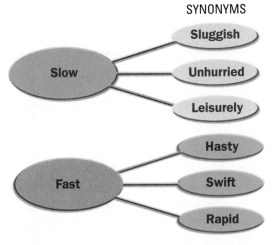

The words *unhurried* and *leisurely* generate more positive feelings than *sluggish*. *Leisurely* and *sluggish* have different **connotations**—in other words, they bring different emotions to the reader's mind. Of the three synonyms for *fast*, which one implies that fast is not always good?

For more on connotation, see p. 406.

Think of a synonym as meaning "similar to," not "the same as." Watch for shades of meaning among synonyms for a word.

PRACTICE Finding Synonyms

Think of one synonym for each of the following words. Then use each in a different sentence. Try to make each sentence reflect the exact shade of meaning of the word you use.

1. **finish** the assignment
2. **bother** your brother
3. the **last** day
4. **under** the porch
5. washed the **cars**
6. **ruined** the drawing
7. bought his **food**
8. a **book** of biographies
9. a **short** answer
10. **stuff** from the store

VOCABULARY

LESSON 5 · Using References

❶ Dictionaries

Sometimes context clues and word parts aren't enough to help you figure out a word. Then it's time to turn to the dictionary. Dictionaries do more than just furnish the definition for a word. They also provide the pronunciation of a word, its **etymology** (origin), and connotations that might concern the reader.

offense / ogle

of • fense (ə-fĕns′) *n.* **1.** The act of offending. **2.** A violation of a moral or social code. **3.** A crime. **4.** (ŏf′ĕns′). *Sports.* A team in possession of the ball or puck. [< Lat. *offendere*, offend.]

of • fen • sive (ə-fĕn′sĭv) *adj.* **1.** Disagreeable to the senses. **2.** Causing anger, resentment, or affront. **3.** Making an attack. **4.** (ŏf′ĕns-. *Sports.* Relating to the offense. **—of • fen′sive • ly** *adv.* **—of • fen′sive • ness** *n.* **Syns:** *disgusting, loathsome, nasty, repellent, repulsive, revolting* **adj.**

of • fer (ô′fər, ŏf′ər) *v.* **1.** To present for acceptance or rejection. **2.** To present for sale. **3.** To present as payment; bid. **4.** To present as an act of worship. **5.** To put up; mount. **6.** To produce or introduce on the stage. [< Lat. *offerre* : *ob-*, to + *ferre*, bring.] **—of′fer** *n.*

of • fi • ci • ate (ə-fĭsh′ē-āt′) *v.* **—at • ed, -at • ing. 1.** To perform the functions of an office or position of authority, esp. at a religious service. **2.** *Sports.* To serve as a referee or umpire. **—of • fi′ci • a′tor** *n.*

of • fic • i • nal (ə-fĭs′ ə-nəl) *adj.* **1.** Readily available in pharmacies; not requiring special preparation. **2.** Recognized by a pharmacopoeia: *an official herb.*

Guide words , or first and last words on page

Entry word divided into syllables

Different **pronunciations** for different definitions

Label identifying special usage

Synonyms

Part of speech being defined

Definitions

Etymology, or history of word

Other forms of entry word

Endings for irregular verbs and for verbs that change their spelling

CHAPTER 33

578

Dictionaries frequently list several definitions for the same word. How do you know which definition is the right one for you?

> **Here's How** **Choosing the Right Definition**
>
> • Read through all the definitions in the dictionary entry.
> • Decide which definition best fits the meaning of the sentence in which you found the word. For example, "an offensive smell" probably matches the first definition listed on the left; "an offensive play in football" probably refers to the fourth definition.

Many textbooks have a **glossary**—a type of mini-dictionary—at the end to help you learn new words in that subject.

❷ Thesauruses

A **thesaurus** is a dictionary of synonyms. Some thesauruses also include definitions, sample sentences, antonyms, and other related words. Notice the difference between the thesaurus entry below and the dictionary entry for the same word, to the left. The thesaurus entry has no definitions to help you understand the differences between synonyms.

offensive *adj.* utterly unpleasant or distasteful to the senses or sensibilities **syn** atrocious, disgusting, evil, foul, hideous, horrible, horrid, icky, loathsome, nasty, nauseating, noisome, obscene, repellent, repugnant, repulsive, revolting, sickening, ungrateful, unwholesome, vile **ant** inoffensive, unoffensive

| Part of speech |
| Definition |
| Synonyms |
| Antonyms |

Don't pick just any synonym or antonym from a thesaurus. Be sure you know the dictionary definition and the positive or negative feelings the word brings to your audience's minds.

Student Help Desk

Developing Vocabulary at a Glance

Look for context clues.	Analyze the parts of a word.	Look for related words.	Use a dictionary.
Calm and collected, she **dispassionately** argued her case.	dis passion ate ly **dis = not** **ate = to make** **ly = in what manner**	dis**passion**ate **passion**ate com**passion**	**dis pas sion ate** (dĭs-păsh'ə-nĭt) *adj.* Not influenced by emotion or bias.

Building Blocks

semiautobiographical: relating to a work that falls between fiction and autobiography, as in partly true and partly made up.

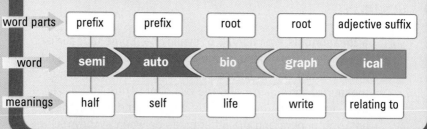

word parts → prefix	prefix	root	root	adjective suffix
word → **semi**	**auto**	**bio**	**graph**	**ical**
meanings → half	self	life	write	relating to

Suffixes and Parts of Speech

	Suffix	Meaning	Examples
Nouns	-er, -ist, -or	one who does	teacher, cyclist, governor
	-ation, -ism, -ment	action or process	narration, heroism, development
Verbs	-ate, -en, -fy, -ize	to make	activate, darken, satisfy, terrorize
Adjectives	-able, -ible	capable of	readable, gullible
	-ate	state or quality of	fortunate, passionate
Adverbs	-ily, -ly	in what manner	speedily, slowly

Some Word Origins in English

Many English words came from other languages. Knowing a word's origin can help you figure out its meaning.

Old English (Anglo-Saxon)
Words in our daily life: man, woman, child, eat, drink, sleep, house, love, life, death
Hunting/gathering/farming terms: meat, cow, sheep, pig, farmer, fisherman, hunter, shepherd

Old French (Norman)
Words related to government, culture, and society: president, congress, mayor, constitution, city, state, nation, religion, art, poetry, court, army, navy, dance, fashion, physician, attorney

Latin
Abstract ideas: independence, loyalty, honor, unity
Technical terms: data, quarter, century, criteria, annual, gradual

Greek
Words related to science: architect, astronaut, hydrophobia, microscope, photograph, telescope, thermometer, psychology

The Bottom Line

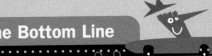

Checklist for Developing Vocabulary

Have I . . .

____ looked at the context in which a word appears to figure out its meaning?

____ analyzed all the parts of a word?

____ tried to think of other words in the same word family?

____ thought of synonyms to replace overused words?

____ used a dictionary or a thesaurus to help me understand a word?

____ begun to use new words in my conversation and writing?

VOCABULARY

Student Resources

Exercise Bank

Boost your grammar fitness! Use the circled arrows ➡ to find the answers to the Self-Check items. In addition, you can complete exercises in this section to get extra practice in a skill you've just learned.

① The Sentence and Its Parts

1. Complete Subjects and Predicates (links to exercise on p. 7)

➡ **1.** Complete subject: *Frank Lloyd Wright;* complete predicate: *designed an unusual home in the Pennsylvania woods*
2. Complete subject: *The owners;* complete predicate: *called the house Fallingwater*

In separate columns on a sheet of paper, write the complete subjects and complete predicates of these sentences.

1. Albert Frey was a world-famous architect.
2. The talented Mr. Frey was 94 years old in 1998.
3. He lived modestly in a 16-by-32-foot house on a mountain in southern California.
4. The architect built his desert house in 1964.
5. This amazing house is a rectangular glass-walled shed with a corrugated aluminum roof.
6. A large boulder is in the center of the house!
7. The unusual house has a single room for dining, living, and sleeping.
8. Mr. Frey deliberately built his house with low-maintenance materials.
9. Aluminum was one of the materials he used.
10. This durable material does not need to be repainted or repaired.

2. Simple Subjects (links to exercise A, p. 9)

➡ **2.** Lodges   **5.** rodents

Write the simple subject of each sentence.

1. Arctic seals spend most of their lives in water.
2. In the winter, they live under the ice.
3. The female digs out a lair, or den, in a snowbank.
4. The lair is on top of the ice but under the snow.
5. The seal creates a hole down to the ocean below.
6. First she breathes on the ice from underneath.

7. Next, the female nibbles on the softened ice.
8. Then, with her flippers, she scoops out the ice.
9. She also makes air holes through the ice.
10. Her "igloo" will have a wide floor for her and her cub.

3. Simple Predicates, or Verbs (links to exercise A, p. 11)

➡ **1.** lived   **2.** traveled

Write the simple predicate, or verb, in each sentence.

1. In the 1800s four sisters claimed 1,920 acres of land on the Great Plains.
2. Settlers dug wells as soon as possible.
3. Many families built windmills.
4. These windmills pumped water from the wells.
5. Some families had no wells.
6. Women carried water several miles to their sod houses.
7. Farmers often used dried buffalo droppings for fuel!
8. Many homesteaders came from Europe.
9. Hundreds of African-American families settled on the plains.
10. These "exodusters" were former slaves.

4. Verb Phrases (links to exercise A, p. 13)

➡ **1.** was developed   **2.** could communicate

Write the verb or verb phrase in each sentence below.

1. Using a kit, you can build a house like the graceful Japanese country houses of the 16th century.
2. Large-diameter poles support your finished house.
3. Each house is surrounded by a large veranda.
4. The veranda should provide a pleasing view of nature.
5. Glazed tiles from Japan are supplied for the roof.
6. Only wood from replaceable trees has been chosen for the kits.
7. These graceful houses can be built in all climates.
8. They have been constructed in the United States, the Caribbean, Europe, and Southeast Asia.
9. Such houses have recently survived hurricanes in the West Indies.
10. They have also been winning architectural awards.

5. Compound Sentence Parts (links to exercise A, p. 15)

➤ **1.** *Space stations* and *platforms*
   2. *may design* and *build*

Write and identify the compound subject (CS) or compound verb (CV) in each sentence.

1. Since the 1950s, pesticides and pollution have almost wiped out the peregrine falcon.
2. Peregrines and some other birds of prey live high up in cliffs.
3. They swoop down and eat smaller birds and rodents.
4. In the 1980s scientists and researchers introduced falcon pairs to skyscrapers.
5. The birds now nest and breed on ledges of tall buildings.
6. There they have no natural predators and can see lots of prey on the ground below.
7. City falcons hunt and eat pigeons and starlings.
8. They kill and consume mice as well.
9. Some peregrines have been attacked by other falcons or even eaten by them.
10. Office workers and apartment dwellers can now watch the birds from their high-rise windows.

6. Kinds of Sentences (links to exercise A, p. 17)

➤ **1.** INT   **2.** D

Identify each of the following sentences as declarative (D), interrogative (INT), exclamatory (EXC), or imperative (IMP).

1. Look at that big yellow and black bee.
2. That's a bumblebee!
3. Did you know they can live as far north as the Arctic Circle?
4. The buzzing sound is a bumblebee fanning its wings.
5. Tell me how they build their nests.
6. The queen constructs a pot of wax and fills it with honey.
7. She lays her eggs in another pot of wax.
8. What happens to the eggs?
9. They hatch and become worker bees.
10. Some hives are a foot wide and have up to 700 workers!

7. Subjects in Unusual Order (links to exercise A, p. 20)

➤ **1.** Subject: *benefits;* verb: *are*
   2. Subject: *fans;* verb: *sit*

In separate columns on a sheet of paper, write the subjects and the verbs or verb phrases in these sentences.

1. There are the two skiers in the starting gates.
2. Give the signal for the giant slalom race to begin.
3. Down the steep slope race the athletes.
4. From their skis sprays snow.
5. Watch the next one jump off the top of that ridge.
6. Did the one on the right miss a gate?
7. Across the hill tumbles the first skier.
8. There is the winner of the giant slalom.
9. Are you skiing in this event?
10. Avoid that icy turn near the third gate.

8. Complements: Subject Complements (links to exercise A, p. 22)

➜ **1.** highways, PN   **2.** difficult, PA

Write the underlined word in each sentence, and identify it as a predicate noun (PN) or a predicate adjective (PA).

1. The Arctic National Wildlife Refuge is an <u>area</u> in northeastern Alaska.
2. It is among the largest <u>refuges</u> in the United States.
3. Half of the Arctic National Wildlife Refuge is a <u>tundra</u>, or treeless plain.
4. The tundra is so <u>cold</u> that the ground never thaws completely.
5. The refuge is <u>home</u> to many animals, including caribou, polar bears, snowy owls, and lemmings.
6. Lemmings are mouselike <u>creatures</u> that live on the tundra.
7. The arctic fox is a <u>predator</u> that hunts lemmings.
8. Caribou are <u>migratory,</u> traveling more than 1,000 miles each spring to the coastal plain in the refuge.
9. The snowy owl is a large <u>bird</u> that lives in the Arctic during the entire year.
10. Environmentalists are <u>protective</u> of the land and creatures of the Arctic National Wildlife Refuge.

9. Complements: Objects of Verbs (links to exercise on p. 24)

➜ **1.** house, DO   **2.** inhabitants, IO; level, DO

Write the objects in these sentences, identifying each as a direct object (DO) or an indirect object (IO).

1. The United States, Russia, and 14 other nations are building a space station.

2. This space station will orbit the earth at 17,500 miles per hour.
3. It will give astronauts a place to live and work in space.
4. Scientific and medical experiments aboard the space station will offer people new insights into life in space.
5. Engineers are constructing the modules of the space station.
6. Rockets and space shuttles are giving these modules a lift into space.
7. During space walks, astronauts will connect the various parts of the space station.
8. A Russian rocket lifted the first section, Zarya, into orbit in November 1998.
9. In December 1998 the crew of the U.S. space shuttle *Endeavour* connected the Unity module to Zarya.
10. Solar panels will give astronauts power for the space station.

10. Fragments and Run-Ons (links to exercise A, p. 27)

➡ **1.** CS **2.** F

Identify each of the following groups of words as a fragment (F), a run-on (RO), or a complete sentence (CS).

1. The Anasazi, a Native American people.
2. Represented by present-day Pueblo people.
3. *Anasazi* is a Navajo word.
4. It may mean "ancient ones" it may also mean "enemy ancestors."
5. Anasazi groups have lived in the Southwest for at least 1,800 years.
6. Built huge dwellings in sandstone cliffs.
7. These dwellings are impressive, you can still see them today.
8. One cliff palace has 150 rooms!
9. Around 1300 A.D. these dwellings were abandoned, nobody knows why.
10. Mysterious but true.

2 Nouns

1. Kinds of Nouns (links to exercise A, p. 38)

➡ **1.** *things,* C; *planet,* C; *sequoias,* C
2. *Sequoya,* P; *scholar,* C; *leader,* C

Write the nouns in these sentences, identifying each as common or proper. Then identify three collective nouns in your list.

1. The Gateway Arch soars high above St. Louis, Missouri.
2. It is made of stainless steel.
3. A competition was held, and the architect Eero Saarinen was chosen to build the landmark.
4. His idea was to construct a giant arch like those built in ancient Rome.
5. The span was constructed by raising sections with cranes.
6. The two sides of the curving arch rose beside the Mississippi River.
7. Safety was an important concern, and no one in the crew was injured during the construction.
8. Unfortunately, the steel expanded in the sun, and the two sides did not meet at the top.
9. A team sprayed cool water on the structure until it shrank to the right size.
10. The population of St. Louis watched on television as the Gateway Arch was completed.

2. Singular and Plural Nouns (links to exercise A, p. 40)

➡ **1.** engineers   **4.** rays

Write the plural forms of the underlined nouns.

1. The Statue of Liberty was a gift from the <u>citizen</u> of France.
2. France wanted to symbolize the similar <u>belief</u> of the two <u>country</u>.
3. The statue was designed to be 151 <u>foot</u> (15 <u>story</u>) high.
4. The iron frame was covered with <u>sheet</u> of copper.
5. Different <u>part</u> were made in design <u>studio</u> throughout Paris.
6. The statue was loaded into a ship in <u>section</u>.
7. Many <u>New Yorker</u>—<u>man</u> and <u>woman</u>, <u>boy</u> and <u>girl</u>—had raised money to build a base for the statue to stand on.
8. Seventy-five <u>worker</u> took six <u>month</u> to put Liberty together.
9. Many workers hung from <u>rope</u> to fit the frame and the copper <u>plate</u> together.
10. <u>Visitor</u> were able to climb <u>step</u> into Liberty's torch.

3. Possessive Nouns (links to exercise A, p. 43)

➡ **1.** *Missouri's,* singular   **3.** *country's,* singular

Write the possessive form of each underlined noun. Label it as singular or plural.

1. Stonehenge is a circle of stone monuments on <u>England</u> Salisbury Plain.

2. This monument of an unknown <u>people</u> religion is believed to be more than <u>5,000</u> years old.
3. <u>America</u> Stonehenge copies are younger and smaller.
4. <u>Sam Hill</u> Stonehenge sits overlooking <u>Washington</u> Columbia River.
5. Hill built the monument in World War I <u>soldiers</u> honor.
6. <u>Georgia</u> Stonehenge copy, called the Georgia Guidestones, has six granite slabs.
7. The <u>slabs</u> carvings are in 12 languages and suggest that <u>readers</u> lives will be better if they "avoid useless officials."
8. Carhenge, an arrangement of cars in Alliance, Nebraska, forms that <u>town</u> tribute to Stonehenge.
9. With some standing upright and others lying across them, the cars reproduce the <u>stones</u> arrangement in the real Stonehenge.
10. In Alliance, <u>residents</u> pride in Carhenge is suggested by their gift <u>shop</u> sign: "We sell Carhenge souvenirs."

4. Compound Nouns (links to exercise A, p. 46)

➡ 1. *foodstuffs,* plural; *South Dakota,* singular
2. *cornstalks,* plural

Write the compound nouns in the sentences below. Identify each compound as singular or plural.

1. In 1968 the Lorraine Motel in Memphis, Tennessee, became the backdrop of a tragedy.
2. Dr. Martin Luther King, Jr., a gifted public speaker, was killed on the motel's balcony.
3. The site is now a landmark, a museum of the struggle for civil rights.
4. In one exhibit schoolchildren can view a burned-out bus.
5. Rosa Parks rode such a bus in the Montgomery bus boycott.
6. Another exhibit celebrates college students who participated in a sit-in.
7. They quietly demanded their rights at a lunchroom in a department store and were arrested and locked up in the jailhouse.
8. Similar displays honor those who fought segregation at public schools, swimming pools, and drinking fountains.
9. Sightseers hear stories of courageous acts that helped to change public policy across the United States.
10. They leave with vivid mental snapshots of those who struggled for freedom.

5. Nouns and Their Jobs (links to exercise A, p. 48)

→ **1.** *Vietnam War,* subject; *country,* complement; *sorrow,* complement

   3. *Veterans,* subject; *war,* object of a preposition

Identify each underlined noun as a subject, a complement, or an object of a preposition.

1. <u>Francis Johnson</u> began wrapping a twine <u>ball</u> in 1950.
2. <u>Johnson</u> added <u>twine</u> for four <u>hours</u> each day until his death in 1989.
3. A <u>crane</u> lifted the huge <u>ball</u> off the <u>ground</u> as it grew larger.
4. The finished <u>object</u> is roughly 38 <u>feet</u> around.
5. The huge <u>sphere</u> brought <u>Darwin</u>, Minnesota, <u>fame</u>.
6. Johnson's <u>ball</u> of twine was a <u>challenge</u> to <u>Frank Stoeber</u>.
7. He rolled his own <u>creation</u> of over 1.6 million feet of material.
8. Stoeber's huge <u>ball</u> grew to be only slightly smaller than Johnson's.
9. But <u>death</u> brought an <u>end</u> to Stoeber's <u>project</u>.
10. Stoeber's Kansas <u>neighbors</u> set up the huge <u>object</u> as a roadside <u>attraction</u>, anyway.

3 Pronouns

1. What Is a Pronoun? (links to exercise A, p. 59)

→ **1.** its   **3.** their, them

Write the personal pronouns used in these sentences. Identify each as a subject, an object, or a possessive form.

1. The discovery of King Tutankamen's tomb and its treasures was a great event in the history of archaeology.
2. The archaeologist Howard Carter discovered the tomb. At the time, he was searching Egypt's Valley of the Kings.
3. The ancient Egyptians built fabulous tombs for their dead kings and queens.
4. Carter knew that many sites had been robbed, but he was not discouraged.
5. We know that in 1922 Carter's crew uncovered a set of stairs in the sand.
6. The stairs led them to King Tut's treasure rooms.
7. They found more than 5,000 objects, many made of solid gold.
8. You may have seen pictures of the magnificent gold mask that covered the mummy's head and shoulders.

9. King Tut's tomb is unique because its treasures were undisturbed by robbers.
10. Carter's discovery gave us new knowledge about ancient Egypt.

2. Subject Pronouns (links to exercise on p. 62)

➡ **1.** I   **2.** they

Write the correct pronoun form to complete each sentence.

1. When Howard Carter's workers uncovered King Tut's tomb, (they, them) also uncovered a mystery.
2. The first in my family to read about Carter was (I, me).
3. Carter began working in Egypt when (him, he) was only 17.
4. (Him, He) met a British lord, the earl of Carnarvon, who gave him money to explore Egypt's past.
5. Medical researchers found that Tut had died at the age of 18, and (they, them) suggested that he may have been murdered.
6. (Him, He) had many powerful enemies who may have wanted a new king.
7. The circumstances of King Tut's death are suspicious, but (us, we) may never know the truth.
8. If people want to find out more about King Tut's life and death, (they, them) can read several good books.
9. (Me, I) have read an especially good one, called *Gods, Graves, and Scholars,* by C. W. Ceram.
10. My friend Kyra wants to explore too. (Her, She) and I plan to go to Egypt someday.

3. Object Pronouns (links to exercise on p. 64)

➡ **1.** *him,* object   **2.** *He,* subject

Write the correct pronoun form to complete each sentence. Identify each as a subject pronoun (SP) or an object pronoun (OP).

1. The mystery surrounding the disappearance of Amelia Earhart makes (I, me) wonder if her fate will ever be known.
2. In 1932 (she, her) became the first woman to fly alone across the Atlantic Ocean.
3. Because of her daring adventures, newspapers gave (she, her) the name First Lady of the Air.
4. It was (she, her) who wanted to be the first woman to fly around the world.
5. Earhart would take with (she, her) a navigator, Fred Noonan.
6. The one who would plan the route was (him, he).

7. In 1937 Earhart and (he, him) set out on the historic round-the-world flight.

8. Earhart's plane disappeared in the Pacific Ocean. Time has given (us, we) few clues about what happened.

9. The disappearance of Amelia Earhart has mystified (us, we) ever since.

10. Earhart's husband, the publisher G. P. Putnam, wrote a biography of (she, her), called *Soaring Wings*.

4. Possessive Pronouns (links to exercise A, p. 67)

➡ **1.** you're   **2.** their

Write the correct pronoun or contraction for each sentence.

1. Why would anybody want to study (your, you're) garbage?

2. (It's, Its) an odd fact, but archaeologists are able to learn a lot about a society from the rubbish it leaves behind.

3. In fact, (you're, your) probably not aware that some scientists make a career of analyzing ancient refuse.

4. Recently, however, some scholars have turned (they're, their) attention to modern garbage.

5. (They're, Their) working in a new field called garbage archaeology, or garbology for short.

6. This new field had (it's, its) beginning in 1973, when William Rathje began the Garbage Project at the University of Arizona.

7. Rathje has used the garbage of some households in Tucson to study what (they're, their) buying and eating.

8. Since then the project has expanded (its, it's) scope to include dozens of other cities as well.

9. Scientists have learned a lot about how (you're, your) spending your money.

10. They know about (your, you're) eating and buying habits, and, of course, about the amount of garbage you throw out!

5. Reflexive and Intensive Pronouns (links to exercise on p. 69)

➡ **1.** *himself,* reflexive   **2.** *itself,* intensive

Write the reflexive or intensive pronoun in each sentence, labeling it *reflexive* or *intensive.*

1. We like to entertain ourselves by doing yo-yo tricks.

2. Have you yourself ever tried tricks like "walk the dog," "around the world," and "lunar loops"?

3. I myself did not know much about the history of the yo-yo until Beth told me about it.

4. The word itself may come from a Philippine word meaning "to return."
5. Beth likes to keep herself informed on all kinds of subjects.
6. She told me that the toy itself was developed in prehistoric times in the jungles of the Philippines.
7. People taught themselves how to make a type of weapon by tying a piece of cord around a grooved rock.
8. They used these early yo-yos to hunt animals and to protect themselves.
9. I taught myself how to do yo-yo tricks.
10. Beth herself practices yo-yo tricks a little every day.

6. Interrogatives and Demonstratives (links to exercise A, p. 72)

➡ **1.** what **4.** Who

Write the correct demonstrative or interrogative pronoun to complete each sentence.

1. From (who, whom) did you get this book, *The Atlas of Mysterious Places?*
2. (This, These) are the most amazing pictures I've seen!
3. One photograph shows stone statues on Easter Island in the Pacific Ocean. (That, Those) look like ancient guardians of the land.
4. (That, Those) are the cylinder-shaped stones that rest on some of the statues' heads like hats.
5. (Who, Whom) carved these 15-foot-tall human busts?
6. (Who, Whom) would spend the time and energy needed to create them?
7. (Whose, Who's) was the face depicted on the giant figures?
8. (Who, Whom) do the statues honor?
9. (Whom, What) caused the sculptors to abandon their work and leave many statues unfinished?
10. (This, These) are some of the questions that have yet to be answered about the mysterious statues.

7. Pronoun Agreement (links to exercise on p. 75)

➡ **1.** She, Agatha Christie; them, mysteries
   3. them, trips

Write the pronouns in these sentences, along with their antecedents.

1. Imagine over a hundred people completely vanishing from their village.

2. Such a disappearance occurred in Virginia in the late 1500s. It still has not been explained.
3. In 1587 John White sailed for Virginia with his fellow passengers—116 men, women, and children.
4. White's daughter and her husband were among the people aboard the ship.
5. A baby girl named Virginia Dare was born in Virginia. She was the first English child to be born in North America.
6. The child was born on Roanoke Island, the place where White and his group landed.
7. White sailed back to England for supplies, but he didn't return until three years later.
8. White searched for the English colonists but did not find them.
9. The colonists may have died, or they may have decided to live among a group of Native Americans.
10. The mystery has baffled many researchers. It remains unsolved.

8. Indefinite-Pronoun Agreement (links to exercise on p. 78)

➡ **1.** their   **3.** her

Choose the pronouns that agree with the indefinite-pronoun antecedents.

1. Do you know anyone who has made (their, his or her) own Möbius strip?
2. Many have created this amazing object by first cutting a narrow strip of paper. (He or she, They) then gave one end a half twist before taping the two ends together.
3. Most who experiment with a Möbius strip will be astonished by (his or her, their) experience.
4. Few will fail to notice that the strip's behavior does not meet (his or her, their) expectations.
5. Ask someone to draw a pencil line around the "outside" of the strip. (He or she, They) will discover that the line also goes around the "inside" of the strip.
6. Nobody who cuts a Möbius strip in two lengthwise will end up with two rings. (He or she, They) will have only one ring!
7. Anyone who tries to color one edge of the strip will discover to (his or her, their) surprise that both edges wind up being colored.
8. Many find the Möbius strip mysterious. However, (his or her, their) questions could easily be answered by a topologist.
9. That is the name for someone who studies the properties of shapes. Using (his or her, their) mathematical skills, a

topologist can explain why a Möbius strip has only one side.

10. Everyone has seen a Möbius strip, whether (he or she, they) knows it or not. It is a symbol that appears on many recyclable products.

9. Pronoun Problems (links to exercise A, p. 80)

→ **1.** us

Write the correct pronoun form to complete each sentence.

1. (We, Us) mystery fans have started a club at our school.
2. The name Rue Morgue Society appealed to (we, us) club members, since the first American detective story was *The Murders in the Rue Morgue* by Edgar Allan Poe.
3. If anyone loves solving crime puzzles, it is (we, us) amateur detectives.
4. Sometimes, (we, us) students even talk about trying to help the local police solve real crimes.
5. People who listen to (we, us) mystery fans sometimes wonder if we're talking about real or fictional crimes.

Correct the unclear pronoun reference in the following sentences by replacing each underlined pronoun with a noun.

6. Luis and Rob saw a movie version of Poe's *The Murders in the Rue Morgue.* <u>He</u> thought the ending was disappointing.
7. Poe and his hero C. Auguste Dupin shared a love of mystery. <u>He</u> had a brilliantly logical mind.
8. In the bedroom, the window and door are both closed. Yet <u>it</u> must have been opened by the murderer.
9. The police and family members are baffled by the murders. <u>They</u> arrest a tradesman for the crime.
10. In the end, an orangutan, not the tradesman, turns out to be the killer. <u>He</u> lived in an East Indian forest and was brought to France by a sailor.

10. More Pronoun Problems (links to exercise A, p. 82)

→ **1.** I   **2.** me

Write the correct pronoun to complete each sentence.

1. My friends and (I, me) were talking about alien life.
2. We wondered whether life on earth, in all its many forms, had (its, their) origin in space.
3. Miguel and Jake, friends of my brother's, said that (he, they) think alien life is a joke.

4. They laughed at Denise and (I, me) when we disagreed.
5. (She, Her) and I have read about projects that search for alien life in space.
6. Some scientific projects, such as SETI, are clear about (its, their) goal—finding and contacting extraterrestrials.
7. I believe that the SETI program, which uses radio telescopes to detect signals from space, interests (me, I) the most.
8. SETI stands for "Search for Extraterrestrial Intelligence," Denise and (I, me) explained to Jake.
9. Scientists at NASA have (its, their) own organization to explore questions about extraterrestrial life.
10. This group is called the Astrobiology Institute, the librarian told Denise and (I, me).

4 Verbs

1. What Is a Verb? (links to exercise A, p. 94)

→ **1.** may be   **3.** sail

Write the verb in each of the following sentences.

1. *Antz* is an example of feature-length animation.
2. The filmmakers created the graphics on computers.
3. The ants in the movie behave a lot like people.
4. Real ants, of course, are nothing like the ones in this film.
5. In the movie, a worker ant falls in love with a princess ant.
6. The worker and the princess escape to the outside world.
7. However, their home colony faces a serious threat.
8. The whole ant population appears in danger of destruction.
9. The worker and the princess return to the colony just in time!
10. The humble worker becomes a hero to the other ants.

2. Action Verbs and Objects (links to exercise A, p. 97)

→ **1.** *people,* direct object
   2. *members,* indirect object; *assignments,* direct object

Write the 15 complements in these sentences, identifying each as a direct object or an indirect object.

1. Steven Spielberg has given us many hit movies, including *Jaws, Raiders of the Lost Ark*, and *E.T. the Extra-Terrestrial*.
2. Spielberg made his first film at the age of 12.
3. He staged the wreck of two toy trains.
4. That experience gave him a taste for spectacular stunts.

5. He used everyone around him in his movies.

6. He gave his mother starring roles in many home movies.

7. When he was 13, Spielberg joined a Boy Scout photography program.

8. He made the scout troop a three-minute movie about a stagecoach robbery.

9. The movie won Spielberg his first filmmaking award—a merit badge.

10. At the age of 16, Spielberg made *Firelight*, his first science fiction movie.

3. Linking Verbs and Predicate Words (links to exercise on p. 99)

➡ **1.** *are,* linking verb; *scary,* predicate adjective

3. *was,* linking verb; *hit,* predicate noun

Identify each linking verb, predicate noun, and predicate adjective in the sentences below.

1. The job title "continuity clerk" may seem unimpressive.

2. But a continuity clerk is an important person on a movie set.

3. The order in which scenes are shot is not the order in which they will appear in the film.

4. Footage from different days can be part of the same scene.

5. Such footage must appear continuous.

6. The continuity clerk's tasks are very tedious.

7. Most people would grow bored by all the details.

8. Good continuity clerks, however, are perfectionists.

9. They remain attentive to the tasks.

10. Some continuity clerks even become directors.

4. Principal Parts of Verbs (links to exercise on p. 101)

➡ **1.** present   **2.** past participle

Identify each underlined principal part as the present, the present participle, the past, or the past participle.

1. Photography has <u>existed</u> for only about 150 years.

2. Eadweard Muybridge <u>created</u> some of the first stop-action photographs.

3. In 1877 he <u>arranged</u> 12 cameras in a row.

4. Then he <u>snapped</u> photos, in sequence, of a galloping horse.

5. Some people had <u>claimed</u> that a running horse always has two feet on the ground.

6. Muybridge's photos <u>proved</u> that all four feet are off the ground at some points.

7. A real horse never <u>assumes</u> a rocking-horse position, with two legs stretched forward and two back.
8. By 1900 Muybridge had <u>mastered</u> the art of stop-action photography.
9. He had <u>produced</u> many series of photos of people running and jumping.
10. Readers are still <u>enjoying</u> these photos in books and magazines today.

5. Irregular Verbs (links to exercise on p. 104)

➡ **1.** seen   **4.** made

In the sentences below, choose the correct forms of the verbs in parentheses.

1. The popular musical *Annie Get Your Gun* was (wrote, written) about a real person, Annie Oakley.
2. Annie Oakley had (grown, growed) up on a farm in Ohio.
3. She (beginned, began) teaching herself to hunt at an early age.
4. She (brought, bringed) home game to feed her family.
5. At the age of 15, she (winned, won) a shooting contest against Frank E. Butler, a well-known target shooter.
6. Before long, she had (given, gave) Butler her hand in marriage.
7. The two (shot, shooted) targets together in circuses and shows.
8. Oakley was so accurate with a rifle that she (hit, hitted) dimes thrown into the air.
9. If someone tossed a playing card into the air, she could riddle it with holes before it (fell, fallen) to the ground.
10. When Oakley performed with Buffalo Bill's Wild West Show, audiences (knew, knowed) her as Little Sure Shot.

6. Simple Tenses (links to exercise A, p. 107)

➡ **1.** future   **3.** present

Identify each underlined verb form as present, past, future, present progressive, past progressive, or future progressive.

1. Gwilym Hughes <u>watched</u> his first movie at the age of seven.
2. After that, he <u>was viewing</u> movies on a regular basis.
3. In the next 46 years he <u>watched</u> more than 24,000 feature films.
4. That <u>is</u> a record.
5. It <u>represents</u> more than one-tenth of all the feature films ever made.
6. Hughes <u>lives</u> in a remote corner of Wales.

7. The nearest theater <u>is</u> 20 miles away.
8. Yet Hughes <u>sees</u> nearly 20 movies every week.
9. He says he <u>will keep</u> up that pace.
10. He <u>will hold</u> the record for many years.

7. Perfect Tenses (links to exercise A, p. 110)

➡ **1.** *had looked,* past perfect
   2. *have found,* present perfect

Identify the verb in each sentence, and indicate whether its tense is present perfect, past perfect, or future perfect.

1. Audiences have watched motion pictures for more than a century.
2. Before 1900, movies had lasted as little as a minute or two.
3. These brief films had showed simple scenes, such as ocean waves.
4. Since the 1903 film *The Great Train Robbery,* movies have featured complete stories.
5. Westerns and thrillers have attracted audiences ever since that time.
6. Even a century from now, thrillers will surely have lost none of their appeal.
7. Before the maturation of the film industry, most producers had filmed movies in New York and New Jersey.
8. Because of its year-round good weather, southern California has become the biggest movie-making center in the United States.
9. By the year 2050, however, several other parts of the country will probably have developed into important centers of film production.
10. The movie business has come a long way since *The Great Train Robbery.*

8. Using Verb Tenses (links to exercise A, p. 114)

➡ **1.** were using   **2.** lacked

In each sentence, choose the correct verb form in parentheses.

1. Television (had been, has been) around for less than 70 years.
2. Experiments with television broadcasting (begin, began) in the early 1930s.

3. Before TV sets became available commercially, scientists (will have demonstrated, had demonstrated) television at the 1939 New York world's fair.
4. Color television (made, will make) its first appearance in 1954.
5. Now virtually all television programs (air, aired) in color.
6. Early home TV sets (have, had) large cabinets but very small screens, never larger than 12 inches.
7. Some of today's televisions (feature, will feature) screens more than 60 inches in width.
8. In the near future, thin, flat TVs (will become, became) common.
9. Since the 1960s communications satellites (will enable, have enabled) television broadcasts from anywhere in the world.
10. In 1969 viewers (see, saw) one of the greatest thrills of the television era: astronauts on the moon.

9. Troublesome Verb Pairs (links to exercise A, p. 117)

➡ **1.** can **5.** sat

Choose the correct word or words in parentheses in each of the following sentences.

1. Do the most talented artists (raise, rise) to the top?
2. In Hollywood, they (may not, cannot).
3. Most studio heads don't want to (sit, set) down with anyone who hasn't made a successful commercial movie.
4. But film festivals give young filmmakers a chance to (lie, lay) their reputations on the line.
5. They (raise, rise) the hopes of artists who might otherwise not have a chance.
6. They (sit, set) their sights on quality instead of money.
7. Winning at a festival can help a filmmaker (raise, rise) money for distributing his or her film.
8. Success (lies, lays) ahead for some of these artists.
9. They (sit, set) a festival's tone with movies about important themes.
10. Festival participation might not help, but it (may not, cannot) hurt.

5 Adjectives and Adverbs

1. What Is an Adjective? (links to exercise on p. 128)

➡ **1.** some, inventors; successful, inventors; mature, scientists
3. cold, ears; red, ears; harsh, winters; Northeastern, winters

Write each adjective and the noun it modifies. Do not include articles.

1. Alison DeSmyter is an inventive teenager from Texas.
2. Alison has a muscular disability and uses a wheelchair.
3. She invented a portable ramp that helps disabled people move over curbs.
4. She had only a few weeks to create an original design for a local contest.
5. She first considered and rejected an awkward ramp made of rubber.
6. Then she imagined an inflatable ramp, but who would blow it up?
7. Finally Alison created a lightweight metallic ramp and named it the Rampanion (ramp companion).
8. Alison made the exact measurements herself, and her father helped her build the ramp of aluminum.
9. The Rampanion weighs four pounds and comes in a handy bag.
10. Her invention won the grand prize for the fifth grade in a statewide contest.

2. Predicate Adjectives (links to exercise A, p. 130)

➡ **1.** common, wipers   **2.** dangerous, trolleys

Write each predicate adjective and the noun or pronoun it modifies.

1. Many inventions have been useful to the food industry.
2. In a refrigerator, an apple remains tasty for a long time.
3. Thanks to canning, foods do not become spoiled.
4. But if they smell moldy, they should not be canned!
5. Dried foods stay edible for a long time.
6. Dried fruits are tasty even after long storage.
7. Dried eggs become usable when water is added.
8. Freeze-dried meals are expensive in comparison with other forms of dried food.
9. But they also taste better.
10. Of course, fresh food always seems best of all.

3. Other Words Used as Adjectives (links to exercise A, p. 132)

➡ **1.** Most; human   **3.** Our

Write each noun or pronoun that is used as an adjective.

1. What if you did not have clothing fasteners or book-bag snaps?
2. All zippers, buttons, clasps, and laces on your belongings are important.
3. But a more recent invention is replacing these fasteners.
4. Velcro was invented in 1955, long before its widespread use.
5. One of George de Mestral's nature walks led to a startling idea.
6. He found many burs with their tiny hooks clinging to his pants.
7. Burs carry seeds from their parent plants.
8. De Mestral spent some years creating Velcro, which makes our lives more comfortable.
9. A Velcro fastener consists of a hook strip and a loop strip.
10. Perhaps someday most fasteners will be made of Velcro.

4. What Is an Adverb? (links to exercise A, p. 136)

➡ **1.** experimentally, were flying (verb)
    2. yet, had flown (verb); successfully, had flown (verb)

Write each adverb and the word it modifies. Then label each modified word as a verb, an adjective, or an adverb. There may be more than one adverb in a sentence.

1. If you have ever failed at inventing something, join the club.
2. The history of invention is full of extremely embarrassing events.
3. Robert Goddard eventually invented the liquid-fueled rocket.
4. But Goddard's first rocket rose rapidly upward and then crashed into his aunt's garden!
5. John Baird made highly important contributions to the invention of television.
6. He also tried to make self-warming socks, a device that failed quite miserably.
7. In 1882 Henry Seeley invented a very early version of the electric iron.
8. But hardly any homes had electricity, so Seeley sold few irons!
9. Hubert Booth cleverly invented an early vacuum cleaner.
10. Because it was too large to move by hand, horses pulled it from house to house!

5. Making Comparisons (links to exercise A, p. 139)

➡ **2.** more important **4.** newest

Choose the correct comparative or superlative form to complete each sentence.

1. The traffic signal is one of the (more important, most important) of all safety inventions.
2. The three-way traffic signal was not the (earlier, earliest) form of traffic control.
3. However, it was (more practical, most practical) than the previous model.
4. Garrett Morgan, who was granted a patent for the traffic signal in 1923, was one of the (more inventive, most inventive) minds of this century.
5. Because Morgan was black, however, his inventions were received (less enthusiastically, least enthusiastically) than those of white inventors.
6. For example, Morgan invented a gas mask that allowed rescue workers to enter gas-filled tunnels (more safely, most safely) than before.
7. In 1916 Morgan and some volunteers who were (braver, bravest) than average wore his masks to rescue 32 men after an underground explosion.
8. Two men with Morgan gas masks were (more effective, most effective) in the first 15 minutes of fighting a fire than a whole company without the masks.
9. Yet when Morgan brought his (later, latest) gas mask to the South, a white companion had to demonstrate it.
10. In World War I, soldiers used Morgan's gas masks to protect themselves from the (deadlier, deadliest) battlefield poison— chlorine gas.

6. Adjective or Adverb? (links to exercise on p. 141)

➡ **1.** really (adverb)

For each sentence, choose the correct modifier from those given in parentheses. Identify each word you choose as an adjective or an adverb.

1. What makes an invention (good, well)?
2. Is a new device (real, really) good if people use it (bad, badly)?
3. The writer Jared Diamond describes the history of some (really, real) helpful inventions that were not used (good, well) at first.

4. For example, the wheel was not a (real, really) advantage for the people of ancient Mexico.
5. Without animals to pull vehicles, they (real, really) couldn't use wheels.
6. An inventor may create something unique without knowing what it is (good, well) for.
7. This happened to Thomas Edison, who did very (good, well) as an inventor.
8. But his plans for the phonograph give us a (good, well) laugh today.
9. Some (bad, badly) ones included using it to teach speech or to record the words of dying people.
10. When businesspeople began playing music on the phonograph, Edison thought this was a (real, really) mistake!

7. Avoiding Double Negatives (links to exercise A, p. 143)

➡ **1.** can   **3.** are

Write the word in parentheses that correctly completes each sentence.

1. No one (can, can't) expect all new inventions to be successful.
2. Consider the poor inventor of the "parachute hat," who (had, hadn't) no luck.
3. The invention didn't (ever, never) work, and the inventor broke his neck trying it out!
4. In 1912 Mr. S. I. Russell (couldn't, could) give no reason why his electric heating pad burned.
5. The reason was that the wiring in the device (wasn't, was) no good.
6. Thomas Adams (had, hadn't) no luck in turning chicle into a substitute for rubber.
7. He tried to use chicle for toys and boots, but he (could, couldn't) hardly succeed.
8. Chewing chicle one day, Adams regretted that it barely (had, hadn't) any flavor.
9. He added flavor and invented chewing gum, but doctors warned that it wouldn't be (no, any) good for people.
10. Today chewing gum is very popular, but you (should, shouldn't) never chew too much.

6 Prepositions, Conjunctions, Interjections ....

1. What Is a Preposition? (links to exercise on p. 154)

➜ **1.** to, fires **2.** from, miles

Write the preposition in each sentence, along with its object.

1. Many people are afraid of bugs.
2. They run from anything "creepy."
3. True, some types of insects are deadly.
4. But very few insects are actually harmful to people.
5. Ant tunnels let air into the soil.
6. Without insect predators, pests would devour farm crops.
7. Bees and butterflies carry pollen between plants.
8. Plants cannot produce fruits or vegetables without pollination.
9. Spiders destroy thousands of flies and other insects.
10. Bugs are a vital link in our ecosystem.

2. Using Prepositional Phrases (links to exercise A, p. 157)

➜ **1.** of spiders, kinds (adj. phrase)
   2. to people, dangerous (adv. phrase)

Write the prepositional phrase in each sentence, along with the word it modifies. Then indicate whether the phrase is an adjective phrase or an adverb phrase.

1. Most people are afraid of tarantulas.
2. They are actually less harmful to people than wasps or bees.
3. They would probably run from you and not attack.
4. Many people keep them as pets.
5. The goliath tarantula is the largest spider in the world.
6. It can grow to be a foot in length.
7. However, this spider tips the scales at only about two ounces.
8. If you meet a goliath tarantula, beware the sharp barbs on its abdomen.
9. It can flick the barbs at attackers, causing an itchy rash.
10. Luckily for us, South America is the goliath tarantula's home.

3. Conjunctions (links to exercise A, p. 160)

➜ **1.** and (lenses, light waves)
   2. but (Light waves show the details of ordinary objects, the waves are too long to reveal the smallest structures)

Write the conjunction in each sentence, along with the words or groups of words that it joins.

1. The firefly and the lightning bug are the same insect.
2. Females lay eggs in soil, and four weeks later the eggs hatch into larvae.
3. These larvae, or glowworms, are carnivorous.
4. Despite their small size, they can eat slugs and snails.
5. Not only adults but also some larvae glow.
6. The larvae spend the winter in small tunnels and come out again in spring.
7. Adult fireflies feed on pollen and nectar.
8. Both male and female fireflies light up.
9. On summer days fireflies rest on plants or in trees.
10. Fireflies produce light, yet they don't produce heat.

7 Verbals and Verbal Phrases ....

1. Gerunds (links to exercise on p. 171)

➡ **1.** riding   **4.** Waiting

Write the gerunds in these sentences.

1. Helping people in wheelchairs is one job of service dogs.
2. People who are dedicated and good with animals are needed for educating the dogs.
3. Loving the animals is the first requirement for trainers.
4. Training a dog in obedience takes two to three months.
5. The next few months are devoted to teaching special skills.
6. The dog focuses on learning exactly the tasks it will need to perform for its new owner.
7. Retrievers are especially good at fetching things for disabled people.
8. Their favorite activity is helping people.
9. Matching each dog with a particular person is important.
10. New owners learn about feeding and exercising their dogs.

2. Participles (links to exercise on p. 173)

➡ **1.** *acting,* participle
   3. *Training,* gerund

Write the participles in these sentences, identifying each as a present participle or a past participle. Also write the noun or pronoun that each participle modifies.

1. Indian Red was a horse living in Ontario.
2. Walking along a road one night, he stopped suddenly.
3. Chilled and fatigued, he should have been seeking shelter.
4. Instead he neighed and whinnied, trying to get cars to stop.
5. Only a few speeding drivers were out on that cold night.
6. Those who came by ignored the horse, driving right past him.
7. Finally, one driver, his curiosity aroused, stopped to see what was wrong.
8. Searching a snow-covered ditch near the horse, the man discovered an old woman.
9. The woman, now numbed by the cold, had fallen into the ditch.
10. Not even knowing her, Indian Red wanted to get help for her.

3. Infinitives (links to exercise A, p. 175)

➡ **2.** To play   **4.** to let

Write the infinitives in these sentences. Identify whether each is used as a noun, an adjective, or an adverb.

1. Jackie Geyer liked to feed raccoons in her yard.
2. One day a badly injured raccoon came to eat.
3. The raccoon needed to limp to the feeding station because its right hind leg was injured.
4. "Chloe" seemed a good name to give the raccoon.
5. One day Chloe was missing, and Jackie began to worry.
6. Finally Chloe appeared, using only her front legs to walk to the food bowl.
7. Jackie was surprised to see that Chloe's other hind leg was now injured.
8. Luckily, to walk on her "hands" was not very hard for a talented raccoon like Chloe.
9. Chloe had decided that Jackie's was the only place in town to eat.
10. Chloe's injured legs were quick to heal, and she has now been dining at Jackie's place for eight years.

4. Verbal Phrases (links to exercise A, p. 177)

➡ **1.** *Strolling around the neighborhood,* gerund phrase
   2. *slightly spoiled,* participial phrase

Write the verbal phrases in these sentences, identifying each as a gerund phrase, a participial phrase, or an infinitive phrase.

1. Many animals, including chimpanzees and elephants, have learned to draw or paint.

2. A chimp named Alpha preferred drawing pictures to eating meals.
3. She would beg visitors, fascinated by her behavior, to give her paper and a pencil.
4. Researchers asked a chimp named Moja to draw various things, including a basketball.
5. Seeing vertical zigzags on the paper, they thought that she had just scribbled.
6. Then they realized that the zigzags might represent the ball's up-and-down bouncing.
7. An elephant named Ruby loves to paint abstract pictures.
8. Choosing colors is a creative act for her.
9. A visitor who enjoyed watching Ruby paint fell ill, and paramedics in blue uniforms came to help him.
10. After they left, Ruby expressed herself by painting a blue blob surrounded by a swirl of red.

8 Sentence Structure

1. What Is a Clause? (links to exercise A, p. 187)

➡ **1.** dependent clause   **5.** independent clause

Identify each underlined group of words as an independent clause or a dependent clause.

1. <u>Dalié Jiménez was concerned</u> that disadvantaged children were not getting books read to them often enough.
2. She had learned in her psychology class <u>that reading to young children was very important</u>.
3. Children need this experience <u>so that their brains can develop properly.</u>
4. <u>When she was 14 years old</u>, Dalié began volunteering at a Head Start program in her hometown of Miami, Florida.
5. She liked this work <u>because she was interested in children</u>.
6. When she told her friends about her work, <u>they wanted to volunteer too</u>.
7. Dalié and about 30 of her friends started a children's library <u>that consisted of donated books</u>.
8. They used puppets to act out stories <u>while they read</u>.
9. When Dalié heard that Head Start's funding was going to be cut by one-third, <u>she lobbied lawmakers</u>.
10. <u>Because they worked so hard</u>, she and her friends were able to help save the Head Start program.

2. Simple and Compound Sentences (links to exercise A, p. 190)

➡ **1.** simple   **2.** compound

Identify each sentence as simple or compound.

1. Justin Lebo of Saddle Brook, New Jersey, loved bikes.
2. He and his dad shared an interest in bicycle racing.
3. They had their garage set up like a bike shop; they worked there on their bikes all the time.
4. Justin bought a couple of rundown bikes, and he fixed them up.
5. The bikes looked as good as new, but Justin didn't need any more bikes himself.
6. He decided to donate them to the Kilbarchan Home for Boys.
7. Justin liked the idea of people fixing up bikes for those less fortunate, so he continued to do so in his spare time.
8. Many people offered him their old bikes for free.
9. The donations were helpful for a time, but soon Justin ran out of space in his small garage.
10. Justin fixed 250 bikes, and he gave them all away.

3. Complex Sentences (links to exercise A, p. 193)

➡ **1.** Independent clause: *many people do not know about it;* dependent clause: *Although the Foster Grandparent Program is more than 30 years old*
2. Independent clause: *This program was established;* dependent clause: *so that hospitalized and institutionalized children could get special attention*

Write these sentences on a sheet of paper. Underline each independent clause once and each dependent clause twice.

1. National Youth Service Day is not well-known, although it has been celebrated for more than ten years.
2. This national event was founded so that young people's volunteer work would be recognized.
3. National Youth Service Day is a two-day event that brings together student volunteers working on community projects.
4. After they work on a project, the volunteers have a deep sense of satisfaction.
5. In Washington, D.C., an old building was turned into a community center so that children would have a safe place to go.
6. Because they wanted to help beautify their city, some volunteers in Atlanta, Georgia, painted a playground.
7. Although adult volunteers helped, most of the work was done by elementary-school and middle-school students.

8. Since they were interested in identifying major problems in their neighborhood, about 90 high school students in San Francisco conducted a community survey.
9. Because they wanted to improve the environment, volunteers in Troutdale, Oregon, planted new vegetation at a state park.
10. Nearly 3 million volunteers worked on one recent National Youth Service Day, so that many communities benefited.

4. Kinds of Dependent Clauses (links to exercise A, p. 197)

➡ 1. *who are visually challenged,* adjective clause
2. *because they help the people get around in daily life,* adverb clause

Write these sentences on a sheet of paper. Underline each dependent clause, identifying it as an adjective clause, an adverb clause, or a noun clause.

1. Christian Miller, who is a young animal lover, cared for sea turtles on a beach near his home in Palm Beach, Florida.
2. You may know that sea turtles are endangered.
3. Until he received training from the Florida Department of Natural Resources, Christian could not work with the turtles.
4. During the turtles' nesting season, which lasts from May to October, Christian help the turtles for two to three hours a day.
5. After the turtles hatch in the sand, they head for the ocean.
6. Baby turtles that have a hard time digging themselves out of the sand may need extra help.
7. Those that were in need of help were lucky to have Christian to assist them.
8. Christian knows where most of the 400 to 600 nests on his beach are.
9. He keeps careful records of his beach patrols so that he can send his findings to the U.S. Department of Natural Resources.
10. Although the job of monitoring sea turtles is hard, Christian finds it very rewarding.

5. Compound-Complex Sentences (links to exercise A, p. 199)

➡ 1. complex   2. compound

Identify each sentence as compound, complex, or compound-complex.

1. When she was four, Mandy Van Benthuysen learned that she had muscular dystrophy.
2. Later she volunteered for the Muscular Dystrophy Association, which works to find treatments for neuromuscular diseases.

3. Neuromuscular diseases are diseases that affect both the nerves and the muscles.
4. Mandy, who was a college student, traveled around the country, and she urged other young people to volunteer.
5. She said that volunteering helps those in need; it also "makes you a better person all around."
6. For more than 30 years, the comedian Jerry Lewis has hosted a telethon that raises money for the Muscular Dystrophy Association.
7. Celebrities who want to help volunteer to be on the show.
8. Among the stars who have volunteered are Mariah Carey, Jason Alexander, Judge Judy, and Cher.
9. Television viewers call in with pledges while they watch the show.
10. Millions of dollars have been raised, and this money has helped many Americans with neuromuscular diseases.

9 Subject-Verb Agreement

1. Agreement in Number (links to exercise A, p. 210)

➜ 1. have   2. create

Rewrite these sentences so that verbs agree in number with their subjects. If a sentence contains no error, write *Correct.*

1. According to legend, the model for *kente* cloth were a spider's web.
2. The word *kente* come from *kenten,* which means "basket."
3. *Kente* cloth resembles the woven pattern of a basket.
4. This finely woven cloth are made on homemade looms.
5. Weavers moves the looms with strings tied to their big toes.
6. Traditionally, *kente* cloth is made from silk.
7. These days the cloth don't always contain silk.
8. Rayon threads serves as an inexpensive substitute.
9. Weavers creates four-inch strips of cloth and then weaves the strips together to make larger garments.
10. Every design has a name, such as "crocodile tears."

2. Compound Subjects (links to exercise A, p. 212)

➜ **1.** Correct   **2.** A basket or pot serves a practical function, such as food storage.

Write the verb form that agrees with the subject of each sentence.

1. Written reports and speeches (has, have) their limitations.
2. Many politicians and business executives (prefers, prefer) using multimedia presentations.
3. CDs and other technology (provides, provide) new ways of reaching audiences.
4. Text, images, and sound (combines, combine) to convey messages effectively.
5. A photograph, art reproduction, or video clip (grabs, grab) the audience's attention.
6. Recorded speech or music (enlivens, enliven) a presentation.
7. Charts and graphs (allows, allow) people to absorb information quickly.
8. Skill and imagination (contributes, contribute) to a presentation's success.
9. Either fuzzy images or poor sound quality (makes, make) a presentation less effective.
10. Poor organization and dull ideas also (displeases, displease) audiences.

3. Agreement Problems in Sentences (links to exercise A, p. 215)

➜ **1.** Do your classmates collect posters?
  2. Correct

Rewrite these sentences so that verbs agree with their subjects. If a sentence contains no error, write *Correct*.

1. Posters is an effective way to sell goods and services.
2. Has you ever seen a poster that sells war?
3. Propaganda posters during wartime has performed this function.
4. Such posters are sometimes an important part of a war effort.
5. There is many examples from the two world wars.
6. The slogan on one of the World War I posters are "Food *is* ammunition—Don't waste it."
7. There is wartime posters designed to promote patriotism.
8. Hatred and fear are other emotions that can be stirred up by propaganda posters.
9. Through posters is recruited many volunteers for the military.
10. Advertising specialists and artists hired by the government are the creative force behind wartime posters.

4. Indefinite Pronouns as Subjects (links to exercise A, p. 218)

➡ **1.** Many know the saying "A picture's   **2.** Correct
worth a thousand words."

Rewrite these sentences so that verbs agree with their subjects. If a sentence contains no error, write *Correct*.

1. One glimpses 19th-century slum life in Jacob Riis's *How the Other Half Lives.*
2. Another of his influential books are *Children of the Poor.*
3. Each of these books contain photographs that convey the problems of immigrants.
4. Many of the photographs document conditions in New York City tenements.
5. All of Riis's photographs exposes the horrors of overcrowding and malnutrition.
6. Both of these problems was common in 19th-century cities.
7. Few has captured urban poverty as vividly as Riis did.
8. None of the written accounts so dramatically demonstrate the plight of the urban poor.
9. Most of Riis's photographs illustrates problems caused by rapid growth.
10. Nearly everyone credit Riis with helping to improve conditions.

5. Problem Subjects (links to exercise A, p. 221)

➡ **1.** describes   **2.** travels

Write the form of the verb that agrees with the subject of each sentence.

1. Three and a half years (seems, seem) a short amount of time for planning and finishing the Vietnam Veterans Memorial.
2. Economics (is, are) always a concern in designing a large project.
3. About eight months (is, are) how long it actually took to construct the memorial.
4. The public (lines, line) up to view the wall and nearby statues at this popular site.
5. "Heroes in Black Stone" (is, are) a song about Vietnam veterans and the people who visit the memorial.
6. Politics (is, are) not the point of the wall.
7. A committee of distinguished sculptors and architects (is, are) to be congratulated for choosing such an effective tribute.
8. Only 600 feet (separates, separate) the wall from the Lincoln Memorial.

9. *Offerings at the Wall,* a book by Thomas Allen, (contains, contain) pictures of items left at the wall by visitors.
10. The National Park Service staff (collects, collect) personal items left at the wall.

10 Capitalization

1. People and Cultures (links to exercise on p. 232)

➜ **2.** Mr. Jones, Knight, Glubok, Tamarin

Write the words and abbreviations that should be capitalized but are not in these sentences. Capitalize each correctly.

1. Last week coach jackett told us a story about one of the most interesting tennis matches of the 20th century.
2. It all started with a man by the name of robert larimore riggs.
3. bobby riggs, as he was known in the tennis world, won the Wimbledon title in 1939.
4. Our coach said that mr. riggs won three U.S. Open championships but became famous for his weird tennis matches.
5. My friend roberta said that her aunt a.j. once played a match against riggs while he sat on a chair.
6. The one event that i found most interesting occurred when riggs challenged the australian margaret court to a tennis match.
7. Most people—including my aunt, who was a tennis fan— expected court to beat riggs because she was 25 years younger than he.
8. Riggs won that tennis match but later met another female challenger, billie jean king, who defeated him easily.
9. The match became one of the most publicized events in american sports, attracting 50 million viewers.
10. Years later, in another gender battle, riggs and vitas gerulaitis lost a doubles match to martina navratilova and pam shriver.

2. First Words and Titles (links to exercise A, p. 235)

➜ **1.** How, Equipment, Baseball, Bat   **2.** Whoever

Write the words that should be capitalized but are not in these sentences, capitalizing them correctly. If there are no errors in a sentence, write *Correct.*

1. on July 20, 1998, the Special Olympics celebrated its 30th anniversary.

2. *the today show* and *parade magazine* have featured inspiring stories about the courage of athletes in the Special Olympics.
3. The Special Olympics oath is "let me win. but if I cannot win, let me be brave in the attempt."
4. In 1997 a Christmas album benefiting the Special Olympics was produced, with songs like "blue christmas" and "the christmas song."
5. The Special Olympics has its own magazine, entitled *spirit*.
6. On February 11, 1990, the television drama *life goes on* devoted an hour-long episode to the Special Olympics.
7. In 1987 more than 4,700 athletes participated in the Special Olympics, the year's largest amateur sports event.
8. The event was covered in *sports illustrated* and *time*.
9. For information on how to get involved, write a letter to Special Olympics headquarters, beginning "dear Sir or Madam."
10. If you would like to research the Special Olympics, you may want to make an outline that begins like this:
    I. general information
       a. athletes
       b. families
       c. volunteers
       d. national and worldwide chapters

3. Places and Transportation (links to exercise A, p. 239)

➜ **1.** North America   **3.** Appalachian Mountains

Write the words that should be capitalized but are not in these sentences, capitalizing them correctly. If there are no errors in a sentence, write *Correct*.

1. Have you ever wondered where the word *marathon* originated?
2. The first marathon was held during the first modern Olympics in athens, greece, in 1896.
3. The race was named for an ancient battle near the Greek town of marathon.
4. According to legend, the soldier Pheidippides raced from marathon to athens (about 25 miles) with news of the Greeks' victory over the Persians and then immediately died.
5. Today, marathons are held all over the world, in places like london, england; sydney, australia; and dublin, ireland.
6. Whether in the northern or the southern part of the country, on the east coast or the west coast, you'll find marathons.
7. For example, the one in new york city begins on staten island, at the verrazano-narrows bridge, and ends in central park.

8. There's even a marathon called Grandma's Marathon in duluth, minnesota, with a scenic course along lake superior.
9. Perhaps you'd be more interested in the Rock 'n' Roll Marathon, with a course that travels through the san diego zoo and along highway 163.
10. Known for its difficult course, the Boston Marathon begins in hopkinton and ends in copley square.

4. Organizations and Other Subjects (links to exercise on p. 241)

➜ **1.** North Side Junior High

Write the words that should be capitalized but are not in these sentences, capitalizing them correctly. If there are no errors write *Correct.*

1. Records show that as early as 400 b.c. the Chinese were playing a game similar to soccer.
2. Some early footballs were stuffed with hair or rags.
3. The term *soccer* was first used at oxford university.
4. James Richardson Spensley, founder of the genoa cricket and football club, introduced the game of soccer to Italy in 1893.
5. On may 21, 1904, an international soccer federation was formed in paris, France.
6. The first world cup finals were held in Uruguay, but the teams could not agree on the size of the ball; therefore, different-sized balls were used in the two halves.
7. During world war II (1939–1945), the world cup was canceled.
8. The oneidas of boston, the first organized soccer club in America, were undefeated from 1862 to 1865.
9. The first series of games known as the women's world cup was played in China in 1991.
10. On saturday, july 10, 1999, the U.S. women's team won its second world cup title in Pasadena's rose bowl stadium.

11 Punctuation

1. Periods and Other End Marks (links to exercise A, p. 252)

➜ **1.** ?   **2.** !

Write the punctuation end mark that should replace each numbered blank.

You don't have to use a code to keep a message secret_1_ You can use invisible ink. What substance should you use_2_ Well, lemon juice works well_3_ No kidding_4_ Dip a toothpick or brush into the juice and use it to write your message. Let the juice dry_5_ Your message will be invisible. Now, hold the paper so that it touches a hot light bulb. Be careful_6_ Don't burn yourself. The words of your message will appear. Amazing_7_ Do you want to try a different kind of ink_8_ Write your message in milk and let it dry. Now, empty pencil-sharpener shavings over the flat paper_9_ The shavings will stick to the invisible words and make the message appear_10_

2. Commas in Sentences (links to exercise on p. 255)

➡ Think of this, readers,

Rewrite this paragraph, adding commas where they are needed.

Some cultures lived in America for many centuries but then they disappeared. They left tools pottery and other artifacts behind. They also left carvings and paintings on rocks called rock art. Petroglyphs (rock carvings) show human figures animals and some designs that are not easily explained. Artists made petroglyphs with small pointed rocks or flat stones. They used these as knives picks and chisels to carve shapes on large stones. Pictographs (rock paintings) on the other hand were made with paint from berries or vegetables. Native American artists may have painted for pleasure or they may have painted to communicate with one another. In any case the pictures are like a form of code to us.

3. Commas: Dates, Addresses, and Letters (links to exercise A, p. 257)

➡ New York, NY   February 20, 2000

Rewrite the following letter, adding missing commas.

April 27 2000

Manuel Rojas
123 Maple Ave.
Los Angeles California

Dear Manny

Today I learned another interesting fact about secret codes. I found out how spies sent secret messages through the mail during World War II. It worked like this. A spy in London England might write a normal letter that contained no secret information. The spy would then address the envelope to his or her superior in Paris France. In the upper right-hand corner of the envelope, the spy would write a tiny message in code. When the spy placed a stamp over the message, no one could detect the message. When the letter arrived, the recipient would steam off the stamp and decode the message. Even if enemy agents opened the letter, it would not arouse suspicion.

By the way, I read in the newspaper that a speaker will give a presentation at our local library about how information is coded in computers. The presentation is on May 18 2000. Would you like to go with me when you visit?

Your friend who loves codes

Jack

4. Quotation Marks (links to exercise A, p. 261)

➡ "Are you nuts?"   "I do," said Jay," and

Rewrite the following passage, correcting errors in the use of quotation marks.

"Some codes are spoken rather than written, Julia said. A whole town once used a secret language called Boontling."
"Why was it called that? asked Paul.
"The town was Boonville, California," Julia explained, "and the word *Boontling* stood for *Boonville lingo*".
Paul asked, "Is lingo the same as slang?"
"That's right! Julia exclaimed. "From the 1880s to the 1930s, nearly everyone who lived in Boonville could speak the lingo." She went on to say that "a few people still know it today."
"Give me some examples," Paul said, of Boontling words."
"Some combine parts of English words," said Julia. "For example, a schoolteacher is a schoolch." A rail fence is a relf."
Paul pointed out that "those words weren't too hard to decipher."
"No," said Julia, but other words are less obvious. A storyteller is called a bearman because the best storyteller in town hunted bears."

5. Semicolons and Colons (links to exercise A, p. 263)

➡ messages: a folk song;

Rewrite this paragraph, correcting errors in the use of semicolons and colons.

The ancient Celts used: a form of written communication called the ogham alphabet. This alphabet can still be seen in inscriptions on stones in fact, more than 350 such stones have survived. They are found in: Ireland, Wales, Scotland, southern England, and the Isle of Man. During the time of ogham's use (about 600 B.C. to 700 A.D.), few people could read and write. To write a message in ogham, a person would draw or chisel a long, straight line. Each letter would be represented by one to five short lines, which might extend to the left of, to the right of, or completely through the long line. A message could also be written on a stick, the letters were cut into its edge. The ogham alphabet had 20 letters, each named for a tree; a shrub or other plant, or a natural element, like lightning or the sea. Among the trees represented were the following, the birch, the oak, and the hawthorn. Nose ogham and shin ogham were variations in which people used their fingers to form the cross-strokes of the letters against the straight line of their nose or shinbone.

6. Hyphens, Dashes, and Parentheses (links to exercise on p. 265)

➜ 1. —   2. -

Indicate what punctuation mark—hyphen, dash, or parenthesis—should replace each numbered blank in this paragraph. If no mark is needed, write *None*.

Imagine living in the Victorian era __1__ a time when messages had to be carried hundreds of miles on horseback or sent on ships that traveled across the ocean __2__. It may have taken days, weeks, or even months for a message to reach its destination. This was how people communicated over long distances in the 1800s. What a tremendous improvement __3__ a leap in technology __4__ the invention of the telegraph was to the people of the Victorian era. Samuel Morse was one of the inventors of the telegraph. In 1844, at the age of fifty __5__ three, Morse demonstrated that messages could be sent quickly from Washington, D.C., to Baltimore, Maryland, __6__ by using his electric telegraph. Morse also invented his own code __7__ the Morse code __8__, which is a system of long and short clicks used to transmit messages by means of the telegraph. When Morse code is written out, the letters of the alphabet appear as groups of dots and dashes. The most famous message in Morse code is (· · · – – – · · ·), or SOS, the widely recognized distress call.

7. Apostrophes (links to exercise A, p. 267)

➜ another's,   Cryptoanalysts

Rewrite this paragraph, correcting errors in the use of apostrophes and possessive pronouns.

Its easy to make a simple cipher called a scytale, which was invented by the Spartan's in ancient Greece. To make you're own scytale, youll need a long strip of plain paper and a cylinder, such as a pencil or the cardboard tube from a paper-towel roll. Wrap the strip of paper in a spiral around the cylinder. Then begin writing your message along the length of the cylinder. Write each letter on a different part of the paper spiral. Dont use punctuation. When you reach the end of a line, continue writing on the next line until your message is complete. Now unroll the paper from the cylinder. It'll look like a long strip of letters in a single column. To read your message, the recipient must wrap the strip of paper around a cylinder of the same size that you used in writing the message. Whose going to read your message? Lysander, an ancient Greek military leader, once received a scytale and used the information in it to win an important battle for the Greek's.

8. Punctuating Titles (links to exercise A, p. 269)

➡ Polygraphia   The Journal of Cryptology

Read this paragraph and rewrite the titles in it, using either quotation marks or underlining as appropriate.

Countries have spied on each other for centuries. In China 2,500 years ago, Sun Zi described how to organize military intelligence in his book The Art of War. In his epic poem the Iliad, Homer discussed spying during the Trojan War. Spying helped the Allies win World War II, as William Stevenson explains in his book A Man Called Intrepid. Codebreaking helped the Allies sink the German battleship *Bismarck*. Broadcast over the BBC, the first lines of Paul Verlaine's poem Chanson d'Automne warned the French Resistance that the Normandy invasion was imminent. Shortly after the war, an American engineer developed information theory in an article called A Mathematical Theory of Communication. Even works of entertainment, like the 1960s TV show Secret Agent, have depicted the pressures of being a spy who can trust no one. Johnny Rivers sang about this dangerous life in the show's theme song, Secret Agent Man. Contemporary movies, such as Mission Impossible and Tomorrow Never Dies, still thrill audiences with their tales of espionage.

Model Bank

Book Review

I enjoyed reading *Roll of Thunder, Hear My Cry* by Mildred D. Taylor even though a lot of it is very sad and some parts of it made me angry. The story is about a black family during the Great Depression. The kids and adults in the family suffer different kinds of discrimination through the course of the book. Sometimes they just have to deal with insulting things like having to wait in stores until the white people have been helped. At other times, the discrimination happens in much more violent ways, like people being burned or lynched.

There is some justice for the characters, though. My favorite scene is when the kids get sick of the school bus driver constantly speeding too close to them and running them off the road as they walk to school. They skip lunch and dig a huge hole on the road that wrecks the bus.

For me, the book is so effective because it is told by Cassie, who is in the first grade and is experiencing most of this racism for the first time. She is just discovering that by being black she is considered to be very different from white people. She gets angry when white people treat her as though she doesn't matter just because she's black. She doesn't know why that should make any difference.

Since I have not experienced racism firsthand, my point of view is similar to Cassie's. I hear a lot about racism on the news and in school, but reading this book from Cassie's point of view made it all very clear and made it feel personal. I felt like Cassie, seeing for the first time the way the world is, and not being able to do anything about it.

RUBRIC IN ACTION

❶ Clearly identifies the book and author and tells something about the story

❷ Gives specific examples to support a point

❸ Explains why the book was effective

❹ Sums up this writer's feeling about the book

Editorial

The Board of Education announced this week that starting next September, this school would be in session year-round. As expected, the moan of the student body could be heard throughout the building. Kids argued that having school all year, especially in the summer, was inhuman.

❶ Clearly identifies the topic of the editorial

This reaction is understandable, but it's probably based more on gut feeling than on the facts. The problem is that when most students hear the words "school all year," the first idea they get is that it means no summer vacation. This simply isn't true.

❷ Answers a major objection to the new schedule

The new schedule calls for three solid months of school at a time, followed by a one-month break. There are really many advantages to this schedule over the traditional one, if students will stop and think about it.

If students were to be completely honest with themselves, they would have to admit that a three-month summer break can get very long and very boring after awhile. With the new schedule, the three-month summer break will be broken up so that there will be one month-long break in March, one in July, and another in November. These breaks will be long enough to allow for trips as well as relaxation at home, but won't be so long that kids will start to get antsy and bored.

❸ Provides information and examples to support this writer's position

There also won't be the endless tunnel of school. When kids get back to school they can say, "Just three months of this and then another month off!"

So, kids don't need to worry about there being no summer vacation. This new schedule could make the year go a lot faster and strike a nice balance between school and vacation. Students should give it a chance and consider the possibilities the new schedule has to offer. Who knows? They may just love it.

❹ Summarizes her position and uses examples to argue her ideas

Business Letter

180 Nemic Street
Boston, MA 02118

April 7, 2001

❶ Sender's address and date

Joe Naglar
PBG Music Club
1 Beach Place
Stamford, CT 06904

❷ Addresses a specific person

Dear Mr. Naglar:

 I'm writing to ask you about five CDs I ordered but never received. I ordered these selections over four months ago. My parents' credit card has been charged for them, but they still have not arrived.

❸ Explains the complaint

 If there is some problem with the availability of these selections, or some other problem with my order, please let me know. As it is now, it looks like I've been charged for things I never received and then I've been forgotten about.

 I hope that whatever the problem was, it has been cleared up and that I will soon receive my CDs, or that my parents' card will be credited.

❹ Asks for specific action

Sincerely,

Charles Terhune

Charles Terhune

❺ Signature above the typed name

Problem-Solution Essay

RUBRIC
IN ACTION

The talk around school lately has been the problem students are having with their lockers. They are so narrow that most students find them much too small to hold their coats along with their binders and books. Also, they are so close together that kids almost have to wait in line to get to their lockers. This causes many kids to be late for class.

❶ This writer clearly identifies the problem.

Principal Sayre has been aware of this problem and is trying to solve it. She says that the main difficulty is obvious: If the school installed wider lockers, they would take up more room and there wouldn't be enough space to have a locker for each student.

❷ Gives an answer to the problem that reveals another problem

My solution to this problem is just as obvious. Currently there are only lockers in the halls of the main building. The music building, however, has no lockers in its halls. The belief is that kids wouldn't want to go outside and walk all the way over to the music building just to get their things. This aspect of the problem could be made easier by assigning the music building lockers to kids who have regular music or drama classes. They would be spending a good part of the day over there anyway, so it wouldn't be such a hassle for them.

❸ Provides a solution and explains why it would work

Since solving the problem is not a matter of money, but of space, we students should work hard to make this compromise. True, it seems like a hassle for some kids to have to walk to the music building to get their things, but other schools in the area have similar setups and their students don't even seem to notice a problem. And really which is worse, having to walk an extra fifty yards to get to your big, roomy, accessible locker, or being late for class because you couldn't get to your narrow, cramped, and crowded locker?

❹ Offers more support for his solution and appeals to the readers' desire for bigger lockers

Process Description

In our science lab this week, we performed an experiment to discover the mechanical advantages of an inclined plane. The materials we used were a wooden board with a pulley at one end, seven textbooks, a spring scale, three feet of string, and a ruler.

❶ Identifies the purpose of the experiment and names the materials needed

We began by setting up our materials for the experiment.

First, we made a stack of six books. Then we rested one end of the board, the end with the pulley, on the stack. We let the other end rest on the table, making a ramp. The first illustration on the right shows these steps.

❷ Gives a step-by-step sequence to prepare for the experiment and indicates an illustration

Then we tied one end of the string around another book and tied the other end to the spring scale. Suspending the book from the spring scale we found the weight of the book. We recorded the weight on a chart as the resistance force.

Next, we measured the height of the stack of books and recorded this as the resistance distance. We then measured the length of the board to find the effort distance.

Now that our materials were set up, we were ready to perform the experiment.

❸ Uses a transition sentence to move to the next part of the sequence

First, we rested the book at the bottom of the inclined board and ran the string over the pulley at the top of the board.

Next, we held the spring scale and slowly pulled the book up the board. As we did, we noted the measurement on the spring scale and recorded that as the effort force.

❹ Identifies each step in the experiment, using transition words and phrases

Next, we removed three of the books from the stack to lower the incline. We measured this new height and recorded this new resistance distance down in our chart. The second illustration shows this setup.

We pulled the book up the incline again and recorded the new effort force from the spring scale.

When both of these experiments were complete, we compared all our data. We learned that the mechanical advantage increased as the height of the incline decreased.

❺ Ends by giving the results of the experiment

Illustration 1

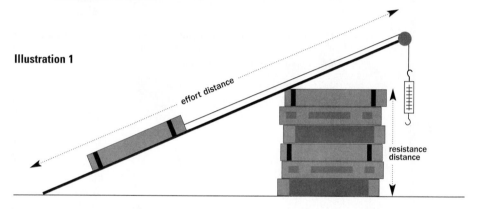

effort distance

resistance distance

Illustration 2

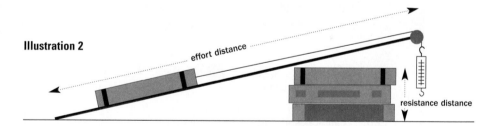

effort distance

resistance distance

Quick-Fix Spelling Machine

QUICK–FIX SPELLING MACHINE: PLURALS OF NOUNS

SINGULAR	RULE	PLURAL
skateboard painting ticket	Add -s to most nouns.	skateboards paintings tickets

WATCH OUT The exceptions to this rule are nouns whose plurals are formed in special ways such as *man (men)*, *woman (women)* and *child (children)*.

SINGULAR	RULE	PLURAL
hiss dish ditch box buzz	Add -es to nouns that end in *s, sh, ch, x,* or *z.*	hisses dishes ditches boxes buzzes
auto igloo radio	Add -s to most nouns that end in *o.*	autos igloos radios
potato tomato mosquito	Add -es to a few nouns that end in *o.*	potatoes tomatoes mosquitoes
flurry deputy battery dairy	For most nouns ending in *y,* change the *y* to *i* and add -es.	flurries deputies batteries dairies
alley play turkey	Just add -s when a vowel comes before the *y.*	alleys plays turkeys
calf thief wife leaf knife	For most nouns ending in *f* or *fe,* change the *f* to a *v* and add -es or -s.	calves thieves wives leaves knives
belief muff safe	Just add -s to a few nouns that end in *f* or *fe.*	beliefs muffs safes
series sheep species aircraft	Keep the same spelling for some nouns.	series sheep species aircraft

QUICK–FIX SPELLING MACHINE: POSSESSIVES

NOUN	RULE	POSSESSIVE
moon	Add an apostrophe and -s to a singular noun.	moon's light
student		student's locker
club		club's president
restaurant		restaurant's menu
school		school's teachers
bank		bank's assets
college		college's facilities
dog		dog's fur
garden		garden's scents
catalog		catalog's merchandise
museum		museum's exhibit
flower		flower's fragrance
book		book's cover
holiday		holiday's traditions
turkey		turkey's drumstick

The exception to this rule is that the *s* after the apostrophe is dropped after *Jesus'*, *Moses'*, and certain names in classical mythology. Dropping the -*s* makes these possessive forms easier to pronounce.

NOUN	RULE	POSSESSIVE
x-rays	Add an apostrophe to a plural noun that ends in *s*.	x-rays' envelopes
organizations		organizations' budgets
teams		teams' coaches
buildings		buildings' windows
cities		cities' mayors
airports		airports' schedules
babies		babies' toys
groceries		groceries' prices
violets		violets' buds
necklaces		necklaces' clasps
butterflies		butterflies' wings

NOUN	RULE	POSSESSIVE
deer	Add an apostrophe and -*s* to a plural noun not ending in *s*.	deer's hoofs
oxen		oxen's load
salmon		salmon's gills
stepchildren		stepchildren's names
sheep		sheep's wool
mice		mice's nests
people		people's languages

SPELLING

QUICK–FIX SPELLING MACHINE: WORDS ENDING IN SILENT e

WORD	RULE	CHANGE
home engage hope tune shame state	Keep the silent *e* when a suffix beginning with a consonant is added to a word that ends in a silent *e*.	homeless engagement hopeful tuneless shameful statement

WATCH OUT Some words that are exceptions include *truly, awful, argument, ninth,* and *wholly.*

| peace
courage
manage
salvage
outrage
charge | Keep the silent *e* when a suffix beginning with an *a* or an *o* is added to a silent *e* word if the *e* follows a soft *c* or *g*. | peaceable
courageous
manageably
salvageable
outrageous
chargeable |

| agree
woe | Keep the silent *e* when a suffix beginning with a vowel is added to a word ending in *ee* or *oe*. | agreeable
woeful |

| flake
elevate
haze
institute
shake
create | Drop the silent *e* from the base word when you add a suffix beginning with *y* or a vowel. | flaky
elevation
hazy
institution
shaky
creative |

WATCH OUT Exceptions to this rule are such words as *changeable* and *courageous.*

QUICK–FIX SPELLING MACHINE: WORDS ENDING IN *y*

WORD	RULE	CHANGE
happy thirty merry greedy sneaky deputy	Change the *y* to *i* to add a suffix to a word ending in *y* if the *y* follows a consonant.	happiness thirtieth merriest greedily sneakier deputies
rally marry tally fry	Keep the *y* when adding *-ing* to a word ending in *y* if the *y* follows a consonant.	rallying marrying tallying frying
joy pay boy	Keep the *y* when adding a suffix to a word ending in a vowel and *y*.	joyous payable boyish

QUICK–FIX SPELLING MACHINE: WORDS ENDING IN A CONSONANT

WORD	RULE	CHANGE
mat slip hit dim	If a one-syllable word ends in a consonant preceded by a vowel, double the final consonant before adding a suffix beginning with a vowel.	matting slipped hitter dimmest
heap steal scoot meat	If a one-syllable word ends in a consonant preceded by two vowels, do not double the final consonant.	heaped stealing scooted meaty
transfer admit allot permit	Double the final consonant in a word of more than one syllable only if the word is accented on the last syllable.	transferring admitted allotting permitting

SPELLING

QUICK-FIX SPELLING MACHINE: ADVERBS

ADJECTIVE	RULE	ADVERB
sudden bad rapid	Add *-ly*.	suddenly badly rapidly
true	Drop *e*, add *-ly*.	truly
angry heavy steady	Change *y* to *i*, add *-ly*.	angrily heavily steadily

QUICK-FIX SPELLING MACHINE: COMPOUNDS

	SINGULAR	RULE	PLURAL
One word	dishcloth supermarket airport	Add *-s* to most words.	dishcloths supermarkets airports
Two or more words	feather bed atomic bomb attorney general	Make the main noun plural. The main noun is the noun that is modified.	feather beds atomic bombs attorneys general
Hyphenated words	son-in-law half-dollar vice-president	Make the main noun plural.	sons-in-law half-dollars vice-presidents

QUICK-FIX SPELLING MACHINE: OPEN AND CLOSED SYLLABLES

An *open syllable* ends in one vowel and has a long vowel sound.	baby labor fable cedar	ba by la bor fa ble ce dar
A *closed syllable* ends in a consonant and has a short vowel sound.	ladder mischief problem plunder	lad der mis chief prob lem plun der

QUICK-FIX SPELLING MACHINE: CONTRACTIONS

WORDS	RULE	CONTRACTION
I am	Combine a personal pronoun with a verb by adding an apostrophe in place of the missing letters.	I'm
you are		you're
he is		he's
she is		she's
it is		it's
we are		we're
they are		they're
I would		I'd
you would		you'd
he would		he'd
she would		she'd
we would		we'd
they would		they'd
I will		I'll
you will		you'll
he will		he'll
she will		she'll
it will		it'll
we will		we'll
they will		they'll
I have		I've
you have		you've
we have		we've
they have		they've
I had		I'd
you had		you'd
he had		he'd
she had		she'd
we had		we'd
they had		they'd
do not	Otherwise, combine two words into one by adding an apostrophe in place of the missing letters.	don't
where is		where's
there is		there's
could not		couldn't
would not		wouldn't
should not		shouldn't
is not		isn't
was not		wasn't
who is		who's

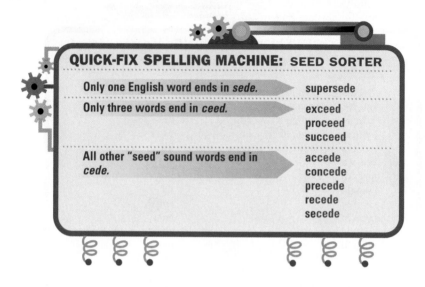

QUICK-FIX SPELLING MACHINE: SEED SORTER

Only one English word ends in *sede*.	supersede
Only three words end in *ceed*.	exceed proceed succeed
All other "seed" sound words end in *cede*.	accede concede precede recede secede

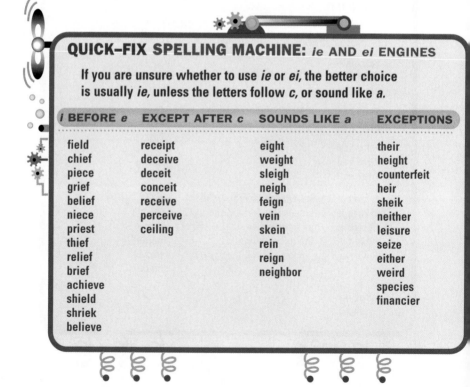

QUICK-FIX SPELLING MACHINE: *ie* AND *ei* ENGINES

If you are unsure whether to use *ie* or *ei*, the better choice is usually *ie*, unless the letters follow *c*, or sound like *a*.

i BEFORE *e*	EXCEPT AFTER *c*	SOUNDS LIKE *a*	EXCEPTIONS
field	receipt	eight	their
chief	deceive	weight	height
piece	deceit	sleigh	counterfeit
grief	conceit	neigh	heir
belief	receive	feign	sheik
niece	perceive	vein	neither
priest	ceiling	skein	leisure
thief		rein	seize
relief		reign	either
brief		neighbor	weird
achieve			species
shield			financier
shriek			
believe			

QUICK-FIX SPELLING MACHINE: BORROWED WORDS

Over the centuries, as English speakers increased their contact with people from other lands, English speakers "borrowed" words from other languages. The English language began to grow in new directions, and became the colorful tapestry we know today.

Spelling follows certain patterns in every language. For example, some letter patterns in French, Spanish, and Italian appear in words commonly used in English.

PATTERN	WORD

Some borrowed words keep their original spellings and pronunciations.

PATTERN	WORD
In many words taken from French, a final *t* is silent.	ballet beret buffet
In both English and French, a soft *g* is usually followed by *e, i,* or *y*.	mirage region energy
A hard *g* is followed by *a, o,* or *u*.	vague
Many words taken from the Dutch language have *oo* in their spellings.	cookie snoop hook caboose
Many words borrowed from Spanish end in *o*.	taco tornado rodeo bronco
Many words that were plural in Italian end in *i*.	spaghetti macaroni ravioli

Some words from other languages were changed to fit English rules of pronunciation and spelling.

Many words in Native American languages contain sound combinations unlike those in English words. English speakers found these words to be useful but difficult to pronounce, so they used more familiar sounds and letter combinations.	topaghan = toboggan tamahaac = tomahawk pakani = pecan squa = squaw wampumpeag = wampum qajaq = kayak

Commonly Misspelled Words

A
abbreviate
accidentally
achievement
analyze
anonymous
answer
apologize
appearance
appreciate
appropriate
argument
awkward

B
beautiful
because
beginning
believe
bicycle
brief
bulletin
business

C
calendar
campaign
candidate
caught
certain
changeable
characteristic
clothes
column

committee
courageous
courteous
criticize
curiosity

D
decision
definitely
dependent
description
desirable
despair
desperate
development
dictionary
different
disappear
disappoint
discipline
dissatisfied

E
eighth
eligible
eliminate
embarrass
enthusiastic
especially
essay
exaggerate
exceed
existence
experience

F
familiar
fascinating
favorite
February
foreign
fourth
fragile

G
generally
government
grammar
guarantee
guard

H
height
humorous

I
immediately
independent
irritable

J, K, L
judgment
knowledge
laboratory
library
license
lightning

literature
loneliness

M
mathematics
minimum
mischievous

N
necessary
nickel
ninety
noticeable
nuclear
nuisance

O
obstacle
occasionally
once
opinion
opportunity
outrageous

P
parallel
particularly
people
permanent
persuade
pleasant
pneumonia

possess
possibility
prejudice
principal
privilege
probably
psychology
pursue

R
realize
receipt
receive
recognize
recommend
reference
rehearse
repetition
restaurant
rhythm
ridiculous

S
sandwich
schedule
scissors
separate
sergeant
similar
sincerely
souvenir
specifically
strategy
success
surprise
syllable
sympathy
symptom

T
temperature
thorough
throughout
tomorrow
traffic
tragedy
transferred
truly
Tuesday
twelfth

U
unnecessary
usable

V
vacuum
vicinity
village

W
weird

Commonly Confused Words

Good writers master words that are easy to misuse and misspell. Study the following words, noting how their meanings differ.

accept, except *Accept* means "to agree to something" or "to receive something willingly." *Except* usually means "not including."
Did the teacher *accept* **your report?**
Everyone smiled for the photographer *except* **Jody.**

advice, advise *Advice* is a noun that means "counsel given to someone." *Advise* is a verb that means "to give counsel."
Jim should take some of his own *advice.*
The mechanic *advised* **me to get new brakes for my car.**

affect, effect *Affect* means "to move or influence" or "to wear or to pretend to have." *Effect* as a verb means "to bring about." As a noun, *effect* means "the result of an action."
The news from South Africa *affected* **him deeply.**
The band's singer *affects* **a British accent.**
The students tried to *effect* **a change in school policy.**
What *effect* **did the acidic soil produce in the plants?**

all ready, already *All ready* means "all are ready" or "completely prepared." *Already* means "previously."
The students were *all ready* **for the field trip.**
We had *already* **pitched our tent before it started raining.**

all right *All right* is the correct spelling. *Alright* is nonstandard and should not be used.

a lot *A lot* may be used in informal writing. *Alot* is incorrect.

borrow, lend *Borrow* means "to receive something on loan." *Lend* means "to give out temporarily."
Please *lend* **me your book.**
He *borrowed* **five dollars from his sister.**

bring, take *Bring* refers to movement toward or with. *Take* refers to movement away from.
I'll *bring* **you a glass of water.**
Would you please *take* **these apples to Pam and John?**

can, may *Can* means "to be able," or "to have the power to." *May* means "to have permission to." *May* can also mean "possibly will."

We *may* **not use pesticides on our community garden.**
Pesticides *may* **not be necessary, anyway.**
Vegetables *can* **grow nicely without pesticides.**

capital, capitol, the Capitol
Capital means "excellent," "most serious," or "most important." It also means "seat of government." A *capitol* is a building in which a state legislature meets. *The Capitol* is the building in Washington, D.C., in which the U.S. Congress meets.
Going to the beach is a *capital* **idea.**
Is Madison the *capital* **of Wisconsin?**
Protesters rallied at the state *capitol.*
A subway connects the Senate and the House in *the Capitol.*

desert, dessert
Desert (des´ ert) means "a dry, sandy, barren region." *Desert* (de sert´) means "to abandon." *Dessert* (des sert´) is a sweet, such as cake.
The Sahara in North Africa is the world's largest *desert.*
The night guard did not *desert* **his post.**
Alison's favorite *dessert* **is chocolate cake.**

fewer, less
Fewer refers to numbers of things that can be counted. *Less* refers to amount, degree, or value.
Fewer **than ten students camped out.**
We made *less* **money this year on the walkathon than last year.**

good, well
Good is always an adjective. *Well* is usually an adverb that modifies an action verb. *Well* can also be an adjective meaning "in good health."
Dana felt *good* **when she finished painting her room.**
Angela ran *well* **in yesterday's race.**
I felt *well* **when I left my house.**

its, it's
Its is a possessive pronoun. *It's* is a contraction for *it is* or *it has.*
Sanibel Island is known for *its* **beautiful beaches.**
It's **great weather for a picnic.**

lay, lie
Lay is a verb that means "to place." It takes a direct object. *Lie* is a verb that means "to be in a certain place." *Lie,* or its past form *lay,* never takes a direct object.
The carpenter will *lay* **the planks on the bench.**
My cat likes to *lie* **under the bed.**

lead, led *Lead* can be a noun that means "a heavy metal" or a verb that means "to show the way." *Led* is the past tense form of the verb.

Lead is used in nuclear reactors.
Raul always *leads* his team onto the field.
She *led* the class as president of the student council.

learn, teach *Learn* means "to gain knowledge." *Teach* means "to instruct."

Enrique is *learning* about black holes in space.
Marva *teaches* astronomy at a college in the city.

leave, let *Leave* means "to go away from" or "to allow to remain." *Leave* can be transitive or intransitive. *Let* is usually used with another verb. It means "to allow to."

Don't *leave* the refrigerator open.
She *leaves* for Scotland tomorrow.
Cyclops wouldn't *let* Odysseus' men *leave* the cave.

like *Like* used as a conjunction before a clause is incorrect. Use *as* or *as if*.

Ramon talked *as if* he had a cold.

lose, loose *Lose* means "to mislay or suffer the loss of something." *Loose* means "free" or "not fastened."

That tire will *lose* air unless you patch it.
My little brother has three *loose* teeth.

passed, past *Passed* is the past tense of *pass* and means "went by." *Past* is an adjective that means "of a former time." *Past* is also a noun that means "time gone by."

We *passed* through the Florida Keys during our vacation.
My *past* experiences have taught me to set my alarm.
Ebenezer Scrooge is a character who relives his *past*.

peace, piece *Peace* means "a state of calm or quiet." *Piece* means "a section or part of something."

Sitting still can bring a sense of *peace*.
Here's another *piece* of the puzzle.

principal, principle *Principal* means "of chief or central importance" or refers to the head of a school. *Principle* means "a basic truth, standard, or rule of behavior."

Lack of customers is the *principal* reason for closing the store.
The *principal* of our school awarded the trophy.
One of my *principles* is to be honest with others.

raise, rise	*Raise* means "to lift" or "to make something go up." It takes a direct object. *Rise* means "to go upward." It does not take a direct object.
	The maintenance workers *raise* the flag each morning.
	The city's population is expected to *rise* steadily.
set, sit	*Set* means "to place" and takes a direct object. *Sit* means "to occupy a seat or a place" and does not take a direct object.
	He *set* the box down outside the shed.
	We *sit* in the last row of the upper balcony.
stationary, stationery	*Stationary* means "fixed or unmoving." *Stationery* means "fine paper for writing letters."
	The wheel pivots, but the seat is *stationary.*
	Rex wrote on special *stationery* imprinted with his name.
than, then	*Than* is used to introduce the second part of a comparison. *Then* means "next in order."
	Ramon is stronger *than* Mark.
	Cut the grass and *then* trim the hedges.
their, there, they're	*Their* means "belonging to them." *There* means "in that place." *They're* is the contraction for *they are.*
	All the campers returned to *their* cabins.
	I keep my card collection *there* in those folders.
	Lisa and Beth run daily; *they're* on the track team.
to, too, two	*To* means "toward" or "in the direction of." *Too* means "also" or "very." *Two* is the number 2.
	We went *to* the mall.
	It's *too* risky riding without a helmet.
	***Two* amusement parks are offering reduced rates for admission.**
whose, who's	*Whose* is the possessive form of *who. Who's* is a contraction of *who is* or *who has.*
	***Whose* parents will drive us to the movies?**
	***Who's* going to the recycling center?**
your, you're	*Your* is the possessive form of *you. You're* is a contraction of *you are.*
	What was *your* record in the fifty-yard dash?
	***You're* one of the winners of the essay contest.**

MLA Citation Guidelines

Forms for Source Cards and Works Cited Entries

The following examples show some basic forms of bibliographic entries for research sources. Use these forms on source cards for your working bibliography and in the list of works cited at the end of your report.

Whole Books

The following models can also be used for citing reports and pamphlets.

A. One author

Blackwood, Gary. The Shakespeare Stealer. New York: Dutton, 1998.

B. Two authors

Cummings, Pat, and Linda Cummings. Talking with Adventurers. Washington: Natl. Geographic Soc., 1998.

C. Three authors

Silverstein, Alvin, Virginia Silverstein, and Laura Silverstein Nunn. The California Condor. Brookfield: Millbrook, 1998.

D. Four or more authors

The abbreviation *et al.* means "and others." Use *et al.* instead of listing all the authors.

Brown, Richard G., et al. Algebra 1: Explorations and Applications. Evanston: McDougal, 1998.

E. No author given

Webster's Word Histories. Springfield: Merriam, 1989.

F. An editor but no single author

Silverberg, Robert, ed. The Science Fiction Hall of Fame. Garden City: Doubleday, 1970.

G. Two or three editors

Colbert, Jan, and Ann McMillan Harms, eds. Dear Dr. King: Letters from Today's Children to Dr. Martin Luther King, Jr. New York: Hyperion, 1998.

H. An author and a translator

Pressler, Mirjam. Halinka. Trans. Elizabeth D. Crawford. New York: Holt, 1998.

I. An author, a translator, and an editor
Hugo, Victor. <u>The Hunchback of Notre-Dame</u>. Trans. Walter J.
 Cobb. Ed. Robin Waterfield. London: Penguin, 1996.

J. An edition other than the first
Gibaldi, Joseph. <u>MLA Handbook for Writers of Research Papers</u>.
 5th ed. New York: MLA, 1999.

K. A book or a monograph that is part of a series
Latta, Sara L. <u>Allergies</u>. Diseases and People. Springfield: Enslow,
 1998.

L. A multivolume work
If you have used only one volume of a multivolume work, cite only
that volume.

Gonen, Amiram, ed. <u>Peoples of the World: Customs and Cultures</u>.
 Vol. 3. Danbury: Grolier, 1998. 10 vols.

If you have used more than one volume of a multivolume work,
cite the entire work.

Gonen, Amiram, ed. <u>Peoples of the World: Customs and Cultures</u>.
 10 vols. Danbury: Grolier, 1998.

M. A volume with its own title that is part of a multivolume work with a different title
Dué, Andrea, ed. <u>The Modern World</u>. Danbury: Grolier, 1999. Vol.
 6 of <u>People and the Earth: An Environmental Atlas</u>. 6 vols.

N. A republished book or a literary work available in several editions
Give the date of the original publication after the title. Then give
complete publication information, including the date, for the
edition that you have used.

Lewis, C. S. <u>The Voyage of the Dawn Treader</u>. 1952. New York:
 Harper, 1994.

0. A government publication

Give the name of the government (country or state). Then give the department if applicable, followed by the agency if applicable. Next give the title, followed by the author if known. Then give the publication information. The publisher of U.S. government documents is usually the Government Printing Office, or GPO.

United States. Dept. of Health and Human Services. Natl. Center for Health Statistics. Health, United States, 1996–1997, and Injury Chartbook. Washington: GPO, 1997.

Parts of Books

A. A poem, a short story, an essay, or a chapter in a collection of works by one author

Wilder, Laura Ingalls. "Whom Will You Marry?" A Little House Reader: A Collection of Writings by Laura Ingalls Wilder. Ed. William Anderson. New York: Harper, 1998. 130–43.

B. A poem, a short story, an essay, or a chapter in a collection of works by several authors

Angelou, Maya. "Still I Rise." I, Too, Sing America: Three Centuries of African American Poetry. Ed. Catherine Clinton. Boston: Houghton, 1998. 107–08.

C. A novel or a play in an anthology

Stone, Peter. Titanic. The Best Plays of 1996–1997. Ed. Otis L. Guernsey, Jr. New York: Limelight-Proscenium, 1997. 157–89.

D. An introduction, a preface, a foreword, or an afterword written by the author(s) of a work

Bradbury, Ray. Afterword. Fahrenheit 451. By Bradbury. New York: Ballantine, 1982. 167–73.

E. An introduction, a preface, a foreword, or an afterword written by someone other than the author(s) of a work

Allende, Isabel. Foreword. Where Angels Glide at Dawn: New Stories from Latin America. Ed. Lori M. Carlson and Cynthia L. Ventura. New York: Lippincott, 1990. ix–xii.

Magazines, Journals, Newspapers, and Encyclopedias

A. An article in a magazine, a journal, or a newspaper

Allen, Jodie. "Working Out Welfare." Time 29 July 1996: 53–54.

Abelson, Philip H. "Preparing Children for the Future." Science 13 Dec. 1996: 1819.

Voedisch, Lynn. "Have You Done Your Homework Yet?" Chicago Tribune 9 Oct. 1997, sec. 5: 5.

Fintor, Lou. "Cancer Control Efforts Reach Out to 'Culturally Isolated.'" Journal of the National Cancer Institute 90 (1998): 1424–27.

B. An article in an encyclopedia or other alphabetically organized reference work

Give the title of the article, the name of the reference work, and the year of the edition.

"Sioux Indians." The World Book Encyclopedia. 1999 ed.

C. A review

Crain, Caleb. "There but for Fortune." Rev. of Hearts in Atlantis by Stephen King. New York Times Book Review 12 Sept. 1999: 10.

Miscellaneous Print and Nonprint Sources

A. An interview you have conducted or a letter you have received

Sosa, Sammy. Letter to the author [or Personal interview]. 20 Oct. 1998.

B. A film

Ever After Screenplay by Susannah Grant and Andy Tennant. Dir. Tennant. Perf. Drew Barrymore, Anjelica Huston, and Dougray Scott. 20th Century Fox, 1998.

C. A work of art (painting, photograph, sculpture)

Escher, M. C. Sky and Water I. National Gallery of Art, Washington.

D. A television or a radio program

Give the episode name (if applicable) and the series or program name. Include any information that you have about the program's writer and director. Then give the network, the local station, the city, and the date of the airing of the program.

"The Idol Maker." Narr. Vicki Mabrey. <u>60 Minutes II</u>. Prod. Aaron Wertheim. CBS. WBBM, Chicago. 29 Sept. 1999.

E. A musical composition

Mendelssohn, Felix. Symphony no.4 in A major, op.90.

F. A recording (compact disc, LP, or audiocassette)

If the recording is not a compact disc, include *LP* or *Audiocassette* before the manufacturer's name.

Johnson, James P. "Fascination." Perf. Marcus Roberts. <u>If I Could Be With You</u>. RCA, 1993.

Prado, Perez. "Mambo #8." <u>Que Rico Mambo</u>. Audiocassette. Rhino, 1989.

G. A lecture, a speech, or an address

Give the name of the speaker, followed by the name of the speech or the kind of speech (*Lecture, Introduction, Address*). Then give the event, the place, and the date.

Lowry, Lois. Speech. Newbery-Caldecott Awarda Banquet. ALA Annual Conference. Convention Center, Miami Beach, 26 June 1994.

Electronic Publications

The number of electronic information sources is great and increasing rapidly, so please refer to the most recent edition of the MLA Handbook for Writers of Research Papers *if you need more guidance. You can also refer to the page "MLA Style" at the Modern Language Association Web site <http://www.mla.org/>.*

Portable databases (CD-ROMs, DVDs, laserdiscs, diskettes, and videocassettes)

These products contain fixed information (information that cannot be changed unless a new version is produced and released). Citing them in a research paper is similar to citing printed sources. You should include the following information:

- Name of the author (if applicable)

- Title of the part of the work used (underlined or in quotation marks)
- Title of the product or the database (underlined)
- Publication medium (CD-ROM, DVD, laserdisc, diskette, or videocassette)
- Edition, release, or version if applicable
- City of publication
- Name of publisher
- Year of publication

If you cannot find some of this information, cite what is available.

Burke, James. "Yesterday, Tomorrow and You." <u>Connections</u>. Video. BBC. Prod. Ambrose, 1978.

<u>Antarctica</u>. Dir. John Weiley. 1991. DVD. Slingshot, 1999.

"Boston Tea Party." <u>Encarta 98 Encyclopedia</u>. CD-ROM. 1998 ed. Redmond: Microsoft, 1998.

<u>Nerds 2.0.1: A Brief History of the Internet</u>. Prod. Oregon. 3 videocassettes. PBS, 1998.

Online Sources

Sources on the World Wide Web are numerous and include scholarly projects, reference databases, articles in periodicals, and professional and personal sites. Not all sites are equally reliable, and therefore material cited from the World Wide Web should be evaluated carefully. Entries for online sources in the Works Cited list should contain as much of the information listed below as is available.

- Name of the author, editor, compiler, or translator, followed by an abbreviation such as *ed., comp.,* or *trans.* if appropriate
- Title of the material accessed. Use quotation marks for titles of poems, short stories, articles, and similar short works. Underline the title of a book.
- Publication information for any print version of the source
- Title (underlined) of the scholarly project, database, periodical, or professional or personal site. For a professional or personal site with no title, add a description such as *Home page* (neither underlined nor in quotation marks).
- Name of the editor of the scholarly project or database

- For a journal, the volume number, issue number, or other identifying number
- Date of electronic publication, of the latest update, or of posting
- For a work from a subscription service, list the name of the service and—if a library is the subscriber—the name of the library and the town or state where it is located.
- Range or total number of pages, paragraphs, or other sections if they are numbered
- Name of any institution or organization that sponsors or is associated with the Web site
- Date the source was accessed
- Electronic address, or URL, of the source. For a subscription service, use the URL of the service's main page (if known) or the keyword assigned by the service.

Scholarly project
Donlan, Leni, and Kathleen Ferenz. "Student page." America Dreams Through the Decades. 21 Feb. 1999. Lib. of Congress American Memory Fellows Program. 6 Oct. 1999 <http://www.internet-catalyst.org/projects/amproject/ student.html>.

Professional site
UNICEF. United Nations Children's Fund. 10 Oct. 1999 <http://www.unicef.org>.

Personal site
Tomarkin, Craig. "World Series History." 6 Feb. 1998. BaseballGuru.com 10 Oct. 1999 <http://members.aol.com/ thebbguru/baseball/bbws1.html>.

Book
Twain, Mark. The Adventures of Tom Sawyer. New York: Harper, 1903. The Electronic Text Center. Ed. David Seaman. Aug. 1993. U of Virginia Library. 10 Oct. 1999 <http://etext.lib.virginia.edu/etcbin/ toccer-new?id=Twa2Tom&tag=public&images=images/ modeng&data=/texts/english/modeng/parsed&part=0>.

Article in reference database
"Aztec." Encyclopedia.com. 1999. Infonautics Corp. 10 Oct. 1999 <http://www.encyclopedia.com>.

Article in journal

Kientzler, Alesha Lynne. "Fifth- and Seventh-Grade Girls' Decisions about Participation in Physical Activity." <u>Elementary School Journal</u> 99.5 (1999): 391-414. 15 Oct. 1999 <http://www.journals.uchicago.edu/ESJ>.

Article in magazine

Warrick, Joby. "Death in the Gulf of Mexico." <u>National Wildlife</u> June/July 1999. 11 Oct. 1999. <http://www.nwf.org/nwf/natlwild/1999/mexico.html>.

Work from a subscription service

"Glasnost." <u>Merriam-Webster Collegiate Dictionary</u>. 1996. America Online. 7 Oct. 1999. Keyword: Collegiate.

Glossary for Writers

Alliteration : the repetition of beginning sounds of words in poetry or prose; for example, the "c" sound in "creeping cat"

Allusion : a reference to a historical or literary person, place, event, or aspect of culture

Analogy : a comparison used to explain an idea or support an argument. For example, an analogy for how a government works might be how a family works.

Analysis : a way of thinking that involves taking apart, examining, and explaining a subject or an idea

Anecdote : a brief story told as an example to illustrate a point

Argument : speaking or writing that expresses a position or states an opinion with supporting evidence. An argument often takes into account other points of view.

Audience : one's readers or listeners

Autobiography : a biography (life story) told by the person whose life it is

Bias : a leaning toward one side in an argument; to be unbiased is to be neutral

Bibliography : a list of sources (articles, books, encyclopedias) in a paper or report, used to document research or to recommend further study

Body : the main part of a composition, in which its ideas are developed

Brainstorming : a way of generating ideas that involves quickly listing ideas as they occur, without stopping to judge them

Cause and Effect : the relationship between an event (the cause) and an event it helps to bring about (the effect)

Characterization : the way people (characters) are portrayed by an author

Chronological : organized according to time sequence

Clarity : the quality of being clear and easy to understand

Classification	a way of organizing information by grouping or categorizing items according to some system or principle
Cliché	an overused expression, such as "quiet as a mouse"
Clustering	a brainstorming technique that involves creating an idea or topic map made up of circled groupings of related details
Coherence	connectedness; a sense that parts hold together. A paragraph has coherence when its sentences flow logically from one to the next. A composition has coherence when its paragraphs are connected logically and linked by transitional words and phrases.
Collaboration	the act of working with other people on projects or to problem solve
Comparison and Contrast	a pattern of organization in which two or more things are related on the basis of similarities and differences
Conclusion	a judgment or a decision that is based on evidence, experience, and logical reasoning; also, the final section of a composition, which summarizes an argument or main idea, and points the reader toward action or further reflection
Connotation	an idea or feeling associated with a word, as opposed to the word's dictionary definition (denotation)
Context	the setting or situation in which something happens; the parts of a statement that occur just before and just after a specific word and help determine its meaning
Controversy	a disagreement, often one that has attracted public interest
Critical Thinking	what a writer *does* with information; thinking that goes beyond the facts to organize, analyze, evaluate, or draw conclusions about them
Criticism	an analysis (usually an essay) of something (usually a literary or artistic work) that evaluates how it does or does not succeed in communicating its meaning

Deductive Reasoning	the process of arriving at a specific conclusion by reasoning from a general premise or statement
Denotation	the dictionary definition of a word, as opposed to the ideas and feelings the word carries (connotation)
Descriptive Writing	an account of what it is like to experience some object, scene, or person; writing that usually gives one basic impression and emphasizes sensory detail
Dialect	a form of a language (usually regional) that has a distinctive pronunciation, vocabulary, and word order
Dialogue	spoken conversation of fictional characters or actual persons; the conversation in novels, stories, plays, poems, or essays
Documentation	the identification of documents or other sources used to support the information reported in an essay or other type of analysis; usually cited in footnotes or in parentheses
Editorial	an article in a publication or a commentary on radio or television expressing an opinion about a public issue
Elaboration	the support or development of a main idea with facts, statistics, sensory details, incidents, examples, quotations, or visual representations
Evaluation	writing that purposefully judges the worth, quality, or success of something
Expository Writing	writing that explains an idea or teaches a process; also called informative writing
Expressive	characterized by expression; refers to descriptive communication of ideas that are full of meaning or feeling, often used by writers in personal writing to explore ideas
Fiction	made-up or imaginary happenings as opposed to statements of fact or nonfiction. Short stories and novels are fiction, even though they may be based on real events; essays, scientific articles, biographies, and news stories are nonfiction.

Figurative Language	language that displays the imaginative and poetic use of words; writing that contains figures of speech such as simile, metaphor, and personification
Formal Language	language in which rules of grammar and vocabulary standards are carefully observed; used in textbooks, reports, and other formal communications
Freewriting	a way of exploring ideas, thoughts, or feelings that involves writing freely—without stopping or otherwise limiting the flow of ideas—for a specific length of time
Gender Free	refers to language that includes both men and women when making reference to a role or a group that consists of people of both sexes. "A medic uses his or her skills to save lives" and "Medics use their skills to save lives" are two gender-free ways of expressing the same idea.
Generalization	a statement expressing a principle or drawing a conclusion based on examples or instances
Graphic Device	a visual way of organizing information. Graphic devices include charts, graphs, outlines, and cluster diagrams.
Idea Tree	a graphic device in which main ideas are written on "branches" and related details are noted on "twigs"
Imagery	figurative language and descriptions used to produce mental images
Inductive Reasoning	a method of thinking or organizing in which a general conclusion is reached by reasoning from specific pieces of information
Inference	a logical guess that is based on observed facts and one's own knowledge and experience
Informative Writing	writing that explains an idea or teaches a process; also called expository writing
Interpretation	an explanation of the meaning of any text, set of facts, object, gesture, or event. To interpret something is to try to make sense of it.
Introduction	the opening section of a composition, which presents the main idea, grabs the reader's attention, and sets the tone

Invisible Writing	writing done with a dimmed computer screen or with an empty ballpoint pen on two sheets of paper with carbon paper between them
Irony	a figure of speech in which the intended meaning is the opposite of the stated meaning—saying one thing and meaning another
Jargon	the special language and terminology used by people in the same profession or with specialized interests
Journal	a record of thoughts and impressions, mainly for personal use
Learning Log	a kind of journal used for recording and reflecting on what one has learned and for noting problems and questions
Literary Analysis	critical thinking and writing about literature, presenting a personal perspective
Looping	a repetitive process for discovering ideas on a topic through freewriting, stopping to find promising ideas, freewriting about those ideas, and repeating the loop several times
Media	various forms of mass communication, such as newspapers, magazines, radio, television, and the Internet; the editorial voice and influence of all of these
Memoir	an account of true events told by a narrator who witnessed or participated in the events; usually focuses on the personalities and actions of persons other than the writer
Metaphor	a figure of speech that makes a comparison without using the word *like* or *as.* "All the world's a stage" is a metaphor.
Monologue	a speech by one person without interruption by other voices. A dramatic monologue reveals the personality and experience of a person through a long speech.
Mood	the feeling about a scene or a subject created by a writer's selection of words and details. The mood of a piece of writing may be suspenseful, mysterious, peaceful, fearful, and so on.

Narrative Writing	writing that tells a story—either made up or true. Some common types of narrative writing are biographies, short stories, and novels.
Onomatopoeia	the use of words (usually in poetry) to suggest sounds; examples are "the clinking of knives and forks," and "the hissing of the fans of the losing team."
Order of Degree	a pattern of organization in which ideas, people, places, or things are presented in rank order on the basis of quantity or extent. An example is listing items in order from most important to least important.
Paraphrase	a restatement in one's own words that stays true to the ideas, tone, and general length of the original passage
Parenthetical Documentation	the placement of citations or other documentation in parentheses within a report
Peer Response	suggestions and comments on a piece of writing, provided by peers or classmates
Personal Writing	writing that focuses on expressing the writer's own thoughts, experiences, and feelings
Personification	a figure of speech in which an object, event, abstract idea, or animal is given human characteristics
Persuasive Writing	writing that is intended to convince the reader to believe a particular point of view or to follow a course of action
Plagiarism	the act of dishonestly presenting someone else's words or ideas as one's own
Point of View	the angle from which a story is told, such as first-, second-, or third-person point of view
Portfolio	a container (usually a folder) for notes on work in progress, drafts and revisions, finished pieces, and peer responses
Proofreading	the act of checking work to discover typographical and other errors; usually the last stage of the revising or editing process
Propaganda	any form of communication aimed at persuading an audience, often containing false or misleading information; usually refers to manipulative political material

Prose	the usual language of speech and writing, lacking the characteristics of poetry; any language that is not poetry
Sensory Details	words that appeal to any of the five senses—the way something looks, sounds, smells, tastes, or feels
Sequential Order	a pattern of organization in which events are presented in the order in which they occur, as in telling a story chronologically or describing the sequence of steps in a process
Simile	a figure of speech that uses the word *like* or *as* to make a comparison. "Trees like pencil strokes" is a simile.
Spatial Order	a pattern of organization in which details are arranged in the order that they appear in space, such as from left to right
Style	the distinctive features of a literary or artistic work that collectively characterize a work of a particular individual, group, period, or school
Summary	a brief restatement of the main idea of a passage
Symbol	something (word, object, or action) that stands for or suggests something else. For example, a flag can stand for or symbolize a nation; a withered plant may suggest or symbolize a failing relationship.
Theme	the central idea or message of a work of literature
Thesis Statement	a statement in one or two sentences of the main idea or purpose of a piece of writing
Tone	a writer's attitude or manner of expression—detached, ironic, serious, or angry, for example
Topic Sentence	a sentence that expresses the main idea of a paragraph
Transition	a connecting word or phrase that clarifies relationships between details, sentences, or paragraphs
Tree Diagram	a graphic way of showing the relationships among ideas; particularly useful in generating ideas; also known as an idea tree or spider map
Trite Phrase	an overused phrase whose use suggests a lack of imagination on the part of the user

Unity   a quality of oneness. A paragraph has unity if all its sentences support the same main idea or purpose; a composition has unity if all its paragraphs support the thesis statement.

Venn Diagram   a way of visually representing the relationship between two items that are distinct but that have common or overlapping elements

Voice   an expression of a writer's personality through such stylistic elements as word choice and tone

Index

A

A, 127, 485
Abbreviations
  capitalization in titles, 230
  capitalization of time, 240
  periods with, 251
Abstract nouns, 37
Action verbs, 10
  complements required by, 23–24,
    95–98
  transitive and intransitive, 96
Active listening, 538–540
  evaluating content and delivery,
    540
  for information, 539
  reasons for, 538
Active reading strategies, 508–509
A.D.
  capitalization of, 240
  periods with, 240
Addresses
  commas in, 56
  periods with abbreviations in, 251
Adjective clauses, 196, 198, 205
Adjective phrases, as prepositional
  phrases, 167
Adjectives, 126–132, 137–141,
  144, 145, 148, 149
  adverbs confused with, 140–141,
    149
  adverbs formed from, 135, 632
  adverbs modifying, 134
  articles, 127
  commas between two or more,
    254
  comparatives and superlatives,
    137–139, 149, 293
  demonstrative pronouns as, 131,
    148

in description, 144–145
for expressing feeling and adding
  detail, 126, 128, 144–145
indefinite pronouns used as, 131
nouns used as, 132, 148
other parts of speech used as,
  131–133, 148
possessive pronouns used as,
  131, 132, 148
predicate, 28, 129–130
pronouns used as, 131, 132, 148
proper, 127
Adverb clauses, 196–197
  function of, 205
Adverb phrases, as prepositional
  phrases, 167
Adverbs, 134–136, 137–139,
  140–141, 144–145, 148, 149
  adjectives confused with,
    140–141, 149
  adverbs modifying, 134
  comparatives and superlatives,
    137–139, 149, 293
  comparisons, irregular, 138
  comparisons, regular, 137–138
  forming from adjectives, 135, 632
  intensifiers, 134–135
  -ly ending of, 135, 632
  position of, 134
  prepositions used as, 153
Advertisements, 532–533, 558,
  559–560
Agreement. *See* Pronoun-antecedent
  agreement; Subject-verb
  agreement.
Airplane names, capitalization of,
  238
Alphabetic order, for works cited list,
  485

source cards for, 479

Brainstorming, 311, 417. *See also* Ideas; Prewriting

in topic selection, 311, 417

Brand names, capitalization of, 241

Bridge names, capitalization of, 238

Building names, capitalization of, 238, 246

Business letters. *See* Letters (documents)

But

comma with, 204, 253

as coordinating conjunction, 14, 158, 204

C

Calendar items, capitalization of, 240, 246

Call numbers, 495, 496

Can, may, 116

Capitalization, 228–247

abbreviations, 230, 240

airplane names, 238

automobile names, 238

awards, 241, 246

bodies of the universe, 237

brand names, 241

bridge names, 238

building names, 238, 246

calendar items, 240, 246

checking during editing, 244

closing of letters, 234, 236

days of the week, 240, 246

deities, 231

ethnic groups, 232

family relationships, 231, 246, 247

first words, 233, 234–235, 246, 247

geographical directions, 238

geographical names, 237, 246

historical documents, 240

historical events, 240, 246

historical periods, 240

holidays, 240, 246

institution names, 240

landmarks, 238

languages, 232

letters (documents), 234

months, 240, 246

names and initials, 36, 230, 246

nationalities, 232

nouns, 36, 51, 127, 230, 232, 246

organization names, 240–241

outlines, 234, 236

parts of a letter, 234

personal titles and abbreviations, 230

place names, 237, 246

planets, 237

poetry, 233, 234, 246, 247

pronoun *I*, 231

proper adjectives, 232

proper nouns, 36, 51, 127, 230, 232, 246

and quotation marks in dialogue, 233, 259

quotations, 233, 259

races, 232

regions, 237, 238

religions and religious terms, 231

salutations (openings) of letters, 234, 236

sentences, 233, 246

ships, 238

special events, 241, 246–247

time abbreviations, 240

titles of works, 234–235, 244, 246, 247

train names, 238

transportation vehicle names, 238

Case, of pronouns, 58, 88, 291

checking during editing, 426

Cause-and-effect essay, writing workshop for, 438–445

Cause-and-effect order

for composition organization, 369

for paragraph organization, 356–357, 360–361

transitional words and phrases for, 356–357, 361, 373

Cause-and-effect relationships, 525, 531

CD-ROMs, as reference works, 479
CDs
    italics for titles of, 268
    for sound effects, 546
Chapter titles, quotation marks for, 268
Character description, writing workshop for, 422–448
Charts. *See also* Graphics; Visual aids
    for elaboration, 382–383, 385
    reading and analyzing, 508–509
Chronological order
    for composition organization, 369
    for paragraph organization, 352–353, 360–361
    for personal narrative, 414
    transition words and phrases for, 353, 361
Circular reasoning, 530–531
Cities
    capitalization of, 237
    comma separating from state, province, or county, 256
Clarity
    for effective language, 404–405, 410
    organizing for, 352–353, 360
Clauses, 186–205. *See also* Independent clauses; Subordinate (dependent) clauses
    punctuating, 204
    types of, 186–188, 196–199, 204–205
Clichés, 301, 409, 411
Closing of a letter, 234, 256
Cluster diagram, for narrowing topic, 312
Coherence
    of compositions, 369
    of paragraphs, 340, 343, 348
Collaboration, 311, 543–544. *See also* Peer response
Collective nouns, 37, 38
    subject-verb agreement with, 216, 226

Colons, 262–263
    between hours and minutes, 263
    for introducing a list, 262
    after salutation of business letter, 263
Commands, 18, 397. *See also* Imperative sentences
Commas, 253–257, 295
    in addresses, 256
    between adjectives, 254
    with appositives, 255, 295
    between city and state, 256
    in compound sentences, 26, 189, 204, 253, 295
    before a coordinating conjunction, 26, 189, 204, 253
    in dates, 256
    with direct address, 254
    between independent clauses, 26, 204, 253
    with interrupters, 254
    with introductory elements, 254, 295
    in letters, 256
    with names, 254
    with nonessential adjective clauses, 204, 295
    in place names, 256
    with quotation marks, 258, 295
    with quotations, 258, 259, 295
    in series, 253, 295
    to avoid confusion, 255
    with *who, that,* and *which,* 295, 334–335, 337
Comma splices, 26, 287
Common nouns, 36, 37, 51, 247
Comparative degree, 137–139, 149, 293
Compare-and-contrast order
    for composition organization, 369
    for paragraph organization, 358–359
    transitional words and phrases for, 358, 361, 373
Comparison-contrast essay, writing workshop for, 446–453

INDEX

in poetry interpretation, 436
  quotation marks with, 258, 275
  in research reports, 481
Discovery drafting, 315
Discussions, in groups, 543, 544
Divided quotations
  capitalization in, 233, 259
  quotation marks for, 259
Do, as helping verb, 12, 93
Documentation, for research reports,
    484–485. *See also* MLA
    citation guidelines
Doesn't, don't, subject-verb
    agreement with, 209
Double comparisons, 149
Double negatives, 142–143, 149
Drafting, 315–319. *See also*
    Compositions
  of cause-and-effect essay, 441
  of character description, 425
  of comparison-contrast essay, 449
  discovery drafting, 315
  of literary analysis, 433
  organizing ideas, 314, 369–370
  of personal narrative, 417
  of poetry, 469
  of poetry interpretation, 433
  of proposal, 457
  of research report, 483
  of response to literature, 433
  of short story, 465
Dramatic reading, 320, 548–549
Dramatic works, italics for titles of,
    268
Drawing conclusions, 528–529

E

East, 38
Editing and proofreading, 319, 321,
    322
  of cause-and-effect essay, 442
  of character description, 426
  of literary analysis, 434
  of personal narrative, 418
  of poetry, 470
  of poetry interpretation, 434

proofreading symbols, 319
  of proposal, 458
  of research report, 486
  of response to literature, 434
  sentence structure, 325–337,
    387–397
  of short story, 466
  for word choice and usage, 319,
    322
Elaboration, 375–385
  charts, 382–383, 385
  diagrams, 382, 385
  examples, 434
  facts, 380–381, 384
  graphs, 382–383, 385
  reasons for, 377
  sensory details, 378–379, 384
  sources for, 381, 384
  for supporting opinions, 377
  statistics, 380–381, 384
  to answer questions, 377
  to describe, 377, 378–379
  to explain, 377
  uses of, 377
  visuals, 382–383, 385
  ways to elaborate, 384
  when to elaborate, 376
  why to elaborate, 377, 384
Electronic media, 554–555
  for publishing your writing, 320,
    323
Electronic reference works, 499
  World Wide Web, 499, 504
E-mail
  partner, for peer review of writing,
    316
  for publishing your writing, 320
Emotional appeals, 532–533
  bandwagon, 533
  loaded language, 532
  name calling, 532–533
  snob appeal, 533
Encyclopedias, 498
End marks, 250–252. *See also*
    Exclamation points; Periods;
    Question marks

English
  nonstandard vs. standard, 403
  Old, as basis for modern English,
    581
Epic poem titles, italics for, 268
Essay test questions, 519, 520
Essay titles, quotation marks for, 268
Essential (restrictive) adjective
    clauses, 205
Essential (restrictive) appositives,
    255
Essential (restrictive) details,
    334–335, 337
Ethnic groups, capitalization of, 232
Evaluation. *See also* Critical listening;
    Critical thinking
  of content and delivery, 540
  of draft, 317–318
  of information, 540
  of a media product, 558
  of speeches, 540
  of Web information, 500–501
  of a Web site, 499
Evidence, for generalizations,
    529–530
Exaggeration, 530, 532, 535
Examples, as context clues, 571
Exclamation points, 251
  with exclamatory sentences, 16,
    251
  with imperative sentences, 16,
    250
  with interjections, 251
  with quotation marks, 258, 275
Exclamatory sentences, 393, 397
  exclamation points for, 16, 251
Expository writing. *See* Research
    reports
Eye contact, in delivering a speech,
    547

F

Facial expression, 547, 550
Facts
  for elaboration, 380–381, 384
  identifying, 526

opinions distinguished from,
    526–527, 534
  types of, 526
Facts and opinions, 526–527,
    528–529, 534
  analyzing, 528–529, 534
  distinguishing, 526–527, 534
  identifying, 526–527, 534
Families of words, 576
Family relationships, capitalization of,
    231, 246, 247
Feedback. *See* Peer response
Figurative language, 303, 408–409
  to add interest to writings, 303
  for effective language, 401,
    408–409
  in poetry, 467, 469, 472
  as style element, 401, 408–409
Figures of speech, for style, 408–409
  avoiding clichés, 409
  metaphors, 408
  personification, 409
  simile, 409
Fill-in-the-blank questions, 518
Films
  capitalization of titles, 234
  italics for titles, 268
First-person pronouns, 58
First words, capitalization of, 233,
    234–235, 246, 247
Flow charts, 562
For
  as coordinating conjunction, 158
  in prepositional phrases, 95
Formal language
  informal language compared with,
    402–403, 410
  as style element, 401
Fractions
  hyphens in spelled-out, 264
  as singular or plural, 217
  subject-verb agreement for,
    217–218, 222
Fragments. *See* Sentence fragments
Freewriting
  for character description, 425
  for personal narrative, 417

for poetry interpretation, 433
in topic selection, 311
Future perfect tense, 108–110
  using, 113
Future progressive tense, 105, 106
  using, 113
Future tense
  as simple tense, 105, 106, 123
  using, 105, 113

G

Gender, pronoun-antecedent
  agreement in, 74, 89
Gender-free language, 74, 89
Generalizations, 529–530
General pronoun reference, 290
Geographical directions, capitalization
  of, 238
Geographical names, capitalization
  of, 237
Gerund phrases, 176–177
Gerunds, 170–171, 182
  for description, 170
  possessive pronouns modifying,
    183
  present participles distinguished
    from, 172
Gestures, 547, 550
Good
  and *bad,* 138, 140
  and *well,* 138, 140
Graphic organizers. *See also*
    Prewriting
  cluster diagram, 312
  flow chart, 562
  Venn diagram, 359
Graphics
  charts, 509
  diagrams, 510
  for elaboration. *See* Elaboration
  graphs, 509
  maps, 509, 510, 546
  for oral presentation, 546
  reading and analyzing, 508–509,
    510–511
  scales, 511

tables, 511
types of, 510–511
in Web site design, 555
Graphs
  for elaboration, 382–383
  reading and analyzing, 508–509
Greek
  origins of English words, 581
  word roots, 575
Greeting of a letter
  capitalization of, 234
  colon after, 263
  comma after, 256
Group communication, 534–544
  skills in groups, 544, 551

H

Have, as helping verb, 12, 93
Helping (auxiliary) verbs, 12–13, 93,
    208–209
Here
  subject position in sentences
    beginning with, 19
  subject-verb agreement in
    sentences beginning with, 219,
    227
  and *this, that, these,* and *those,* 71
His or her, as singular, 74, 89
Historical documents, events, and
    periods, capitalization of, 240,
    246
Holidays, capitalization of, 240, 246
Hyphenated words, 264
Hyphens, 264–265
  in hyphenated words, 264
  for line breaks, 264

I, J, K

I, capitalization of, 231
Ideas
  categorizing, 524–527
  for cause-and-effect essay, 441,
    444
  for character description, 425,
    427

INDEX

M

Magazines
    capitalization of titles, 234
    on CD-ROM, 499
    citation form for, 476, 485
    italics for titles, 268
    in library collection, 494, 497
    as news medium, 556
    online versions, 499
    for publishing your writing, 320, 323
    source cards for, 479
    as source for elaboration, 384
    targeting the audience for, 564
Main clauses. See Independent clauses
Main idea, 340, 341. See also Topic sentences
Main verb, 12
Matching test questions, 517
Mathematics, word problems, 222–223
May, can, 116
Meaning, 570–571
Measurement
    periods used with, 251
    subject-verb agreement with, 217–218
Media, 553–565. See also Books; Magazines; Movies; Multimedia presentations; World Wide Web
    audience for, 557–558, 564
    comparing, 554–556
    creating media products, 554
    documentary, 555, 559
    electronic, 554–555
    elements of media, 554
    evaluating, 557–558, 559–560
    influence of, 557–558
    messages in the media, 559–560
    news, 554
    persuasive techniques, 554, 556, 557, 558, 559, 560, 565
    print, 556
    purposes, 557
    targeting the audience, 557–558, 559, 560, 564
    techniques, 554
    types of, 554–556
    using media to communicate, 554
    verbal/nonverbal elements of media, 554
    visual persuasion, 554, 555, 556, 557, 558, 559, 560
    Web sites, 555
Media Center, 494
Message
    evaluation of, 559–560
    in oral communication, 539, 540
Metaphors, 408
MLA citation guidelines, 640–647
Modifiers, 327. See also Adjectives; Adverbs
    comparisons, 137–139, 145, 148, 293
    for details, 327
    double, 293
    problems with, 293
Months, capitalization of, 240, 246
Mountains, capitalization of, 237
Movies
    capitalization of titles, 234
    italics for titles, 268
Multimedia presentations, 561–565
    choosing media elements, 561
    designing, 562
    developing, 561
    evaluating and revising, 565
    planning and organizing, 562
    preparing the script, 563
Music
    capitalization of titles, 234
    italics for titles of long compositions, 268
    review, 560

N

Names, capitalization of, 36, 230, 246
Narrative/literary writing. See also Personal narrative, writing workshop for; Poetry; Short story, writing workshop for

paragraphs in, 345
Nationalities, capitalization of, 232
Negatives, 142–143
News, 554. *See also* Media;
    Newspapers
Newscasts, television, 554
Newspapers
    capitalization of titles, 234
    citation forms for, 479
    indexes of, 497
    in library collection, 494
    as news medium, 556
    online versions, 499
    for publishing your writing, 320
    source cards for, 479
    as source for elaboration, 384
Nominative case, for personal
    pronouns, 88
Nonessential (nonrestrictive)
    adjective clauses, 205
Nonessential (nonrestrictive)
    appositives, 255
Nonstandard English, 403
Nonverbal elements
    of delivering a speech, 547
    of media, 554
Nor, 211, 226
North, 238
Note cards, 480, 514, 546
Note taking
    for research reports, 480–481,
        483
    for studying, 509, 510–514
Noun clauses, 197–198
    function of, 205
Nouns, 34–53. *See also* Predicate
    nouns
    abstract, 37
    as adjectives, 132
    collective, 37, 38, 216
    common, 36, 37, 38, 51, 247
    as complements, 47, 48, 49
    compound, 45–46
    concrete, 36, 37
    as objects, 79
    as objects of prepositions, 47, 48

plural, 39, 40–41, 216–217, 628,
    629
possessive, 42–44, 51, 629
proper, 36, 51, 127, 230, 232, 246
singular, 39, 216–217
as subjects, 47, 79
types of, 36–37, 38, 51
Number
    personal pronouns, 58
    pronoun-antecedent agreement in,
        73, 89
    subject-verb agreement in,
        208–209

O

Objective case, of personal pronouns,
    63–64, 88
Objective test questions, 516–518
Object of a preposition
    nouns as, 47, 48
    in prepositional phrases, 95, 153
    pronouns as, 63, 70
    whom as, 70
Objects of verbs, 23–24, 95–97. *See
    also* Direct objects; Indirect
    objects
    types of, 23–24
    whom as, 70
Online services, 499–501
Opinions
    facts distinguished from,
        526–527, 534
    identifying, 526–527
Or, as coordinating conjunction, 14,
    211, 226, 395
Oral communication, 543–551
    in groups, 543–544
    individual, 543
    interviewing, 541–542
    reports, 545–547
    speeches, 545–550
Organization
    of compositions, 369
    of information, 314
    of paragraphs, 351–361

INDEX

Possessive pronouns, 58–59, 65–67, 88, 131
  as adjectives, 131, 132
  apostrophes for forming, 65–66, 629
  contractions distinguished from, 65–66
  personal, 58–59, 88
  uses of, 65, 88
Posture, in delivering a speech, 547, 550
Precise language, 401, 404–405
Predicate adjectives, 28, 98–99, 129–130
  position of, 129
Predicate nouns, 47–49, 79, 98
Predicate pronouns, 61, 89
  subject-verb agreement with, 220, 227
Predicates, 10–11
  complete, 6–7, 10, 326
  compound, 14–15
  simple, 10–11, 12–13
Prefixes, 573, 574, 580
  common, 573
Prepositional phrases, 153–157, 167
  for adding detail, 154
  adjective phrases, 167
  adverb phrases, 167
  commas after introductory, 254
  for description, 154
  placement of, 156
  subject-verb agreement when inserting between subject and verb, 81, 220, 226
Prepositions, 152–157, 166. *See also* Prepositional phrases
  as adverbs, 153
  capitalization in titles, 234, 247
  commonly used, 152
  object of, 47–48, 152
Presentation portfolio, 321
Present participle, 172
  gerunds distinguished from, 172
  as principal part of a verb, 100
Present perfect tense, 108–110, 111

Present progressive tense, 105–106, 111
Present tense
  of irregular verbs, 102–103
  as principal part of a verb, 100
  as simple tense, 105, 106, 123
  using, 105, 111
Prewriting, 310–314
  brainstorming, 311, 417, 477
  of cause-and-effect essay, 441, 444
  of character description, 425, 427
  of comparison-contrast essay, 449, 452
  determining purpose, audience, and form, 310–314
  drafting, 315
  exploring and limiting a topic, 312–314
  finding a topic, 310–311
  freewriting, 311
  graphic organizers, 312, 359, 425, 441, 449, 457, 465
  of literary analysis, 433, 436
  observing and recording, 310
  organizing information, 314–315, 482
  of personal narrative, 417, 420
  of poetry, 469, 471
  of poetry interpretation, 433, 436
  of proposal, 457, 460
  of research report, 482, 488
  of response to literature, 433, 436
  of short story, 465, 471
Primary sources, 478–481, 495–497
Print media. *See also* Books; Magazines; Newspapers; Periodicals
  as news source, 556
  publishing in, 320
Progressive verb forms, 105
Pronoun-antecedent agreement, 73–78, 290, 486
  in gender, 74, 89
  with indefinite pronouns as antecedents, 76–78

in number, 73, 89
in person, 73–74, 89
Pronoun reference, 290
Pronouns, 56–89. *See also* Indefinite
    pronouns; Personal pronouns;
    Possessive pronouns
    agreement with antecedent. *See*
        Pronoun-antecedent agreement
    antecedent of, 58. *See also*
        Pronoun-antecedent agreement
    case of, 58, 88, 291, 426
    demonstrative, 71, 131, 132
    first-person, 58
    intensive, 68–69, 88
    interrogative, 70, 88
    objective, 58–59, 63–64, 81, 88
    plural, 58–59, 61, 63–64, 65–67,
        71, 76–78
    problems with, 79–83
    reference of, 290
    reflexive, 68–69, 88
    relative, 334–335, 337
    second-person, 58
    singular, 58–59, 61, 63–64,
        65–67, 76–78
    subject, 58–59, 61–62, 81, 88
    third-person, 58
    types of, 58, 88
Proofreading
    others' writing. *See* Peer response
    own writing. *See* Editing and
        Proofreading
Propaganda. *See* Emotional appeals;
    Logical fallacies; Media,
    evaluating
Proper adjectives, 127
    capitalization of, 232
Proper nouns, 36, 51, 127, 230,
    232, 246
    proper adjectives formed from,
        127
Proposal, writing workshop for,
    454–461
Publishing, 320–321, 323
    of cause-and-effect essay, 445
    of character description, 428
    of comparison-contrast essay, 453

in electronic media, 320, 323
for general audiences, 320, 323
for literary analysis, 437
for personal narrative, 421
for poetry, 472
for poetry interpretation, 437
for proposal, 461
for research report, 489
for response to literature, 437
for short story, 472
for specific audiences, 320
Punctuation, 248–275. *See also*
    Colons; Commas; Exclamation
    points; Periods; Question
    marks; Quotation marks;
    Semicolons
    apostrophes, 266–267
    checking during editing, 418, 434
    for clauses, 262
    dashes, 264
    hyphens, 264–265
    parentheses, 264–265
    of parenthetical information, 264
    in poetry, 470
    of titles, 268–269
Purpose
    of cause-and-effect essay, 441
    of character description, 425
    of comparison-contrast essay, 449
    of personal narrative, 417
    of poetry, 469
    of poetry interpretation, 433
    of proposal, 457
    of research report, 477
    of response to literature, 433
    of short story, 465

Q

Question marks, 250
    with interrogative sentences, 16,
        250
    with quotation marks, 258, 275
Questions, 397. *See also*
    Interrogative sentences
    order in, 18
    for sentence variety, 397

the subject and verb, 81, 220, 226

Subordinate (dependent) clauses, 186–187, 196–199, 204–205
adjective clauses, 196, 205
adverb clauses, 196–197, 205
in complex sentences, 192
in compound-complex sentences, 194–195
noun clauses, 197–198, 205
for sentence variety, 193
subordinating conjunctions introducing, 186, 192
Subordinating conjunctions, 186, 192
Suffixes, 574
Summarizing of information, 513
Superlative degree, 137–138, 149
Supporting details
for the main idea, 300, 524
types of, 300
Supporting opinions, 377
Suspense, 463
Synonyms, 577
thesaurus for finding, 579

T

Tables, reading and analyzing, 511
Television
capitalization of titles of shows, 234
as news medium, 554
TV commercial, 559
Tenses of verbs, 13, 294
checking during editing, 114
future, 13, 105, 113
past, 13, 105, 112
perfect, 108–110
present, 13, 105, 111
progressive, 105, 106, 111
shifts in, 106, 111
simple, 105–107
verbs phrases for expressing, 12
Tests, 507–521
active reading strategies, 508–509
essay questions, 519, 520

objective questions, 516–518
reading directions for, 519, 521
short-answer questions, 518
study and review strategies, 507–521
understanding the prompt, 519
The, 127, 485
Thesaurus, 597
Thesis statement, 364–368, 372
the body of a composition developing, 368
in introduction of composition, 364–365, 366–367, 368
of research report, 482
restating in conclusion of composition, 371
Thinking skills, 523–535
Third-person pronouns, 58
Time abbreviations
capitalization of, 240
periods with, 251
Time expressions, colons with, 263
Titles (of works)
capitalization of, 234–235, 246, 247
italics for, 268, 274
quotation marks for, 268, 274
subject-verb agreement with, 217
Titles (personal), capitalization of, 230
To, in infinitives and prepositional phrases, 95
Topics
for cause-and-effect essay, 441, 444
exploring and limiting, 312–314
finding, 310–311, 322
for research reports, 477, 488
Topic sentences, 340–343, 348, 364, 369
Towns, capitalization of, 237
Train names, capitalization of, 238
Transitional words and phrases
for cause-and-effect order, 356–357, 361
for coherence in compositions, 369

for comparison-contrast order,
358, 361, 452
for sequential order, 353, 361
for spatial order, 355, 361
Transitive verbs, 96
Transportation vehicle names,
capitalization of, 238
True-false test questions, 516
TV. *See* Television

U, V

Underlining. *See* Italics
Unity, in compositions, 341–342,
348, 368–369
Us, with a noun, 79–80, 89
Variety in sentences, 19–20, 28–29,
193, 298–299, 392–393, 397,
450
Vehicle names
capitalization of, 238
italics for, 268
Venn diagrams, 359
Verbal cues, 545, 547, 550
Verbals, 168–183
gerunds, 170–171
infinitives, 174–175
participles, 172–173
Verb phrases, 10–11, 12–13, 93
in simple predicates, 10
subject-verb agreement for,
208–209, 226
time expressed by, 13
Verbs, 10–11, 90–123, 172
action, 10, 92–93, 95, 97
compound, 14–15, 253
in compound predicates, 14–15
helping (auxiliary), 12–13, 93,
208–209
intransitive, 96
in inverted sentences, 18–19
irregular, 100, 102–104, 115–116
linking, 10, 61, 92, 93, 98, 129
main, 12
principal parts of, 100–101,
102–104, 122, 294

progressive forms, 105, 106, 111
regular, 100, 122
in simple predicates, 10–11
tenses, 105–114, 118–119, 123,
294
transitive, 96
troublesome verb pairs, 115–117
types of, 92–93, 96
Visual aids, 546. *See also* Graphics
Visualization, elaboration for,
382–383, 384
Vocabulary, 567–581
analyzing word structure,
573–575, 580
antonyms, 579
reference books, 578–579
strategies for building, 568, 569,
570
synonyms, 577, 579
understanding related words,
578–579
understanding shades of meaning,
577
using context clues, 570–572
using the dictionary, 578–579
using the thesaurus, 579
using word parts, 573–575, 580
word origins, 574–575, 578, 581
Voice
in compositions, 317, 318, 399,
410
in oral presentations, 547, 550

W, X, Y, Z

We, with a noun, 79–80, 89
Web, the. *See* World Wide Web
Well, good, 138, 140
West, 238
Which, for combining sentences,
334–335, 337
Who, 292
for combining sentences,
334–335, 337
in questions, 70
as subject, 70, 89

Acknowledgments

For Literature and Text

Atheneum Books for Young Readers: Excerpt from "Eleanor Roosevelt," from *Great Lives: Human Rights* by William Jay Jacobs. Copyright © 1990 by William Jay Jacobs. Reprinted by permission of Atheneum Books for Young Readers, an imprint of Simon & Schuster, Inc.

Susan Bergholz Literary Services: Excerpt from *The House on Mango Street* by Sandra Cisneros. Copyright © 1984 by Sandra Cisneros. Published by Vintage Books, a division of Random House, Inc., and in hardcover by Alfred A. Knopf. Reprinted by permission of Susan Bergholz Literary Services, New York. All rights reserved.

Brandt & Brandt Literary Agents and A. M. Heath: "The Serial Garden," from *Armitage, Armitage, Fly Away Home* by Joan Aiken. Copyright © 1966 by Macmillan & Co., Ltd. Copyright © 1969 by Joan Aiken Enterprises, Ltd. Copyright renewed © 1994 by Joan Aiken Enterprises, Ltd. Reprinted by permission of Brandt & Brandt Literary Agents, Inc., and A. M. Heath & Co., Ltd., on behalf of the author.

Candlewick Press: "What Do Fish Have to Do with Anything?" from *What Do Fish Have to Do with Anything?, and Other Stories* by Avi. Copyright © 1997 by Avi Wortis. Reprinted by permission of Candlewick Press, Cambridge, MA.

Britney L. Chilcote: "Fallen Ballerina" by Britney L. Chilcote. First printed in *Statement, Journal of the Colorado Language Arts Society,* Vol. 33, No. 2, Spring 1997. Reprinted by permission of Britney L. Chilcote.

Cobblestone Publishing: Excerpt from "Ask Uly" by Lawrence Krumenaker, from *Odyssey's* November 1992 issue, *Handshakes in Space.* Copyright © 1992 by Cobblestone Publishing Company, 30 Grove Street, Suite C, Peterborough, NH 03458. Reprinted by permission of the publisher.

Farrar, Straus & Giroux: Excerpt from "Thank You, M'am," from *The Langston Hughes Reader,* by Langston Hughes. Copyright © 1958 by Langston Hughes, renewed 1986 by George Houston Bass. Reprinted by permission of Farrar, Straus & Giroux, Inc.

Farrar, Straus & Giroux and David Higham Associates: Excerpt from *Boy: Tales of Childhood* by Roald Dahl. Copyright © 1984 by Roald Dahl. Reprinted by permission of Farrar, Straus & Giroux, Inc., and David Higham Associates.

Ian Frazier: Excerpt from "It's Hard to Eat Just One" by Ian Frazier, from *Outside,* April 1997. Copyright © 1997 by Ian Frazier. Used by permission of the author.

Golden Books Family Entertainment: Excerpt from *Weather* by Paul E. Lehr, R. Will Burnett, and Herbert S. Zim. Copyright ©1987 by Western Publishing Company, Inc. Reprinted by permission of Golden Books Family Entertainment.

Grove/Atlantic: Excerpt from "The Turtle," from *Dream Work* by Mary Oliver. Copyright © 1986 by Mary Oliver. Reprinted with permission of Grove/Atlantic, Inc.

Houghton Mifflin Company: Excerpt from *The American Heritage Dictionary of the English Language,* 3rd ed. Copyright © 1996 by Houghton Mifflin Company. / Excerpt from *Across the Centuries,* Teacher's Edition in Houghton Mifflin Social Studies, by Armento et al. Copyright © 1991 by Houghton Mifflin Company. / Reprinted by permission of Houghton Mifflin Company. All rights reserved.

Marshall Editions: Excerpt from *Weather Explained, A Beginner's Guide to the Elements* by Erek Elsom. Copyright © 1997 by Marshall Editions Developments Ltd. Reprinted by permission of Marshall Editions, Ltd.

Naomi Shihab Nye: "The Rider" by Naomi Shihab Nye, from *Invisible.* Reprinted with permission of the author.

Orchard Books: "A Crush," from *A Couple of Kooks and Other Stories About Love* by Cynthia Rylant. Copyright © 1990 by Cynthia Rylant. Reprinted by permission of the publisher, Orchard Books, New York.

Oxford University Press: Excerpt from *A History of US: War, Peace, and All That Jazz* (book 9) by Joy Hakim. Copyright © 1995 by Joy Hakim. Used by permission of Oxford University Press, Inc.

Random House: Excerpt from *Living Out Loud* by Anna Quindlen. Copyright © 1988 by Anna Quindlen. Reprinted by permission of Random House, Inc.

Simon & Schuster: Excerpt from *The Merriam-Webster Thesaurus.* Copyright © 1978 by G. & C. Merriam Co. Reprinted by permission of Simon & Schuster.

Stone Soup: "The Floodgates of the Sky" by Rachel Smith, age 12, from *Stone Soup,* January/February 1998. Copyright © 1998 by The Children's Art Foundation. Reprinted with permission from *Stone Soup, the magazine by young writers and artists.*

Viking Penguin: "Mooses," from *Under the North Star* by Ted Hughes. Copyright © 1981 by Ted Hughes. Used by permission of Viking Penguin, a division of Penguin Putnam, Inc.

World Book Publishing: Excerpt from "Mongoose" from *The World Book Encyclopedia.* Copyright © 1999 by World Book, Inc. Used by permission of the publisher.

Table of Contents

viii *top* Illustration by Todd Graveline; *bottom* Copyright © Daryl Solomon/ Photonica; **x** Copyright © Reporters/Verpoorten/Leo de Wys, Inc.; **xi** Illustration by Todd Graveline; **xii** Copyright © Dick Young/Unicorn Stock Photos; **xiii** *top* Copyright © 1999 Harry Walker/AlaskaStock.com; *bottom* Illustration by Todd Graveline; **xiv** The Purcell Team/Corbis; **xv** Copyright © 1999 PhotoDisc, Inc.; **xvi** *background* Copyright © Andrea Pistolesi/The Image Bank/PNI; **xvii, xviii** *top left* Illustration by Todd Graveline; **xviii** *bottom right* Copyright © Bill Bachmann /PhotoNetwork/PNI; **xix** Craig Lovell/Corbis; **xx** *bottom right* Photo by Sharon Hoogstraten; **xxi** Illustration by Todd Graveline; **xxii** *center* Photo by Sharon Hoogstraten; *bottom* Copyright © 1999 PhotoDisc, Inc.; **xxiv, xxviii** *center left* Photo by Sharon Hoogstraten; **xxviii** *bottom* Copyright © 1999 PhotoDisc, Inc.; **xxx** Copyright © Bob Daemmrich/Stock Boston/PNI; **xxxi** Copyright © Richard Shock/Tony Stone Images; **xxxiii** Illustration by Todd Graveline.

Illustrations by Todd Graveline

6, 8, 16, 17 *top right,* 27, 32, 33 *top, center,* 38 *center left,* 39, 43, 44, 52, 55, 71, 76–77, 88, 89, 105, 113, 116, 123, 130, 143, 148, 152, 156 *top,* 167, 177, 182, 183, 189, 204, 205, 227, 235, 236, 246, 247, 257, 272 *bottom right,* 274, 276, 284, 286, 316, 322, 323, 328 *top,* 330 *top left,* 331, 333, 335, 336, 337, 342, 349 *top, center,* 360, 361, 372, 384 *bottom,* 389, 391, 392, 394, 396, 401, 403, 405 *top,* 406, 410, 411, 420, 421, 520 *center right,* 521, 528, 532, 533, 534, 535, 550 *top left, top right,* 551, 560 *top,* 565, 569 *center right,* 574.

Art Credits

COVER *top right* Copyright © David O'Connor/Graphistock; *center* Tabletop photo by Sharon Hoogstraten; *bottom left* Copyright © 1997 Stephen Simpson/FPG International.

CHAPTER 1   2–3 Copyright © William Swartz/Index Stock Imagery/PNI; **4** Copyright © Reporters/Verpoorten/Leo de Wys, Inc.; **7** Richard A. Cooke/Corbis; **8** Copyright © 1999 Harry Walker/AlaskaStock.com; **15** Corbis; **17** *bottom, FoxTrot* copyright © 1988 Bill Amend. Reprinted with permission of Universal Press Syndicate. All rights reserved; **25** Copyright © Pacific Pictures/John Penisten/ Liaison Agency; **29** Copyright © SuperStock.

CHAPTER 2   34 Illustration by John Roman; **36** Copyright © Art Wolfe/AllStock/ PNI; **38** *bottom right, Farcus®* is reprinted with permission from LaughingStock Licensing Inc., Ottawa, Canada. All rights reserved; **40** American Jewish Joint Distribution Committee Photo Archives; **41** The Purcell Team/Corbis; **48** Copyright © David Burnett/Contact/Camp; **49** Illustration by John Condon; **50** *top* Copyright © Rob Boudreau/Tony Stone Images; **50–51** Illustration by John Roman; **51** *bottom right* Copyright © Donovan Reese/Tony Stone Images.

CHAPTER 3   56 Copyright © Photofest; **59** Copyright © Paul Chesley/NGS Image Collection; **60** Copyright © Michael Melford, Inc./The Image Bank/PNI; **61** Copyright © National Museum of Natural History, Smithsonian Institution; **63** Copyright © Owen Franken/Stock Boston/PNI; **66** Copyright © Victor H. Mair; **69** Corbis; **72** Roman Soumar/Corbis; **74** Corbis-Bettmann; **78** AP/Wide World Photos; **79, 80** Copyright © 1999 PhotoDisc, Inc.; **83** *top* Corbis.

CHAPTER 4   90, 93, 99 Copyright © Photofest; **101** AP/Wide World Photos; **108** Copyright © Photofest; **111, 112** Copyright © Photofest; **118** Photos by Sharon Hoogstraten; **120** Copyright © Time-Life Films/The Museum of Modern Art/Film Stills Archive.

CHAPTER 5   124 *left, center* Corbis-Bettmann; *top right* Copyright © George Hall/Check Six/PNI; **126, 131** Copyright © 1999 PhotoDisc, Inc.; **139** *left* David G. Houser/Corbis; *center* Galen Rowell/Corbis; *right* Lowell Georgia/Corbis.

CHAPTER 6   150 Copyright © Dr. Morley Read/Science Photo Library/Photo Researchers, Inc.; **153** Corbis; **154** The Granger Collection, New York; **156** *bottom* Copyright © 1994 Kim Taylor/PNI; **157** Copyright © 1999 PhotoDisc, Inc.; **158** *left* Copyright © K. G. Vock/OKAPIA 1989/Photo Researchers, Inc.; *right* Copyright © Andrew Syred/Science Photo Library/Photo Researchers, Inc.; **161** Copyright © 1983 FarWorks, Inc. All rights reserved. Reprinted with permission; **162** *background* Photo by Sharon Hoogstraten; **163** Copyright © Des & Jen Bartlett/NGS Image Collection; **164** Copyright © Mervyn Rees/Tony Stone Images.

CHAPTER 15 **350** *top left* Copyright © Ronnie Kaufman/The Stock Market; *top right* Copyright © Paul Cherfils/Tony Stone Images; *bottom left* Copyright © Chris Shinn/Tony Stone Images; *bottom right* Copyright © Christopher Bissell/Tony Stone Images; **351** *background* Copyright © 1999 Gregg Mancuso/PNI; *foreground* Illustration by Todd Graveline; **352** *Calvin and Hobbes* copyright © 1991 Watterson. Dist. by Universal Press Syndicate. Reprinted with permission. All rights reserved; **355** Copyright © 1998 First Light/Zephyr Images; **357** Photo by Arthur Rothstein. Courtesy of the Library of Congress; **359** *left* NASA; *right* Corbis.

CHAPTER 16 **362** Copyright © 1999 PhotoDisc, Inc.; **363** Photo by Sharon Hoogstraten; **365** Historical Picture Archive/Corbis; **367** Christel Gerstenberg/Corbis; **369** Corbis; **370** Illustration by the studio of Wood Ronsaville Harlin, Inc.

CHAPTER 17 **374** Copyright © 1999 PhotoDisc, Inc.; **375** *background* Robert Holmes/Corbis; *foreground* Illustration by Todd Graveline; **376** *FoxTrot* copyright © 1991 Bill Amend. Reprinted with permission of Universal Press Syndicate. All rights reserved; **377** Copyright © Will & Deni McIntyre/Tony Stone Images; **379** Paul A. Souders/Corbis; **384** *center* Copyright © 1999 Johnny Johnson/AlaskaStock.com.

CHAPTER 18 **386** *background* Copyright © 1999 PhotoDisc, Inc.; *foreground* Copyright © Simon Battensby/Tony Stone Images; **387** *background* Copyright © A. Bolesta/H. Armstrong Roberts; *foreground* Illustration by Todd Graveline; **388** *Peanuts* reprinted by permission of United Feature Syndicate, Inc.; **390** Photo by Dane Penland (SI Neg. No. 80-3070); Copyright © National Air and Space Museum, Smithsonian Institution, Washington, D.C.

CHAPTER 19 **398** David Lees (David Lees/Corbis); **399** *bottom* Copyright © 1999 PhotoDisc, Inc.; *top* Photo by Sharon Hoogstraten; **400** Copyright © Daniel Heuclin-Bios/Peter Arnold, Inc.; **405** *bottom* Copyright © Jim Cammack/Black Star/PNI; **407** Copyright © 1999 PhotoDisc, Inc.; **408** *Bizarro* copyright © 1994 by Dan Piraro. Reprinted with permission of Universal Press Syndicate. All rights reserved.

CHAPTER 20 **412–413** Tecmap Corporation/Corbis; **419** Photos by Sharon Hoogstraten.

CHAPTER 21 **427** Photos by Sharon Hoogstraten.

CHAPTER 22 **435** Photos by Sharon Hoogstraten.

CHAPTER 23 **443** Photos by Sharon Hoogstraten.

CHAPTER 24 **451** Photos by Sharon Hoogstraten.

CHAPTER 25 **459** Photos by Sharon Hoogstraten; **460** *Calvin and Hobbes* copyright © 1993 Watterson. Dist. by Universal Press Syndicate. Reprinted with permission. All rights reserved.

CHAPTER 26 **471** Photo by Sharon Hoogstraten.

CHAPTER 27 **487** *background* Corbis; *foreground* Photo by Sharon Hoogstraten.